Sermons (125) Preached from the Pulpit of Machiasport, Maine,

1991-2010

By

François Kara Akoa-Mongo

Trafford rev. 02/04/2011

 www.trafford.com

North America & international
toll-free: 1 888 232 4444 (USA & Canada)
phone: 250 383 6864 ♦ fax: 812 355 4082

DEDICATION

I dedicate this book to my late father, the Rev. François Akoa Abômô, who was an excellent preacher and church leader in the Presbyterian Church of Cameroon, and a Cameroonian statesman for more than 60 years. Even though he preached all over the Republic, very few of his written sermons were kept.

I also dedicate this sermon collection preached from the pulpit of the First Congregational Church of Machiasport, from 1991 to 2010 to my late father-in-law, Harold Martin Young, who influenced me as a man of faith and contentment, and to my wife, Kathy Akoa, as we have grown together in faith and the Lord's service over the years.

Machiasport, January 11, 2010.

FOREWORD:
HOW THESE 125 CAME TO BE:

François K. Akoa-Mongo was ordained as the Minister of the Word and Sacrament by the Presbyterian Church of Cameroon on July 1ˢᵗ 1967. Up to 1981, he preached most of his sermons either in French, or in his native Cameroonian dialect. While teaching at Washington Academy, the pulpit of the First Congregational Church of Machiasport became vacant. He applied and got the job as their Pastor in November 1991.

In order to preach in English, he wrote out his messages. From that time, he developed the habit of writing the core of all his sermons. They are refined thoughts revealed to him through his work for the spiritual enrichment of his congregation over 19 years. They contain good biblical quotations and Protestant theology.

He is thankful to the congregation of Machiasport for loving him enough to be their pastor for so many years, in spite of his French accent, a different background in culture, and his inability to speak as a person from Down East. He has more than 500 sermons on tape, which he may someday record on CD'S.

The presentation of this book is purposefully different from a regular book. Texts of sermons are Dr. Akoa-Mongo's notes from his office's work used as instrument of his messages Sunday after Sunday. They are important theological, biblical, and practical features that he used to nourish spiritually his congregation in 25-35 minutes.

When reading any of these sermons, what would be missing is the oral development of main points found along the way. Any line or paraphrase deserves to be expended in one way or the other. If one had an opportunity to listen to the same messages on tape, after reading it on paper, one would see the following differences: (a) the spoken message would not go line per line as presented on paper. (b) All biblical references found in the written text would not be quoted during the delivery; (c) the written text would have neither illustrations, nor expended development as the oral one. This difference is the work of the Holy Spirit revealing to him whatever is needed on the pulpit. - During research and the work in his office, Dr. Akoa-Mongo believes that the Spirit of God worked with him; but when delivering his sermons on the pulpit, he lets the Holy Spirit lead him and speak freely, remaining more obedient to the Spirit on the pulpit than in the office.

The following are some advantages of written sermons (a) Would one wish to study the Rev. Dr. François Akoa Mongo's theology on specific aspects, this is the place to do so. As many know, the problem churches are facing today is that people no longer know what used to be called "**heresy**". A church, which doesn't know which doctrines are heretics is without faith. Those who believe in something are heretics, as far as those who don't. The faith in God must be based on 'specifics' the foundation, which makes some heretics, and separates them from those who don't believe in Jesus Christ in the same way. (b) These sermons may be used for Bible Studies. They have questions, answers, main points, sub-points and biblical references. (c) Their messages go right on the heart of the matter. Each deals with a specific theme with an introduction, divisions, and the conclusion. (d) Dr. Akoa-Mongo uses three questions to lead the reader. The first part of the sermon tries to answer the question: "**what?**"

In order to bring the reader to be a part of the sermon from the start, having in mind the reader as well as the congregation, who may be asking him, "**What are you saying?**"; he works drawing the reader's interests on the subject. Once he is sure that the has reached that goal, he deals with the second question, which is " **why?**" having in mind that the reader or the congregation is asking him, "**Why this topic, should be important to me?**" "**Why are you devoting your time and effort to speak about this? Why the Bible and the Holy Spirit want us to be interested on this subject with you?**" This is what François would have in mind vis-à-vis of his congregation at this point. Here, the Bible, the Holy Spirit, and God speak to the reader. The last question he strives to answer is, "**What this has to do with me?**" Here, he involves the reader or the audience to know the message and mission given by the Lord. This in an invitation to go out and work to change the problem and do the will of our Father who is in heaven. (e) About the conclusion. He summarizes the whole message so that the reader would have in mind what the Lord wanted him/her to hear that day.

ACKNOWLEDGMENT

The Rev. Dr. François Kara Akoa-Mongo asks forgiveness to his wife and children for not always being their for them most of the time. Even when he was present with them, he would keep himself busy in his office, or dealing with church and school business. He remembers missing or changing family's plans for his church's obligations on Sunday. Monday through Friday was the time he spent in school, and Saturdays were used to finish writing and rewriting his sermons. He hopes his family has forgiven or will forgive him someday. Even now that the children are gone, and he has retired from teaching, he still sees himself sitting in the living room with his wife working on his laptop. . He is sorry and is asking forgiveness.

François thanks Mr. Bart Brizée, who made all the grammatical and spelling corrections from his written sermons each Sunday before saving them in his computer. He also thanks Mr. and Mrs. John and Carrie Gardner, who took the time to read his final manuscripts.

May the Lord bless them individually.

OTHERS PUBLICATIONS
BY THE AUTHOR

The Life of Akoa-Mongo Kara, from Cameroon to the United States…

<u>Will publish soon:</u>

This book translated in French: Les Sermons (125) Préchés à Machiasport.

100 Hymnes Traduits en Bulu. – Music in his native language

Les Méditations (365) pour Les Couples Chrétiens,

Qui était le Rév. François Akoa Abômô? –L'Homme et l'Oeuvre.

THE AUTHOR

The Rev. Dr. François Kara Akoa-Mongo was born in Cameroon. There, he graduated from Dager Theological Seminary with the Bachelor in Divinity, then in the United States with the Master of Divinity from Bangor Theological Seminary, the Master of Arts in Teaching Foreign Languages and the Ph.D in Social Studies from the University of Maine at Orono.

Akoa-Mongo is an ordained minister of the Presbyterian Church of Cameroon, serving from 1967 to 1971, and from 1977 to 1987 as parish minister as well as Principal in many High Schools, teacher of English and an Adjunct professor of Education at the University of Yaoundé. François, his wife Kathy, and their 9 children now live in the United States. Since 1987 he taught French, Spanish, Latin, and Social studies at Washington Academy and Narraguagus High Schools in Maine. He has been serving as Pastor of the First Congregational Church of Machiasport for the last 20 years.

François speaks, French, English, Spanish, three African dialects and reads Greek, Hebrew and Latin. He has been married to his lovely wife Katherine A. Young for the last 33 years.

ETERNAL LIFE

Eternal life; what does it entail?
'Tis endless life, that will never fail.
But friend, it means so much more than this,
It's life in Heaven; it's total bliss.
A Promise fulfilled, it does mean,
No man, nor Satan, can come between.
'Tis ours, the moment we do believe,
When we trust Christ to save us, and Him receive.
Christ promised life, abundantly,
We can claim this Promise, victoriously.
A full meaningful life, in His will,
Spirit controlled, with hope to instill.
This 'life' is yours, when you do believe,
It starts on Earth, 'till Heav'n we receive.
Only thru' Christ, can you have this 'life',
Without Christ, sin and evil are rife.
Life in Heav'n is coming, soon I know,
No tears, pain nor suffering, no woe.
Only the joy of serving our Lord,
Loving Him always; that won't be hard.
I praise my dear Saviour, ev'ry day,
Eternal life is mine, for always!
The joy and peace He puts in my heart,
And the hope of Heav'n, will ne'er depart.

****

By: Connie Kramer Apr.20,1996 # 210
Scripture verses for above poem:
(Jn.3:15-18,36; 5:24; 8:24; 10:10;14:27; 17:3; 20:31;
Ac.13:52; Ep.5:18; 1 P.1:8)

A HARD LIFE

Living for Christ is not easy to do,
When you walk close to Him, folks watch you!
Ready to jump on you if you slip,
At times you feel like deserting the ship!
With love like our God; we are to love,
'Tis hard in this world of push and shove.
Repaying good, for evil folks do,
I surely need Him, to see me thru'.
Curse not, but bless; love your enemy,
Only with Christ can we have victory.
Our brother we are to truly forgive,
If we want forgiveness, as we live.
Lord Jesus, we can't do it alone,
We would fail completely, on our own.
Please Lord Jesus, stay close by our side,
Love and forgive, and be there to guide.

****

By: His servant, Connie Kramer Mar.8,1996 # 160

Scripture verses for above poem:
(Jn.15:18; Phil.4:13,19;
Mt.10:22; 5:21-22,27-28,31-35,38-39,43;44; 6:14-15)

REVIEW ON THE BACK COVER

The following are some advantages of reading these sermons from the Rev. Akoa-Mongo (a) they define his theology on specific aspects. As many know, the problem churches are facing today is that people no longer know what used to be called "**heresy**". A church, which doesn't know which doctrines are heretics is without faith. Those who believe in something are heretics, as far as those who don't. The faith in God must be based on 'specifics' the foundation, which makes some heretics, and separates them from those who don't believe in Jesus Christ in the same way. (b) With questions, answers, main points, sub-points and biblical references, these sermons can be used in churches for Bible Studies (c) With a specific theme, an introduction, divisions, and conclusions, their messages go right on the heart of the matter.

Dr. Akoa-Mongo uses three questions to lead the reader through. The question: "what?" makes the reader a part of the sermon from the start. The second question " why?". He let the Bible, the Holy Spirit, and God speak to the reader. The last question he answers is, "What about me?". He involves the reader or the audience to know the message and the mission the Lord gives to them through this message. This is an invitation to go out and change the problem in the people's lives and to do the will of our Father who is in heaven. (e) About the conclusion. He summarizes the whole message so that the reader would have in mind what the Lord wanted him/her to hear for the day.

(1)

THEME: THE OLD TESTAMENT AND JESUS.

INTRODUCTION: Have you heard someone asking why Christian Church has their Holy Book called the Bible divided into two parties: These are Old and the New Testaments. You should know that the first half called Old Testament has as its principal role to prepare what was about to take place in the New Testament. The Principal character that first part of the Bible is dealing with is Jesus Christ, the coming of the Messiah who is going to be the Savior of the Word.

In order to speak about what was about to happen, the Spirit of God entered for a moment the mind of some individuals we call "**PROPHETS**". Prophets were people God opened the eyes and mind for a certain period of time in order to see and write about things, which will take place in the future. Therefore, we are going to study what prophets predicted about the person called the Messiah or Christ. They predicted that:

I – JESUS IS ETERNAL:

Micah 5:1-2 (NIV) Marshal your troops, O city of troops, for a siege is laid against us. They will strike Israel's ruler on the cheek with a rod. 2 "But you, Bethlehem Ephrata, though you are small among the clans of Judah, out of you will come for me one who will be ruler over Israel, whose origins are from of old, from ancient times."

John 1:1 (NIV) in the beginning was the Word, and the Word was with God, and the Word was God.

II – JESUS IS THE SON OF GOD:

Psalms 2:7 (NIV) I will proclaim the decree of the LORD: He said to me, "You are my Son; today I have become your Father.

NT. Matthew 3:17 (NIV) and a voice from heaven said, "This is my Son, whom I love; with him I am well pleased."

IV- JESUS WOULD BE THE SEED OF A WOMAN. He would crush

the serpent's head. Genesis 3:15 And I will put enmity between you and the woman, and between your offspring and hers; he will crush your head, and you will strike his heel."

Galatians 4:4 But when the time had fully come, God sent his Son, born of a woman, born under law, 1 John 3:8 He who does what is sinful is of the devil, because the devil has been sinning from the beginning. The reason the Son of God appeared was to destroy the devil's work.

V- JESUS WILL BE BORN IN BETHLEHEM:

Micah 5:1 Marshal your troops, O city of troops, for a siege is laid against us. They will strike Israel's ruler on the cheek with a rod. 2 "But you, Bethlehem Ephrata, though you are small among the clans of Judah, out of you will come for me one who will be ruler over Israel, whose origins are from of old, from ancient times."

Matthew 2:1 After Jesus was born in Bethlehem in Judea, during the time of King Herod, Magi from the east came to Jerusalem

VI -JESUS WOULD BE CRUCIFIED

Psalms 22:16 Dogs have surrounded me; a band of evil men has encircled me, they have pierced my hands and my feet. Matthew 27:35 when they had crucified him, they divided up his clothes by casting lots. Luke 24:39 "Look at my hands and my feet. It is I myself! Touch me and see; a ghost does not have flesh and bones, as you see I have." Jesus' dying words were prophesied in Psalms 22:1." A psalm of David. My God, my God, why have you forsaken me? Why are you so far from saving me, so far from the words of my groaning? Psalms 31:5 into your hands I commit my spirit; redeem me, O LORD, the God of truth.

Matthew 27:46 about the ninth hour Jesus cried out in a loud voice, "Eliot, Eliot, lama sabachthani?"--which means, "My God, my God, why have you forsaken me?"

Mark 15:34 and at the ninth hour Jesus cried out in a loud voice, "Eloi, Eloi, lama sabachthani?"--which means, "My God, my God, why have you forsaken me?"

Luke 23:46 Jesus called out with a loud voice, "Father, into your hands I commit my spirit." When he had said this, he breathed his last. Jesus' death would atone for the sins of mankind.

Isaiah 53:5-7 But he was pierced for our transgressions, he was crushed for our iniquities; the punishment that brought us peace was upon him, and by his wounds we are healed. 6 We all, like sheep, have gone astray, each of us has turned to his own way; and the LORD has laid on him the iniquity of us all. 7 He was oppressed and afflicted, yet he did not open his mouth; he was led like a lamb to the slaughter, and as a sheep before her shearers is silent, so he did not open his mouth.

Isaiah 53:12 therefore I will give him a portion among the great, and he will divide the spoils with the strong, because he poured out his life unto death, and was numbered with the transgressors. For he bore the sin of many, and made intercession for the transgressors.

Mark 10:45 for even the Son of Man did not come to be served, but to serve, and to give his life as a ransom for many."

John 1:29 the next day John saw Jesus coming toward him and said, "Look, the Lamb of God, who takes away the sin of the world!

John 3:16 "For God so loved the world that he gave his one and only Son, that whoever believes in him shall not perish but have eternal life.

VII - JESUS WOULD RISE FROM THE DEAD THE THIRD DAY

Hosea 6:2 after two days he will revive us; on the third day he will restore us that we may live in his presence.

Conclusion: There is no doubt that the central figure of the Old Testament was Jesus. Not to lead and understand the Old Testament as well as the New will make Christians ignorant of the purpose, the preparation and the coming of the One who is their Savior Jesus Christ, the Messiah, the One who was sent by his Father to save all humankind.

Read and understand the Old Testament and you will understand who your Savior is.

Amen. Maschiasport November 1st, 2009

4

(2)

Readings Isaiah 53 and Luke 24:36-49

Text Luke 24:44 "Then he said, 'When I was with you before, I told you that everything written about me by Moses and the prophets and in the Psalms must all come true.

THEME: **THE MESSIANIC PROPHECIES FULFILLED IN JESUS.**

INTRODUCTION: Last week, we talked about "what is a prophecy in the Old Testament." <u>A prophecy is an inspired vision of the future, revealed to people called prophets in the Old Testament.</u>

Today we will speak about a specific kind of prophecy called MESSIANIC. Messianic because they deal with the person, an individual person who was promised to come and SAVE. In the beginning, it was about saving the children of Israel. But at the end, it became his assignment to save all humankind. His name in the Old Testament was MESSIAH. That Hebrew name is translated in Greek by CHRIST.

There are more than 100 COMPILED PREDICTIONS REGARD-ING THE MESSIAH IN THE OLD TESTAMENT. They are called Messianic Prophecies.

That name is given to them because they name places, which did not exist those years, and recite sentences word by word as they will be used by Jesus Christ.

They cite events just as they will take place in the future

These are ACCURATELY recorded in the Old Testament.

These were recorded in a period of 1,000 years ahead.

These were fulfilled here on earth by Jesus Christ our SAVIOR.

II – LET US SEE WHAT THOSE MESSIANIC PROPHESIES WERE ABOUT AND HOW THEY WERE FULFILLED BY JESUS IN THE NEW TESTAMENT:
IT WAS PREDICTED THAT:

1. JESUS WILL BE BORN IN BETHLEHEM (Micah 5:2, - 750 B.C.

   Fulfilled in Matthew 2:1; Luke 2:4-7)

2. HIS MOTHER WILL BE A VIRGIN - (Isaiah 7:14; 700-680 B.C.
   The Lord will give a sign: The virgin will be with a son
   Fulfilled Matthew 1:21-23)

3. THAT CHILDREN WILL BE KILLED IN RAMAH -Jeremiah 31:15 626-580 BC. This is what the Lord says: A voice is heard in Ramah; mourning and great weeping, Rachel weeping for her children and refusing to be comforted because her children are no more.
   Fulfilled in Matthew 2:16-18)

4. HE WILL LIVE IN EGYPT AS A BABY (Hos. 11:1, 715 BC

   Fulfilled in Matt2:14-15)

5. A MAN WILL GO AHEAD TO PREPARE THE WAY (John the Baptist) (Isaiah 40:3-5; Malachi 3:1) 700-680 ; 460 B.C

The voice of one calling in the desert "prepares the way for the Lord, make straight in the wilderness a highway for our God."

Fulfilled in; Matthew 3:1-3)

6. HE'LL BE ANOINTED (Isaiah 11:2); 700 BC.

ι The Spirit of the Lord will rest on him. The Spirit of wisdom and Understanding, the Spirit of counsel and of power; the Spirit of Knowledge and have fear of the Lord.

Fulfilled in Matthew 3:16-17.

7. HE WILL PREACH THE GOOD NEWS FOR THE SALVATION OF HIS PEOPLE (Isaiah 61:1; 700 BC.

The Spirit of the Sovereign Lord is on me

Because the Lord has anointed me to preach good news to the

Poor. He has sent me to bind up the brokenhearted, to

Proclaim freedom for the captives and release from darkness

For the prisoners. To proclaim the year of the Lord's favor.

Fulfilled in Luke 4:14-21)

8. THAT HE WILL PERFORM MIRACLES (Isaiah 35:5-6; 700 BC.

Then will the eyes of the blind be opened and the ears of the

Deaf unstopped. Then will the lame leap like deer;

And the mute tongue shouts for joy.

Fulfilled in Matthew 9:35)

9. THAT HE WILL MINISTER IN GALILEE (Isaiah 9:1; 700 B.C.

He will honor Galilee of the Gentiles, by the way of the sea, along The Jordan.

Fulfilled in Matthew 4:12-16)

10. HE WILL ENTER JERUSALEM ON A DONKEY

(Zechariah 9:9; 520 BC.

Rejoice greatly O daughters of Zion!

Shout daughters of Jerusalem! See your king come to you,

Righteous and having salvation, gentle and riding on a donkey.

Fulfilled in Matthew 21:4-9)

11. THAT HE WILL BE REJECTED BY HIS PEOPLE, THE JEWS

(Psalm 118:22; 1,000 BC.

Fulfilled in 1 Peter 2:7)

12. HE WILL DIE A HUMILIATING DEATH (Psalm 22; Isaiah 53 – 1,000;700 BC)

(a) Rejection (Isaiah 53:3;

He was despised and rejected by men. A man of sorrows,

And familiar with suffering.

Fulfilled in John 1:10-11; 7:5, 48),

(b) Betrayal by a friend (Psalm 41:9;

Even my close friend, whom I trusted, he who shared my

bread has lifted up his heel against me.

Fulfilled in Luke 22:3-4; John 13:18),

(c) Sold for 30 pieces of silver (Zechariah 11:12; Matthew 26:14-15),

(d) Silence before His accusers (Isaiah 53:7; Matthew 27:12-14),

(e) Being mocked (Psalm 22: 7-8; Matthew 27:31),

(f) Beaten (Isaiah 52:14; Matthew 27:26),

(g) Spit upon (Isaiah 50:6; Matthew 27:30),

(h) Piercing His hands and feet (Psalm 22:16; Matthew 27:31),

(i) Being crucified with thieves (Isaiah 53:12; Matthew 27:38),

(j) Praying for His persecutors (Isaiah 53:12; Luke 23:34),

(k) Piercing His side (Zechariah 12:10; John 19:34),

(l) Given gall and vinegar to drink (Psalm 69:21, Matthew 27:34,

(m) No broken bones (Psalm 34:20; John 19:32-36),

(n) Buried in a rich man's tomb (Isaiah 53:9; Matthew 27:57-60),

(o) Casting lots for His garments (Psalm 22:18; John 19:23-24).

13. <u>HE WILL RISE FROM THE DEAD</u> (Psalm 16:10;

Because you will not abandon me to the grave,

Nor will you let YOUR HOLY One see decay.

Fulfilled in Mark 16:6; Acts 2:31)

14. <u>THAT HE WILL ASCEND INTO HEAVEN</u> (Psalm 68:18;

When you ascended on high,

Fulfilled in Acts 1:9)

15. <u>HE WILL SIT AT THE RIGHT HAND OF GOD</u> (Psalm 110:1;

The Lord says to my Lord, Sit at my right hand

Until I make your enemies a footstool for your feet.

Fulfilled in Hebrews 1:3)

<u>CONCLUSION</u>: All these predictions revealed to the holy prophets hundred years ahead were fulfilled in the lifetime of Jesus Christ so that you and I living today may be certain that Jesus Christ was the Messiah. That Jesus Christ is the only Savior of all mankind. That you and I we should not wait for another. Our Savior has come and now he is sitting at the right hand of God interceding for us. Amen. Nov.8. 2009

(3)

Readings. Isaiah 40:21-41:1 and I Thessalonians 1:4-10.

Text. Isaiah 40:30-31 even youths grow tired and weary, and young men stumble and fall. BUT THOSE WHO HOPE IN THE LORD, will renew their strength, they will soar on wings like eagles; they will run and not grow weary; they will walk and not be faint.

THEME: DESCRIPTION OF THE WAITERS
   (THE HOPEFUL ON THEIR GOD)

INTRODUCTION: Modern man has a problem. All of us here present, we have a problem. That problem is about waiting. We don't like to wait at any waiting room. We don't like standing on line anywhere. We don't like traffic jam, it drives us nuts. We don't like flight cancellations when we have to travel. Yes, we love fast food eateries. We love instant gratifications. WE love drive through in Banks. We love ATM machines, being paid every Friday, using Credit Cards but not checks.

In our daily life the way we live now, we don't think about tomorrow; We don't want to save anything for others; We love to eat it all, to have it all, to spend it all and RIGHT NOW. TODAY IS THE MOST IMPORTANT DAY IN OUR LIVES IN EVERYTHING WE DO. QUE SERA, SERA!

This attitude of our centuries is contrary to the spirit of CHRISTIANITY; TO THE SPIRIT OF CHRISTIAN RELIGION, WHICH IS BASED ON HOPE, ON WAITING, ON TOMORROW. AND ON OVERTHERE, NOT HERE NOT NOW!

WAITING IS AN IMPORTANT BIBLICAL CONCEPT. ONE CAN'T CALL ONESELF CHRISTIAN WITHOUT UNDERSTANDING THIS BASIC PRINCIPLE ABOUT HOPE, WAITING, AND EXPECTATION.

I - FROM THE OLD TESTAMENT AND MOSTLY FROM ABOUT 1,000 YEARS, THE TIME OF THE PROPHETS, ISRAEL LIVED THROUGH WAITING, HOPING FOR THE MESSAIAH

ALL THE PROPHETS LOOKED IN THE FUTURE
THE NEW TESTAMENT AIMED AT THE FUTURE
THE KINGDOM OF GOD JESUS CAME TO ESTABLISH
BUT ITS FULFILLMENT IS YET TO COME – His return!
Philippians 3:20-21— OUR CITIZENSHIP IS NOT HERE

THE BELIEVERS ARE EAGERLY WAITING TO GO HOME
REMEMBER WAITING CAN BE HARD:
1 Thessalonians 1:9-10 — waiting can be hard.
There are moments of frustration
There are moments of discouragement
There are moments our human side tries to take over.

THAT'S WHY WE HAVE TENTION, HIGH BLOOD PRESSURE
TAKE ANTIDEPRSSANT DRUGS DRINK ALCOHOL HAVE MENTAL ILLNESS DON'T LOSE HOPE. WAIT! ARE YOU WAITING?

II – THE DESCRIPTION OF THE WAITERS, THE HOPEFUL:

(1) THE WAITERS MUST TRUST IN GOD

Psalm 40:1-4 —I wait patiently for the Lord;

He turned to me and heard my cry

He lifted me out of the slimy pit, out of the mud and mire.

He set my feet on a rock, and gave me a firm place to stand.

He put a new song in my mouth,

A hymn of praise to our God.

They will see and fear and put their trust in the Lord.

BLESSED IS THE MAN WHO TRUSTS IN THE LORD.

(2) THE WAITERS ARE ALSO THE HOPEFUL. Psalm 130:5-8 —

I wait for the Lord; my soul waits and in his word I put my hope.

My soul waits for the Lord more than watchmen wait...

(3) WAITING IS AN ATTITUDE OF THE SOUL – INNER SELF.

(4) THE WAITERS ARE AT PEACE WITHIN THEMSELVES:

Psalm 62:1-2 — my soul finds rest in God alone.

My salvation comes from him.

He alone is my rock and my salvation.

(5) REST, PEACE, SALVATION GO TOGETHER

(6) THE WAITHERS ARE COURAGEOUS:

Psalm 27:14 — Wait for the Lord,

Be strong and take heart

And wait for the Lord.

(7) WHEN EVERYBODY ELSE IS PANICKING, THE WAITER WAITS.

YOU NEED COURAGE TO BE ABLE TO WAIT.

(8) THE WAITERS ARE OBEDIENT, THEY HAVE ENDURANCE

Psalm 37:34 — Wait for the Lord and keep his way.

He will exalt you to inherit the land

When the wicked are cut off, you will see it.

BECAUSE OF THEIR PATIENCE:

1) The waiters will inherit the Promised Land.

2) The man waiting for the Lord is not sleeping

above saying "Now serving:" and a sign on the counter INSTEAD

WAITING FOR THE LORD IS AN ACTIVE GODLY LIFE

III -REMEMBER: IMPATIENCE IS A FORM OF

(1) UNBELIEF

(2) A SUPERFICIAL DENIAL

(3) RUNNING AHEAD OF GOD

(4) TAKING THINGS IN ONE'S OWN HANDS

(5) DENYING GOD THE POWER TO DO WHAT IS RIGHT

Luke 21:19 "By your endurance (patience) you will gain your lives."

(1) PATIENCE IS DOING THE WILL OF GOD

(2) PATIENCE IS THE FRUIT OF FAITH AND IMPATIENCE IS THE FRUIT OF UNBELIEF...

(3) THERE IS A RELATIONSHIP BETWEEN GOD'S PROMISES AND WAITING

13

IV– THINKS THE LORD IS DOING FOR THE BELIEVERS
WHEN THEY ARE STILL HERE ON EARTH WHILE WAITING
HIS COMING. Isaiah 40:31-32
THOSE WHO WAIT (HOPE) FOR THE LORD
THEY WILL RENEW THEIR STRENGTH
THEY WILL SOAR ON WINGS LIKE EAGLES
THEY WILL RUN AND NOT GROW WEARY
THEY WILL WALK AND NOT BE FAINT.

CONCLUSION: The Old as well as the New Testaments teach us Christians that one of the fundamental principles of our faith is TO BE WAITERS, TO BE HOPEFUL, TO BE PATIENT, TO BE OBEDIENT, TO BE THE ENDURERS, THE COURAGEOUS, HAVING A GODLY ACTIVE LIVING WHILE WAITING FOR THE LORD

WHEN WE WAIT, WE AFFIRM OUR BELIEF NOT THE UNBELIEF, WE LET GOD, AND FOLLOW HIM NOT GOING AHEAD OF HIM; WE BELIEVE HIS PROMISES HE WILL FULFILL IN DUE TIME.

DURING THE TIME WE ARE WAITING,
GOD WILL RENEW OUR STRENGTH,
WE WILL SOAR ON HIS WINGS LIKE EAGLES,
WE WILL RUN AND WALK BY HIS POWER.
ARE WE WAITING? LET'S WAITH FOR THE LORD.... Amen.

Machiasport, November 15, 2009

(4)

Scripture Readings. Matthew 3:1-12 and Philippians 2: 2-13

Text. Matt. 3:7-and Phil. 2:5 but when he saw many of the Pharisees and Sadducees coming where he was baptizing, he said to them: "YOU BROOD OF VIPERS! WHO WARNED YOU TO FLEE FROM THE COMING WRATH? PRODUCE FRUIT IN KEEPING WITH REPENTANCE....YOUR ATTITUDE SHOULD BE THE SAME AS THAT OF JESUS CHRIST.

THEME: DO YOU WANT TO WIN? CHAGE YOUR MIND.

INTRODUCTION: Some of us would rather change anything but their mind. You know names we give to people who can't change their mind. We call them - -Stubborn, - hardheaded, - obstinate - mule-headed.
Paul encourages the Philippians in the passage we read saying, "Let the same mind be in you that was in Christ Jesus, who though he was in the form of God, did not regard equality with God as something to be exploited, but emptied himself taking the form of a servant, being born in human likeness." (Philp. 2: 5-7)

Paul is inviting Philippians to CHANGE THEIR MIND. To be a Christian is to be a person who has a CHANGED MIND.

THE SOURCE OF OUR DIFFICULY IS CHANGING OUR MIND:
1-LOOK AT OUR NATURE: a human being doesn't want to make sacrifice. The SACRIFICIAL ATTITUDE IS NOT A PART OF OUR NATURE. But this is what Christ is inviting us to do. In order to reach that level in our Christ like life, WE HAVE TO CHANGE OUR MIND FIRST

2. WE SHOULD CHANGE OUR MIND BECAUSE CHRIST DID SO Christ Jesus changed himself from a divine Son of God to a human being born on earth so that our sin be forgiven and we be part of God's Kingdom.

(a) CHRIST JESUS IS OUR REDEEMER:

(b) JESUS HEALED OUR SOULS.

His grace purified me; His power saved me -

His truth illuminated to deal with all spiritual issues

my emotionality, my relational and mental health status.

3. WE MUST CHANGE TO HARMING OURSELVES

HEALTH ISSUES START WITH THE MIND. Almost all of us know what to eat, what to drink, what to do to stay healthy, to be safe, to avoid mistakes, to be out of troubles this doesn't happen because WE DO NOT CHANGE OUR MIND.

IT IS SAID THAT THE AVERAGE PERSON

(a) **Has 67 pounds** of muscle,

(b) **40 pounds** of bone, and

(c) **3.5 pounds** of brain –

ARE WE FOOLISH? Are we dumb? What is wrong with us? Why are we walking in darkness in the middle of the day? Why do we choose death over being alive and healthy? Why does a man love suffering, problems, prison, war, and pain AND NOT peace, happiness, joy, freedom, and living in harmony with others?

THERE IS ONLY ONE REASON: WE DON'T WANT TO **CHANGE OUR MIND.**

II – LET 'S SEE WHAT THE MIND DOES TO US ALL.

1) THE MIND INFLUENCES DECISIONS AND CONITIONS

Worry, - fear, - insecurity, - anxiety, - uncertainty, - excitement and a host of other thoughts and emotions can influence the body in a variety of ways, including:

Heart attacks - migraine headaches - hypertension - ulcers - backaches - accidents.

2) BEING HEALTHY OR SICK DEPENDS ON THE MIND:

-It is believed that 90% of all headaches – including migraine headaches – occur when the person is experiencing feelings of anxiety, tension, anger, frustration, fear or powerlessness

3) MUST PEOPLE TAKE CARE OF THEIR BODIES RUINING THEIR MINDS

(1) What people watch to TV and read poisons their mind.

Angry thoughts - resentful thoughts - negative thoughts - self-pitying

Thoughts condemning thoughts - anxious thoughts - depressing thoughts

Jealous thoughts -- dwelling in the past - hatred - fear -• blaming others

III - WHAT TO DO IN ORDER TO WIN THIS MIND' BATTLE?

1) IT MUST BE A SPIRITUAL BATLE WHERE THE LORD FIGHTS

not a man with his poor strategies

2) <u>WE ADAM AND EVE'S CHILDREN</u>

Since the Fall, our minds love sinning than the will of God

3) <u>REMEMBER YOUR CULTURE EN AND ENVIRONMENT.</u>

4) <u>REMEMBER, WE ARE DIFFERENT FROM GOD</u>

5) <u>BE READY FOR THE SPIRITUAL BATTLE</u>

Paul talks about <u>BEING ALERT.</u>

<u>THINGS TO DO IN ORDER TO BE ALERT</u>
<u>SETTING OUR MIND ON THINGS ABOVE</u>
<u>STAYING IN FELLOWSHIP WITH THE SPIRIT OF GOD</u>

<u>CONSEQUENCES:</u>

(1) WE WILL BECOME COMPASSIONATE,

(2) WE WIL BECOME A LOVING PEOPLE.

(3) WE WILL HAVE THE FULL MIND, WHICH WAS IN CHRIST.

<u>THIS MIND OF CHRIST IS WHAT REPENTANCE IS ALL ABOUT.</u>
<u>JOHN THE BAPTIST CAME TO PREPARE THE WAY FOR THE LORD</u>

1) IN ORDER TO MAKE STRAIGHT HIS WAY **(Isaiah 40:1-5)**
1. A HIGH WAY FOR OUR GOD
2. EVERY VALLEY RAISED UP
3. EVERY MOUNTAIN AND HILL MADE LOW
4. THE ROUGH GROUND BE LEVELED
5. THE RUGGED PLACES TRANSFORMED INTO PLAIN
6. THEN THE GLORY OF THE LORD WILL BE REVEALED

WE NEED THE MIND, WHICH WAS IN CHRIST TODAY.

CONCLUSION: As people who believe in Christ Jesus; as people who still live in this world; as people who are surrounded by a culture which is contrary to the Kingdom of God we have elected to be members, we should never forget that we have a battle to fight. That battle is not against the flesh; this battle is not against outsiders; it is a battle, which is against us, our mind.

NOW IS THE TIME WE MUST CHANGE OUR MIND. This is the time we must RECEIVE THE MIND OF CHRIST and be in his LIKELINESS.

1) Remembering that we are children of Adam and Eve. There is nothing we can do to please God. We need repentance, which is a MIND CHANGING CONDITION...

Remembering that we can't fight this fight by ourselves, we must let the Spirit of God take over the battle and we will be winners.

We must reject all human attitudes, which have brought us all kinds of problems:

LET'S CHANE OUR MIND AND GOD TAKE OVER

A mind set for things above becomes in the likeness of Christ

IF YOU DO THAT TODAY, YOU WILL WIN THE BATTLE.

DO YOU TO WIN? CHANGE YOUR MIND. Amen

Machiasport, December 6, 2009.

(5)

Texts: 1 Samuel 13:8, 14; 16:7; Psalms 51

<u>THEME</u>: **FIVE (5) LESSONS TO BE LEARNED FROM DAVID.**

INTRODUCTION: Christians tend to be far more impressed with a person's failures than with his or her successes. This tendency can be illustrated in many ways. For example, consider the two common statements made by one Christian to another: "Yes, but do you know what he (she) did (or was)?" Though he or she obviously repented evidenced by his/her redirection of life, the past still lives as the most important measure of him or her.

<u>I- CHRISTIANS ARE MORE IMPRESSED WITH SOMEONE'S FAILURES THAN SUCCESSES</u>: consider the man David for example. Most Christians are more likely to remember David from the incident of adultery with Bathsheba (2 Samuel 11)

    1) See David's compassionate courage at the incident of Keilah (1 Samuel 23)

    2) What about DAVID FAITH in his flight from King Saul. [Expressing faith in God is what a person devoted to righteous is supposed to do; APPLICATION: I don't say that we should not remember sins people have committed. But we should also look and value the way God has used those

sinners and show his grace through their lives. We are born sinners, but by grace, we become saints through the blood of Jesus. Therefore, today, we will speak about positive sides of David's life.

II –DAVID IS A GOOD EXAMPLE OF WHAT FRIENDSHIP IS: SOULS OF TWO BEST FRIENDS ARE BOUND:

1) "When David had finished speaking to Saul, the soul of Jonathan was bound to the soul of David, and Jonathan loved him as his own soul. Saul took him that day and would not let him return to his father's house. Then Jonathan made a covenant with David, because he loved him as his own soul. Jonathan stripped himself of the robe that he was wearing, and gave it to David, and his armor, his sword his bow and his belt." (1 Samuel 18:1-4)

2) THE LIFE BETWEEN TWO FRIENDS IS A COVENANT: Then Jonathan and David met in secret. Jonathan begged David to come back to the palace, but David was afraid for his life. So they made a plan: Jonathan would go home and try to find out what his father was thinking. If his father had cooled down, he would let David know it was safe.

For as long as the son of Jesse lives upon the earth, neither you nor your kingdom shall be established." (1 Samuel 20:30)
Jonathan immediately ran from the table. And, that night, he went to tell David the sad news.

3) THE LOVE BETWEEN FRIENDS IS GREATER THAN THE LOVE BETWEEN MAN AND A WOMAN:
"David rose from beside the stone heap and prostrated himself with his face to the ground. He bowed three times and they kissed each other and wept with each other; David wept the more. Then Jonathan said to David, 'Go in peace, since both of us have sworn in the name of the Lord, saying, "The Lord shall be between me and you, and between my descendants and

your descendants, forever." ' He got up and left; and Jonathan went into the city." (1 Samuel 20:41-42)

4) <u>THE LOVE BETWEEN TWO FRIENDS IS FOR GENERATIONS:</u>

The story of David adopting Jonathan's son Mephibosheth is found in 2 Samuel 9. For examples of how some other monarchs dealt with the potential heirs to the throne, 2 Kings 10:1-11 and 11:1-3, 13-16. Because of the covenant, the love, deep friendship between David and Jonathan, David adopted MEPHIBOSHETH who ate at his table for the rest of his life.

<u>APPLICATION:</u> WOULD YOU LIKE TO HAVE A FRIEND?

(1) Two souls bound? (2) A life covenant made?

(3) Love more than husband or wife? (4) A generational love.

<u>III- DAVID: GOOD EXAMPLE OF GOD'S SERVANT</u>

1) THE REASON TO FIGHT: GOLIATH DID NOT BELONG TO THE LORD the enemy of the living God is also your enemy. (1 Samuel 17:26, 46, 47).

- FIGHT AND WIN THE NON-BELIEVERS

2) THE REASON NOT TO KILL SAUL WAS THAT THE ANOINTED MAN (when David was dependent on God (1 Samuel 24:6). GOD WILL DO IT, NOT ME.

- KNOW WHO OR WHAT IS HOLY – SET APART.

3) DAVID KNEW HIS LIMITATIONS - HIS SIN. – FINGER AT HIMSELF because The prophet Nathan confronted him, David immediately acknowledged his failure and was willing to die for what he had done 2 Sam. 12:13, 14

BE RESPONSIBLE FOR YOUR SINS – REPENT.

<u>IV -WHY WAS DAVID CALLED "A MAN AFTER GOD'S OWN HEART?"</u> Was it because he was perfect? Obviously not! Then why? Four reasons are given for your consideration.

<u>BECAUSE:</u>

1) DAVID UNDERSTOOD THAT HUMAN EXISTENCE IS ABOUT GOD NOT ABOUT SELFISH AMBITIONS. Even if ambitions are rooted in acts of God, God determines your purposes, [like David's refusal to kill King Saul].

2) DAVID KNEW WHO MUST CONTROLE HIS LIFE He made some horrible choices! However, consciously rejecting God was not one of them!

3) DAVID BECAME RESPONSIBLE FOR HIS ACTION/ MISTAKES

4) DAVID WAS READY TO REPENT FROM HIS MISTAKES. There was no justification of failure! "I sinned! It is my fault!"

<u>CONCLUSION:</u>

Don't always be impressed with people's failures. Look on the way God has used his grace and love in their lives.

Do you have a friend or would you like to have a friend. Model your friendship after David and Jonathan. (a) Their souls were bound; (2) they live a covenantal life; (c) their love was more than marital one; and (4) their friendship love was for generation.

Be a good servant of the Lord: (1) Fight against all the Goliaths because they don't belong to God; (2) Don't stand against the anointed, whoever or whatever is set apart for the Lord, and (3) Be responsible of your sins – repent if you sin.

Be a person whose heart is like God's:(1) live for God; (2) Let God control your life, and (3) Accept your responsibilities, always repent for your sins to God. Amen. 09/3/09

(6)

Scripture Readings: Genesis 27:1-29; Matthew 22:29-33

THEME: SIX (6) LESSONS TO BE LEARNED FROM JACOB.

INTRODUCTION: The road we are treading today as Christians has been followed by many for generations. We may even count of our families, races and nations many before us who have followed that road we call CHRISTIANITY.

The Bible gives us some of the names of those who were faithful to God in the past the Book of Hebrew, chapter 11 is full of those names. As we said last week, we will study some biblical characters these following weeks. Last Sunday, we studied about Abraham. These were the seven lessons we learned from him:

ABRAHAM LIVED A LIFE OF COMPLETE FAITH. IN GOD.

ABRAHAM WAS OBEDIENT TO GOD leaving home and going to...

ABRAHAM SACRIFIED HIS LIFE TO GOD – Not staying in Egypt

ABRAHAM OBEID GO TO GO TO CANAN

ABRAHAM OBEYED GOD IN STAYING IN EGYPT

ABRAHAM BELIEVED THAT GOD WILL KEEP HIS PROMISES

ABRAHAM GAVE GOD EVERYTHING HE HAD

TODAY < WE'LL 5 LESSONS FROM JACOB

TODAY < WE'LL 5 LESSONS FROM JACOB

GENERATION: There is always something about the third generation. That generation is different from the first and the second.

I <u>JACOB, WAS THE FAVORITE CHILD OF HIS MOTHER, REBECCA.</u> Isaac called Esau and told him that the time of his death was near. He would like to bless him. Therefore, Esau should go and find an animal, cook it and bring it to him, and then he (his father) would bless him. Esau was Isaac's favorite son. But his wife, Rebecca has Jacob as her favorite one.

When Isaac was talking to his favorite son Esau, his wife Rebecca was listening. After hearing this and Esau gone, Rebecca called her favorite son Jacob, and made the entire plan to deceive Isaac, and let Jacob get all the blessings.

APPLICATION: The majority of our families have this problem. When a parent doesn't love all his or her children in the same way, it is a disaster in preparation. Many families have been destroyed by parents not by their children. Isaac and Rebecca destroyed their own family because one favored one child and the other parent favored the other child. What a blessing if both could sit down and plan.

<u>THE FIRST LESSON</u> Parents should work together and love their children in the same manner, not favor some and hate some. Parent, if you do, don't wonder why your family is or will be divided. You are the cause of the hatred, fights, conflicts and divisions your family is going through today. Be careful about what you say and do to your children. It can be interpreted somehow by others and that will hurt you later on.

Rebecca loved Jacob. After Jacob left when Esau promised to kill him after the death of their father, Jacob FLED and both parents died when he was away.

II – THE NAME OF JACOB MEANS "SURPLANTER "– the one who takes the place of another by TRICKING HIM.

Jacob was a very profit oriented person. His brother Esau was a hunter. One day, Esau came back hungry from hunting. Jacob just finished cooking a pottage of lentils. His brother asked him to have some. Jacob said "if you want some, sell me your birthright". Thinking that his brother was just joking, Esau said, "You have it. Give me the food". Jacob gave him the pottage of lentils, and really considered himself as the one who deserved to be blessed and he planned everything with his mother, and he got all the blessings from his father Isaac.

Have you known people when this are right with them,

They don't care about whom they hurt

They don't care about what people will say.

They don't care about tomorrow.

They don't care about right and wrong.

They don't care about the consequences.

If they have it and it is theirs, it is fine and they are happy...

THE SECOND LESSON: Don't live a life of self-centered, me, me and me. Don't always put yourself first.

Think about who you are hurting.

Think about what people are saying,

Think about tomorrow,

Think about what I am doing, is it right or wrong.

Think about what will happen next?

III-WHAT JACOB DID TO ESAU, LABAN DID IT TO HIM TOO.

After Jacob left his father and mother, he reached his Uncle Laban's home. He fell in love with his younger daughter Rachel. Laban told him that he should work for him for 7 years. After 7 years, Rachel will be your wife. Jacob agreed. After 7 years, they have a marriage ceremony. When it was time to go to bed, the married girl went to the bedroom followed by her husband. In the morning, when Jacob looked at his wife's face, it was not Rachel, but Leah, the oldest of the family was given to him for his wife. When he complained, Laban told Jacob that according to the tradition, the younger girl couldn't be married before the elder one. Therefore, if he really wanted to marry Rachel, he had to work for 7 more years; which he did. Therefore, Laban also tricked Jacob as he tricked his father...

After 14 years of work, Laban said to Jacob, continue working for me. All the spotted or speckled or dark-colored lambs, goats or sheep will be yours. As soon as Laban said that, Laban removed all the MALE spotted, speckled, dark-colored sheep goats and lambs from the livestock, as well as all the females.

JACOB TRICKED LABAN BY taking fresh cut branches from an almond tree and made white stripes on them, peeling the bark and exposing the white inner wood of the branches. When female goats, sheep and lambs came to drink water, they would look at these stripes colored trees inside the water fountains. Almost all the newborn animals were dark-colored, speckled, and spotted. Therefore, Jacob's livestock grew and Laban's diminished.

LESSON: 3: WHAT GOES UP ALWAYS COMES DOWN. WHAT YOU DO TO OTHERS, SOMEONE WILL DO THAT TO YOU OR TO ONE OF YOURS.

IV- JACOB'S ENCOUNTER WITH GOD AT BETHEL. After Jacob left his father, mother and brother behind, he slept at BETHEL. There he dreamt. He saw a stairway resting on the earth with its top reaching to heaven and the angels of God were ascending and descending. "I am the Lord, the God of Abraham and of your father Isaac. I will give to your descendants the land on which you are lying....I am with you and will watch over you wherever you go, and I will bring you back to this land. I will not leave you until I HAVE DONE WHAT I HAVE PROMISED YOU. (Gen. 28:10-15)

LESSON 4: DON'T THINK THAT YOU CAN FLEE FROM GOD. GOD'S PLAN IS NOT ABOUT YOU AND HE WILL FINISH HIS PLAN

V- THERE ARE BAD CONSEQUENCES FOR BAD CHOICES:
(1) JACOB STOLE BLESSINGS FROM HIS BROTHER ESAU.
   CONSEQUENCE: Today's situation in the middle East
(2) JACOB FLED AS ADVISED BY HIS MOTHER
   CONSEQUENCE: She died when Jacob was away
(3) LABAN TRICKED JACOB AS JACOB TRICKED ESAU, AS JACOB TRICKED LABAN.
   CONSEQUENCE: THEY NEVER TRUST EACH OTHER.
   (1) Jacob left his country young; he came back old.
   (2) Jacob left his country single; he came back married.
   (3) Jacob left his country poor; he came back rich.
   (4) Jacob left his country healthy; he came back lame.
   (5) Jacob's name changed into Israel.
   (6) Jacob came back reconciled to his brother.
   (7) Jacob came back reconciled with God.

(8) He left his country walking away from God; he came back walking with God.

IV-JACOB, THE WRESTLER, THE ENCOUNTER THAT CHANGED HIM AND HE BECAME ISRAEL (THE PRINCE OF GOD) AT JABBOK (Gen.32.23-32)

Jacob came back from Haram rich. 2 wives, (Leah and Rachel) concubines: Bilhah, Zilpah and many herds of animals, and 12 children.

- HE DID NOT HAVE PEACE

(2) His father's blessings – THE BLESSINGS HE STOLE

- HE DID NOT HAVE PEACE -

When he met the Lord, he wanted his blessings and he fought for it all night long.

APPLICATION: LESSONS JACOB DID LEARN

JACOB FOUND OUT THAT POSSESSIONS ARE NOTHING.

JACOB NEEDED ONE THING: FORGIVENESS

JACOB NEEDED GOD'S BLESSINGS NOT MAN'S.

JACOB WANTED A NEW BIRTH. HE BECAME ISRAEL - THE PRINCE OF GOD.

LESSON 5: GO TO JABBOK! FIND A JABBOK IN YOUR LIFE!

(1) MATERIAL THINGS WILL BE NOTHING.

(2) YOU MUST ASK FORGIVENESS FOR YOUR SINS

(3) YOU WILL RECEIVE GOD'S BLESSINGS

(4) YOU WILL HAVE A CHANGED NAME. . Amen. 9/20/09.

(7)

Reading of the Scripture: Genesis 12:1-9, 22:1-14

Text. Genesis 22: 11-13 But the angel of the Lord called out to him from heaven, "Abraham! Abraham!" Here I am", he replied. "Do not lay a hand on the boy," he said, "Do not do anything to him. Now I know that you fear God, because you have not withheld from me your son, your only son."

THEME: SEVEN (7) LESSONS ABRAHAM

INTRODUCTION: I invite each one of us to read autobiographies of other people. I am writing my own at this moment. I want my children and grandchildren to read it. I am certain that they will learn many things about me, which even those who think they know me will discover.

We will study some Biblical Characters these coming Sundays. We start today with Abraham. Let's learn some lessons from him and try to apply them in our lives. Don't be surprised if you do become an Abraham of our generation.

I chose 7 lessons we can learn about Abraham today:

I--LIVE A LIFE OF COMPLETE FAITH IN GOD this is what God said to Abraham and he believed it: Genesis 12:1

Leave your country, your people and your father's household and go to the
land I will show you.

God made a covenant with Abraham:

I will make you into a great nation

I will bless you

I will make your name great

You will be a blessing

I will bless those who bless you,

   and whoever curses you I will curse

And ALL PEOPLES ON EARTH will be blessed through you.

APPLICATION: Abraham believed all this and had complete faith in
God

OBEY GOD REGARDLESS Genesis 12:4-9

By faith Abraham DEPARTED from Haram and went to Canaan

There Abraham built an ALTAR unto the Lord who appeared to him and
promised to give the land unto his seed. (Verse 7)

APPLICATION: Not only that Abraham left Haram and went to Canaan,
but there, he built an altar and continued worshipping the Lord who also
affirmed his promise to give to his seed the land he promised in chapter 12

BE WILLING TO GIVE YOUR LIFE FOR HIM Gen. 12:10-20

Abraham went down to Egypt because of the famine in the land of Canaan.
Down there, Abraham lied about his wife Sarah to Pharaoh saying that she
was his sister. He forgot that if you belong to God, you are no longer a man
of this world. LIE, NO! TELL THE TRUTH NO MATTER WHAT.

APPLICATION: Abraham should have given his life and see what God
would do. God would never let Pharaoh kill Abraham. Abraham took

things into his own hand. Those who believe in God don't take things into their own hands; they give them to God, what Abraham did not do.

CHAPTER 13 DIVINE RESTORATION. God restored Abraham –
Abraham left Egypt rich, wealthy.
Abraham went back to where he had built the altar to God before.

APPLICATION: When God forgives us, he restores us at the previous position when we ask forgiveness.

GO WHERE HE SENDS YOU
In Chapter 12: God told Abraham to leave his country and his household. He did when problems arose between Lot's herdsmen and Abraham's herdsmen, this is what Abraham said to Lot, "Let's not have any quarreling between you and me or between your herdsmen and mine, for WE ARE BROTHERS. Is not the whole land before you? Let's part company. IF you go to the left, I'll go to the right. If you go to the right, I'll go to the left.

LOOK THE WAY LOT ACTED: Lot looked up and saw that the whole plain of the Jordan was well watered, like the garden of the Lord, like the land of Egypt, toward Zoar. (This was before the Lord destroyed Sodom and Gomorrah). So Lot chose for himself the whole plain of the Jordan and set out toward the east.....Abraham lived in the land of Canaan, while Lot lived among the cities of the plain and pitched his tents near Sodom.

APPLICATION: Lot chose for HIMSELF, Abraham let God choose. Let God choose for you as Abraham.

STAY IN GOD'S WILL AND "OUT OF EGYPT"
Abraham left Egypt and went back to Canaan, the Promised Land.

APPLICATION: We live for two worlds: Egypt and the Promised Land. Christians don't belong to Egypt; they belong to the Promised Land. We may have famine in the Promised Land – sickness, temptations – but don't visit Egypt, but return to the Promised Land as Abraham did.

GOD WILL KEEP HIS PROMESSES ANYWAY.

God reconfirmed the covenant with Abraham 8 times in these Chapters 12-21:

Great nation, Gen. 12:2

To his offspring he will give the land of Canaan, (Gen.12:7)

After Abraham and Lot departed, God promised to Abraham that he would give him the land where he was staying to his offspring forever as his heritage, God told Abraham that his heir will be a son coming from his own body and that his descendants will be as numerous as the stars in heaven. (Gen.15:2-5)

Promise that his children with be foreigners

And they will be mistreated for 400 years, (Gen. 15:14-16)

Ishmael was born in Chapter 16 because his wife Sarah did not believe that she will have a child. (Gen. 16). God changed Abraham's name. It went from Abram to Abraham. He was 99 year old – the father of many nations - (Gen. 17:5)

God even changed his wife's name from Sarai into SARAH = princess.

The Lord even named the child to be born, ISAAC. In (Gen. 17:9)

ISAAC was born in Chapter 21 when Abraham was 100 year old – 25 years later.

APPLICATION: IF GOD SAID IT, IT WILL BE DONE. JUST BELIEVE!

GIVE TO THE LORD WHATEVER HE WANTS FROM YOU.

The test of faith - MAKE YOUR FAITH EQUAL TO THE TEST.

God's commands Abraham to give what? His only son. Abraham obeys

GOD PROVIDES THE SUBSTITUTE - Gene. 22:13

APPLICATION: Is anything too expensive to give to God?

    Is there anything too personal to me I can't give to God?

    What do I have that doesn't belong to God?

LOOK AHEAD TO THE CITY LIKE ABRAHAM

ABRAHAM LIVED A LIFE OF COMPLETE FAITH. IN GOD.

ABRAHAM WAS OBEDIENT TO GOD leaving home and going to...

ABRAHAM SACRIFIED HIS LIFE TO GOD – Not staying in Egypt

ABRAHAM OBEYED GO TO GO TO CANA'AN

ABRAHAM OBEYED GOD BY STAYING IN EGYPT

ABRAHAM BELIEVED THAT GOD WILL KEEP HIS PROMISES

ABRAHAM GAVE TO THE LORD WHATEVER ASKED.

Learn and apply these lessons in your life. Amen.

Machiasport, Sept. 13, 2009

(8)

Scripture Reading. Matthews 21:1-11

Text. Matt. 21:10-11 When Jesus entered Jerusalem, the whole city was stirred and asked, "WHO IS THIS?" The crowd answered, "THIS IS JESUS, THE PROPHET FROM NAZARETH IN GALILEE"

THEME: WHO IS JESUS? WHO IS THIS MAN? GIVE AN ANSWER.

INTRODUCTION: When Jesus was entering Jerusalem the day we call PALM SUNDAY, Matthew tells us that the whole city was stirred and asked, WHO IS THIS? We can also formulate this question saying, "WHAT IS GOING ON HERE?"

Those who ignored who Jesus was asked this question

Pharisees who did want to hear asked.

The inhabitants of the city Jesus came to sake asked.

Those who joined the crowed yelling asked who he was

HOSANNAH, BLESSED BE THE ONE WHO COMES IN THE NAME OF THE LORD. HOSANNA IN THE HIGHEST!"

These people's real question was "**WHO IS THIS KING OF GLORY?**" As Psalm 24:8 and Isaiah 63:1 ask. The answer is, "**THE LORD, STRONG AND ALMIGHTY LORD IN BATTLE**" People should lift up their hearts to him.

THE CROWD GAVE AN ANSWER. Verse 11, "THIS IS JESUS, THE PROPHET FROM NAZARETH IN GALILEE". WRONG! WRONG ANSWER!

Yes, every question needs an answer; but don't give a wrong answer to every question. Many of those who followed Jesus that day, many who put the cloth on the road so that Jesus will walk triumphal over them, many who yelled, "HOSANNA, and BLESSED BE THE ONE WHO COMES IN THE NAME OF THE LORD" that day did not know the real answer of the question asked "WHO IS THIS MAN?"

Today, my brother and sister, I want you to have and to know the real answer to this question and you will be able to give a RIGHT ANSWER EVERY DAY to the ignorant, the destroyers, and all those who are still seeking the WAY. Know that many are still lost and many are still looking at places and things for their SALVATION:
THIS IS JESUS THE ANSWER! JESUS THAT LORD AND KING

I - JESUS IS THE MESSIAH OF THE OLD TESTAMENT

WE HAVE MORE THAN 300 PROPHECIES FULFILLED IN THE N.TESTAMENT PROPHECY FULFILLMENT

1. JESUS IS THE CRUSHER OF SATAN'S HEAD IN EDEN.
Gen. 3:13 He will crush your head, and you will strike his hill.

2. JESUS IS THE - DESCENDENT OF ABRAHAM Genesis 18:18"

3. JESUS IS THE. DESCENDENT OF ISAAC Genesis 17:19"

4. JESUS IS THE. DESCENDENT OF JACOB
Numbers 24:17 Fulfilled Luke 3:34

5. JESUS IS THE DESCENDENT OF JUDAH
Genesis 49:10, fulfilled Luke 3:33

6. JESUS WILL BE BORN IN BETHEHEM
Micah 5:2 fulfilled in Matthew 2:1

7. JESUS'. MOTHER WILL BE A VIRGIN
Isaiah 7:14 fulfilled in Matthew 1:18

8. JESUS WILL BE REJECTED BY HIS PEOPLE THE JEWISH
Isaiah 53:3 fulfilled John 1:11 "He came to that which was his own, but his own did not receive him."

9. HE WILL ENTER JERUSALEM ON A YOUNG DONKEY
Zechariah 9:9 " fulfilled in John 12:13-14 "They took palm branches and went out to meet him, shouting, 'Hosanna!' 'Blessed is the King of Israel!' Jesus found a young Donkey and sat upon it, as it is written."

10. THEY PREDICTED HIS DEATH WITH SINNERS.
Isaiah 53:12 fulfilled in Matthew 27:38 "Two robbers were crucified with him, one on his right and the other on his left. His hands and feet will be pierced.

11. HE WILL BE RESURRECTED FROM THE DEAD
Psalm 16:10 fulfilled Matthew 28:9 "Suddenly Jesus met them.' Greetings, he said. They came to him, clasped his feet and worshiped him.

12. HE WILL ASCEND INTO HEAVEN.

Psalm 68:18 "When you ascended on high, you led captives in your train; you received gifts from men, even from the rebellious--that you, O Lord God, might dwell there." Luke 24:50-51 "When he had led them out to the vicinity of Bethany, he lifted up his hands and blessed them. While he was blessing them, he left them and was taken up into heaven."

II- THIS IS WHAT THE NEW T. SAY ABOUT JESUS:

1. JESUS WAS GOD – SAME NATURE AND ESSENCE AS GOD:

John 8:28-29 "So Jesus said, 'When you have lifted up the Son of Man, then you will know who I am and that I do nothing on my own but speak just what the Father has taught me. The one who sent me is with me; he has not left me alone, for I always do what pleases him.'"

2. HE WAS A MAN BUT NEVER SINNED:

John 8:46-47 "Can any of you prove me guilty of sin? If I am telling the truth, why don't you believe me? He who belongs to God hears what God says. The reason you do not hear is that you do not belong to God."

3. THAT HIM AND GOD WERE ONE PERSON:

Not one of several ways, but the one and only way. Not to teach the way, but to be the way to God. Nobody has ever made claims like that before and backed them, but Jesus did through his love, balanced life, and miracles.

4. HE WAS AT THE SAME TIME THE WAY, THE TRUTH, AND THE LIFE.

John 14:6 "I am the way, the truth, and the life. No one comes to the Father but by me."

Matthew 11:27 "All things have been committed to me by my Father. No one knows the Son except the Father, and no one knows the Father except the Son and those to whom the Son chooses to reveal him."

5. JESUS TAUGHT US THAT HE FROM HEAVEN

John 17:5 "And now, Father, glorify me in your presence with the glory I had with you before the world began."

6. THAT HE ON EARTH TO TAKE AWAY ALL OUR SINS:

Luke 5:20-21 "When Jesus saw their faith, he said, 'Friend, your sins are forgiven.' The Pharisees and the teachers of the law began thinking to themselves, 'Who is this fellow who speaks blasphemy? Who can forgive sins but God alone?'"

7. HE CAME TO ESTABLISH HIS KINGDOM:

John 18:36-37 "Jesus said, 'My kingdom is not of this world. If it were, my servants would fight to prevent my arrest by the Jews. But now my kingdom is from another place.' 'You are a king, then!' said Pilate. Jesus answered, 'you are right in saying I am a king. In fact, for this reason I was born, and for this I came into the world, to testify to the truth. Everyone on the side of truth listens to me.

8. HE CAME TO GIVE US EVERLASTING LIFE.

John 6:40 "For my Father's will is that everyone who looks to the Son and believes in him shall have eternal life, and I will raise him up at the last day."

John 6:47 "I tell you the truth, he who believes has everlasting life."

9. THAT JESUS WILL COME BACK AND RAISE HIS BELIEVERS

Matthew 25:31-32 "When the Son of Man comes in his glory, and all the angels with him, he will sit on his throne in heavenly glory. All the nations will be gathered before him, and he will separate the people one from another as a shepherd separates the sheep and the goats."

III- WHAT DID THE DISCIPLES FIND IN ESUS?

JESUS HAS TRANSFORMED THEIR LIVES

THEY HAVE FOUND JOY AND PEACE IN CHRIST

THEIR LIVES HAVE FOUND A PURPOSE

THEY HAVE HAD A POSITIVE IMPACT IN THE WORLD

THEY KNOW WHERE THEY ARE GOING AFTER HERE.

THOSE WHO BELIEVE IN HIM HAVE NOW A MASTER.

CONCLUSION:

ACCORDING TO YOU, WHO IS JESUS?

IS HE A PROPHET AS MUHAMMED TAUGHT HIS PEOPLE?

WAS JESUS JUST A MORAL TEACHER AS SOME THINK?

JESUS IS YOUR SAVIOR AND KING

DID JESUS COME TO DIE AND GIVE YOU ETERNAL LIFE? IF YES, RECEIVE HIM TODAY SAYING "

HOSANNA, BLESSED BE THE ONE WHO COMES IN THE NAME OF THE LORD. HOSANNA TO THE HIGHEST!

LET JESUS REIGN IN YOUR HEART FROM TODAY AND FOREVER.

Amen. Machiasport, Palm Sunday April 4th, 2009

(9)

Scripture Reading: John 17:6-19

THEME: JESUS IS PRAYING FOR HIS DISCIPLES.

INTRODUCTION: I have heard many people praying. Myself in my Christian life, I pray all the time. I know the importance of prayer in the life of the believers. Prayer is where we communicate with God, where we hear God, where God listens to us; these are special moments, even though we live in the presence of God all the time, moments we shot ourselves off from the world and stay in intimate communication and live in the presence of our Lord.

We have used those moments to praise, to thank, and to magnify the name and the power of God. During those moments we have shown and demonstrated that we believe and trust him. These also are moments we ask forgiveness for our sins; we seek his face; we renew our commitment and look forwards for good and new relationships with him

Prayer time is those moments we present our supplications and intercessions to God. For many, it looks like the only thing they do in prayers is to ask God to DO THIS, DO THAT to their brothers, sisters their, children, friends, themselves, their families, their towns, their countries and so forth. Sometimes, we don't even remember what we asked first and last to God. Ask, ask, ask becomes the central piece of our prayer that way. Prayer is more than that.

There are many lessons we can learn from Jesus Christ's prayer to his Father as it is found in John chapter 17. But this morning, I would like to center our message on the THINGS Jesus was praying for his disciples. Remember, everyone who is the follower of Jesus is his or her disciple and this passage is addressing to you. Jesus then, in the past prayed and now is praying for you...

WHY DID JESUS PRAY FOR HIS DISCIPLES: (vv.6-10)
We can understand why Jesus prayed for himself but why would he pray for these men and women also? Jesus is praying for them because they are his disciples. But how did they come to be in that relationship with him?

I – JESUS' PRAYER WAS BASED ON RELATIONSHIPS
   THE REALITY AND THE IMPORTANCE OF RELATIONSHIP.
   A TRIANGULAR ONE: - FATHER - SON- DISCIPLES

CONSIDER THESE TWO ELEMENTS:
   (1) THE FORCE OF A TRIANGLE AMONG ALL FIGURES.
   (2) THE PLACE OF RELATIONSHIP WITHIN EACH UNIT.
   Jesus consecrated the whole chapter 17 of John to pray for relationships.

II - THERE ARE FOUR IMPORTANT CONSIDERATIONS HERE:
(1) THE DISCIPLES ARE THE POSSESSION OF THE FATHER:
   Before the disciples, before you and me are given to Jesus, we belong to the Father "They were yours", says Jesus. All creation belongs to God.
   We were given to Jesus "out of the world".
God chose us OUT OF THE WORLD AND GAVE US TO JESUS

(2) THE DISCIPLES AS A GIFT FROM THE FATHER TO THE SON:

THE FATHER'S GIFT TO THE SON – (vv.6, 9)

A GIFT SHARED BY THE FATHER AND THE SON (v.10).

THE FATHER IS SAVING THE WORLD THROUGH THE SON

THE GIFT WHICH BRINGS GLORY TO THE FATHER.

(3) THE DISCIPLES ARE NOW BELIEVERS THROUGH FAITH

THE DISCIPLES HAVE EXPERIENCED WHO JESUS IS

THE DISCIPLES HAVE OBEYED JESUS

THE DISCIPLES HAVE THE FATHER'S WORD. (v.6).

THE DISCIPLES HAVE ACCEPTED THE WORD (v.8).

The disciples have experienced the Word

They are witness after RECEIVING JESUS

THE DISCIPLES ARE IN THE WORLD BUT NOT OF THE WORLD. (They are hated by the world (v.14)

THERE ARE ONLY THREE THINGS WHICH CAN BRING ABOUT A DIFFERENCE BETWEEN THE DISCIPLES OF JESUS AND THE PEOPLE WHO ARE IN THE WORLD:

WHETHER THE DISCIPLES ARE PROTECTED

WHETHER THE DISCIPOLES ARE UNITED

WHETHER THE DISCIPLES ARE SANCTIFIED.

THIS PRAYER IS FOR THE CALLED, SET APART PEOPLE

THIS PRAYER IS FOR THE KNOWERS OF GOD AND HIS SON

THIS PRAYER IS FOR THOSE WHO HAVE BELIEVED THE WORD.

THIS PRAYER IS FOR THE MISSIONARIES – THE WITNESSES

- THIS IS JESUS' COMFORT.

-THIS IS JESUS' SECURITY

-THIS IS THE JOY OF THE FATHER AND OF THE SON –

THIS PRAYER IS FOR A MISSION ACCOMPLISHED!

II- JESUS PRAYED:

THAT THESE PEOPLE BE THE PROTECTED (vv.11-16
   (1) BECAUSE THEY NO LONGER BELONG TO THIS WORLD
   (2) BECAUSE THEY LIVE IN A TROUBLED WORLD-.
   (3) BECAUSE THE EVIL IS IN THIS WORLD "the evil one" (v.15).
HE HAS A MISSION
HE IS THE ENEMY
WE MUST BE PROTECTED FROM THE EVIL ONE
REMEMBER, WE CAN'T EVADE THE WORLD.
OUR PROTECTION IS THROUGH THE POWER OF THE SON

"Protect them", Jesus prays, "by the power of your name" (v.11)

APPLICATION: As Jesus' disciples, we should never forget that Jesus knows that we are in the world; that Satan is around and within us, BUT WE ARE PROTECTED BY THE HOLY SPIRIT. LISTEN TO THE HOLY SPIRIT; LIVE ACCORDING TO THE HOLY SPIRIT OUR PROTECTOR.

III- JESUS PRAYED.
THAT THESE PEOPLE BE UNITED
THAT THEY BE ONE AS HE IS ONE WITH HIS FATHER
DEVIL'S STRATEGY IS TO DIVIDE GOD'S PEOPLE" (v.11)

IV- JESUS PRAYED
THAT THESE PEOPLE BE SANCTIFIED LIVING IN THE WORLD BUT NO LONGER IN WORLD. (Verses.17-19)
   (1) WE DON'T HAVE TO BE HOSTILE TO THE WORLD
   (2) WE MUST LIVE THE TRUTH IN THE WORLD

A DEMONSTRATION THAT WE BELONG AND ARE PART OF A NEW KINGDOM (Verses.6-10.)

WE BEAR FRUIT OF THE SPIRIT HERE ON EARTH. (Verse.19)

WE ARE PEOPLE WE DO THE WILL OF THE FATHER HERE.

QUESTIONS:

(1) HAS JESUS' PRAYER FOR YOU BORNE FRUIT IN YOUR LIFE?

(2) WHY DO WE THE CHURCH OF CHRIST, HAVE ALL THESE PROBLEMS? -

NO PROTECTION, NO UNITY – NO SANCTIFICATION

Jesus knew what will destroy and nullify his DIVINE MISSION. If the Church will let herself be PROTECTED by the Holy Spirit, if she will be UNITED by the Holy Spirit, and if she will let herself be SANCTIFIED by the Holy Spirit, THE DIVINE MISSION WILL REACH THE END OF THE WORLD AND SATAN WILL HAVE NO EFFECT AS IN THE TIME JESUS HIMSELF WAS ON EARTH..

But because we do our own things, seek our own goals and don't have any daily and hourly relationship with the Father, the Son and the Holy Spirit, there is no protection, no unity and no sanctification among the disciples of Jesus Christ today.

LESSON: Jesus is praying today as he prayed before going to the cross that we LET THE HOLY SPIRIT PROTECT US that we stay UNITED and that we be SANCTIFIED and his DIVINE MISSION WILL BE SUCCESSFUL.

JESUS IS PRAYING FOR YOU TODAY: BE PROTECTED, BE UNITED, AND BE SANCTIFIED AS HIS DISCIPLE. Amen.

Machiasport, March 29, 2009.

(10)

John 14:1-21

Text: 14:6"Jesus said unto him, I am the WAY, the TRUTH, and the LIFE: NO ONE COMES TO THE FATHER EXCEPT THROUGH ME."

THEME: JESUS IS THE TRUTH,

INTRODUCTION: Jesus is the great I Am. Jesus is the way to eternal life. He is the TRUTH and He is eternal life to all God's children.

Paul writing to the Ephesians Christians from his prison wrote those great chapters on God's amazing Grace and in that little book of only six chapters, Paul stated, "...as the truth is in Jesus." Ephesians 4:21

Paul continued to say in Ephesians 4:17-21 "If I tell you this, and insist on it in the Lord, that you must no longer live as the Gentiles do, in the futility of their thinking. They are darkened in their understanding and separated from the life of God because of the ignorance that is in them due to the hardening of their hearts. Having lost all sensitivity, they have given themselves over to the sensuality so as to indulge in every kind of impurity, with a continual lust for more.

You, however, did not come to know Christ that way. Surely you heard of him and were taught in him in accordance with the TRUTH THAT IS IN JESUS"

-SATAN IS AGAINST JESUS, AGAINST GOD:

From the beginning until the end, until the return of the Lord, there is only one problem which divides this world: THE DEFINITION OF WHAT IS THE TRUTH". Everyone who doesn't believe in Jesus as the truth is the follower of the anti-Christ (II John, v. 7).

THERE ARE CERTAIN BIBLICAL TRUTHS WHICH WILL STAND FOREVER: These truths summarize what we, Christians believe as TRUTH. In JESUS.

(1). What you believe determines whether you follow the anti-Christ or the Lord Jesus

If a person is wrong about Jesus Christ, it doesn't matter what else he is right about.

2). Jesus came to reveal the Father. He came as the final revelation of God to humankind

Even though Pilate asked, Jesus "What is Truth?" himself did not find anything wrong with Jesus. John 18:38. How sad, the truth is standing before Pilate and he did not recognize it. This is still true today as it has been through the ages. Men love darkness rather than Light. Proverbs 4:19 says "The way of the wicked is as darkness; they know not at what they stumble."

I - HERE IS WHAT WE KNOW, AND BELIEVE ABOUT JESUS

1. JESUS WAS A WALKING TRUTH ON EARTH:

When you and I received him and he became our Savior and Redeemer, we embraced the truth and the truth came to reside in us forever.

JESUS, EMMANUEL, GOD WITH US FOREVER.

APPLICATION: WALK IN THAT TRUTH EVERY DAY

2. NOBODY COULD CONVINCE HIM OF SIN!

Jesus himself said these words to the Pharisees in John 8:45-46 "Yet, because I tell you the truth, you do not believe me. Can any of you prove me guilty of sin

And if I am telling you the truth, why don't you believe me?" John 8:45-56.

3. THE COURT COULD NOT CONVINCE HIM OF SIN.

(a) "When Pilate saw that he was getting nowhere, but that instead uproar was starting, he took water, and washed his hands in front of the crowds and said I am innocent of that man's blood." Matthew 27:24

(b) "Then said Pilate to the Chief Priests and to the people, I find no fault in this man." Luke 23:4

CONCLUSION: Then, Pilate who asked "What Is Truth?" was also the one who said, "I find no fault in this man". Therefore, even Pilate, knew and believed the TRUTH

4. JESUS WAS NOT CRUCIFIED AS A CRIMINAL!

-Two criminal thieves were one on each side of Jesus. But not Jesus as criminal.

-Jesus was crucified as the perfect and innocent one.

-Jesus died for sinners.

-Jesus died as Lord of men, Lord of Angles, Lord over devils.

BECAUSE OF HIS DEATH ON THE CROSS:

Every knee will bow down in front of him

He is coming again as King of Kings and Lord of Lords

5. JESUS' TEACHINGS WERE NOTHING BUT THE TRUTH.

People were astonished of his teachings: for he taught them as one having authority, and not as the scribes." Matthew 7:28-29

Jesus never lied about anything.

6. JESUS NEVER SINNED IN ALL HIS LIFE

No one has ever lived like Jesus.

And never has been person a like the Lord Jesus Christ.

THIS IS THE WAY JESUS LIVED:

(1) Jesus loved and was full of compassion.

He went about doing well. Jesus loved all kinds of people. "For God so loved the world..."

(2) His life was a life of forgiving sinners.

(3) Jesus taught the way of salvation.

He is the Friend of sinners.

(4). Jesus went about healing the sick and diseased

(5) Jesus lived a perfect, pure, sinless, holy life without spot or blemish.

(6) Jesus was the perfect Lamb of God and men perfect Substitute and Sacrifice.

APPLICATION: Let's thank God for the life Jesus lived, His death on the cross and His glorious resurrection from the dead gave us ETERNAL LIFE WE HAVE TODAY.

7. JESUS IS THE TRUTH:

SOMEONE SAID: "The name of Jesus is honey to the mouth, music to the ears, and gladness to the heart." I remember this song we used to sing in our Sunday School Classes:

"Take the name of Jesus with you

Child of sorrow and of woe;

it will joy and comfort give you,

Take it then wherever you go."

REF: Precious name, Oh, how sweet! Hope of earth and joy of heaven (bis) Closing this message, let ALL YOUR ACTIONS, ALL YOUR LIVING BE UNDERTAKEN IN THE NAME OF JESUS as Colossians 3:17 says: "And whoever you do, whether in word or deed, DO IT ALL IN THE NAME OF JESUS, GIVING THANKS TO GOD THE FATHER THROUGH HIM."

In all our days may our prayer be "Father, glorify thy name." John 12:28

Amen! Machiasport March 22nd, 09

(11)

John 21:1-19

THEME: JESUS: THE SAVIOR OF THE FALLEN

It Happened to Peter, It can also happen to ME.

INTRODUCTION: If you are a follower of Jesus, you should really know why we call him SAVIOR. He did not come to save the saints but the sinners. He came in the world because he loves the fallen sinners and his work cannot be completed if he has not yet rescues a sinner.

There have been many occasions when I had to come to the Lord confessing my sins and failures and seeking forgiveness and restoration. Each time, I have found Him to be a faithful Friend to those who have fallen by the wayside. While the focus of this chapter is on the Lord Jesus, there is also major emphasis placed on the interaction between Jesus and Peter. It is that theme that I would like to zero in on this morning. As I do, I would like to speak directly to those who aren't as close to the Lord today as you should be. Maybe the things of God aren't as sweet as they used to be. Maybe there isn't a hot, burning love for the Lord, His House, His Word and His People like there used to be. Maybe even your church attendance is no longer your priority. My duty this morning is to tell you that it does not have to remain that way! Jesus Christ is still the Friend of the fallen this morning. As we look into what the Lord did for Peter,

I want you to know that He can and will do the same for you if you will respond in the correct manner. With that in mind, let's take a few minutes to consider together Jesus: The Friend of the Fallen.

1Matt. 26:69-75 PETER'S FAILURE what really happened to Peter, those strong, boasting disciples of our Lord Jesus? How come that the Bible tells us that Peter fell?

I - PETER FELL BECAUSE OF THE PLACE HE WAS IN.

CONGREGATION: SAY: DON'T FOLLOW JESUS AFAR OFF" The day Jesus was arrested, Peter, as the rest of the disciples abandoned his mast, Matt. 26:56. But Peter decided to follow Jesus "afar off."
    -When Peter found himself surrounded by the Lord's enemies, it became hard for him to stand by his earlier boast confession for his Master

APPLICATION: All those who have started backsliding have started by following Jesus "AFAR OFF " Instead of staying as close to the Lord they follow AFAR OFF,
Being in the wrong place is dangerous! Just ask David - 2 Sam. 11:1-17.)
Stay forever close to your Lord no matter what is in your life.

(1) THIS WAS PAINFUL TO PETER –
CONGREGATION: SAY, "IT IS PAINFUL TO FOLLOW JESUS AFAR OFF
When Peter denied Jesus, he CRIED, HE WEPT BITTERLY, HE WAS MISERABLE"

APPLICATION: When every child of God has abandoned him, he is miserable.

If you decide today to abandon your God, you will feel what Peter felt that night so it is with every child of God who decides to walk away from the will of God. You will soon realize that sin brings with it pain, suffering and misery, Pro. 13:15.

(2) HIS FAILLURE COST HIM A LOT
CONGREGATION: WE SHOULD FOLLOW JESUS AFAR OFF

Peter lost contact with his Master

2) Peter lost his joy and peace;

Peter lost his blessings from the Lord

Peter became a REBEL "He became a dead child of God in his SIN.

The one the Lord is looking for John 5:16, I Cor. 5:5

APPLICATION: Peter failed and he failed big! However, many of us say that we would never do anything like that, but we are guilty of denying the Lord also! I am certain that there are several who need to come before the Lord today and make some things right with Him. If this is you, you still have a Friend!)

I. Peter's Failure

II - V. 3 HIS FAILLURE MADE HIM LOOK FOOLISH

TO THE CONGREGATION: SAY TO YOUR NEIGHBOR, IF YOU FOLLOW JESUS AFAR OFF, YOU WILL BE FOOLISH.

(1) PETER WAS FOOLISH TO TAKE OTHERS WITH HIM

After the resurrection, Peter must have assumed that his ministry was over. He had denied the Lord and so he decided to return to the old way of life. I am sure that he might have tried to justify it by saying, "Well, I have a family to support." Whatever the motivation, Peter had been called to forsake all those things and to follow Jesus, Matt. 4:19. The Lord's call had been a call to come and be a fisher of men!

APPLICATION: Brother, sister, if you have decided to leave Jesus, don't try to take other disciples with you.

Don't try to take others who need salvation with you.

Don't destroy the Church of Christ because many people have known that you are Christian and they will believe that that is the way of the Church of Christ.

(2) FOOLISHED TO EXPECT BLESSINGS:

CONGREGATION: "THERE IS NO BLESSING OUT THERE"

Peter and his fishermen fished all the nightlong and did not catch a single fish! Most of these men had been professional fishermen before they met the Lord and this must have been a devastating thing to have to deal with. They toiled and labored all the night and produced nothing of value!

APPLICATION: Talk to many people who have failed Christ about the life they live outside their Savior. If they trust you, they will tell you how MISERABLE THEY ARE. There is not success outside there. You may think that: money, joy, peace, goods, happiness and so on are there, THERE IS NO BLESSING WITHOUT CHRIST IN THE CENTER. PETER AND HIS FRIENDS DID NOT CUT ANY FISH.

III-. 4-17 BUT PETER HAS A FRIEND IN JESUS

CONGREGATION" BUT PETER HAS A FRIEND: JESUS.

THAT FRIEND WAS JESUS

(2)Verses. 4-7 JESUS LOOKED AND FOUND PETER

    Verse. 5 JESUS FORCED HIM T ADMIT HIS FAILURE

    THAT FRIEND REHABILITATED PETER THERE

IV.<u>LOOK AT PETER'S FUTURE</u>
CONGREGATION: FROM THERE, PETER SACRIFIICED HIMSELF TO THE LORD: HE BECAME THE HEAD OF THE CHURCH OF JERUSALEM

B. V. <u>19b PETER'S LIFE WAS DEVOTED TO THE LORD THERE PETER SURRENDERED TO THE LORD FOREVER.</u>
The last thing Jesus does is to give Peter this command, "Follow Me!" The last call is the same as the first. When Jesus found Peter and called him the first time, this was His command. When he re-commissions Peter, He issues the same call. This tells us that the Lord hasn't changed His mind about Peter, or about Peter's duty before the Lord

<u>APPLICATION</u>
Regardless of how deep you may have fallen into sin, please know today that the Lord hasn't changed His mind about you!
-God gives the same command to you today that He gave to Peter then, "Follow me!" All Jesus wants from you is a surrendered life.
Peter surrendered and he was changed by the power of the Cross.

<u>CONCLUSION I</u>- Right now, you have a place next to Jesus, keep it forever
(2) Don't try to follow Jesus AFAR OFF" You may end up like Peter-
(3) If you fail, don't take others with you; don't expect blessings there.
(3) REMEMBER, YOU HAVE A FRIEND, JESUS. He is looking and will find you.
He is willing to REHABILITATE YOU as he did Peter.

IF JESUS HAS FOUND YOU, LISTEN TO HIS ADVICE.
COMMIT AND SURRENDER YOURSELF TO THE MASTER LIKE PETER.
YOUR FUTURE WILL NOT BE DIFFERENT FROM THE LIFE OF PETER. Amen

(12)

John 6:1-13

Text: John 6:5 Jesus looked up and saw a great crowd coming toward him, he said to Philip? "Where can we buy bread for these people to eat? He asked this only to test him, for he ALREADY HAD IN MIND WHAT HE WAS GOING TO DO.

THEME: LET GOD DO WHAT YOU CAN'T

GIVE HIM YOUR PROBLEM; HE ALREADY HAS THE SOLUTION

Introduction: When you are overwhelmed with a problem, a situation you don't know how to get out of safely, what do you do? Where do you go? If at this moment, you hear that your house has burned down, what will you do? If you hear that all your investments have disappeared as we know that economics is not well these days; what will you do? Have you seen people being overwhelmed by situations and events; have you asked yourself a question: How did they get out and smile?

OUR PROBLEM whatever name we attach to it, is totally overwhelming in our eyes. When this happens, the general tendency is to just quit. I would like to remind you that you have someone who can carry all your burdens and give you rest; He is your God! He is your Creator; He is your Master of the Sea, the Lily of the Valley, The Bright and Morning Star.

He is the One who was, who is and who is to come! He is still God and we need to remember this very important fact.

The passage we just finished reading pictures a scene that is absolutely impossible in the eyes of man, but to God, it is merely an opportunity to display His awesome power... It is an opportunity for Him to showcase His ability to overcome any and all situations, without exception!

Today, take whatever burden you carry, whether it be personal, work, church or related to someone else. Look at that burden, and then look at the greatness and power of your God. KNOW THAT JESUS CAN HANDLE IT. BRING THAT BURDEN AT THIS ALTAR AT THE END OF THIS SERVICE AND PUT IT ON THE SHOULDERS OF YOUR LORD HERE. LET YOUR GOD DO WHAT YOU CAN'T

I. Verses.1-7 THE SITUATION:

Jesus went to the other side of the sea. He was followed by a multitude of men, women and children. It was already late in the evening. No food was available. People have to eat. Jesus' disciples were OVERWHELMED BY THE SITUATION.

FIRST: REMEMBER THAT GOD KNOWS ALL SITUATIONS YOU AND I ARE IN: There is no situation, no circumstance which can happen without the knowledge of God. He knows what you face; He knows what you are going through.

SECOND: KNOW THAT GOD KNOWS HOW HE WILL HANDLE IT: He is God; He loves you; He cares for you. He can't give you a burden you can't bear. He knows all your weaknesses and all your strengths. Be careful. He has the solution!

II – JESUS ASKED PHILIP A QUESTION: WHERE: THE WAYS WE REACT TO ALL OUR PROBLEMS:

Jesus asked Philip: WHERE ARE WE GOING TO BUY FOOD FOR THESE PEOPLE

(1) Listen to Philip's answer EIGHT MONTHS WAGES WOULD NOT BUY ENOUGH BREAD FOR EACH ONE TO HAVE A BITE!

MONEY! MONEY! MONEY! Jesus asked WHERE? Philippe brings in MONEY.

APPLICATION: Just as you and I, think that IF YOU HAVE MONEY, YOU WILL SOLVE ALL PROBLEMS. - Things will be easy if we have money

(2) Listen to Andrew: "Here is a boy with five small barley loaves and two small fish, but how far will they go among so many "

I HAVE NOTHING! I HAVE NOTHING! I DON'T HAVE ENOUGH!

APPLICATION:

Andrew was just as you and I; MINIMIZE WHATEVER WE HAVE

To deal with the situation. You can't perform miracles. What you have is what you have and it is what God has given you.

DAVID KILLED GOLIATH WITH WHAT?

MOSES AND THE CHILDREN OF ISRAEL AT THE RED SEA

GIDEON WITH THE PHILISTINES

ABRAHAM IN THE MOUNT MORIAH

Listen to all the other disciples' answer: Mark 6:35-36 and Matt 15:23 "The disciples said to Jesus, "THIS IS A REMOTE PLACE, AND IT IS ALREADY VERY LATE. SEND THE PEOPLE AWAY SO THEY CAN

GO TO THE SURROUNDING COUNTRY-SIDE AND VILLAGES
AND BUY THEMSELVES SOMETHING TO EAT."

PROBLEM, GO AWAY! WHY ME? WHY ME? THERE ARE
OTHERS.

Jesus "Philip, "WHERE CAN WE BUY FOOD FOR THESE
PEOPLE?"

THE SOLUTION GOD IS GOING TO USE WILL COME FROM
YOU!

APPLICATION: These disciples, just like you and I, WANTED TO GET
RID OF THE

PROBLEM. It is not our problem. We don't need that. We can't do
anything

JESUS KNOWS ALL SITUATIONS BEFORE US; GOD KNOWS
HOW HE IS GOING TO HANDLE THEES SITUATIONS; GOD
LOVES US AND CAN'T PUT US IN A SITUATION WE CAN'T
COPE WITH. REMEMBER THAT! KNOW THAT EVERY
SITUATION IS A TEST FROM GOD. HE WOULD LIKE TO SEE
HOW MUCH YOU TRUST HIM.

Verse 6:6 HE ASKED THIS ONLY TO TEST HIM, FOR HE ALREADY
HAD IN MIND WHAT HE WAS GOING TO DO.

HERE IS WHERE ALL OF US FALL SHORT "GOD HAS THE
SOLUTION."

Before the situation, the event, GOD ALREADY HAS A
SOLUTION."

(1) Don't panic!

(2) Don't look for money

(3) Don't say that this is not my problem

(4) Don't say "I can't" I don't have this or that

III – WHAT JESUS WAS ASKING PHILIP TO DO?

WHAT GOD REQUIRES OF US IN EVERY SITUATION IS FAITH
IN HIM:

(1) What do you think of ABRAHAM and his Son Isaac on the mount
   Mariah?

(2) What do you think of Moses at the Red Sea…

(3) What do you think of David in front of Goliath…

(4) What do you think of Peter and Barabbas in front of the
   paralytic.

(5) What do you think of Jesus at Lazarus' tomb…

   LET US HAVE FAITH IN HIM.

YES! IT IS TRUE:

a) Verses 8-9 THE SUPPLIES MAY BE INSUFFICIENT (Andrew)

b)Verse 9 THE SIZE OF THE GIFT MAY BE SMALL - (5 biscuits
and 2 sardines)

TODAY, GOD IS LOOKING FOR THE GIVERS

GOD IS LOOKING FOR THOSE WHO CAN SACRIFICE WHAT
THEY HAVE –

He gave all he had. This is all God asks of any of us - Give Him all, whether
it be great or small and He will use it for his glory.

c)Verse 9 OUR DOUBTING MIND. We should not have any doubt
in our mind about what God can do: If only we believe and trust God, a
lot will be possible and done in the world today.

When the disciples talked about what the boy had, they were just
joking" A BOY HOLDING FIVE SMALL BARLEY LOAVES AND

TWO SMALL FISH, BUT HOW FAR WILL THEY GO AMONG SO MANY". They did not believe that Jesus could do something with these.. I am certain that the disciples were saying that when they were sitting people down on the grass.

HERE IS WHERE WE ALL FALL SHORT: WE NEED FAITH! JESUS WANTED THE DISCIPLES TO JUST HAND HIM WHAT THEY HAD!

IV- LET US SEE WHAT GOD CAN DO WITH A LITTLE GIFT:
JESUS TOOK THE BREAD AND THE FISH (He made them) HE PRAYED.
THEN, HE GAVE THAT FOOD TO THE PEOPLE TO GIVE TO THE PEOPLE.

APPLICATION:
HE WILL TAKE WHAT YOU HAVE
HE WILL BLESS WHAT YOU HAVE
HE WILL USE WHAT YOU HAVE.
WHAT YOU HAVE WILL BECOME SUFFICIENT.

V – LET'S SEE WHAT HAPPENED TO WHAT WAS TAKEN FROM THE BOY
EVERY NEED WAS MET, PEOPLE WERE SATISFIED: Every need was met, possibly 20,000+ people were fed, Matt. 14:21. Jesus took the little bit and turned it into a lot! (Eph.3:20) Place your little bit in the Lord's hand and He will multiply it.
Verses 10-13 THE SURPLUS WAS ABUNDANT Jesus was not disturbed by the circumstances - Ill. v.10 - You'll never have a problem greater than God's ability!)

(3). THE FAITHLESS WERE STUPEFIED - 12 baskets - 1 for each doubting disciple. When God does move in your situation, look out, it will amaze you and everyone who sees - 1 Cor. 2:9 (Your doubts will seem ridiculous then!)

CONCLUSION: Do you look at the things you face in life and say, "There's no way!" Brothers and sisters, as long as there is a great God Who sits on the throne of Heaven, there is ALWAYS A WAY! Jesus himself said "I am the way!" John 14:6! GIVE ALL YOUR PROBLEMS TO JESUS. PUT THEM TODAY IN HIS HANDS; NOT ONLY THAT WILL HE HANDLE THEM, BUT HE WILL FIND THE WAY.

REMARK: You know what is going on in your life at this moment.

Asking that to go away will not solve it.

Having a lot of money will not solve it.

Looking yourself for the way how you will deal with it will not solve it.

Text: John 6:5 Jesus looked up and saw a great crowd coming toward him, he said to Philip? "Where can we buy bread for these people to eat? He asked this only to test him, for him ALREADY HAD IN MIND WHAT HE WAS GOING TO DO.

THEME: LET GOD DO WHAT YOU CAN'T
GIVE HIM YOUR PROBLEM; HE ALREADY HAS THE SOLUTION
GIVE TO JESUS YOUR PROBLEM NOW AND YOU WILL BE AMAZED CONCERNING WHAT HE WILL DO WITH IT TODAY!
Amen. Feb. 22/2009

(13)

Reading of the Scripture John 4:1-39.

Text John 4: 7, 10 When the Samaritan woman came to draw water, Jesus said to her, "Will you give me a drink?...Jesus answered her," If you knew the gift of God and who it is that asks you for water, you would have asked him and he would have given you living water."

THEME HOW CAN WE REACH SINNERS? Example
JESUS AND THE SAMARITAN WOMAN AT THE WELL

INTRODUCTION

1. Most Christians want to share the gospel of Christ with others...

    a. Yet, most of them feel not gifted, not knowing where to start.

    b. Start a Bible class in their churches.

2. Today, let us learn some things from Jesus, the master teacher...

    a. In the N.T., we see him, we see him engaged in personal evangelism over and over preaching the Good News.

    For example, His conversation with the Samaritan woman at Jacob's well - John 4:1-26

IN OBSERVING JESUS, LET US LEARN SEVEN PRINCIPLES HE USED:

I. HE WORKED ON ONE ON ONE: PERSONAL CONTACTS

A. WE MUST ESTABLISH CONTACT WITH THE SOCIETY:

Jesus went through SAMARIA, what many Jews didn't do, and also STOPPED AND SPOKE TO A SAMARITAN WOMAN ALONE John 4:1-6

APPLICATION: Start with social contracts. Luke 5:29-32

IF PEOPLE ARE NOT COMING TO US-CHRIST

LET'S NOT KEEP THE SEED IN THE BARN

B. DO NOT CONFUSE SEPARATION WITH ISOLATION...

1. Yes, we must be separate - 2 Cor. 6:14-18

2. But this does not mean we are to isolate ourselves

   a. Note the prayer of Christ - John 17:15

C. OPPORTUNITIES FOR SOCIAL CONTACT...

1. At school with fellow students

2. at work with fellow employees or employers

3. At home with neighbors, friends, and family . Ac 1:14

Remember, Jesus said "Go into the entire world..." (Mk 16:15). We must go where the people are! Another principle we can glean from Jesus'

II. FIND SOME COMMON INTEREST WITH THAT PERSON:

A. COMMON INTERESTS CREATE A BRIDGE...

1. Note Jesus' first words to the woman - John 4:7-8

   a. He was thirsty

2. Realize the need to build rapport

   a. Meaningful dialogue is not easy, especially involving

   b. Once a bridge for communication has been established, it will be easier to discuss God's word with another person

B. COMMON INTERESTS ARE MANY...

(Such as work, community projects, hobbies)

1. Shared experiences (such as travel, or even

III. STMULATE SPIRITUAL INTERESTS IN HIM

A. THROUGH YOUR ACTIONS...

1. The example of Jesus - John 4:9

    a. As a man He speaks to her, a woman

    b. As a rabbi He speaks to her, an immoral woman

    c. As a Jew He speaks to her, a Samaritan

    d. Having a STRONG FAITH AND HOPE- , 1 Pet. 3:1-2, 15

B. THROUGH YOUR WORDS...

1. The example of Jesus - John 4:10-14

    a. Jesus' statement shifted their conversation to spiritual matters

    b. He led them into a discussion on a common spiritual

    Interest (THE LIVING WATER)

    Conversations to spiritual matters

BUILD TRUST, CONFIDENCE, THE WANT IN THE OTHER.

2) This was the practice of apostolic preaching - Acts 13:16-22

IV. GO SLOWLY WITH HIM: BE SLOW:

A. GIVE A PERSON WHAT THEY ARE READY FOR...

1. Note Jesus' discussion with the woman - John 4:15-16

V. BE NOT JUDGMENTAL

A. THE EXAMPLE OF JESUS...

1. He could have dwelt on her being an adulteress - John 4:17-18

2. He came to save the world, not to condemn it. John 3:17

3. Not to say He will not one day judge the world, but that the primary purpose of His first coming was to offer salvation . John 12:46-47

VI. STAY CENTERED IN CHRIST
A. IN THE CASE OF THE SAMARITAN WOMAN...
B. REMAIN STEADFAST TO YOUR <u>OBJECTIVES</u>.

VII. <u>BE ASSERTIVE WHEN YOU MUST</u>
A. <u>JESUS' EXAMPLE THEN</u>...
1. Finally, Jesus confronted the woman with His identity - John 4:26
2. This came after He had laid the groundwork

B. <u>EXAMPLES FOR TODAY</u>...
1. In trying to set up a home Bible study.
   a. Take advantage of social contacts
   b. Develop common interests
   c. Be open to comments that indicate a spiritual interest,
   While demonstrating your own faith through actions and words
2. during the course of a home Bible study
   a. Continue to develop the social contact
   b. Continue to establish common interests
   c. Look for what can enhance your spiritual life together
   d. Go from common ground to uncommon ground carefully
   e. Stress the good news, and minimize people's shortcomings.
   f. Have one primary objective: to help them understand there

<u>CONCLUSION</u>
1. The result of Jesus' conversation with the Samaritan woman was the conversion of many people in the city of Sychar - John 4:39-42
2. This demonstrates the potential of personal evangelism...
   a. Who knows whether the one person you teach may in turn bring many to Christ?

b. That one person may be like a seed from which seeds may come forth

"Do you not say, 'There are still four months and [then] comes the harvest'? Behold, I say to you, lift up your eyes and look at the fields, for they are white already to harvest!" (John 4:35). Amen.

(14)

Scripture Reading: John 3:1-21

Text John 3:16-17, "FOR GOD SO LOVED THE WORLD THAT HE GAVE HIS ONLY SON, THAT WHOEVER BELIEVES IN HIM SHALL NOT PERISH BUT HAVE ETERNAL LIFE. GOD DID NOT SEND HIS SON INTO THE WORLD TO CONDEMN THE WORLD, BUT TO SAVE THE WORLD THROUGH HIM.

THEME: **IS GOD CAPABLE OF SAVING THE WORLD?**

INTRODUCTION: Jesus Christ has a conversation with Nicodemus. The whole conversation was based on some important statements made by him:
- (1) First Jesus said that he came into the world to provide salvation for all human beings.
- (2) That the salvation is available to every human being regardless of his age, sex, origin, color, level of education and so forth. Anyone born from a woman can be saved by Jesus Christ, the Son of God.
- (3) That everyone who is alive today can be saved today.

Let us recite John 3:16-17, "FOR GOD SO LOVED THE WORLD THAT HE GAVE HIS ONLY SON, THAT WHOEVER BELIEVES IN HIM SHALL NOT PERISH BUT HAVE ETERNAL LIFE. GOD DID NOT SEND HIS SON INTO THE WORLD TO CONDEMN THE WORLD, BUT TO SAVE THE WORLD THROUGH HIM.

I – JESUS WAS SENT TO SAVE THE WORLD:

The purpose of the coming of Jesus on earth was TO SAVE EVERYONE so, to clear up any confusion, I want to tell you what that word means. The word "saved" comes from the Greek word "sozow". This word literally means, "to save, to keep safe and sound, and to rescue from danger or destruction."

1) To save one from injury from peril, from suffering, from perishing, to deliver from penalty, to save from EVIL, TO DELIVER FROM SATAN.
2) To preserve one who is in danger of destruction, to 1)
3) To deliver from the penalties of the Messianic Judgment

Man in his natural state in the world is lost. Because, man in his natural state of sin Rom. 3:23. says "For all have sinned and fall short of God's glory" Rom. 3:23 says "FOR THE WAGES OF SIN IS DEATH, BUT THE GIFT OF GOD IS ETERNAL LIFE.

When you and I and everyone who breathes were burn in this world, what was awaiting for us forever is a DEATH SENTENCE. PUNISHMENT, SUFFERING, PENALITY, PERDICTION, CONDEMNATION, DEATH - A DEPARTURE AND SEPARATION FROM GOD FOREVER.

II HOW COULD WE BE SAVED BEING BORN SINNERS?
JESUS IS THE ANSWER - GOD IS CAPABLE OF SAVING US.
(1) GOD HAS PROMISED SALVATION:

A- <u>SALVATION IS AN OLD PROMISE</u>: - Our ancestors in the Garden of Eden,

> (1) Gen. 3:15. God promised to provide a means of Salvation.
>
> (2) In Rev. 13:8 Jesus is the Lamb slain from the foundation of the world.
>
> Peter says in I Peter 1:20 he was chosen before the creation

<u>BEFORE YOU AND I SINNED</u>, GOD ALREADY MADE A PROMISE TO SAVE US

<u>B.THAT PROMISE IS ETERNAL</u> - Before that promise was pronounced to Adam and Eve; it was already made in ETERNITY. The promise is valid today as it has always been. Note: John 5:24. This promise has never and will never lose its great power. God is a saving God and nothing will ever change that truth!

<u>C. THIS PROMISE IS AN OPEN ONE THIS PROMISE IS OFFERED TO ALL HUMAN BEING - WHOEVER</u>. No sex, no age, no origin, no nationality, no DENOMINATION, NO OTHER CONDITION EXCEPT – To believe in Jesus Christ.

> (1) Roman 10:13 FOR, "EVERYONE WHO CALLS ON THE NAME OF THE LORD WILL BE SAVED."
>
> (2) John 6:57, Rom. 10:13 jus to name a few it is clear
> THAT WHAT THE FATHER GIVES TO ME, WILL COME TO ME AND WHOEVER COMES TO ME, I WILL NEVER DRIVE AWAY.

(3) Listen to what Jesus himself said in John 7:37.

"IN ANYONE THIRSTS, LET HIN COME TO DRINK

(4) NOT THE HEALTHY WHO I NEED THE DOCTOR, BUT THE SICK. I DID COME FOR THE RIGHTEOUS, BUT SINNERS.

APPLICATION: WHO IS NOT A SINNER IN THIS ROOM ? RAISE YOUR HAND. Rom. 3:23; Gal. 3:22. WHO DOESN'T NEED SALVATION? RAISE YOUR HAND.

Isa. 53:6. Says "WE ALL, LIKE SHEEP, HAVE GONE ASTRAY

EACH OF US, HAS GONE HIS OWN WAY

AND THE LORD HAS LAID ON HIM

THE INIQUITY OF US ALL.

II. GOD HAS THE POWER TO SAVE ALL HUMAN BEINGS:

- Not only that the Lord has promised

-That that promise is Eternal,

-That that promise is open to all

But God has the power to fulfill his promise

A-GOD HAS THE POWER TO REACH THE SINNERS.

(1) The Holy Spirit has been reaching someone in order that He will accept Jesus as his Savior.

(2) Rom. 3:11.NO ONE CAN UNDERSTAND, NONE WHO SEEKS GOD

(3) Salvation originates from God John 6:44

"No ne come to me unless the Father who sent me draws him, And I will raise him at the last day"

B. GOD HAS THE POWER TO CONVERT SINNERS - When a sinner places his or her faith in the Lord Jesus Christ for salvation, GOD DOES THE WORK OF GRACE IN THE SINNER'S HEART AND LIFE – Human beings can't do that.

CONVERTED ALL SINNER, SINS ARE AUTOMATICALLY FORGIVEN –

(1) Psa. 103:12; As far as the east is from the west,
   so far as has he removed our transgressions from us.

(2) The Sinner Becomes a Child of God 1 John
   "That we should be called children of God

(3) the Sinner Is Delivered From Sin
   a.) The Power of Sin - Rom. 6:14
   b.) The Penalty of Sin. Rom. 8:1 "Therefore there is no Condemnation for those who are in Christ Jesus

(4) the Sinner Becomes Joint Heir with Christ. Rom. 8:17

(5) The Sinner Inherits a Heavenly Home –
   John 14:1-3 I WILL COME BACK AND TAKE YOU TO BE WITH ME THAT YOU ALSO MAY BE WHERE I AM.

THE SINNER BECOMES A SAINT - When Jesus saves you, He changes you forever –
2 Cor. 5:17. THEREFORE IF ANYONE IS IN CHRIST, HE IS A NEW CREATION, THE OLD HAS GONE, THE NEW HAS COME.
HE CHANGED Saul - Acts 9;
HE CHANGED Nicodemus - John 3, 7,
HE CHANGED Bartimaeus - Mark 10;
HE CHANGED Zacchaeus - Luke 10,
HE CHANGED The Dying Thief - Luke 23;

C. HE WAS THE POWER TO CONSERVE THE SAINT

If God starts the work in any sinner, he will finish it. YOU CAN'T LOSE YOUR SALVATION. GOD CAN'T SAVE YOU AND LOSE YOU.

  (1) 1 Pet. 1:5; THROUGH FAITH THEY ARE SHIELDED BY GOD'S POWER

  (2) Rom. 8:37 NOW IN ALL THESE THINGS, WE ARE MORE THAN CONQUERORS THROUGH HIM WHO LOVED US;

2 Tim. 1:12 I AM CONVINCED THAT HE IS ABLE TO GUARD WHAT I HAVE ENTRUSTED HIM FOR THAT DAY.

SUMMARY:

I. THE GOD WHO HAS PROMISED TO SAVE

II. IS THE GOD WHO HAS THE POWER TO SAVE

III- HE IS THE ONE WHO HAS THE PROVISIONS TO SAVE

  A- JESUS/ APPROPRIATE SUBSTITUTE OFFERED FOR OUR SINS: - In order to save a man who sinned, A MAN HAS TO DIE but it must be a PERFECTMAN, THAT MAN WAS Jesus Christ. In fact, the gift of God in Christ proves God's love for you and me - John 3:16; Rom. 5:6-8.

  When Jesus was on the cross, God transferred your sins to Jesus and He died to pay your price on that cross - 2 Cor. 5:21

  B.- THE SACRIFICE HE MADE ON THE CROSS WAS SUFFICIENT

  (1) Heb. 10:10 WE HAVE BEEN MADE HOLY THROUGH THE SACRIFICE OF THE BODY OF JESUS CHRIST

  (2) Eph. 2:8-9 FOR IT IS BY GRACE THAT YOU HAVE BEEN SAVED, THROUGH FAITH, AND THIS IS NOT FROM YOURSELVES, IT IS A GIFT OF GOD.

THERE IS A PLAN FOR OUR SALVATION

(1) If God promised to save us,

(2) If He has the power to save us

(3) If He has provided the means to save us,

IV –WHAT SHOULD WE DO IN ORDER TO BE SAVED? The answer is found in the verses we read this morning -

John 3:16-17.TO BELIEVE IN JESUS CHRIST Rom. 10:9-10.

(1) NO CREED, (2) NO DENOMINATION,

(3) NO PERSON, (4) NO SELF EFFORT,

(5) NO SELF RIGHTEOUSNESS –

BUT BELIEVE IN JESUS AND BE SAVED Acts 16:31

"BELIEVE IN THE LORD AND BE SAVED Rom. 10:13

"EVERYONE WHO CALLS IN HIS NAME WILL BE SAVED Rom. 6:23. FOR THE WAGES OF SIN IS DEATH, BUT THE GIFT OF GOD IS ETERNAL LIFE IN CHRIST JESUS OUR LORD.

CONCLUSION: (1)Is there anyone here who doesn't understand about those whom Jesus Christ came to save?

(2) Is there anyone here who still doubts that God can save any human being regardless of anything we consider as LIMITATION, OBSTACLE FOR HIS OR HER SALVATION? THERE IS ONLY ONE CONDITION WHICH STANDS BETWEEN YOU AND YOUR SALVATION, YOU AND YOUR CONDEMNATION, YOU AND YOUR PERDITION, YOU AND YOUR DEATH IN SPIRIT, YOU AND YOUR SEPARATION FROM YOUR GOD, YOU AND YOUR ETERNAL LIFE: BELIEVE IN JESUS CHRIST AND YOU WILL BE SAVED TODAY IF YOU BELIEVE, GIVE ALL YOUR TRUST, ALL YOUR HOPE, ALL YOUR HEART, ALL YOUR BURDEN TO JESUS AND RECEIVE HIM AS YOUR SAVIOR AND LORD.

DO YOU BELIEVE IN HIM AS THE BIBLE SAYS? IF "Yes" YOU HAVE ETERNAL LIFE. RIGHT NOW. Amen.

Machiasport, Feb.8, 2009

(15)

Reading of the Scripture John 20:19-30

Text: John 20: 20:20 Thomas said to him "My Lord and my God."

THEME: THOMAS, THE TRANSFORMED DISCIPLE.

INTRODUCTION: Almost every Christian or non-Christian knows names of many of Jesus' disciples. Many know stories concerning Peter, Judas, and Paul. Sure enough, everybody remembers Thomas' story how he wanted to put his finger on Jesus' side and hands in order to believe.

No one knows about Thomas' origin, his early life. But what happened that day Jesus came among his disciples and Thomas was not there, is what everyone remembers: his denial of the resurrection of the Lord and the necessary proof in order that he believed that he had risen from the death. Brother and sister don't forget that Thomas was called as the other eleven disciples to follow Jesus. John 21,

The name Thomas in Aramaic and stands for "Twin". The other name he has in the Bible is "Didymus". This word means "twin" in Greek. Apparently, Thomas had either a twin brother or sister, but that person is not identified in the Bible

Thomas only appears in twelve passages in the Gospel of John. In Matthew, Mark and Luke, Thomas is only mentioned three times. Each time he is mentioned, his name appears when he is listed with the other disciples of Jesus, Matt. 10:3; Mark 3:18; Luke 6:15. He is also mentioned in Acts 1:3 as one of the disciples present in the upper room on the day of Pentecost.

I –THOMAS WAS ABSENT AT THE FIRST JESUS' APPEARANCE

For nearly 2,000 years, Thomas has received a lot of bad press.

He was given the name of "Doubting Thomas".

He has been portrayed as a man filled with doubt and fear

WHAT WAS THOMAS' PROBLEM?: was not his doubting;

Was he fearful NO! He is the one who said to the rest of the Disciples in John "LET'S GO AND DIE WITH HIM "

(1) Thomas was a pessimist!

(2) He was a "glass half-empty" kind of person.

(3) He LOVED to look for the negative side of every situation first.

(4) He loved looking for the "dark side" of things.

(5) He was loyal but with an inquiring spirit.

(6) He was skeptical, but his skepticism was the right kind.

(7) He was a skeptic but open to belief.

I WILL SPEAK ABOUT THE TRANSFORMATION OF THOMAS

Let's see how God changes a man from doubt to shout.

1 John 20:24 says that Thomas, one of the 12 also called DIDYMUS Was not with the disciples when Jesus came.

A. The Context – Why the disciples were where they were, v. 19, and what they were doing there. - Were they supposed to be there but Thomas wasn't?

B. Where was Thomas that day and that moment?
BUT WE KNOW THAT THOMAS LOVED JESUS:

1. John 11:16- Jesus is going to raise Lazarus and Thomas knows that Jesus' enemies are after Him and that Jesus might just die. He is willing to go with Jesus and die with him if necessary. Thomas challenged the rest to go along with Jesus.

2. John 14:5– Jesus has told His disciples that He is going away. He also tells the disciples that they know where He is going and they know how to get there themselves. Thomas responds by saying that he needs more information. He wasn't afraid to ask questions. His questions were not motivated by doubt, but by a desire to know more!

C. THESE TWO PASSAGES SHOW THAT THOMAS WAS NOT A FEARFUL MAN: BUT A BRAVE MAN; A LOVING MAN.

YES, Thomas was disappointed when Jesus died on the cross.

He was not with the other disciples by choice.

He was not there because of his broken-heart; his shattered

D. THE PERSON WHO MISSED THE MOST THAT DAY WAS THOMAS BECAUSE HE WAS NOT THERE THE DAY JESUS CAME

1. v. 19 – He missed the Presence of the Lord.
2. v. 19 – He missed the Power of the Lord.
3. v. 19 – He missed the Peace of the Lord.
4. v. 20 – He missed the Praises of the Lord.
5. v. 21 – He missed the Promotions of the Lord.
6. Verses. 22-23 – He missed the Provisions of the Lord.

Thomas missed a lot when he missed that assembly. Regardless of his excuse for not being there, he missed some things that could never be duplicated. Others told him about it, verses. 25, but Thomas learned the hard way that there are some things you just have to see for yourself.

II –THE GOOD PICTURE OF BEING FAITHFUL TO CHURCH.

You never know what you will miss when you fail to come to church.

I KNOW THAT PEOPLE ALWAYS HAVE SOME GOOD EXCUSES NOT TO COME TO CHURCH:

(1) TODAY'S PEOPLE ARE TOO BUSY – Hectic life.

(2) CHILDREN ARE TOO BUSY – Sports.

(3) TODAY LADIES ARE WORKERS AND HOUSEWIVESs

(4) BECAUSE OF SNOW, PEOPLE GOD SNOWMOBILING

(5) SERMONS ARE TOO LONG

(6) WORSHIP NOT CONTEMPORARY

QUESTION: DO YOU REALLY KNOW WHAT YOU MISS:

1. verse 19 – He missed the Presence of the Lord.

2. verse 19 – He missed the Power of the Lord.

3. verse 19 – He missed the Peace of the Lord.

4. verse 20 – He missed the Praises of the Lord.

5. verse 21 – He missed the Promotions of the Lord.

6. verses 22-23 – He missed the Provisions of the Lord.

III – THE PASTOR MAY ALSO HAVE SOME EXCUSES:

ILLUSTRATION: The Pastor and his wife arose one Sunday morning and the wife dressed for church. It was just about time for the service when she noticed her husband hadn't moved a finger toward getting dressed. Perplexed, she asked, "Why aren't you getting dressed for church?" He said, "Because I don't want to go." She asked, "Do you have any reason?" He said, "Yes, I have three good reasons. First, the congregation is cold. Second, no one likes me. And third, I just don't want to go." The wife replied, wisely, "Well, honey, I have three reasons why you should go. First, the congregation is warm. Second, there are a few people there who like you. And third, you're the pastor! So get dressed!"

NONE OF OUR EXCUSES IS RIGHT – GO TO CHURCH

1. Church attendance is not an optional matter; IT IS A COMMAND FROM THE LORD, Heb. 10:25-26. An absence from church is a vote to close the doors! It is a testimony to the world that your life is more important than His worship.

2. WHEN YOU MISS THE SERVICE, you miss an opportunity that will never present itself again. Ever notice the good service is the one you miss? That problem you have; that need in your life; that question that has been plaguing you; might just be dealt with in one of the services you chose to miss. You never know what you will miss when you don't come to church.

3. GOD HAS SOMETHING SPECIAL FOR EACH ONE OF US WHEN WE MEET. If we come with a clean, open heart, we will receive a blessing from Him, Matt. 18:20.

ILLUSTRATION: The missing Lamps – In a certain mountain village in Europe several centuries ago, a nobleman wondered what legacy he should leave to his townspeople. At last he decided to build them a church. No one saw the complete plans for the church until it was finished. When the people gathered, they marveled at its beauty and completeness. Then someone asked, "But where are the lamps? How will it be lighted?" The nobleman pointed to some brackets in the walls. Then he gave to each family a lamp which they were to bring with them each time they came to worship. "Each time you are here the area where you are seated will be lighted," the nobleman said. "Each time you are not here, that area will be dark. This is to remind you that whenever you fail to come to church, some part of God's house will be dark.

IV- OUR FELLOWSIP MISSES SOMETHING WITHOUT YOU

You need the church and what it offers – When you go to church to worship, you are proclaiming your faith in a risen Lord. You are teaching your children the importance of God's house. You are building a wall of protection around your heart and life. You are strengthening your faith and growing in the Lord. verse. 25 THOMAS THE DOUBTER

A. The Context – Thomas was not there when Jesus appeared. The other disciples were and they told him about all that they had seen when Jesus appeared to them. The little verb "said" is in the "active voice". In other words, they kept on telling him about seeing Jesus and trying to convince him that the Lord was really raised from the dead.

Despite their assurances and testimonies, Thomas cannot bring himself to believe. He goes so far as to say, "I will not believe!" This is a powerful statement. It is a "double negative". Thomas is saying, "I positively will not believe!"

Now, before we come down too hard on Thomas, we need to think about the other disciples. When they first heard the news that Jesus was alive, they didn't believe either, Luke 24:11; Mark 16:11. The whole group was so overcome with grief and disappointment that they could not bring themselves to believe. The only reason the ten believed was because they had seen Jesus for themselves. Thomas was only asking for the same proof they had already received.

Here was Thomas' problem: he was a negative person. He was always looking for the cloud behind the silver lining. He had hoped against hope that Jesus was the Messiah and the Savior. Now, his last memory of Jesus is of a dead man hanging on a cross. His world has fallen down around him and he cannot bring himself to believe anymore. So, he rejects the words of his friends and spends a whole week in self-imposed loneliness and discouragement.

B. There are people in this room who can identify with Thomas. You have a hard time believing what you cannot see with your eyes. For that reason you have put off trusting in Jesus. His claims are amazing! What the Bible says about Him is hard for the human mind to grasp. Still, let me encourage you to delay no longer! Look to Jesus and believe the testimony of His Word and of those who have seen Him for themselves. Look to Him and be saved; He is the only hope you have, John 14:6; Acts 4:12; John 8:24.

C. Others here have lived lives shaken by one disappointment after another. You are disillusioned and think the claims of Jesus are too good to be true. But, the thing that makes them so good is the fact that they are true! Jesus can do for you what He has promised He can do. He can do for you what He has done for others. He can save your soul; forgive your sins; make you a child of God; free you from spiritual death and from the bondage of your sins. He can do it for you, and He will do it for you if only you will believe in Him, Rom. 10:9, 13; Acts 16:31 .

D. There was a time when we were all doubters. But, the Spirit of God convinced us of the truth. We, like the ten disciples, believed and were saved and filled with peace, joy and spiritual life. Those same blessings can be yours, if you will believe. And, you can do that today!

III. v. 26-29 THE WAY THOMAS BECAME THE SHOUTER
A. The Context – Perhaps the disciples begged and pleaded with Thomas to the point where he decided to meet with them on the next Sunday. While they are there, Jesus again appears in their midst. This time, He focuses His attention on Thomas. He repeats the very words of Thomas (v. 25) back to

him and invites him to touch Him and satisfy his need to know. Then Jesus tells him to let go of his doubts and trust what he knows to be true.

There is a difference between doubt and unbelief. Doubt is a problem of the intellect. The person wants to believe, but has questions. Unbelief is a problem of the heart. Unbelief will not believe no matter what it sees. Thomas was plagued by doubt. When his questions were answered, he did not need to touch the risen Jesus; seeing Him was enough. Thomas utters one of the greatest confessions in the Bible. He calls Jesus both "Lord and God" and he claims the Lord as his own. All of his pouts and his doubts are now settled. Thomas receives what the other disciples have been enjoying for a whole week. He gets all the things they got back in verses 19-23.

B. Apparently, Thomas never doubted again. After Pentecost, the Bible never mentions him again. History, however, tells us what happened to the disciples called "Twin". Thomas traveled east, preaching the Gospel through Persia. He finally wound up in India where he had a very fruitful ministry. There are several churches in India today that can trace their history back to the time of Thomas. Eventually, the enemies of the Lord took Thomas and killed him with a spear. He died for the Lord he once doubted.

C. Oh that those who doubt could do what Thomas did.

Oh that you could just get past your doubts,

If you come to him and believe, you'll find that

Jesus can fill your life with peace, joy, praise, and blessing.

He can take you just like you are and transform you like he did Thomas.

He will use you, bless you, keep you, and amaze you.

All you have to do is believe!

No matter who you are; what you have done; or where you have been, you need to know that Jesus Christ can and will save you if you will come to Him, John 6:37. Come to Him and watch Jesus take your pouts and your doubts and transform them into shouts.

Conclusion: In verses 29, Jesus tells Thomas something you need to hear today. He tells Thomas that Thomas had believed because of what he had seen with his eyes. Jesus then says something very important. He says that those who believe without seeing are even more blessed than Thomas. That is good news today! None of us will ever see the physical Person of Jesus in this life. What we must do is believe by faith what the Bible says about Jesus. If we can get passed our doubts and believe Him, we will be saved by Him!

If you are lost, what keeps you from believing in Jesus? What would it take to convince you? What holds you back? Whatever it is, it is not worth the eternal price you will pay for not coming, Mark 8:36-37.

Maybe there are others here like Thomas. You have been allowing yourself to be absent from the place where God meets with and blesses His people.

If the Lord has spoken to you and convinced you of the need to be saved, or of the need to draw closer in your walk with Him, you need to come to Him today and deal with those issues. Let Jesus take your doubts and turn them into shouts for Him and his glory today.

Amen.

(16)

Reading of the Scripture: Luke 4:14-22

THEME: JESUS'S MISSION OUTLINE.

INTRODUCTION: Jesus, just at the beginning of his ministry, let everybody know why he came on this earth and what the main objectives of his job were.

Every time a new position is created in any enterprise, the boss or bosses first seat down and define the kind of employment the new employee will perform. The second thing they do is look on the kind of education and training that person will have to have. They put down a canvas of qualifications...

He, Jesus, is letting everyone know how he is going to accomplish his job. Yes, through His birth, his death and his resurrection he proved repeatedly who He was. Prophecies spoke about him and he came to fulfill them. But his life and his work should demonstrate that he is the one who was the Messiah and the Savior of the world.

Still, men failed to recognize Him for Who He was. Look at verse 22, "Is not this Joseph's son?" Look at what they said about Him in John 8:19, 41. You see, He was and is far more than men could or can see. He is the Son of God. He is the fulfillment of all the types and prophecies of the Old Testament. He is the Son of Man, but He is so much more. He is:

(1) •Abel's Lamb (2) •Noah's Ark (3) •Abraham's Sacrifice (4) •David's Good Shepherd (5) •God's Tabernacle (6) •the Perfect Sacrifice

Here, Jesus makes certain claims regarding why He came. He quotes Isaiah 61:1-2, and applies this scripture to Himself and His ministry. All of these things Jesus quotes were fulfilled in His lifetime. Yet, they continue to be fulfilled everyday that the world stands. What He was doing then, He is still doing! He will never die again, he will never rise from the dead again. No more will men beat Him and spit in His face. But, there are still portions of His ministry that He continues to carry out daily in your life and mine.

LET US BE WELL PREPARED TO CONTINUE THE MAIN MISSION JESUS CAME TO DIE FOR IN ORDER TO BE OUR SAVIOR AND THE MESSIAH PROMISED.

I - THE KIND OF PERSON JESUS WAS, AND WE SHOULD BE

The first thing Jesus needed in order to fulfill his mission was to be filled with the Holy Spirit. That is why he took the text from Isaiah and read the text from Luke 4:18 says, "The Spirit of the Lord is on me"

Here is a question for you. Are you certain that the Spirit of God is on you? Can you witness to others and at any place and any moment that the Spirit of God is on you? You are possessed by that Spirit? You are not alone in your witnessing? This is just what Jesus did. He let everyone in that synagogue that day know that he was in the Spirit of the Most High.

Before we start talking about serving God, we should be sure that we have his Spirit. We are going to do what we do in his name. Jesus was sure. Let us be sure that we are in his Spirit in this life and this world. Don't be ashamed to witness to all that you have his Spirit.

What does it mean that the Spirit of God was on Jesus if not that he was called; he was set apart; he became a different person from the time the Spirit of God came upon him. Was it at his baptism? I am sure that when he left the water everyone who was there saw that Spirit in the form of a dove descending on him and the voice of God being heard, that was the day that Spirit came and dwelt on him forever here on earth.

You are anointed; you are set apart for a special mission just as Jesus. Any one who is in Christ is a new creation. Anyone who has confessed by his mouth that Jesus is his or her Savior has the Spirit of God. You can't, I can't do it if we don't have his Spirit and if his Spirit doesn't dwell in us.

Do you know that you are anointed? Do you know that you are a special person in this life? Do you really know who you are? Jesus knew who he was and he knew his calling too. Do the same. KNOW YOURSELF. There is nothing more important in this life than a person knowing who he or she is.

The next verses are very important because they describe the job Jesus is going to do point by point. Jesus was anointed by God in order that he, first of all, preaches the Good News to the poor. (Luke 4:18b. When we read the Beatitudes, Jesus' sermon on the Mount, (Matt.5:3), he named the poor and qualified which poor. Yes. In Mark 2:12, Jesus healed the paralytic; in Matt.9:33 he gave sight to the blind mute. He fated people, and did many miracles among the poor. The poor he talked about in Luke 4:18b are the poor in Spirit. People we know that they don't have Jesus in their lives. Do you know them in your family, in your work place, some of your friends, people you meet at the market place, on the street, people who are around you. If you have the Spirit of God; if you are called as a Christian (because Christians are little Christs here and now), look, brother, sister, these are people the Good News is meant to reach first.

Second, Jesus said that his job is "to proclaim freedom for the prisoners." The prisoners are not just those who are in physical prisons. I hope that in our towns and cities, all churches have some special ministries in prisons. There are more prisons in our societies than jails. There are emotional prisons. Some people spend more time and effort to satisfy their emotions than anything else. Do things which make them feel good. It may be what they say with their mouth, what they do with their bodies, what they see with their eyes, what they spend their money for. There are mental prisons. What preoccupies your mind? When you go to bed, when you are at the workplace, when you speak to your friend, is Jesus in the center of all that? What do you read from the time you wake up to the time you go to bed? There are many mental prisoners. Are you one? There are many materialistic prisoners. Work, work, work. Money, Money, money. Possessions, possessions, possessions. Promotions, promotions, promotion. As long as there is no profit, no personal gain, nothing can motivate those people. These are prisoners and the Good News, brothers in Christ, is for this group in our societies. Do what Christ came to do and we, his church, should witness to this group of people.

The third group Jesus named is the blind. He came to give sight to the blind. As we said before, he brought sight back to Bartimeus and other blind in the New Testament. These were just an illustration of the kind of blind we have today. We have many people well educated today. Some of them are even members of our congregation. They may be important people in our societies. Brothers, and sisters in Christ, don't be confused, know that you are surrendered by spiritual blind. You know what is going on in your family, in your village and town, in the country and in the world today. If everyone knows about Jesus, if everyone who goes to church, who gives money, who hears and sings Christians hymns, if everyone who has watched T.V. and listened to religious programs on radio could have their eyes open, think about Jesus coming soon and anytime from this moment, the world will be different. Let us consider those blind men and women and bring the Good News to them, brothers and sisters.

I truly believe that our job is to preach the Good News. Our calling is not to change people's hearts. This is what the Holy Spirit does. Our job is not to push people to confess Jesus as their Savior. This is what every individual person has to do. For that, if he or she doesn't, the judgment will fall on them. Now is the time we should risk everything and do everything in order to bring the Good News to the poor, to the prisoners, to the blind, and there is another category, to the oppressed.

The oppressed that are pinned down. They may have the desire, the will to get out but they can't. Sometimes, they have tried but they fall back. It may be because of economy. It may be because of education. It may be because of their origin, their sex, their physical, mental or any other handicap in this life. We know them. They are our children, our brothers and sisters, our friends and many who are looking at us at this moment. Have compassion and the love of Christ in your heart, your eye, and your mind. When you look at them, see Jesus through each one of them. Your calling is to treat them as the oppressed Jesus came to free. Free them yourself.

To the poor; to the prisoners, to the blind and to the oppressed, to the all sinners of our humankind, Jesus came to proclaim the year of the Lord's favor.

This time in history of the world. The period between Jesus ascension and his second coming is the period which is known as the year of God's favor. God is standing extending his arms to the world; calling every sinner to go to him; letting each one of us know that there is only one condition and a very simple one which stands between perdition and our salvation; our rejection and our reception; our death and our eternal life. That condition is just to raise our eyes and look at Jesus Christ. That condition is just to receive him as our Savior. That condition is just to call him "ABBA" Father. This is the year of the Lord's favor. This is the time of grace. Forgiveness is available to anyone who accepts Jesus and he will become automatically the son or daughter of the Most High. He or she will inherit the Kingdom of heaven and because the brother or sister of our Lord Jesus.

John 18:37 Pilate said to Jesus, "You are the king." And Jesus said to him, "Yes, you are right, I am the king. In fact for that reason I was born, and for this I came into the world, to testify to the truth.

STORY: I heard about a man who was in prison for 25 years. When the day of his release was coming close, he told the Jail supervisor that he didn't want to go out because he did not know how to be himself and make right decisions. Therefore, he wanted to stay in jail. He did not know how he could cope outside jail.

CONCLUSION:

Brother, sister, if you feel that way about any situation which has separated you from Jesus, if you are and know that Jesus is far away from you, you should know that his mission and the mission of his church is for you:

(1) TO PREACH THE GOOD NEWS FOR THE POOR

(2)TO SET THE PRISONERS FREE

(3) TO GIVE SIGHT TO THE BLING

(4) TO SET AT LIBERTY THOSE WHO ARE BRUISED.

(5) TO PROCLAIM THE LORD'S FAVOR, GRACE AND MERCY.

DO YOU HAVE THE SPIRIT OF GOD?

YOU ARE AN ANOINTED PERSEON, SET APART.

ARE YOU DOING YOUR JOB: OF FIVE POINTS. Amen.

Jan.25/ 2009

(17)

Reading: Matt. 2:1-12

Text: Matt. 2:2 Magi from the east came to Jerusalem and asked, 'where is the one who has been born King of the Jews? We saw His star in the east, and have come to worship Him.'"

THEME: BELIEVING IS SEEING

INTRODUCTION

1. In the nativity scenes, people called WISE MEN, or MAGI
    a. three in number,
    b. Their names: Melchior, Balthasar, and Caspar
2. Matthew is the gospel writer who records this visit...
    a. Which is found in Matt.2:1-12

I. INTERESTING FEATURES OF THIS STORY

A. FOR WHAT MATTHEW DOESN'T TELL US...

1. "wise men from the East"?
    a. priests from Persia
    b. astrologers from Babylon

2. What was the nature of the "star"?

    a. Was it an actual "star"?

3. Their connection STAR/WISE MEN/ JESUS BIRTH?

B. <u>FOR WHAT LEGENDS HAVE RISEN...</u>

1. "Three kings from the Orient"

2. That their names were Gaspar, Balthasar , and Melchior

3. That they were later baptized by Thomas

We have come to worship, the true God

"Immanuel", or "God with us")!

II. LESSONS TO BE LEARNED

(1). THERE ARE TRUE SERVANTS OF GOD WHERE NOT EXPECTED

    1. Millions some other places hidden

    2. God's people not those you know about, listed in "our" directories

    3. Many faithful Christians in other countries

        a. GOD KNOWS THEM ALL 2 Tim. 2:19 2

(2). WE DON'T KNOW EVERYONE WHO HONOR GOD.

    1. THE MAGI CAME FAR AWAY TO WORSHIP HIM

John 1:11 "He came to his own, and his own received him not"

"He came to His own, and His own did not receive Him" – John 1:11-

2. Christians may often show less love to GOD

Children of Christian parents many children of non-Christians

(3). PEOPLE MAY KNOW JESUS IN THE HEAD, BUT LESS GRACE IN THE HEART...

1. The chief priests and scribes

2. What about us today? 2 Pet. 3:18

(4). BE SPIRITUALLY DILIGENT AS THE WISE MEN

1. Consider what it must have cost them to travel

A. In money

B. In time

C. In dangers

(5) HAVE FAITH AS THE WISE MEN:

1. They believed in Christ..

a. When they had never seen Him in the past..

2. THEY WORSHIP JESUS

1) Without miracles to convince them (except the star)

2) Without much teaching to persuade them

THE FELL DOWN AND WORSHIP THE BABY

3. THEY HAVE FAITH IN JESUS

As Jesus said later, "Thomas, because you have seen Me, you have believed. Blessed are those who have not seen and yet have believed." – John 20:29

4. THEY HAVE – GOD, FRANKINCENSE, and MYRRH.

CONCLUSION

1. May the faith and diligence of the wise men serve to inspire us to greater service to our Lord!

2. Though the world around us may remain careless and unbelieving, let's not be ashamed to believe in Jesus and confess Him

3. We have many more reasons to believe Him and worship Him...

    His miracles, His resurrection from the dead

    His teachings, His death on the cross for our sins

Are we willing to make the effort to find, worship, and serve this great King? As stated on a popular bumper-sticker:

"Wise men still seek Him." Amen.

(18)

Reading: Ecclesiastes 7:1-9 & Philippians 3:1-14 Message of the end of the year 2008.

Text Philip.3:13-14 and Ecc. 7:8 Brothers, I do not consider myself yet to have taken hold of it. But one thing I do: forgetting what is behind and straining toward what is ahead, I press on toward the goal to win the prize for which God has called me heavenward in Christ Jesus....The end of a thing is better than its beginning.

THEME: DON'T PARK THERE! PLEASE, DON'T!

As I reflected on the end of the year and what to say to you in this last Sunday morning sermon of 2008, I thought of Solomon's words in Ecclesiastes 7:8 "THE END OF A THING IS BETTER THAN ITS BEGINNING;"

I - THE END OF THE TRIP IS BETTER THAN ITS BEGINNING:
COMING BACK HOME A CAPTAIN OF A SHIP WITH HIS CARGO AN AIRLINE PILOT - Storms, Roads, Problems, Temptations, Medical reports, Deaths in family, Economy, Price of gas and oil , Elections Financial problems, family members, Wars,
THE END OF THE YEAR IS BETTER THAT ITS BEGINNING.

II -FIRST WE SHOULD NOT HAVE ANY REGRETS, SOON THIS YEAR WILL BE A PART OF HISTORY:

III - NOT EVERY END IS BETTER THAN THE BEGINNING:

Not everyone who goes to war comes back with victory.

Not every one who goes to parties comes back without accident

Not every married couple celebrates a golden anniversary.

ILLUSTRATION: I know a couple who left their home and went to celebrate

Christmas with other members of their family. The husband passed away on the 26th. The year did not end better for that family.

SHOULD WE START THIS YEAR WITH PESIMISM?

Ecclesiastes 7:10 says, "DO NOT SAY, "WHY WERE THE FORMER DAYS BETTER THAN THE END?"

IT IS NOT WISE TO WISH TO GO BACK: WHO WOULD WANT TO GO BACK?

(b) REPEAT THOSE EXPERIENCES - NOT I

is better than it's beginning and we truly wouldn't like to go back and live it all over again. We are freed from our past.

IV- DON'T FEAR THE FUTURE! DON'T WONDER IF THE FUTURE WILL REALLY BE ANY BETTER. TO BE SURE, THE END WILL ALWAYS BE BETTER THAN THE BEGINNING.

Lament 3:27 says

A man should bear yoke in his youth.

It's like a girl who saw an eclipse of the sun. She asked her mother, "Why did the sun go out?" That's understandable for a child,

But an adult knows that the sun will shine again. GOD IS IN CHARGE

JEREMIAH says the LORD. "They are plans for good and not for disaster, to give you a future and a hope." God has a plan for you, even in this dark time.

THINK ABOUT JOSEPH.

Sold by his brothers, falsely accused and thrown in prison - his darkest moments of his life Then his high position of power in Egypt if he had not gone to prison.

V- LET US STAND STRONGLY IN OUR FAITH:

WHO BROUGHT YOU THROUGH THAT PAST?

Isaiah," But they that wait upon the LORD shall renew their strength; they shall mount up with wings as eagles; they shall run, and not be weary; and they shall walk, and not faint.

"Now if we died with Christ, we believe that we shall also live with Him, knowing that Christ, having been raised from the dead, dies no more. Death no longer has dominion over Him."

If you can say that the end of your life will be better than the beginning. Before 2008 leaves us forever, I pray that God will touch your heart and cause you to obey Him. The past is history, the future's a mystery, but this moment is called present, and a God' gift.

THE END OF THE YEAR – OPPORTUNITY TO ANALYSE THE PRESSENT

WHAT HAS HAPPENED DURING THE LAST 365 days
THIS TIME HAS BROUGHT US MORE CLOSER TO OUR GOALS
YET, THIS TIME IS ALSO A MOMENT TO SET OUR NEW GOALS.
They're PARKING FOR HANDICAPS: -Have you been tempted to park there?

THE LESSON PAUL IS GIVING US TODAY IS THIS:
No one ever parks in life without paying a price. Life is a way, a road, not a parking lot. Life is a school, not a cemetery. Life is for growth, for movement, for development, for struggle, for progress. So don't park: keep moving. Keep driving.' And don't park because of your handicaps. Many say to themselves 'What's the use - with my handicap?'

A -THINK OF BLIND PEOPLE LIKE:
Milton, Homer, Fanny Crosby, and Louis Braille, who moved past their terrible handicap and became fulfilled human beings, not in spite of, but because of, their blindness

B - THINK OF CRIPPLED PEOPLE LIKE:
- Byron, Dickens, Scott, Balzac, Wilberforce, Poe, Handel, Pasteur, and Franklin Delano Roosevelt. At the age of 39, in the prime of life, polio struck Roosevelt down.

John Günter says that 'polio was God's greatest gift to Franklin Delano Roosevelt.

C - THINK OF THE DEAF:
Beethoven –
The last words of this composer of such majestic music: 'I shall hear in heaven.' If CHARLES DARWIN SAID THAT WE DIFFER IN THE

DEGREE WE USE OUR ABILITIES THAN IN THE SUM TOTAL OF OUR DISABILITIES-

WE ALSO DIFFER IN THE WAY WE USE OUR DISABILITIES:

FOR SOME PEOPLE, THE BLIND MILTON WROTE "A PARADISE LOST "

A little black girl ETHEL WATERS, raped at 12, married at 13 to an older man, who shoplifted to feed herself when she was six. Married at 13 to an older man, used to sing and dance before a mirror, and eventually overcame her past... Today she is remembered as the one who sung the son: 'If his eye is on the sparrow I know he watches me!

FORGETTING WHAT IS BEHIND,
THE YEAR 2009 SHOULD BE THE YEAR WE WILL NOT STOP BECAUSE OF OUR SUCCESSES, OUR FAILURES.
THE MINUTE YOU GET SATISFIED WITH WHAT YOU HAVE GOT, THEN YOU BECOME FROZEN

DON'T STOP – life is a movement; like is a fight, life is failures and successes; life is hope, life is the future, life is looking ahead and not looking back.

DON'T BE SATISFIED WITH THE AVERAGE AND THE GOOD. LOOK FOR THE BEST AND THE BEST IS YET TO COME. DON'T PARK THERE'. BUT DON'T PARK THERE...!

<u>CONCLUSION</u>:

Brothers, I do not consider myself yet to have taken hold of it. But one thing I do:

(1) Forgetting what is behind

(2) and straining toward what is ahead,

a) I press on toward the goal to win the prize

b) for which God has called me heavenward

-in Christ Jesus….

The end of a thing is better than its beginning.

DON'T; DON'T! DON'T PARK THERE. Amen! 12/28/08

(19)

Luke 1:26-38; 2:1-7.

Text: Luke 1:30-33 and the angel said to her, "Do not be afraid, Mary; for you have found favor with God. "And behold, you will conceive in your womb, and bear a son, and you shall name Him Jesus. "He will be great, and will be called the Son of the Most High; and the Lord God will give Him the throne of His father David; and He will reign over the house of Jacob forever; and His kingdom will have no end."

THEME: WHAT CHILD IS THIS?

INTRODUCTION: People ask questions because they want to know. Once a question is answered, no one should continue wondering what should be the answer.

For an answer let's turn our attention to the remarkable prophecy of Jesus' birth in Luke 1—Gabriel's appearance to Mary.

And the angel said to her, "Do not be afraid, Mary; for you have found favor with God. "And behold, you will conceive in your womb, and bear a son, and you shall name Him Jesus. "He will be great, and will be called the Son of the Most High; and the Lord God will give Him the throne of His father David; and He will reign over the house of Jacob forever; and His kingdom will have no end." (Luke 1:30-33)

I am sure that this announcement by God through His angel, Gabriel, is recorded by Luke, not to encourage us to celebrate a man-made holy day to Jesus' birth but to make clear to us at the beginning of his gospel who Jesus is by revealing the mission planned for Him by God.

What child is this? God's messenger answers. He is—Savior of sinful man—"You shall name Him Jesus" Jesus' name was carefully chosen. He was named not by Joseph and Mary but by God; for His very name identifies His mission on earth. Our word "Jesus" is an English transliteration of the Greek word Ihsouj by which Jesus was called by his disciples. That Greek name is in turn a derivative of a common Hebrew name "Yehoshua" which means "the Lord saves". This OT name, "Joshua", reminded every Israelite of their dependence upon the Lord for deliverance from all enemies. The salvation Jesus would bring is spiritual as God makes clear later to Joseph..

BIBLICAL TEXTS:

"And she will bear a Son; and you shall call His name Jesus, for it is He who will save His people from their sins." (Matthew 1:21)

"And you, child, will be called the prophet of the Most High; For you will go on before the Lord to prepare His ways; to give to His people the knowledge of salvation by the forgiveness of their sins, (Luke 1:76-79) OUR WISH IS THAT EVERYONE WHO ADORES HIM, WHO WORSHIPES HIM WILL LOVE HIM AS HIS/ HER SAVIOR. JESUS IS YOUR SAVIOR.

THAT BABY IN THE MANGER IS GOING TO BE THE SACRIFICIAL LAMB, WHICH WILL TAKE AWAY YOUR SINS. THAT BABY IS GOING TO DIE ON THE CROSS TO REDEEM YOU

THAT BABY IS GOING TO BE SIN FOR YOUR RIGHTEOUSNESS

YOU WILL BE HEALED BECAUSE OF HIS BLOOD.. (1 Peter 2:24)
ASK ONCE MORE: WHAT CHILD IS THIS?
THAT CHILD IS THE SAVIOR OF ALL MANKIND.

II – THAT CHILD IS GOD' DIVINE SON

—"He shall be great and will be called the Son of the Most High"

Many children are born every SECOND IN THIS WORLD.

I read this week that BARACK OBAMA was named the person of the year. Where can you go today and pronounce the name " BARACK OBAMA" and people will say " who is Barack Obama?" That name is well known all over the world.

If Barack Obama can be known in history this way today; if his name will be remembered as long as the history of the world will go on, what about Jesus? HE WAS GREAT BECAUSE HE WAS THE SON OF THE MOST HIGH.

WHO IS THE MOST HIGH? - YEHOWAH, ELOHIM,

The Creator of the whole earth.. The Giver of life.

The Omnipotent, the Omnipresent, the Omniscient.

YEHOWAH SHABAOTH, YEHOWAH JIREH,

NO OTHER PERSON IN THE HISTORY OF THE WORLD HAS IMPACT THE WORLD AS JESUS.

BILLIONS OF BOOKS HAVE BEEN WRITTEN ABOUT JESUS IMAGINE SERMONS WHAT HAVE BEEN WRITTEN CONCERNING HIM.

BUT THAT JESUS:

"Here is a man who was born in an obscure village, child of a peasant woman.. He grew up in another obscure village. He worked in a carpenter shop until He was thirty, and then for three years was an itinerant preacher.
"He never wrote a book. He never held an office. He never owned a home

He never had a family. He never went to college. He never put his foot inside a big city. He never traveled two hundred miles from the place where He was born. He never did one of the things that usually accompany greatness. He had no credentials but himself. He had nothing to do with this world except the naked power of His divine manhood." "While still a young man the tide of popular opinion turned against Him. His friends ran away. One of them denied Him. Another betrayed Him. He was turned over to His enemies. He went through the mockery of a trial. He was nailed upon the cross between two thieves. His executioners gambled for the only piece of property He had on earth while He was dying, and that was His coat. When He was dead, He was taken down and laid in a borrowed grave through the pity of a friend. "Nineteen wild centuries have come and gone and today He is the center of the human race and the leader of the column of progress "I am far within the mark when I say that all the armies that ever marched, and all the navies that were ever built, and all the parliaments that ever sat and all the kings that ever reigned, put together, have not affected the life of man upon the earth as powerfully as has this one solitary life."

This child was not only great; he was called the Son of God. What the first chapters of the gospel make clear to us is that, though Jesus was born into the world as a man and possessed the nature of man, he was more than a man. He was God in human body subject to the characteristics of humanity.

THE BIBLICAL PROOFS:

For in Him all the fullness of Deity dwells in bodily form, (Colossians 2:9) No one will, no matter how brilliant, adequately explain the mysteries of the incarnation. God became Man in Jesus in such a way that he did not cease to be God. Think about that awhile.

He demonstrated all the qualities of humanity (body, physical need, subject to temptation out of that need). And yet in the full possession of his divine nature as well (omniscient, omnipotent, omnipresent, eternal).

Because of this he can be: God's mediator for there is one God, and one mediator also between God and men, the man Christ Jesus, (1 Timothy 2:5)

Man's high priest. Therefore, He had to be made like His brethren in all things, that He might become a merciful and faithful high priest in things pertaining to God, to make propitiation for the sins of the people. (Hebrews 2:17)

WHAT CHILD IS THIS?

And He is the image of the invisible God, the first-born of all creation. (Colossians 1:15)

And He is the radiance of His glory and the exact representation of His nature. (Heb 1:3)

HE WAS THE LORD AND CHRIST:

Lord and Christ—"The Lord God will give Him the throne of His father David

III – HE WILL REIGN OVER THE HOUSE OF HIS FATHER DAVID AND HIS REIGN WILL HAVE NO END.

When God chose Israel and delivered them from bondage, He set himself as king over them. When they came to Sinai he made this known by telling them that there were a "kingdom of priests" (Ex. 19:6). Who was the king? God. Later the people impressed with the earthly kingdoms around them clamored for a human king (1 Sam. 8:5). They had rejected the Lord as king. God gave them what they wanted. What Israel learned from this experience was that when men served as their king, unless he was truly a servant of God himself, their nation suffered and their kingdom would not endure. God then began to excite in them the hope that God would give them a righteous king that would rule over them and whose kingdom would not come under the judgment of the Lord because of sin but would instead endure forever.

For a child will be born to us, a son will be given to us; And the government will rest on His shoulders; And His name will be called Wonderful Counselor, Mighty God, Eternal Father, Prince of Peace. There will be no end to the increase of His government or of peace, On the throne of David and over his kingdom, To establish it and to uphold it with justice and righteousness From then on and forevermore. The zeal of the Lord of hosts will accomplish this.(Isaiah 9:6-7) The angel Gabriel declares that these wonderful promises of a holy king over the house of David are now about to be fulfilled and because of His holiness those who serve Him will never again see their kingdom destroyed as before but rather be apart of what would endure forever. This kingdom is the reign of God in the hearts of His church. It is the rule of God through Christ in the hearts of all who accept His word.

HE WILL REIGN FOREVER BECAUSE HE WILL DELIEVER US FROM THE DOMAIN OF DARKNESS AND TRANSFERRED US TO THE KINGDOM OF HIS BELOVED SON (Colossians 1:13)

THAT KINGDOM CANNOT BE SHAKEN (Hebrews 12:28)
WHAT CHILD IS THIS? – HE IS THE KING OF KINGS, THE LORD OF LORDS

CONCLUSION? WHAT CHILD IS THIS?

THAT CHILD IS THE SAVIOR OF ALL MANKIND.

THAT CHILD IS THE SON OF THE MOST HIGH, A DIVINE SON
THAT CHILD WILL REIGN FOREVER IN HIS FATHER'S PLACE
THAT CHILD IS THE ONE WHO CAME TO ACCOMPLISH THE
PROMISE.

HE IS YOUR PERSONAL SAVIOR. RECEIVE HIM TODAY. Amen!
12/21/00

(20)

THEME: THE TRUE MEANING OF CHRISTMAS.

Introduction: Christ is a series of facts and results. CAUSES AND EFFECTS. Nothing happened in the life of Jesus from the time he departed from heaven to the time he will come again without a CAUSE and an EFFECT.

We can ask 10 questions WE WILL ASK 1) QUESTIONS TODAY THE BIBLE WILL ANSWER THEM ALL IN ORDER TO SHOW CAUSES AND EFFECTS IN THE LIFE OF JESUS

QUESTION 1 WHY DID JESUS LEAVE HIS PLACE IN HEAVEN AND COME TO BE BORN AS A MAN. - Why that descend?
JESUS DESCENDED TO DO HIS FATHER'S WILL
John 6:38 For I have come down from heaven not to do my will but to do the will of him who sent me.

In John 14:3 And if I go and prepare a place for you, I will come back and take you to be with me that you also may be where I am.

HIS WILL WAS TO COME AND SAVE US.

QUEST .2 WHY JESUS BECAME POOR? II Cor. For you know the grace of our Lord Jesus Christ, that though he was rich, YET FOR YOUR SAKE he became poor.

James 2:5 Listen, my dear brothers: Has not God chosen those who are poor in the eyes of the world to be rich in faith and to inherit the kingdom he promised those who love him?

HE BECAME POOR THAT WE BECOME RICH:

QUEST .3. WHY JESUS WAS BORN AS A HUMAN BEING? Phil.2:7 but made himself nothing, taken the very nature of a servant being made in human likeness.

EFFECT.

Galatians 4:4-5 God sent his Son, born of a woman, born under law, TO REDEEM THOSE UNDER LAW, THAT WE MIGHT RECEIVE THE FULL RIGHTS OF SONS.

HE WAS BORN AS HUMAN SO THAT WE BE BORN AS SONS OF GOD

QUEST 4. WHY JESUS CHRIST DID NOT HAVE A HOME? Matt. 8:20 Jesus replied "Foxes have holes and birds in the air have nests, but the Son of Man has no place to lay his head.

EFFECT: John 14:2 In my Father's home are many rooms; if it were not so, I would have told you. -

THAT WE HAVE A HOME WITH HIM IN HEAVEN.

QUEST: 5. WHY JESUS WAS HUNGRY?

Matt. 4:2 After fasting forty days and forty nights, he was hungry

EFFECT: John 6:51. I am the living bread that came down from heaven. If anyone eats of this bread. he will live forever.

JESUS WAS HUNGRY SO THAT WE BE FED.

QUEST 6: WHY JESUS WAS THIRSTY (On the Cross) John 19:28 "I am thirsty."

EFFECT: THAT WE BE SATISFIED. He is the living water.

QUEEST.7: WHY JESUS WAS STRIPPED? Matt. 27:28 They stripped him and put a scarlet robe on him.

EFFECT: Gal. 3:27 For all of you who were baptized into Christ HAVE CLOTHED YOURSELVES WITH CHRIST. SO THAT WE BE CLOTHED.

QUEST 8: WHY JESUS WAS SAD? Isaiah 53:3 He was despised and rejected of men, a man of sorrows, and familiar with suffering.

EFFECT: Philip. 4:4 Rejoice in the Lord always. I will say it again: REJOICE!

JESUS WAS SADDENDED SO THAT WE WILL ALWAS REJOICE!

QUEST.9: WHY JESUS CHRIST WAS MADE A SINNER? II Cor. 5:21 God made him, WHO HAD NO SIN TO BE SIN FOR US, SO THAT IN HIM, we might become the righteous of God.

EFFECT: WE BECOME RIGHTEOUS OF GOD.

QUEST.10 WHY DID JESUS COME DOWN THAT NIGHT OF CHRISTMAS,

THE NIGHT WE SHOULD ALWAYS REMEMBER?

EFFECT: I Thess.4:16, 17. For the Lord himself will come down from heaven, with a loud command, with the voice of the archangel and with the trumpet call of God, and the dead in CHRIST will rise first. After that, we who are still alive and are left will be caught up together with them in the clouds to meet the Lord in the air. And so we will be with the Lord forever.

THE GOAL OF JESUS COMING DOWN THAT NIGHT WAS TO TAKE US UP WITH HIM AND BE FOREVER WITH GOD.

HOW CAN YOU FORGET THAT NIGHT!

CHRISTMAS IS THE NIGHT WE WILL NEVER FORGET. Amen.

(21)

Readings: Isaiah 53:1-12; John 11:17-44.

Text Isaiah 53:6 We all, like sheep, have gone astray; EACH OF US has turned to his own way; AND THE LORD HAS LAID ON HIM the INIQUITY OF US ALL.

THEME: THE MESSIAH CAME TO SAVE US.

More than 2,500 years ago, God revealed the greatest message in history to the Hebrew prophet Isaiah. In chapter 53 of the book that bears his name, Isaiah unveils God's message of salvation to the world, and in so doing, he reveals the identity of the Messiah

– The Lamb of God who would lay down His life as an offering for the world's sins.

A human race which once lived in darkness can now move forward with hope: Isaiah 53

"WHO CAN BELIEVE THIS MESSAGE?

NOT THE BLOOD OF ANOTHER HUMAN BEING

NOT THE BLOOD OF THOSE WHO SINNED – Children of Adam

NOT THE BLOOD OF ANIMAL.

BUT THE BLOOD OF THE SON OF GOD HIMSELF

   –HE PAID THE PRICE, HE DIED IN OUR PLACE

   –SUBSTITUE DEATH–

But it was the Lord's good plan to crush him and fill him with grief
He bore the sins of all manking, yours and mine. Isai. 53:12

I - JESUS WAS THE LAMB OF GOD

(1) HE WAS SILENT BEFORE THE ACCUSERS

(2) "He was oppressed and treated harshly, yet he never said a word.

(3) He was led as a lamb to the slaughter. And as a sheep is silent before the shearers, he did not open his mouth." Isaiah 53:7

"Then the high priest stood up and said to Jesus, 'Well, aren't you going to answer these charges? What do you have to say for yourself?' But Jesus remained silent. Mat.26:62-63

(4) HE WAS DESPISED AND REJECTED

He was despised and rejected – a man of sorrows, acquainted with bitterest grief. Isa 53:3

"And Pilate said to the people, 'Here is your king!' 'Away with him,' they yelled. 'Away with him – crucify him!' 'What? Crucify your king?' Pilate asked. 'We have no king but Caesar,' the leading priests shouted back." John 19:14-15

II -JESUS BORE THE SINS OF ALL MANKIND:

(1) "IT IS OUR WEAKNESSES THAT HE CARRIED

"For all have sinned; all fall short of God's glorious standard. Romans 3:23-26

Pilate released Barabbas, the man in prison for insurrection and murder. He delivered Jesus, and Jewish mistreated him Luke 23:23-25

Wounded and Crushed for Our Sins

(2) "BUT HE WAS WOUNDED AND CRUSHED FOR OUR SINS."
Isaiah 53:5

"Then they nailed him to the cross." Mark 15:24

(3) "For God in all his fullness was pleased to live in Christ, and by him God reconciled everything to himself.
THE RESULT OF HIS DEATH, YOU ARE BLAMELESS AS YOU STAND BEFORE GOD TODAY WITHOUT A SINGLE FAULT" Colossians 1:19-22

III- JESUS SUFFERED SO THAT WE MAY HAVE PEACE:
"He was beaten that we might have peace." Isaiah 53:5
(1) HE WAS WHIPPED SO THAT WE MAY BE HEALED" Isaiah 53:5
"He ordered Jesus flogged with a lead-tipped whip, and then turned him over to the Roman soldiers to crucify him." Matthew 27:26

IV-SALVATION THROUGH MESSIAH – WAS GOD'S PLAN:
The last verses of Isaiah 53 continue to describe the life of Jesus Christ:
"But it was the Lord's good plan to crush him and fill him with grief. Yet when his life is made an offering for sin, he will have a multitude of children, many heirs. He will enjoy a long life, and the Lord's plan will prosper in his hands. When he sees all that is accomplished by his anguish, he will be satisfied. And because of what he has experienced, my righteous servant will make it possible for many to be counted righteous, for he will bear all their sins. I will give him the honors of one who is mighty and great, because he exposed himself to death. He was counted among those who were sinners. He bore the sins of many and interceded for sinners." Isaiah 53:10-12
Revelation 5
"And I saw a scroll in the right hand of the one who was sitting on the throne. There was writing on the inside and the outside of the scroll, and it was sealed with seven seals. And I saw a strong angel, who shouted with a loud voice: 'Who is worthy to break the seals on this scroll and unroll

it?' But no one in heaven or on earth or under the earth was able to open the scroll and read it.

V- BECAUSE OF HIS DEEDS THE COMFORT IS OURS

    THE LAMB OF GOD HAS TAKEN OUR SINS AWAY

    THE LAMB OF GOD HAS DIED IN OUR PLACE

    THE LAMB OF GOD HAS GIVEN US PEACE

    THE LAMB OF GOD HAS RECONCILED US WITH OUR FATHER.

VI- THE FINAL VICTORY IS HIS:

"Because of this,

GOD HAS GIVEN HIM THE NAME ABOVE EVERY KNEE WILL BOW AND EVERY TONGUE WILL CONFESS THAT JESUS CHRIST IS LORD TO THE GLORY OF THE FATHER.

Philippians 2:9-11 Amen.

(22)

Reading: I John 5:11-13

THEME: THE STIGMAS ON A SAVED PERSON (MARKS)

INTRODUCTION: After Jesus' resurrection, he had some marks on his hands, on his side, and on his feed. Many people believe that when Jesus returns, he will still have those marks, those STIGMAS ON HIM.

I have known twin girls. They were absolutely identical, except for the fact that one of them had a large birthmark on her cheek. Without that birthmark, it would have been impossible for many people even their parents to tell them apart.

Did you know that all true believers also possess certain marks that set them apart from the rest of humanity? We could rightly call these things that set us apart our birthmarks. They appear when we are saved and they mark us as children of God. Every saved person has every one of the birthmarks of salvation.

In fact, one of the reasons for the writing of this book from which we have read this was to help people know for sure that they had been saved, 1:6; 5:13. As you read First John, it becomes clear that he is trying to help God's people gain absolute assurance of their salvation. He uses the word "know" 39 times. John is trying to tell us that there are some things we can know. One of them is whether or not we are saved.

I want to share the birthmarks of the true believer with you this morning. Identifying the presence, or the lack, of these traits within our lives can help us understand where we stand in relation to God. If you have struggled in this area, there is no need to do so any longer. God can give you assurance, one way or the other, right now. Let's look together at The Birthmarks Of The True Believer.

I. 5:1 STIGMAS ON A SPIRITUAL CONVERSION

1. BELIEVING THAT JESUS IS THE SON OF GOD. Not merely a mental acknowledgment of the facts. But a belief knowing with the head, as an accepted truth into the heart.. It is a saving faith, that Jesus Christ for salvation.

2. BELIEVING THAT HAVING CHRIST IS HAVING ETERNAL LIFE: 1 John 5:12; John 5:24; John 3:16; Acts 16:31; Rom. 10:9-13; Rom. 8:1; Rev. 22:17; Acts 2:21, and hundreds more besides! We also have this principle from Scripture: God is holy and cannot lie, Heb. 6:18. What He promises to do, He will do!

3. BELIEVING THAT YOU ARE A SINNER AND YOU NEED JESUS:(Rom. 3:23; 3:10) That is, have you ever been lost? Until you can see your sins and yourself as a sinner, you cannot be saved. This process is called conviction! It is the Holy Spirit drawing sinner unto Himself, John 6:44; John 16:7-11

4. BELIEVING THAT THE SALARY OF SIN IS DEATH: Rom. 6:23

5. ACKNOWLEDGING THAT CHRIST DIED FOR YOUR SINS: 2 Cor. 5:21;

6. ACKNOWLEDGING THAT CALLING ON HIM GIVES SALVATION, Rom. 10:13

    "Right there is when I trusted Jesus Christ as my Savior and my life was forever transformed!"

II. 1:6-7 STIGMAS ON A SPIRITUAL CHANGE

1. HEN YOU WALK IN THE LIGHT AS HE IS THE LIGHT:
   John 8:12.
   2:29 – THE DESIRE TO WANT WHAT GOD RECOMMANDS
   US TO DO
   5:18 – WHEN WE DO NOT LIVE IN SIN

2. WHEN WE HAVE BEEN CHANGED INSIDE OUT, 2 Cor. 5:17;
   Col. 3:1-17.

III. 4:13 STIGMAS ON A SPIRITUAL COMPANIONSHIP

1. WILLING TO LIVE ACCORDING TO THE HOLY SPIRIT.,
   Rom. 8:9.; 1 Cor. 12:13. His job in us is to seal us, Eph. 4:30; lead us,
   John 16:13; and to give us assurance of our salvation; Eph. 1:13-14; 2
   Cor. 1:22; 2 Cor. 5:5.

2. AVING THE LOVE OF GOD IN HIS HEART, ***Rom. 5:5***.
   Like a mother who wraps her arms around that insecure child everyday
   and expresses her undying love, the Spirit of God does the same things
   for the redeemed child of the Lord.
   C. If there is no peace; if there is no assurance;

Conclusion: I know I have covered a lot of territory this morning.
But, I felt lead of the Lord to preach this message. Why? Because there are
people in this room who are not sure where they stand with God. There
are others who know they are not saved. My friends, if you lack even one
of the birthmarks of the true believer this morning, then this message was
sent this way for your benefit. It's all or nothing! You need to leave the seat
where you are sitting and you need to come to Jesus and get this thing
settled right now and forever. If the Lord is speaking to your heart you

need to come! If you are in doubt you need to come. If you are convinced that you are lost, you need to come. Will you listen to the call of God and come to Him for salvation today? Or, will you continue to live in doubt and fear? God can help you if you will come to Him right now.

You can know! God wants you to know! And, the first step in your coming to know for sure is for you to make your way to Him right now! Amen.

(23)

1 John 1:4; 5:13

THEME: TEST AND GRADE YOURSELF:

HOW DO YOU KNOW THAT YOU ARE SAVED-

Introduction: The early church had been birthed in power. It grew like wildfire and the Lord truly blessed that church. However, it wasn't many days until heresy began to creep into the church. One of the earliest perversions of Christianity to make an appearance was known as Gnosticism.

There were many versions of Gnosticism, but the primary areas of agreement were that knowledge and not the cross was the means to salvation. This meant that Jesus Christ did not really have a flesh and blood body. If matter was evil then Christ could not have had a physical body. It only appeared that He had died. Some did believe that Jesus died, but the spirit of Christ left Him before the cross. This, of course, eliminated the cross and the resurrection as the basis of salvation.

To aid us in knowing for sure whether we are saved or not, John gives his readers a simple test they can take to determine where they stand with the Lord.

You will not need a number two pencil. All you will need is an honest heart. Take the test, see where you stand and if corrections need to be made, they will be allowed. Let's examine the sections of John's test and our own hearts tonight. Let's take a test!

I. THE COMMANDMENT SECTION

A.1 John 2:3-6 – A SAVED PERSON HAS THE DESIRE TO WALK ACCORDING TO THE WORD OF GOD.

- John 14:15. SAYS" IF YOU LOVE ME, YOU WILL OBEY MY COMMANDMENT

B. 1 John 4:6 A SAVED PERSON KNOWS HIS GRACE AND LISTENS TO HIS BROTHERS AND SISTERS

- Pastors, Leaders of the church other brothers in Christ Judge yourself,

Your grade A__B__C__D__F__

II. THE COMPASSION SECTION

A. 1 John 2:9-11 –

A SAVED PERSON DOES NOT HATE HIS/HER BROTHER,. IF HE DOES, HE/SHE IS A MURDERER HE /SHE LOVE THEIR BROTHERS – and FELLOW PERSON

B. 1 John 3:14-22

A SAVED PERSON ACKNOWKLEGES THAT JESUS IS THE SON OF GOD AND HE LIVES IN LOVE WITH ONE ANOTHER.

WE LOVE BECAUSE HE FIRST LOVED US.

CHRISTIANITY IS BASED ON FORGIVENESS AND LOVE.

C. 1 John 4:20-21 – A SAVED PERSON LOVES ALL MEMBERS OF GOD'S FAMILY

JUDGE YOURSELF; YOUR GRADE IS? A__ B___ C___D___ F__

III. THE CHRISTLIKENESS SECTION

A. John 3:40-10 A SAVED ONE DOESN'T LIVE IN SIN...

IV. THE COMPANION SECTION

   A. I John 3:24 A SAVED ONE LIVES IN GOD, FOR GOD.

   B. II Cor.5:17 A SAVED PERSON IS A NEW CREATION

   C. I John 2:6 A SAVED PERSON WALKS AS JESUS DID.

   D. I John 1:8 A SAVED PERSON KNOWS THAT HE IS A SINNER, BUT A FORGIVEN ONE.

     1 John 4:13. SAYS, WE KNOW THAT WE LIVE IN HIM AND HE IN US, BECAUSE HE HAS GIVEN US OF HIS SPIRIT.

V. THE COMMITMENT SECTION

A. 1 John 5:1 A SAVED PERSON IS BORN IN GOD.

B. Acts 16:31 A SAVED PERSON HAS BELIEVED IN THE NAME OF JESUS - HIS SALVATION DEPENDS ON WHAT HE DID NOT ON WHAT HE/SHE DOES TODAY.

C. 1 John 5:13 A SAVED PERSON KNOWS THAT HE/SHE HAS ETERNAL LIFE.

   JUDGE YOURSELF; YOUR GRADE IS? A__ B__ C__D__ F__

CONCLUSION: You have your result. You have tested yourself in four areas:

IN THE AREA OF GOD'S COMMANDMENT – OBEDIENCE.

IN THE AREA OF COMPASSION – LOVE

IN THE AREA OF COMPANIONSHIP WITH GOD

IN THE AREA OF COMMMITMENT RELATION WITH GOD.

A PERSON WHO IS SAVED LOVES WALKING OBEING GOD.

A PERSON WHO IS SAVED LIVES BY LOVE

A PERSON WHO IS SAVED IS LIKE CHRIST

A PERSON WHO IS SAVED IS IN CHRIST.

WHAT IS YOUR GRADE? WHERE DO YOU STAND?

JUDGE YOURSELF; YOUR GRADE IS? A__ B__ C__ D__ F__

Amen. Machiasport Nov.8th, 2008

READING: 1 John 1:4; 5:13

THEME: TEST AND GRADE YOURSEL

I. THE COMMANDMENT SECTION

A. 1 John 2:3-6 - B. 1 John 4:6

   (1) HOW DO YOU DO IN THIS SECTION?

   (2) WHAT IS THE GRADE YOU GIVE TO YOURSELF?

   A_____ B_____ C_____ D_____ F_____

II. THE COMPASSION SECTION

   A. 1 John 2:9-11 B. 1 John 3:14-22 B. 1 John 4:20-21

III. THE CHRISTLIKENESS SECTION

   A. 1 John 3:4-10 B. 2 Cor. 5:17!

   C. 1 John 2:6. D. 1 John 1:8

   HOW DO YOU DO IN THIS SECTION?

   WHAT IS THE GRADE YOU GIVE TO YOURSELF?

   A_____ B_____ C_____ D_____ F_____

IV. THE COMPANION SECTION

A. 1 John 3:24

   (1) HOW DO YOU DO IN THIS SECTION?

   (2) WHAT IS THE GRADE YOU GIVE TO YOURSELF?

   A_____ B_____ C_____ D_____ F_____

V. THE COMMITMENT SECTION

A. 1 John 5:1 and Acts 16:31! B. 1 John 5:13

   (1) HOW DO YOU DO IN THIS SECTION?

   (2) WHAT IS THE GRADE YOU GIVE TO YOURSELF?

   A_____ B_____ C_____ D_____ F_____

WHAT IS YOUR GENERAL AVERAGE? _____

(24)

Reading: 5:1-24; I John 1:5-10.

THEME: PEOPLE WHO WALK WITH GOD –

Genesis 5:22, 24 Enoch walked with God 300 years and had other sons and daughters. All together, Enoch lived 365 years. Enoch walked with God; then he was no more, because God took him away."

INTRODUCTION: Doctors recommend walking. If you do, there are many advantages.

I – SIGNS ON PEOPLE WHO WALK WITH GOD ARE

(1) KEEPERS OF THE LORD'S COMMAND Deut. 5:33
Laws, Commands, Precepts – WHAT THE BIBLE SAYS:

GREAT COMMAND. He (she) LOVES THE LORD
With all his heart, mind, soul and loves others as himself.

(2) THEIR WAYS ARE BLAMELESS Psalm 84:11
- NOT BY MEN, BUT BY GOD.

(4) HE FEARS THE LORD Psalm 128:1-2
The fear of the Lord is the beginning of WISDOM

THEY WALK NOT BY THE WICKED COUSEL Ps. 1:1-3

(5) THEY ARE PRAYER WARRIERS.
KEEP THEMSELVES IN THE PRESENCE OF THE LORD.

II – THE BENEFITS OF WALKING WITH GOD ARE:

THEY LIVE, PROSPER, AND POSSESS THE LAND. Deut 5:33
GOD WILL WALK WITH THEM. Leviticus 26:12

GOD BLESSES THEM. Deut. 30:16

GOD IS THEIR SUN AND THEIR SHIELD

-THEY ARE FAVORED AND HONORS BY GOD
   -GOD GIVES THEM GOOD THINGS I Kings 11:38

THEY ARE FAVORED BY GOD! (I LOVE THAT!)

(1) THEY ARE GUIDED BY THE LORD. Psalm 4:11-12

(2) THEY'LL EAT THE FRUIT OF THEIR LABOR Ps. 128:1,2

IT MAY NOT BE HERE, BUT IN HEAVEN

III – CONDITIONS OF THOSE WALKERS ARE:

THEY HAVE PEACE:

Jesus after his resurrection used to say to his disciples every time he appeared
to them" Receive my peace; peace, I give to you; my peace I give to you."
WHEN PEACE LIKE A RIVER ATTENDETH MY WAY
When sorrows like sea billows roll. Whatever my lot,
Thou has taught me to say. It is well; it is well with my soul.

(2) THEY HAVE HOPE – Hope in God, hope in tomorrows.
   Nothing can separate them with the love which is in God.
   (3) THEY HAVE GOD'S LOVE – ETERNAL LOVE
   - (1) CAN PEOPLE SEE SOME SIGNS OF THAT NOW?
   ARE YOU HAVING THOSE BENEFITS NOW

   ARE YOU LIVING ACCORDING TO THESE CONDITIONS?

Romans 8:38-39 for I am persuaded, that neither death, nor life, nor angels,
nor principalities, nor powers, nor things present, nor things to come, nor
height, nor depth, nor any other creature, shall be able to separate us from
the love of God, which is in Christ Jesus our Lord
(4) THEY HAVE A HOME IN HEAVEN. John 14:1-3
   JESUS IS COMING TO TAKE THEM HOME.

(5) THEY HAVE ETERNEL LIFE.
   ALL THOSE WHO WALK WITH HIM HERE ON EARTH
WILL VE WITH HIM FOREVER IN HIS KINGDOM.

   ENOCH, NOAH, ABRAHAM, JOSEPH,

YOU TO, WALKING WITH THE LORDS HERE

CONCLUSION: JUST A QUESTION FOR YOU:
(1) DEEP, DEEP DOWN IN YOUR HEART,
     WALK WITH YOUR GOD EVERY DAY!
DO YOU KNOW THAT YOU LIVE UNDER HIS PRIVILEGES?
DO YOU HAVE HIS LOVE, HIS PEACE, HIS HOPE? ARE YOU SURE OF YOUR
HOME IN HEAVEN AND ETERNAL LIFE WITH HIM?

YOU WALK WITH YOUR GOD. AMEN! 11 3rd, 2008

(25)

Readings Genesis 19:1-26; Luke 9:51-62

Text Gen. 19:17 As soon as they had brought them out, one of them said, "Flee for your life! Don't look back, and don't stop anywhere in the plan! Flee to the mountains or you will be swept away".

THEME: DON'T LOOK BACK; LOOK AHEAD.

I- SOME PEOPLE IN THE BIBLE LOOKED BACK AND BAD THINGS HAPPENED TO THEM:

Joshua and his men attacked Ai and they set fire on the city. When the men of Ai looke back, the disaster fell on them. Josh 8:20

(2) LOT'S WIFE BECAME A PILLAR OF SALT.

JESUS GIVES US A GOOD ADVICE: JESUS IN LUKE 9:62

NO ONE WHO PUTS HIS HAND TO THE PLOW AND LOOK BACK IS FIT FOR SERVICE IN THE KINGDOM OF HEAVEN. Luke 9:62.

PEOPLE WHO LOOK BACK START USE "IF" IN THEIR SPEECH

IF ONLY......54qw SET YOUR HOPE IN THE LORD

YOUR LORD WILL DELIEVER YOU II Cor. 1:10

GOD NEVER CHANGE, HE IS THE GOD OF GRACE AND MERCY GOD OF LOVE, GOD OF HOPE - HE IS A GREAT GOD I John 3: 20

II - LIFE WITHOUT REGRETS DOESN'T MEAN, LIFE WITHOUT REPENTANCE:

HAVE YOU REPENTED FROM YOUR SINS OF THE PAST?

HAVE YOUR TURNED AWAY FROM THE PAST?

HAVE YOU RECEIVED FORGIVENESS FROM GOD?

The Bible SAYS Anyone in Christ is a new creation.

THE OLD HAS GONE; THE NEW HAS COME. II Cor. 5:17

REMEMBER:

(1) JESUS HAS CLEANSED YOU WITH HYSOP.

(2) JESUS HAS HID HIS FACE FROM YOUR SINS

(3) JESUS HAS CREATED IN YOU A NEW HEART

(4) JESUS HAS NOT CAST YOU FROM HIS PRESENCE

(5) JESUS HAS PUT HIS SPIRIT IN YOU. Psalm 51 : 7-12

III - WHEN WE HAVE EXPERIENCED GOD'S FORGIVENESS:

WE ARE NEW CREATURES

YES, WE HAVE NOT YET REACH. WE ARE ON THE WAY

I do not consider myself as yet taken hold of it. But one thing I do: FORGETTING WHAT IS BEHING; AND STRAINING TOWARD WHAT IS AHEAD; I PRESS ON TOWARD THE GOAL TO WIN THE PRICE FOR WHICH GOD HAS CALLED ME HEAVENWARD IN CHRIST JESUS. Philippians 3:13-14

HEBREWS 12:1-2 says

Let us throw everything that hinders and the sin that so easily ENTANGLES, and let us RUN WITH PERSEVERANCE THE RACE MARKED OUT FOR US. LET US FIX our EYES on Jesus, the author and perfector of our faith.

IV - IF WE HAVE TO LOOK BASCK IN OUR LIVES:

IT MAY BE IN GOD'S PERSPECTIVE – No REMORSE or REGRETS.

WE WILL BE ABLE TO SEE GOD'S HAND IN US IN OUR PAST

WE WILL KNOW FOR SURE THAT

IN ALL THINGS GOD WORKS FOR THE GOOD OF THOSE WHO LOVE HIM, WHO HAVE BEEN CALLED ACCORDING TO HIS PURPOSE. Rom 8:2

CONCLUSION:

DO YOU KNOW ANYONE WHO DOESN'T HAVE A PAST?

HAVE YOU GIVEN YOUR PAST TO GOD?

HAVE YOU REALLY REPENTED AND ASKED FORGIVENESS?

HAVE YOU RECEIVED FORGIVENESS FROM GOD?

HAVE YOU BEEN CREATED ANEW IN JESUS?

FIX YOU EYES ON JESUS

RUN, RUN, RUN, AND FLEE SATAN AND HIS AGENTS.

DON'T STOP, GOD TO THE MOUNTAIN. THAT MOUNTAN IS CALVARY, THAT MOUNTAN IS THE CROSS, THAT MOUNTAIN IS JESUS. HE WILL GIVE YOU REST. Amen. Oct. 26. 2008-

(26)

THEME: THAT IS WHY I SUFFER AS I AM.

I KNOW WHOM I HAVE BELIEVED; I AM CONVINCED THAT HE IS ABLE TO GUARD WHAT I HAVE ENTRUSTED TO HIM FOR THAT DAY.

INTRODUCTION: Few people annoy us more than the know-it-all. As soon as we mention anything to him – anything, whether cars or cameras – he starts yammering as if he were the world's expert. We're especially irked when it becomes evident that the know-it-all knows nothing, nothing whatever about cars or cameras.

Annoying as the know-it-all always is, he's most annoying, downright obnoxious, when he's a religious know-it-all.

Nevertheless, while we're certainly offended by the person who "knows it all", we're never going to be helped by the person who knows nothing. We'd never choose as our lawyer or physician, dentist or mechanic, someone who boasted of her ignorance. In other words, while know-it-all people offend us, people who know nothing can't help us.

WHAT DOES PAUL MEAN IN HIS LETTERS BY "I KNOW "? letters the apostle THAT KNOWING MEANS:

PROFOUND ASSURANCE OF WHAT IS REAL

IT IS AN ACT OF CERTAINTY, NOT A GUESS

133

IT IS SEIZED BY THE TRUTH - STANDING STRONG AND FIRM

I – THE FIRST THING PAUL AND I KNOW IS – NOTHING GOOD IN ME: GOOD HERE MEANS WHAT CAN PLEASE GOD, ULTIMATE GODLINESS. ARE YOU A SINNER?
Every human being who KNOWS what Christ did on the Cross for him, should have as first knowledge, his failing nature in sin making him a sinner 100%
NOTHING GOOD CAN COME FROM YOU ALONE

II: – I KNOW THAT THE GOOD IS CLOSER TO ME ONLY THROUGH THE ONE WHO HAS TAKEN MY SIN AWAY AND CLOTHED ME WITH HIS RIGHTEOUSNESS – JESUS
IT IS THROUGH SOMEONE ELSE
I TRUST THAT PERSON.
I BELIEVE IN THAT PERSON.
HE HAS MADE ME CAPABLE TO PLEASE GOD IN MY SIN
I HAVE WELL INFORMATION OF THAT KNOWLEDGE – H.SPIRIT.

He reminds Timothy, a younger man on whom the older man's experience and wisdom won't be lost. If Paul's realism stopped with his assessment of human perversity, the human condition would be hopeless. But he doesn't stop there. He's certain of the one who can remedy it: "I know the One in whom I have put my trust."

III –I KNOW THAT THE SPIRIT OF GOD IS IN ME:
IF I AM HERE AND DO WHAT I DO, IT IS BECAUSE OF HIM
IF I HAVE THE FAITH I HAVE, IT IS BECAUSE OF HIM,
IF I CALL GOD MY FATHER, IT IS BECAUSE OF HIM,

I RECOGNIZE MY SIN BECAUSE OF HIM
IF I DON'T BELONG TO SATAN, IT IS BECAUSE OF HIM.
UNDERSTAND THE SCRIPTURES, BECAUSE OF HIM.
HE WILL KEEP IT.
HE WILL SAVE IT.
HE WILL REUNITE IT WITH MY BODY THE LAST DAY.
HE WILL RAISE IT FROM THE DEAD.
HE WILL BRING ME TO HIS ETERNAL GLORY.

IV - ONE LAST THING I KNOW: THE ONE WHO STARTED HIS
WORK IN ME WILL FINISH IT: (Philippians 1:6)
HE NEVER STARTS A WORK HE NEVER FINISHES.
HE STARTED CREATING THE WORLD, HE FINISHED IT.
THE CHILDREN OF ISRAEL, FREEDOM, HE FINISHED IT
THE SALVATION OF HUMANKIND, HE FINISHED IT.
WHAT WAS JESUS THE LAST WORD ON THE CROSS,
IT IS FINISHED!
HE WILL FINISH HIS REDEMPTIVE WORK IN ME
I KNOW THAT. I BELIEVE THAT. I AM SURE.

THE DOCTRINE OF THE PRESERVATION OF THE SAINTS:

We Presbyterians are rooted in what's called "The Reformed Tradition." The Reformed Tradition moved from the Sixteenth Century Reformers to the Seventeenth Century Puritans. Our Puritan ancestors used to speak quaintly of "the perseverance of the saints." By this expression they didn't mean that God's people were mysteriously rendered superhuman. By "the perseverance of the saints" they meant "God's perseverance in his saints

YES, LIFE MOVES FROM MOUNTAN TOP TO THE DEEP VALLEY,
GOD WILL ALWAYS TURN; LEMOND INTO LEMONADE, THE

BELIEVER WILL ALWAYS GROW STRONGER IN TRIBULATIONS, ADVERSITIES, TROUBLES, SICKNESS, DEPRAVATIONS, PERSECUTIONS and EVEN DEATH.

THE ONE WHO STARTED ALWAYS FINISHES HIS WORK.

CONCLUSION: WHAT DO YOU KNOW?

(1) DO YOU KNOW THAT YOU ARE A SINNER INCAPABLE TO DO GOOD

(2) DO YOU KNOW THAT GODLINESS IS CLOSER TO YOU NOW.

(3) DO YOU KNOW THE ONE YOU HAVE ENTRUSTED YOUR SOUL

(4) DO YOU KNOW ABOUT THE PRESERVATION OF THE SAINTS

(4) BE CONVINCED, CONVICTED, ASSURED, AND FIRM IN YOUR PROFOUND KNOWLEDGE RECEIVED FROM GOD THROUGH THE HOLY SPIRIT WHICH DWELLS IN YOU. Amen. Oct. 12. 2008

(27)

THEME: HAVE A DIALOGUE WITH YOUR OWN SOUL

TEXT. Psalm 42:11 Why art thou cast down, O my soul? and why art thou disquieted within me? hope thou in God: for I shall yet praise him, who is the health of my countenance, and my God.. What a blessed consolation and evidence of the Divine inspiration of the Word of God—that as soon as life is breathed into the soul by the Holy Spirit—the soul delights in the inspired Word.

Psal 119:15 I will meditate in thy precepts, and have respect unto thy ways.

PSA 119:10-11 With my whole heart have I sought thee: O let me not wander from thy commandments.

PSA 119:49-50 Remember the word unto thy servant, upon which thou hast caused me to hope.. 50 This is my comfort in my affliction: for thy word hath quickened me.. The same Word of consolation is also a reminder of how transparent we are in the sight of Christ..

I - OCCASIONS YOUR SOUL CAN BE CASTEDOWN:
1) WHEN YOU HAVE WANDERED – The Prodigal son.
1) THE PRODIGAL SON TEACHES US A LESSON:
2) WHEN YOU ARE TEMPTED:
3) WHEN THE SELF WANTS OVER.

4) WHEN YOU FEEL ABANDONED, NO LIGHT, NO HOPE, NO TOMORROW.

SOME REASONS OUR SOUL CAN BE CAST DOWN:

Is your soul cast down because of besetting sins and temptations— then counsel your soul to hope in your God and His Word as we read from

2) DOES YOUR FAITH IN TRIALS? – THEY ARE THERE FOR OUR PROFITS.

- You will praise and honor God through them.
- YOUR TRIALS ARE MORE PRECIOUS THAN GOLD.
- KNOW WHERE YOUR HELP IS COMING.

Isa 1:19-20 If you are obedient, you shall eat the good of the land:

Mark 13:31 The word of God will not pass away.

II - THINGS YOU SHOULD REMEMBER AT THOSE MOMENTS: WHEN YOUR SOUL IS CAST DOWN:

1) SPEAK TO YOUR SOUL— ...hope thou in God: for I shall yet praise him, who is the health of my countenance, and my God."

2) ALL WILL PAST AWAY: For the mountains shall depart, and the hills be removed; but my kindness shall not depart from thee, neither shall the covenant of my peace be removed, said the Lord that have mercy on thee.

3) GOD IS HURT WHEN YOU ARE HURT: When our soul is cast down over some straying away from God's approved way— we may counsel with our soul to hear what the prophet said in JER 8:21-22

For the hurt of the daughter of my people am I hurt; I am black; astonishment hath taken hold on me.

4) YOUR HOPE IS IN THE LORD— your hope can rest securely upon our God's eternal covenants which we find recorded in His Word

5) GOD WILL TAKE CARE OF YOU :ISA 54:8-10 In a little wrath I hid my face from thee for a moment; but with everlasting kindness will I have mercy on thee, said the LORD thy Redeemer.

BE CERTAIN:

1) PE 1:5-7 THE POWER OF GOD through faith unto salvation ready to be revealed in the last time.
2) HEB 4:14-16 WE HAVE A GREAT HIGH PRIEST that is passed into the heavens, Jesus the Son of God; let us hold fast our profession
3) OUR FAITH CAN BE REVIVED

LAM 3:25-26 The LORD is good unto them that wait for him, to the soul that seek him.. It is good that a man should both hope and quietly wait for the salvation of the LORD.

PSALM 139

I – WHAT IS DAVID'S EXPERIENCE CONCERNING GOD?

(!) God has search him

(2) God know him   -(a) He sits (b) he rises

                -(b) God perceives his thoughts from afar

                -(c) God is familiar with all his ways

                -(c) Before a word is on his tongue, God knows it completely.

GOD HEMS HIM IN – behind, before.

CONCLUSION: Such knowledge is too wonderful and lofty for me.

II – QUESTION: (Vs 7-12) THE PRESENCE & THE SPIRIT OF GOD
WHERE CAN I GO? – God is present with his Spirit everywhere:
   (1) In heavens (2) in the depts., (3) in the wings of the dawn,
   (4) In the far side of the sea, (5) in the darkness.

III – WHY GOD CAN BE THIS WAY? (Reason) FOR - (Verses 13)
God created my innermost being
God knit me in my mother's womb.

IV- REASONS TO PRAISE GOD:
(1) I am fearfully and wonderfully MADE. (Verse 14)
   -God's works are wonderful. (Do you know any which is not?)
(2) My frame not hidden from God
   - God EYE saw my UNFORMED BODY
(3) All my DAYS ARE ORDAINED.
   - They are written in God's book before they came to be. (V.16)

V – APPRECIATIONS OF WHO GOD IS: (Verses 17)
(1) How precious are your thoughts to me?
   – The sum is vast.
I can't count them – more than the grains of sand

VI – WHICH ABOUT THE ENEMIES- (Verse 19)
IF God would slay the wicked.
Because they speak of God with evil intent.
They misuse God's name.
I have those who HATE GOD. (verse 20)
I abhor those who rise up against God – THEY ADVERSARIES.

They are also my ENEMIES.

CONCLUSION: -(Verses 23-24)

Now that I have this experience from God. – I can't hide from God

That I am so WONDERFULLY CREATE BY GOD,

THAT I WAS CREATED FOR A PURPOSE – PRAISE HIM,

THAT I APPRECIATE HIM SO MUCH

THAT I WISH THAT HE WILL SLAY ALL HIS AND MY ADVERSARIES,

HE SHOULD:

PURIFY MY HEART

TEST MY THOUGHTS

LEAD ME TO THE EVERLASTIN WAY – HIS HOME. Amen.

(28)

Scripture Reading: I Cor. 6:15-20

Text. I Cor.6:15 & 19 "Do you NOT know that your bodies are members of Christ himself?... Do you NOT know that your body is a temple of the Holy Spirit, who is in you, whom you have received from God?

THEME: THEME YOUR BODY BELONGS TO THE LORD.

INTRODUCTION: The Church is not the BUILDING
(2) THE CHURCH IS A MYSTICAL BODY OF CHRIST made up Of EVERY PERSON IT THE PAST, IN THE PRESENT AND IN THE FUTURE – WHO TRUSTS JESUS AS SAVIOR BY FAITH,
-AND HAS BEEN BORN AGAIN INTO THE FAMILY OF GOD.
YOUR BODY BELONGS TO CHRIST!
THE BIBLE USES CERTAIN FIGURES OF SPEECH TO ILLUSTRATE THIS:
(1) BODY, (2) TEMPLE.
THE TEMPLE HAD CERTAIN FUNCTIONS:
DEDICATION If someone was guilty of sins, he went to the temple to give offerings for atonement – RECONSECRATION
The Temple was a place where people WORSHIP – DEVOTION – prostrate,

Spend time in the PRESENCE OF THE LORD –ENCOUNTER HIM
THERE

(3) PLACE OF SERVICE –BONSERVANT

(4) – DEAD IN OURSELVES- ALIVE IN CHRIST.

THEREFORE:

1) – JESUS GLORIFIES IN ME.

2) – I AM AN OBJECT TO WITNESS TO OTHERS.

MY PRAYER IS THAT: If God can give me 1, 10, 20, and 25 more
Years. – LIVE FOR HIM AND – WITNESS TO OTHERS.

I - WHAT OUR BODIES ARE NOT

1. NOT FOR THE FORNICATION –

2. NOT FOR THE UNCLEANNESS - Impurity of thought or life.

3. NOT FOR EVIL DESIRES AND PASSIONS.

4. NOT FOR EVIL LUST, FORBIDDEN ACTS
    (Adam and Eve's fall into sin!)

5. NOT FOR GREED, - DESIRES BEYOUND MEASURES

6. NOT FOR LIES - YOUR MOUTH - YES, YES -- NO, NO

II – WHAT MY BODY IS:

(1) MY BODY IS A PLACE FOR DEDICATION TO THE LORD

A. The earthly Temple was a place wholly dedicated to God and His
glory. It appears from the text, Lev. 10:8-11, that these men were guilty of
drunkenness before the Lord.) Be that as it may, the earthly temple was a
place set apart for God and His glory.

B. These earthly bodies we dwell in are also set apart for His glory!
According to our text, no one in this room has the right to use his/her
body for anything other than that which glorifies the Lord, v. 19b, 20. The
reason? We have been bought with a price!

(2). MY BODY IS A PLACE OF DEVOTION TO THE LORD

B. The temple was a place where men gathered to worship God. They came to the temple and glorified the Lord. It was a place where songs were sung, prayers were prayed, hands were raised, praise was rendered and God was magnified. The temple was a place of worship - Isa. 56:7.

1. Present It as a Living Sacrifice - Rom. 12:1-2, covenant with God that you will use your body for nothing that will dishonor and degrade His Name. (Ill. Make WWJD a standard for living, not just a catchy slogan!)

2. Prostrate It In Prayer - Jer. 33:3, Take you body aside from the world and go to the.

3. Practice His Presence - Heb. 13:5; Matt. 28:20,

4. Praise Him Continually - Heb. 13:15; Psa. 47:1,

5. Place Your Body In His Hand For Service - Rom. 6:16

C. MY BODY IS "A HOUSE OF WORTSHIP" for the Lord.

(3) .MY BODY IS A PLACE OF SERVICE TO THE LORD

D. The temple was a place where men carried out the duties they had been given by the Lord. Things such as the sacrifice, the tithe, the offerings and prayers were all carried out here at the temple. It was a place where duties were performed.

E. These fleshly temples are also places where we are to carry out the duties we have been given by We need to adopt the same mind set as the great Apostle Paul. Even though God was using him to pen the Scriptures and to preach the Gospel under a mighty manifestation of divine power, Paul still referred to himself as a "servant." The word there is literally a "Bond slave." One who has made a conscious decision to give the totality of himself up to Jesus and to His will.

(4). YOUR BODY DEAD IN ITSELF, BUT ALIVE IN CHRIST

You and I are challenged to be dead to certain things in this world. According to the Bible, we have been born again, 1 Pet. 1:23. As a result, we are a totally "new creation", 2 Cor. 5:17. Therefore, we are expected to be dead to our old way of life, and to the way of life held so dear by this world system.

(5). A PLACE DISPLAY THE GLORY OF THE LORD

A. When men saw the temple standing there in Jerusalem, they were reminded of God. They were mad to recall that there is a God in Heaven who loves sinners and has made a way for their redemption.

B. These bodies, as temples of the Lord,

QUESTION: WHY PEOPLE DON'T GO TO CHURCH TODAY?

    Many answers.

THEY DON'T SEE ANY DIFFERENCE IN US FROM THEM.

SAME BIBLE – DIFFERENT MESSAGES

– TOUT CHEMIN MENE A ROME. – If Jesus is not the only TRUE, LIGHT, WAY

WHY BELIEVE IN HIM WHEN ONE CAN BE SAVED SOME PLACE ELSE?

EXHORATION: LET US LIVE IN FULL AS

    1)-MEMBERS OF THE BODY OF CHRIST

    2)-WE ARE HIS TEMPLE.

    3)-WE DON'T BELONG TO OURSELVES, BUT TO HIM.

CONCLUSION YOUR BODY IS THE TEMPLE OF GOD.

    (1) DEDICATE IT

    (2) WORSHIP THE LORD WITH IT:

    (3) DEVOTE YOURSELF TO HIM

(4) SERVE HIM – DUTIES

(5) BE DEAD IN HIM

(6) DISPLAY – WITNESS THE ONE WHO DIED FOR YOU WITH IT. Are you Devotion? Duties, Death, Display – WITNESSING. Some here are not even saved. You are not God's temple, but you can be if you will make your way to this altar and call on God, He will save you by His grace. God is doing business today; will you give Him the right of way in your life? Amen.

(29)

Reading: Esther 4:1-17

THEME: WHY ARE YOU HERE TODAY?
HOW GOD'S PROVIDENCE WORKS

INTRODUCTION:

A. In the days of AHASUERUS, KING OF PERSIA king of Persia, and in the days between the building of the Temple and the wall around Jerusalem, Israel found themselves in a time of great peril.

1. The very existence of their nation was at stake.

2. God through His providence, will save Israel from certain destruction.

DEFINITION OF: GOD DIVINE PROVIDENCE IS:

1. The preservation, care and government which God exercises over all things that He created, in order that they may accomplish the ends for which they were created.

2. NO MIRACLES INVOLVED BUT NATURAL LAWS to accomplish His will.

3. Things that seem to happen by accident, may have happened by providence.

DISCUSSION:

I-. THE STORY OF ESTHER

1. Ahasuerus, after coming home from conquering all of Asia, party that lasts 104 days (1:1-8) When Ahasuerus had become drunken, he calls for his wife, who was very beautiful, to parade around in front of all those gathered (1:9-12)
2. Vashti refused to be made a spectacle, and the king became very angry (1:12)
3. Vashti was removed as queen (1:13-22).
4. Esther is made queen instead of Vashti …Esther 2:17
5. Mordecai uncovered a plot to kill the king (2:19-23)
6. Mordecai's deed was written in the king's chronicle
7. Haman is promoted to a high position in the kingdom and the king makes a decree that all should bow in reverence to him (3:1-2)
8. Mordecai refuses to pay reverence (3:2)
   1) Haman thus hates all the Jews (3:6)
9. Haman goes to the king in order to get revenge (3:7-11)
   b. He tells a lie…
10. The extermination of the Jews is decreed (3:12-15) Esther 3:13
    a). There was a great mourning among the Jews (4:1-3)

II. IF THIS EXTERMINATION TAKES PLACE:

   1) All the promises to Abraham would become void
   2) The Messiah …..
1. MARDECAI ASKS ESTHER TO INTERCED (4:8)
   a. Esther give an excuse ….Esther 4:11.
2. Esther agrees to intercede (4:16) … "if I perish, I perish"
3. The Jews are given the authority to resist their enemies (8:9-14) — The Jews are saved!!!

III. THE NAME OF GOD IS NOT MENTIONED ANYWHERE IN THE WHOLE BOOK OF ESTHER; YET, GOD IS SEEN THROUGH OUT THAT BOOK

QUESTION: ARE YOU DOING YOUR JOB IN TIME LIKE THIS?

WE ARE AT A PERIOD THIS QUESTION MUST BE ANSWERED - WHO KNOW WHY YOU ARE HERE JUST FOR A TIME LIKE THIS

B – YOU HAVE A UNIQUE OPPORTUNITY TO BE ONE OF THOSE WHO SAVE THE KINGDOM OF GOD

-THE CHURCH OF JESUS CHRIST HERE AND EVERYWHERE.

CONCLUSION: CAN YOU IMAGINE?

NOT 104 days of feast.
VASHTI GOING TO THE PARTY
MARDECAI BOWING TO HANNAN
ESTHER NOT INTERCEDING
KING AHASUERUS NOT SAVING THE JEWS?

CAN YOU IMAGINE YOU NOT DOING ANYTHING AFTER HEARING THIS MESSAGE?

WHO KNOWS IF YOU ARE CALLED FOR SUCH A TIME LIKE THIS. Amen.

Machiasport. Aug.3.2008

(30)

Scripture Reading Isaiah 30:15-22

Isaiah 30:21-22 Whether you turn to the right or to the left, your ears will hear a voice behind you saying, " THIS IS THE WAY, WALK IN IT" Then you will defile your idols overlaid with silver and your images covered with gold; you will throw them away like a menstrual cloth and say to them, "AWAY WITH YOU"

THEME: THE SCHOOL TO HEAR GOD'S VOICE NOW.

INTRODUCTION: I have heard many people saying that God has spoken to them.
IN ORDER TO HEAR GOD:

I-WE HAVE TO HAVE A PASSION TO SEEK & PURSUI GOD:
NOT TO FOREGET :Only God can touch our hearts and give us the desire to seek and to know Him, and to want His will & plans & ways above our own:

The Old Testament and New Testament words for "seek" mean: to seek the face of God;

to desire ; to examine or explore ;

to seek earnestly ;

to diligently search for ; to wish for ;

to crave ; to investigate ;

to pursue.

THE BIBLE SAYS:

1) "I will give them a heart to know me." Jeremiah 24:

2) "For it is God who works in you to will and act according to His good purpose." Phil. 2:13

3) INTIMACY WITH GOD, FULL FELLOWSHIP, PARTNERSHIP WITH HIM

Can create the desire and seek to know Him & His plans and will and His ways.

"As the deer pants for streams of water, so my soul pants for you, O God. My soul thirsts for God, for the living God. (Psalm 42:1-2)

THE BIBLE SAYS:
DRAWING NEAR & ENTERING THE PRESENCE OF GOD

4. HEARING AND OBEYING GOD'S VOICE
   1) WHEN WE SEEK HIM , SEEK HIS GUIDANCE, HAVE HIS VISION

   IT IS AN IMPORTANT PART OF OUR RELATIONSHIP WITH HIM

   THE WAY WE KNOW OUR CALLING IN THIS LIFE,

HOW TO KNOW THAT WE ARE CLOSE TO HIM: TO KNOW THE DIFFERENCE BETWEEN WAS IS RIGHT OR TWRONG,

TO SAY WE HAVE HEARD HIS VOICE BEHIND OUR THOUGHTS.

ISAIAH 30:21 GOD SAYING TO US: "THIS IS THE WAY; WALK IN IT."

IT IS THAT PERSON WHO CAN SAY:IN A BIBLICAL MANNER:

1) I LISTEN TO GOD:

2) GOD HAS REVEALED HIMSELF TO ME

3) I FOLLOW GOD

4) I OBEY GOD

III – WE CANNOT BE TRUE DISCIPLES (LEARNER AND FOLLOWER) OF JESUS UNLESS WE LEARN TO HEAR HIS VOICE, FOLLOW AND OBEY HIM:

THE BIBLE SAYS: (I)
MY SHEEP FOLLOW ME BECAUSE THEY KNOW MY VOICE...
MY SHEEP LISTEN TO MY VOICE; I KNOW THEM, AND THEY FOLLOW ME."
Some of us are like Martha –Busy working. Some like Maria - listening–

IV -WHY SHOULD WE LISTEN TO GOD & OBEY/FOLLOW HIM?

JESUS SAID:

"I AM THE WAY, THE TRUTH, AND THE LIFE..." JOHN 14:6 If you want to know the best way through life, if you want to know truth, if you want the abundant life Jesus promised, then you must seek & follow Jesus

PROVERBS 4:20 SAYS: (III)

"MY SON, PAY ATTENTION TO WHAT I SAY; LISTEN CLOSELY TO MY WORDS. DO NOT LET THEM OUT OF YOUR SIGHT, KEEP THEM WITHIN YOUR HEART; FOR THEY ARE LIFE TO THOSE WHO FIND THEM AND HEALTH TO A MAN'S WHOLE BODY."

LUKE 11:28 SAYS: "BLESSED ARE THOSE WHO HEAR THE WORD OF GOD AND OBEY IT."

V- WHAT HAPPENS WHEN WE DON'T SEEK, LISTEN AND OBEY GOD?

1) ISAIAH 64:6-7 - They become like THOSE WHO ARE UNCLEAN
- GOD WILL HIT HIS FACE FROM THEM.
2) JEREMIAH 32:32,35 - THEY PROVOKE THE LORD. -
3) PSALM 81:8, 16 IF YOU WOULD LISTEN TO ME, O ISRAEL,
YOU WOULD BE FED WITH THE FINEST WHEAT
WITH HONEY FROM THE ROCK I WOULD SATISFY YOU.

CONCLUSION

IF GOD IS OUR "TREASURE"; IF HE IS OUR "FIRST LOVE"
IF WE WANT A CLOSE RELATIONSHIP WITH HIM MORE
THAN ANYTHING ELSE

WE WILL HEAR GOD

WE WILL SEEK HIM,

WE WILL PURSUE HIM,

HE WILL HEAR HIM,

WE WILL OBEY HIM

WE WILL HEAR HIS VOICE ALWAYS BEHIND OUR EARS.

QUESTIONS:

1) HAVE YOU LEARNED HOW TO HEAR GOD'S VOICE
   BEHIND YOUR EARS?

2) DO YO HEAR HIM WELL IN YOUR LIFE? AMEN.
   6/29/08

(31)

Text. I Peter 2:8—10 But you are a chosen people, a royal priesthood, a holy nation, a people belonging to God, that you may declare the praise of him who called you out of darkness into his wonderful light. Once you were not a people, but now you are the people of God; once you had not received mercy, but now you have received mercy.

THEME: CHRISTIANS LIVING IN THE WORLD.?

INTRODUCTION: KNOW WHO YOU ARE -
THE IDEA OF A GROUP, BELONGING TO A GROUP. – Perhaps this doesn't make sense to people of this country. GROUPINGS ARE MEANINGFUL TO OTHER SOCIETIES:
Arabs, Europeans, Africans. - I AM AN ENOAH MON AKOA!
What do you mean by: New Yorker? Bostonian? Down-easter ?

= SOME PARTICULARITIES
Peter describes people who have been saved by the blood of Jesus as:
(1) CHOSEN PEOPE, (2) A ROYAL PRIESTHOOD; (3) A HOLY NATION; (4) A PEOPLE BELONGING TO GOD; (5) THOSE WHO ONCE WERE NOT PEOPLE (6) THOSE WHO ONCE DID NOT RECEIVE MERCY.

François Kara Akoa-Mongo

QUESTION: HOW CHRISTIANS LIVE IN THE SECULAR WORLD?

In 1951 Dr. Richard Niebuhr in his work of CHRIST AND CULTURE. As well as Jimmy Young YONG in GENERATING HOPE, they proposed 5 ways Christians can address the secular world:

(1) CHRIST OF CULTURE, or ASSIMILATING CHURCH – In order to reach the world.
Music, Arts, Place of Worship, Programs of Services, dresses and church decoration
(2) CHRIST AND CULTURE – PROTECTING CHURCH – Monasteries, Convents, Isolation.
(3) CHRIST ABOVE CULTURE – UNCHANGING CHURCH - We are MODEL – Traditions; THE TIME DOESN'T HAVE ANY EFFECT ON US.
(4) CHRIST AGAINST CULTURE – BATTLE CHURCH – Let's change people in the government. WE SHOULD ELECT CHRISTIANS IN THE GOVERNMENT
(5) CHRIST THE TRANSFORMING OF CULTURE – INFLUENCING CHURCH.
We have the mission to light in darkness and change the world.

CONCLUSION: YOU CAN MAKE YOUR OWN CHOICE.

II – HOW TO LIVE IN A SECULAR WORLD AS CHRISTIANS?

PETER'S APPROACH IN I PETER:
I. LET OUR ACTIONS SPEAK LOUDER THAN OUR WORDS

I Peter 2:12 Live such good lives among the pagans THAT, though they accuse you of doing wrong, they may see your good deeds and GLORIFY GOD ON THE DAY HE VISITS US.

Most of our Communication is in non-verbal.

2. LET'S HAVE GOOD CONDUCT DOING GOOD THINGS

I Peter 1:15: For it is God's will that by doing GOOD you should silence the ignorant talk of foolish men.

3-LET'S HAVE THE CHARACTER OF GOD IN THE WORLD:

THE FRUIT OF THE SPIRIT: love, joy, peace, patience, kindness, goodness, faithfulness, gentleness, and self-control. Others-humility, forgiveness, joy in trials.

4-LET'S SPEAK AGAINST: EVIL, SLANDER, AS CHRISTIANS

But God has a plan for those people! Even those who might speak out against us may be worn down by our good conduct.

5- LET'S BE READY TO SHARE OUR HOPE IN CHRIST

1 Peter 3:15 for it is God's will that by doing GOOD you should silence the ignorant talk of foolish men. But in your hearts set apart Christ as Lord.

6-LET'S LIVE OUR CHRISTIAN FAITH DAILY.

We can expect to be asked about our faith on a daily basis. What do we need to do? Give a Defense:

7-Let's defend our belief having good conduct, and actions.

If not knowing what to say? Depend on God to come through for us-- Luke 21:12-18

THE HOLY SPIRIT WILL GIVE THE WORD.

We need to understand that we have a New Identity.

III. KNOW THAT WE HAVE AN IDENTITY
Look at verse 2:11 where he calls us Strangers and Aliens- Peter uses two terms:

1. WE ARE STRANGERS IN THIS WORLD.
meaning sojourner or traveler.

2. WE ARE MARTIANS IN THIS WORLD – ALIEN – Not Citizen
The pressure to fit in will be great, but when we know our identity as Strangers and Aliens of this world-we can begin to complete the fourth step to living in a secular world

IV. REMEMBER THAT GOD HAS SET YOU APART-
(1) SET YOUR HEART APART
1 Pet 2:11 Dear friends, I urge you, as aliens and strangers in the world, TO ABSTAIN FROM THE SINFUL DESIRES, WHICH ARE AGAINST YOUR SOUL.

  a) BY ABSTAINING FROM SINFUL DESIRES
     WE ARE AT WAR AGAINST
     PROTECT YOUR SOUL.
  b) KILL YOUR FLESHY DESIRERS
     Galatians 5- selfish, greedy, proud, impatient, angry, envious, or angry. There really is a war going on in our hearts.
  c) By LETTING CHRIST REIGN IN YOUR INNER PERSON
     LET HIM HAVE THE FIRST PLACE IN YOUR HEART

CONCLUSION:

I. WHAT KIND OF CHURCH DO YOU WANT THIS ONE TO BE:

1. The Assimilating Church: In the World and of the World
2. 2. The Protecting Church: Not of the World and Not in the World
3. The Unchanging Church: Not in the World and Oblivious to the World
4. The Battling Church: In the World and Over the World
5. The Influencing Church: In the World but not of the World

II – IN ORDER TO INFLUENCE OUR CULTURE: WE MUST:

1. KNOW YOUR IDENTITY: YE ARE (1) WE ARE CHOSEN PEOPLE, (2) A ROYAL PRIESTHOOD; (3) A HOLY NATION; (4) A PEOPLE BELONGING TO GOD; (5) THOSE WHO ONCE WERE NOT PEOPLE (6) THOSE WHO ONCE DID NOT RECEIVE MERCY.

III – HERE ARE PETER'S APPROACHES IN ORDER TO INFLUENCE OUR CULTURE:

1. LET OUR ACTIONS SPEAK LOUDER THAN OUR WORDS
2. LET US HAVE GOOD CONDUCT DOING GOOD IN THE WORLD.
3. LET'S HAVE THE CHARACTER OF GOD IN THE WORLD:

THE FRUIT OF THE SPIRIT: love, joy, peace, patience, kindness, goodness, faithfulness, gentleness, and self-control. Others-humility, forgiveness, joy in trials.

4-LET'S SPEAK AGAINST: EVIL, SLANDER, AS CHRISTIANS

5- LET'S BE READY TO SHARE OUR HOPE IN CHRIST

6-LET'S LIVE OUR CHRISTIAN FAITH DAILY

7-LET'S DEFEND OUR BELIEF...

IV. LET'S REMEMBER THAT GOD HAS SET US APART-
(1) WE ARE A STRANGERS, AN ALIENS HERE
(2) LET CHRIST REIGN IN OUR INNER PERSONS Amen 6/8/08

(32)

1 Samuel 17:40-51

Scripture Reading I Samuel 17:26-56

Text: I Sam.17 39b, 44 I cannot go in these," he said to Saül, " because I am not used to them"….Then he took his staff in his hand, chose FIVE SMOOTH STONES from the stream, put them in the pouch of his shepherd's bag and, with his sling in his hand, approached the Philistine…. David said to the Philistine, " You come against me with sword and spear and javelin, but I come against you in the name of the Lord Almighty, the God of the armies of Israël.

THEME: THE KIND OF PEOPLE GOD USES TO DEFEAT GOLIATH WITH FIVE SMOOTH STONES ARE COURAGEOUS, CONFIDENT, PREPARED, TRUSTWORLY, AND THE VICTORY IS THEIRS

INTRODUCTION: Over 150 years ago, Henry Varley said, "The world has yet to see what God can do with and for and through and in a man who is fully and wholly consecrated to Him."

A young man named D.L. Moody heard those words and determined in his heart to be that man! He gave himself fully to the will of God for

His life and the Lord used him to shake two continents for Jesus. Moody preached to more than 100 million people during his ministry and many thousands came to know Jesus Christ as their Savior. I don't know about you, but I want to be a person God can use. The Lord is still looking for men, women, boys and girls that He can fill with His Spirit and use to make a difference for Jesus. You and I can be that person that God will take and use for His name's sake.

In our passage, we are told about a young man named David. In his meeting with Goliath, there are some definite principles that teach us about the person God uses. The Kind Of Person God Uses. These verses shed some light on the characteristics they possess.

I. THE PEOPLE GOD USES ARE COMMON PEOPLE
A. Ordinary People Are Used By God - 1 Sam. 16:6-13 –
    1) David was the youngest of his family.
    2) He was almost unknown, a shepherd.
    God does that so that the GLORY WILL BE HIS
B. Obedient People Are Used By God - 1 Sam. 17:17-22 –
    1) David was on a mission
    2 It was an opportunity to serve the Lord.

II. THE PEOPLE GOD USES ARE CONSECRATED PEOPLE
A. He Uses People Who Are Related To Him - David's words, v. 26,29, 37, 45-57, reveal that David has a personal relationship with God.
B. He Uses People Who Are Relying On Him - 1 Sam. 17:37-47
-David voiced his faith and confidence in the Lord.
-David was not looking to man made weapons and resources,
-David had faith in God! (Note: Any battles that are won in our lives will be won by God! If we are ever used in this life, it will be because we are leaning upon Him and His resources for our strength and provision!)

III. THE PEOPLE GOD USES ARE COMMITTED PEOPLE

A. They Are Committed In Spite Of The Obstacles - 1 Sam. 17:4-11, 32 - David was determined to honor the Lord despite the size and power of Goliath. His eyes were not on the problem, but on the Problem-solver!

B. They Are Committed In Spite Of The Opposition - 1 Sam. 17:27-32 - Some said that David couldn't do it. Others questioned his motives, but David was determined to defeat Goliath despite those who stood against him.

Those who go with God are going to face opposition - 2 Tim. 3:12)

C. They Are Committed In Spite Of The Opportunities - 1 Sam. 17:17-26 –

1) David had the chance to walk away, but David had his priorities in order.

2) He had made up His mind that God would come first, no matter what!

IV. THE PEOPLE GOD USES ARE COURAGEOUS PEOPLE

A. They Are Willing To Accept The Risks - 1 Sam. 17:38-51

- David was willing to put his life on the line for the glory of God.

- That is what moved Shadrach, Meshach, Abednego and Daniel!)

B. They Are Willing To Accept The Ridicule - 1 Sam. 17:28, 32-37 –

What were David ARMS TO FIGHT GOLIATH?

humiliation he might suffer because of others.

C. They Are Willing To Accept The Results - 1 Sam. 17:49-51

- David walked confident that he would win.

-While you may not always win in the battles of faith, if your faith is in the Lord above, you can never lose!

What looks like a defeat in our eyes, may just be a victory in the eyes of the Lord!)

CONCLUSION:

Do you want to be the kind of person God uses? I do! Regardless of what it costs in time, energy or reputation, it will be worth it to be used by the Lord. As you have listened to these characteristics exposed and explained, it may be that you have identified certain areas of your life that need correction. If so, please come before the Lord and talk to Him about your needs. He will take your life and use you for His glory if you will get honest with Him. If you do not have a relationship with Jesus, then you come to Him tonight and I will take the world of God and show you how you can be saved. Wherever you may be right now, you can become a person God uses for His glory. Let's determine to pay the price this evening to be that person for the glory of God! Amen.

Machiasport, June 22, 200

(33)

Exodus 3:1-22; and Matthew 7:7-12

Text: Mat. 7:9-11 Which of you, if his son asks for bread will give him a stone? Or if he asks for a fish, will give him a snake? If you, then, though you are evil, know how to give good gifts to your children, how more will YOUR FATHER in heaven give good gifts to those who ask him.

THEME: FATHERS' LESSON FROM THE HEANLY FATHER GOD.

INTRODUCTION: When a baby animal comes to life, he or she learns everything from his mother and father. He or she will eat what they eat. Go where they go. Trust who they trust; follow them all the way. That is why all lions are alike; all monkey act alike; every fish is in water and every chicken a chicken not a duck.

As human beings, we need PROTOTYPES. Mothers should learn how to be mothers from a mother. Fathers should learn how to be fathers from a Father. Leaders should learn how to be leaders from Leaders.

WHY TO TRY TO INVENT AN ALREADY INVENTED WHEEL?
What many of us do in our lives is to live as no one has lived before. To do everything in our own way. Because we don't want to follow models, habits,

traditions, ways which have been proven from generations to generations, look where we stand today? FAILURES IN: (1) raising children, (2) failures in Education; (3) failures in marriage; (4) failures in life in general.

ONE OF THE MOST POPULAR FIGURES OF GOD IN THE BIBLE IS GOD AS THE FATHER.

LET US LEARN HOW GOD FITS THAT IMAGE.
A. THE HISTORY OF THE BIBLE:

1. God called Israel his "MY SON" before he became a NATION
When God sent Moses to speak to Pharaoh, God said to Pharaoh
"Israel is my Son, my firstborn (Exodus 4:22).
LET MY PEOPLE GO.
2. Before Israel entered the Promised Land, God told them,
"You are the children of the Lord your God"
(Deuteronomy 14:1).
3.The prophet Isaiah told Israel to call upon God as "our Father"
(Isaiah 64:8).
The prophet Hosea told Israel that they were "sons of the living God"
(Hosea 1:10).

B- LOOK AT JESUS, GOD BECAME OUR SPIRITUAL FATHER:

1. At Jesus' baptism a voice from heaven said of Jesus,
"This is my beloved Son..." (Matthew 3:17).
2. When Jesus was transfigured, a voice from a cloud said of Jesus,
"This is my beloved Son..." (Matthew 17:5).
3. Jesus frequently referred to God as "my Father" (Matthew 11:26
4. Jesus also taught people that God was their FATHER.
5. Jesus told people to love their enemies in order that they might be
"the sons of your Father who is in heaven" (Matthew 5:45).

6. Jesus told his disciples to pray,

"Our Father, who is in heaven..." (Matthew 6:9).

7. Jesus himself referred to God as "your Father"

(Matthew 6:4, 8; 7:11; 10:20; etc.).

C. LOOK AT PAUL AND THE REST OF THE NEW TESTAMENT:

1. Romans through the rest of the New Testament epistles, God is often referred to as "God our Father," "our God and Father," and God the Father."

2. The Bible teaches us to look at our relationship with God as a parent and child relationship, a Father and son relationship.

II- WHY ARE WE TAUGHT TO LOOK AT GOD AS OUR FATHER.
WHAT SHOULD WE GET FROM THIS IMAGE? ANSWERS:

1. That God becomes the Prototype of the kind of father we should be.

2. GOD IS A GOD OF RELATIONSHIP WITH US.

- Healthy Relationship.
- Loving relationship.
- Caring relationship.
- Positive relationship.
- Protecting relationship.
- Forgiving relationship.
- Guiding relationship

QUESTION: AS PARENT, AS FATHER, DO YOU HAVE SUCH RELATIONSHIP WITH YOUR CHILDREN?

III - THE ROLE OF A FATHER IN THE BIBLE:

1. That should be positive, good image.

2. Fathers in Biblical time were not perfect, that is why the Bible gives these advices

3. But the image of a good father was powerful and positive.

GOOD FATHER PROVIDES:

1 .Protection for the family.

2. Security in an uncertain world.

3. Fair Discipline, but not abuse.

4. Preparation of the child for life

5. Love and Kindness.

Forgiveness and mercy.

IV – BEING A FATHER IS NOT AN EASY JOB: WHEN YOU LOOK BACK OR WHEN YOU THINK OF YOUR JOB AS A FATHER:

A. DO YOU HAVE SOME WISHES?

I wish I had been more involved in my children's lives

I wish I had spent more time with them

I wish I had taken them to church regularly

I wish I did not say this or that around with them

I wish I had given them much more help and support

I told you that I did not know much about small children

B. WHAT DO YOU DO ABOUT IT NOW?

1. DO YOU THINK THAT IT IS TOO LATE? .

2. TO THOSE WHO STILL HAVE CHILDREN:

a) Learn from your Father who is in heaven.

b) Provide protection for the family.

c) Provide security for your child in an uncertain world.

d) Provide faire discipline, but not abuse to your child.

e) Prepare your child for life

f). Love and be Kind to your child.

g) Have a forgiving and merciful heart for your.

CONCLUSION:

1. DON'T LOOK FOR A MODEL SOMEWHERE ELSE
2. OUR FATHER LOVES, FORGES, HAS MERCY ON US.
3. HE CALLED US HIS CHILDREN BEFORE WE WERE CREATED.
4. HE HAS GUIDED US ALL OUR LIVES.
5. HE PROTECTES AND CARES FOR US EVERY DAY.
6. LET US REFLECT HIS ATTRIBUTS AND CARE IN OUR CHILDREN AND BE BLESSED BY OUR FATHER.

THEME: THE LESSON FROM OUR FATHER IN HEAVEN.

Amen. Machiasport, June 15, 2008

(34)

John 15:1-8; Acts 4:1-22

Text. Acts 4:13 WHEN THEY SAW THE COURAGE of Peter and John and REALIZED THAT THEY WERE UNSCHOOLED, ORDINARY MEN, THEY WERE ASTONISHED and THEY TOOK NOTE THAT THESE MEN HAD BEEN WITH JESUS.

THEME JESUS IS ALL THAT YOU NEED TO MAKE A DIFFERENCE.

INTRODUCTION: Each one of us don't want to live and die without making a difference in this world. Whoever we are, we would like to touch other lives, to do something people will be pleased with. To make someone smile. To know that we are worthy.

The Question is, WHAT DO YOU NEED TO DO JUST THAT? Is it money? Is it education? Is it a high position in the society? Will it be to be a man, to be a woman? To be old, to be young, to be A MILLIONAIRE? WHAT DO WE NEED TO MAKE

A DIFFERENCE IN THIS WORD?

Peter and John, those unschooled men were teaching in the name of Jesus and many people were being saved. The rulers, elders and teachers of the law met in Jerusalem. Anna the High Priest and other authorities asked them this question

"BY WHAT POWER OR WHAT NAME DID YOU DO THIS?

QUESTION: HAVE YOU MADE PEOPLE WANDER ABOUT YOUR ACTIONS?

TAKE ADVANTAGE OF THEIR ASTONISHMENT AND EXPLAIN TO THEM:

WHY DO WE NEED JESUS?
I- WE NEED JESUS BECAUSE:
A- JESUS PAID THE HIGHEST PRICE FOR OUR SALVATION-
Calvary. - THE CROSS - HE DIED FOR THEM ALL
JESUS LOVES US (Ill. Isa 52:14; Isa. 50:6 ; - Rom. 5:8.

B. JESUS MADE (5) PRECIOUS PROMISES FOR THE SAVED
Among them are these:

1. JESUS CAN SAVE ANYONE - John 3:16; John 12:46
   -That was his purpose to come on earth
   - He came to save THE SINNERS - Luke 5:31-32.)

2. JESUS CAN FORGIVE ANY SIN Any Sin Can Be Forgiven - John 6:37.
   Remember the criminal with him on the Cross Luke 23:40-43.;

3. JESUS GIVES ETERNAL LIFE TO ANYONE WHO BELIEVES
   FOR ETERNITY John 10:28-29
   THEY WILL NEVER PERISH, John 5:24

4. JESUS DELIVERES ANYONE FROM HELL -
   SAVED FROM THE WRATH OF GOD - Rom. 5:9

5. JESUS PROMISES ETERNITY IN HEAVEN TO ANY BELIEVER

JESUS WENT TO PREPARE A PLACE FOR THEM John 14:1-3–
SPENT ETERNITY WITH HIM THERE- 1 Cor. 2:9;

II – RAISONS JESUS IS ALL THAT WE NEED (3)

1... ALL THAT OUR SOCIETY NEEDS TODAY IS JESUS

WE NEED THE BIBLE TO GUIDE OUR SOCIETY:

THE TRUTH OF THE BIBLE

JUSTICE OF GOD

THE LOVE OF GOD

We can't pattern our lives to anything or any body else

2... ALL THAT WE NEED IS THE BLOOD OF JESUS

WHO ELSE or WHAT ELSE CAN People's HEARTS CHANGE

WHAT CAN TRANSFORM OUR SOCIETY - 2 Cor. 5:17, 2 Cor. 4:7.

3... WHAT WE NEED IS THE BLESSINGS OF JESUS:

WHERE CAN WE GET OUR BLESSINGS

III. THE ONE WE NEED TO SERVE TODAY IS JESUS John 15:5

A. JESUS IS THE ONE WHO WILL GIVE US THE ABILITY TO SERVE

- Phil. 4:13 – I can do anything through HIM WHO GIVES ME STRENGTH

B. JESUS IS THE ONE WHO WILL MOTIVATE US TO SERVE HIM-

JESUS WILL OPEN DOORS - SHUT DOORS TO SERVE HIM

IV.ARE YOU LOOKING FOR SATISFACTION? GO TO JESUS.

IMPORTANT THING WE NEED IS SATISFACTION

- I WOULD LIKE TO FILL MY HEART'S DESIRES.

- IT CAN BE DONE ONLY IN JESUS.

- I NEED JESUS and JESUS ALONE -

1-HE WILL SATISFY YOU HERE ON EARTH: -John 4:14.

<u>APPLICATION</u> Sadly. Many Christians are just like the Israelites. Even though they have been delivered from the bondage of Egypt (sin) they still long for the leek and onions (pleasures) of the old life, Num. 11:5-6.

2. HE WILL SATISFY YOU IN HEAVEN - Luke 16:19-31; .

Eternally saved, eternally happy and eternally alive with the Lord in Heaven.

Where do you want to go to when you die? Jesus promises a satisfying eternity.

<u>CONCLUSION:</u>

1. Jesus paid the highest price for us.

2. Jesus made important promises to those who will believe in him.

3. Jesus is the one we need today in our society and in the whole world

4. Jesus is the only one we should serve.

5. Jesus is the only one who can satisfy our needs.

6. Who else do you need in your life except Jesus?

7. Who else does our society need today, other than Jesus?

8. We need Jesus. He will make a big difference in our lives.

" I am the vine, and you are the branches. If a man remains in me, and I in him, he will bear more fruit. Apart from me, you can do nothing. If anyone doesn't remain in me, he is like a branch that is thrown away and withers. Come to Jesus today. Amen..

Machiasport, June 1st 2008

(35)

Scripture Readings I Corinthians 11:23-34

Text. I Cor. 11:24 And when he had given thanks, he broke it and said," Take, eat: this is my body, WHICH IS BROKEN FOR YOU: THIS DO IN REMEMBRANCE OF ME….This cup is THE NEW TESTAMENT IN MY BLOOD: THIS DO, AS OFTEN AS YOU DRINK IT, IN REMEBRANCE OF ME.

THEME: REMEMBER; REMEMBER. DON'T FORGET

INTRODUCTION:

<u>1-. THE PROBLEM WITH OUR MIND:</u>

We have tendency or not to remember, or to remember only good things or only the bad.

IT IS GOOD TO REMEMBER THE PAST – WHAT
HAPPENED WHY IT HAPPENED and BECAUSE
IT HAPPENED WHERE WE ARE TODAY

THE REMEMBRANCE AND GOOD REMEMBRANCE IS SYMBOLIC MEMORIAL DAY' CELEBRATION IS SYMBOLIC. THE EXPERIENCE REMEMBERED CAN'T BE REPEATED

THE EXPERIENCE REMEMBERED BECOMES MEANINGFUL. IT IS A TIME OF REMEMBRANCE. A TIME TO BRING BACK TO OUR

MEMORY, TO OUR LIVES WHAT HAPPENED SOME TIME AGO. THERE ARE FOUR DIFFERENT VIEWS CONCERNING COMMUNION

1. Transubstantiation - The bread and wine literally change into the body and blood of the Lord Jesus Christ. The recipient actually eats the Lord's body and drinks His blood, because Jesus is literally being sacrificed in the mass. This is the Roman Catholic view and it is non-biblical!

2. Consubstantiation - The bread and wine actually contain the body and blood of Jesus, but do not literally change. Christ is actually present "with, in and under" the elements. According to this view, the recipient receives the forgiveness of sins and the confirmation of their faith through the elements. This is the Lutheran view and it too is unbiblical.

3. Reformed - Christ is not literally present in the elements, but there is the spiritual presence of Christ. The recipient receives grace through partaking of the elements. This is the Presbyterian and Reformed Church view

4. Memorial - This view teaches that Jesus is present neither physically nor spiritually in the elements, but that the Lord's Supper stands as a symbolic reminder of what Jesus did for man as the cross and the tomb. This is the Baptist and Mennonite view

II – THE LORD SUPPER AS ANY OTHER COMEMORATION IS A REMINDER, SO THAT WE WILL NEVER, NEVER FORGET CERTAIN FACTS:

1. THE SACRIFICE OF CHRIST FOR OUR SINS:

2. V. 24-25 THE AGONY OF CHRIST TO SAVE US FROM SIN- The blood and juice represent the broken body and shed blood of the Lord Jesus Christ. As we partake of this observance, we need to remember the awful price that Jesus paid to save our souls. Please remember that when He died on the cross, He was dying in your place, and that He suffered greatly when He did, Isa. 52:14.

3. V. 26 REMEMBER HIS ACHIEVEMENT, HE AROSE. Those three days later, He arose from the dead. He lives, Matt. 28:1-6;.

4. V. 26 THE PRESENCE OF CHRIST -HE IS WITH US TODAY-After Jesus rose from the dead, He ascended back to Heaven and sat down at His Father's right hand to wait the day when He will return to this earth to receive His people unto Himself. Every time we take the Lord's Supper, we are declaring to a lost world that we believe in a returning Lord.
We should have it in HIGH REGARD
Through what he did WE WERE SAVED.

III- THERE ARE CERTAIN CONSEQUENCES IN US WHEN WE WELL REMEMBER; WHEN WE DON'T FORGET
1– WHEN WE REMEMBER, WE WITNESS - IT IS TRUE –

IV WE RECOGNIZE A SPECIAL SERVICE RENDERED TO US:

2- IT IS AN OPPORTUNITY FOR US TO REPENT

1) REPENT FROM OUR SINS: - v. 27-30 –

2) REPENT FROM OUR SELFISHNESS

3) BE COMMITTED TO OUR RENEWAL - The Lord's Supper service is a wonderful time for the child of God to his vows and his vision. It is a great time to remember why we are here. It is a good time to renew our vows unto the Lord. Many allow sin to creep into their lives and hinder their walk with the Lord. This is a good time to get all of that fixed up and get back on track with the Lord.

4) 17-22 CONSECRATE OURSELVES TO A SOLEMN SERVICE Verse 28 tells us that we are to examine ourselves. That verb is in the imperative mood. It is a command and not an option! Before you partake of the Lord's Supper, be certain of a few necessary things.

5) BE CERTAIN OF OUR SA LVATION - This is a service for Christians. If you are lost, you can neither understand nor appreciate when we are doing here this morning. If you are lost, then I want to invite you to come to Jesus and be saved today.

6) BE CERTAIN WE ARE RIGHT WITH THE LORD- If you are saved, then be sure you examine yourself and that you confess your sins before the Lord. He will receive you and forgive you and make you ready to receive the Lord's Supper.

7) BE CERTAIN THAT THE HOLY SPIRIT GUIDES US - This is a time of worship and not a time to take things lightly. Please focus your heart and mind on the Lord and do your best to be in communion with Him as you receive His Supper.

CONCLUSION:

1)-FOR THE COMMUNION, NO ONE IS WORTHY TO PARTAKE
   THE LORD SUPPER. YOU MUST BE SAVED AND LIVE FOR
   CHRIST WHO DIED FOR YOU
2)-WE NEED TO WELL REMEMBER AND NOT FORGET WHAT
   HAPPENED
      (1) THE SACRIFICES - (2) THE SUFFERINGS - (3) THE
ACHIEVEMENTS (4) THE BENEFITES (5) THE VALUE (6) NEW
         CONDITION WE ARE IN TODAY
3) WE WILL REPENT, MAKE NEW COMMITMENT leading to:
   (1) OUR NEW CONSECRATION TO THE CAUSE
   (2) OUR CERTITUDE CONCERNING OUR SALVATION

THEME: REMEMBER; REMEMBER. DON'T FORGET. Amen.

Machiasport May 25, 2008

(36)

Scripture Readings: John 20:10-18

Text John 20:15,-126 "Woman, "he said, "why are you crying? Who is it you are looking for?...She said," Sir, if you have carried him away, tell me where you have put him, and I will get him". Jesus said to her, " Mary... "She turned toward him and cried out in Aramaic, "Rabboni ! (which means Teacher?) ... "I have seen the Lord."

THEME: JESUS AROUND FOR 40 DAYS AFTER EASTER?

To Restore his disciples, to build their faith @ to commission them.

I – THE DIFFERENCE BETWEEN

RESURRECTION: bring someone back to life after death..

RESUSCITATION: Actions to restore breathing and circulation.

IN THE OLD TESTAMENT:

1. Elijah raise the son of a widow from the dead (I Kings 17:17-22)

2. Elisha raised the son of the woman from the dead (2 Kings 4:32-35).

3. A man was raised when his body touched Elisha's bones (2 Kings 13:20,

4. Jesus raised the widow's son from the dead (Luke 7:11-15).

5. Jesus raised the daughter of Jairus from the dead (Luke 8:41, 42, 49-55).

6. Jesus raised Lazarus from the dead (John 11:1-44).

7. Peter raised Dorcas from the dead (Acts 9:36-41).

8. Eutychus was raised from the dead by Paul Acts 20:9, 10).

II – JESUS APPEARED 14 TIMES TO HIS DISCIPLES TO RESTORE THEM - TO BUILD UP THEIR FAITH

QUESTION: HAVE EVER RESTORED ANYTHING?

I remember the DJ. Chapel

1. To Mary Magdalene Mk. 16:9

2. To the women returning from the tomb Mt. 28:8-10

3. To Peter later in the day Luke. 24:34;

    It is true, the Lord has risen and has appeared to Simon. I Cor. 15:5:

4. To the disciples going to Emmaus in the evening Luke. 24:13-31

5. To the apostles (except Thomas) Luke. 24:36-45;

6. To the apostles a week later (Thomas present) John. 20:24-29

7. In Galilee to the seven by the Lake of Tiberias John. 21:1-23

    - Made them have a big catch of fish

    - Gave them breakfast on the shore

    - Share communion with them there

    IN ORDER TO RESTORE PETER - John 21:15-19.

8. In Galilee on a mountain to the apostles and 500 believers 1 Cor. 15:6

9. At Jerusalem and Bethany again to James 1 Cor. 15:7

10. At Olivet and the ascension Acts 1:3-12

11. To Paul near Damascus Acts 9:3-6;

12. To Stephen outside Jerusalem Acts 7:55

13. To Paul in the temple Acts 22:17

14. To John on Patmos Rev. 1:10-19

    JOHN CLOSES HIS GOSPEL BY THESE WORDS: 21:25

Jesus did many other things as well. If everyone of them were written down, I suppose that even the whole world would not have room for the book that would be written.

II – TO TEACH HIS DISCIPLES HOW THE SCRIPTURES WERE FULFILLED.

HE SPENT THAT TIME TO TEACH TO BETTER UNDERSTAND

THE SCRIPTURE - HOW EVERYTHING WHICH WAS SAID BEFORE IN

THE OLD TESTAMENT WAS ABOUT HIM.

Application: Study the Scripture.

Improve your understanding of the Word of God

Learn HOW HE SPEAKS TO HIS PEOPLE.

III-JESUS STAYED TO GIVE SOME CHARGES TO HIS DISCIPLES

1) STAY IN JERUSALEM AND WAIT FOR THE HOLY SPIRIT.

YOU CAN'T DO ANYTHING WITHOUT THE HOLY SPIRIT

2) ONCE YOU HAVE RECEIVED THE HOLY SPIRIT

GO ALL OVER THE WORLD STARTING FROM:

JERUSALEM – Your home

JUDEA - Your people, friends, relatives

SAMARIA, Your enemies, foreigners etc.

THE ENDS OF THE WORLD.

CONCLUSION:

I – HAVE YOU BEEN CONVINCED ENOUGH THAT CHRIST WAS RAISED

FROM THE DEAD BY HIS FATHER AND THAT HE IS ALIVE NOW.

II – HAVE YOU BEEN RESTORED IN YOUR FAITH, YOUR HOPE?

III – DO YOU UNDERSTAND THE RELATIONSHIP BETWEEN JESUS AND ALL THE WORK OF GOD IN THE WORLD TODAY?

IV- ARE YOU READY TO RECEIVE THE HOLY SPIRIT AND GO ON WITH THE GREAT COMMISSION?

-ARE YOU NOW TRULY ENGAGED IN THAT MISSION:

1) AT HOME, - Family members, children, husband/wife

2) IN YOUR TOWN? – Neighbors, any one ?

3) WITH YOUR FRIENDS

4) PEOPLE WHO DON'T LIKE YOU?

5) ARE YOU INVOLVED IN FOREIGN MISSIONS ?

HERE ARE THE 3 MAIN REASONS JESUS DID NOT ASCEND RIGHT AWAY:

TO RESTORE HIS DISCIPLES,

TO BUILD UP THEIR FAITH AND HOPE

TO PREPARE THEM FOR THE GREAT COMMISSION.

April 13, 2008

(37)

THEME: HE DID IT ALL FOR YOU. Luke 23:13-46; 24:36-43.

INTRODUCTION When I read the account of the death of Jesus on the cross, there is always a question that forms in my mind: that question is, Why? Why did Jesus leave Heaven to be born in Bethlehem? Why did the Creator come in the image of the creature, live in poverty, be rejected by those He came to save and then die a cruel death on the cross? Why? Well, Jesus Himself answered that question the night before He died. If there had ever been any doubt as to why He came to this world, it was dispelled forever as He and His disciples observed the Passover together in the upper room. Look in Luke 22:19-20. There we find two small, seemingly insignificant words that solve the riddle as to why He came to die. Those words are: "for you". Jesus came for you. Jesus died for you and Jesus rose again for you. That is why He did what He did: just for you!

Let's look into our text today and consider what He did just for you.

I. 23:13-LOOK AT HIS CONDEMNATION - JUST FOR YOU

A. V. 18-23 See Him Rejected - (Ill. John 19:4-7; 34-43) The very people He came to redeem and deliver from their sin and bondage were the ones who turned their backs upon Him, fully and finally, John 1:11.

B. V. 35-39 See Him Ridiculed - (Matt. 27: 39-44) With one accord, His enemies mocked and ridiculed the King of Kings. Yet, He did not revile them! He endured their cruel mockeries because that was part of the price He was destined to pay for you and me, 1 Pet. 2:23; Isa. 53:7. (Note: It is interesting to recall what the Lord said about those who sinned against Him, Psa. 2:4; Pro. 1:26. The Lord promised to mock and laugh at those who sided with sin against Him. However, as part of the plan to redeem the lost, Jesus became a laughing stock before those He came to redeem! What irony! What utter depravity that would laugh at the Creator as He died for the creature.)

II. 23:33 LOOK AT HIS CRUCIFIXION - JUST FOR YOU

A. See His Crown - (Matt. 27:27-31) Never did a King wear such a cruel crown of mockery and infamy! Yet, He allowed Himself to be crowned as an amusement to the soldiers, because He was in fact a King! A King Who one day would wear many crowns upon His lovely head, Rev. 19:12

B. See His Cross - (John 19:16-17) Never did a King occupy such a gruesome throne as He occupied that day. It was to write in agony on a rough piece of wood, after having been beaten with a scourge, after being tried and convicted, after being beaten by the soldiers, after being mocked and made to bear his cross taken to the place of his execution. It was a horrible death! Yet, it was this death that He was destined for. Isaiah the prophet wrote of His death, Isa. 53:4-6. David the Psalmist wrote of His death.

III. 23:44-46 LOOK AT HIS CONQUEST - JUST FOR YOU

A. See Him Redeeming - Matt. 27:45-46 As Jesus hung on the cross, something mysterious and divine took place. The sky was darkened and the precious Lamb of God literally became the sin of the entire world, 2

Cor. 5:21. He did not just take our sins upon Himself; He literally became our sin on that cross! God judged Jesus as if He were the literal sins that you and I were born in and commit day after day. God saw His Son as if He were my wretched sins and He was subjected to the wrath of God on the cross. His work on the cross opened the way to God, Matt. 27:51, and (Ill. The veil in the Temple had stood as a barrier between God and man for centuries, Heb. 9:7

THE DAILY LIFE OF THE PEOPLE WHO USE THIS WORD.

1. A Servant's Word - Used when a task had been completed.
2. A Priest's Word - Used when a sacrificial animal was found to be worthy.
3. A Farmer's Word - Used when a perfect specimen had been born into the flock.
4. An Artist's Word - Used when the final touches had been applied to a masterpiece.
5. A Merchant's Word - Used when a deal had been struck and all the haggling had ended. Its usage meant that both parties were satisfied.

CONCLUSION: JESUS DID IT ALL JUST FOR YOU! That is why the King of Glory left Heaven, was born in Bethlehem, lived in poverty, died in shame and agony and arose in victory. He did it just for you! He did all that He did SO THAT YOU MIGHT CALL HIM BY FAITH AND BE SAVED BY HIS GRACE. HE DID IT SO THAT YOU MIGHT MISS HELL AND ENTER HEAVEN.
WHAT HE DID OPENED AN EXCLUSIVE WAY INTO A SAVING RELATIONSHIP WITH GOD John 14:6; Acts 4:12.

NOW, WHAT HAVE YOU DONE ABOUT YOUR LIFE? HAVE YOU TRUSTED HIM AS YOUR SAVIOR? TODAY IS THE DAY YOU SHOULD DO THAT IF YOU NEVER HAVE AND SAY, "THANK YOU LORD FOR DOING ALL YOU DID FOR ME". Amen. 3/23/2008

(38)

Matthew 26:36-46

40 Then he returned to his disciples and found them sleeping. "Could you men not keep watch with me for one hour?" he asked Peter. 41 "Watch and pray so that you will not fall into temptation. The spirit is willing, but the body is weak."

42 He went away a second time and prayed, "My Father, if it is not possible for this cup to be taken away unless I drink it, may your will be done."

THEME: WHY HAD JESUS TO SUFFER FOR US?

Why was the Passion of the Christ necessary?
MANY OF US, WE BELIEVE THAT WE ARE GOOD PEOPLE:
WE KNOW THE DIFFERENCE OF GOOD AND BAD.

STATISTICS 80% OF AMERICANS ARE CHRISTIANS.

WE SAY JUST AS THIS PHARISEE: "God, I thank you that I am not like all other men—robbers, evildoers, adulterers—or even like this tax collector. I fast twice a week and give a tenth of all that I get."

187

ANSWER:

I - CHRIST HAD TO DIE FOR US BECAUSE WE ARE SINNERS:

"Every inclination of man's heart is evil from childhood" (Genesis 8:21).

"I have seen this people, and they are a stiff-necked people" (Deut. 9:13).

"The heart is deceitful above all things and beyond cure" (Jere. 17:9).

"I know how your offenses and how great your are sins" (Amos 5:12).

"All have sinned and fall short of the glory of God" (Romans 3:23).

"The wages of sin is death" (Romans 6:23).

WE SHOULD ALL SAY AS THE TAX COLLECTOR ALL DAY LONG "GOD, HAVE MERCY ON ME"

II - OUR SINS ARE ALWAYS BEFORE YOU?

LOOKING BACK IN MY LIFE, I SEE? – SHAME! GUILT!

David who pleads

God not to remember his sins and rebellious ways (Ps 25:7).

The Passion is necessary because we are all guilty, and some one has to pay for those sins. Someone's suffer is necessary.

III – ASK CERTAIN PEOPLE WHO WALKED WITH GOD:

(1) ASK KING DAVID, "Surely I was sinful from birth, sinful from the time my mother conceived me"(Psal 51:5).

GUILTY FROM THE MOMENT WE WERE CONCEIVED ENEMIES OF GOD – LIVE UNDER HIS WRATHT

(2) LISTEN TO PETER:

Peter, who was struggling.

(1) "The spirit is willing, but the body is weak." Jesus commended Peter. He believed. The Spirit was working in him making him willing

to do God's will. But he still had the sinful flesh that was weak, it was unable to do God's will, it held him back from what the Spirit wanted him to do.

(3) LISTEN TO PAUL: "The good that I would, I do not, and the evil that I would not do, that I do"(Ro 7:18).

IT WAS NECESAARY: NO MATTER HOW HARD WE TRY, WE ALWAYS FALL SHORT OF GOD'S STANDARD

LET US ASK JESUS HIMSELF: WHY DID HE HAVE TO SUFFER FOR US? A

LISTEN TO JESUS ANSWER: He said,

"Greater love has no one than this, that a man lay down his life for his friends."

JESUS HAS A GREAT LOVE FOR YOU.

God already revealed that in the Garden of Gethsemane.

Jesus was sorrowful and troubled.

IV – THERE IS NO DOUBT THAT JESUS SUFFERED:

LISTEN TO WHAT HE SAID:

(1) "My soul is overwhelmed with sorrow to the point of death" (Mark 14:34).

(2) LISTEN WHAT LUKE SAID ABOUT HIM IN GETHSEMANE:

"his sweat was like drops of blood falling to the ground" (Luke 22:44).

YET

Yet he went to the Garden, knowing that he would be arrested there

YET

HE LET HIMSELF TO BE ARRESTED BECAUSE HE LOVED

murderers (2) adulterers, (3) thieves (4) cheaters, and all of us here today.

YET

HE WAS SENTENCED TO DEATH BECAUSE OF YOU AND ME
TRULY
HE DIED, HE DIED, AND HE REALLY DIED FOR YOU AND ME!
BECAUSE, BECAUSE, BECAUSE HE LOVED YOU AND ME SO, SO
MUCH TO DIE ON THE CROSS!

JESUS' PASSION, JESUS' SUFFERING WAS NECESSARY BECAUSE
HE HAD TO PAY THE PRICE YOU COULD NOT PAY IN ORDER
TO GIVE YOU THE LIFE YOU DON'T DESERVE: ETERNAL LIFE.
DO YOU LOVE HIM? Amen.

March 2nd, 2008

(39)

READING: John 17:6-26

Text John 17:9, I pray for them. My prayer is not that you take them out of this world but that you protect them from the evil one. They are not of this world, even as I am not of it. Sanctify them by the truth; your Word is truth.

THEME: JESUS' PRAYER FOR ALL HIS DISCIPLES

(1) Their protection from the evil one; (2) Their sanctification by the Word. -
INTRODUCTION: This Sunday is the third one I preach on this text. The first Sunday I preached on Jesus praying for his glorification. "Father, I have finished the work you sent me to do. Glorify your Son with the glory he had from the beginning. I want those I came to save to see me in my glory."

The second Sunday, I preached on Jesus' requests concerning those who will believe the witnessing of his disciples; those who will hear the Good News from them, those who will read their words and believe in Jesus Christ as their Savior and Lord. He prayed for our Unity; he prayed that we will also BEHOLD HIS GLORY at the end of time; and he prayed that we will be LOVED BY HIS FATHER as he was loved.

I will preach of his requests concerning his disciples sitting in front of him at that time.

<u>BECAUSE WE ARE A PROTESTANT CHURCH, WE BELIEVE THAT EACH ONE OF US IS DISCIPLE AND A PRIEST; THESE RESQUESTS ARE GOING TO BE FOR US AS WELL.</u>

Yes! JESUS HAS PRAYED FOR OUR UNITY, I DON'T WANT TO COME BACK TO THAT HERE HE PRAYED:

(1) FOR OUR PROTECTION IN THE WORD AGAINST THE EVIL ONE.

(2) FOR OUR SANCTIFICATION BY HIS HOLY WORD.

<u>APPLICATION:</u> I used to listen to my mother praying. After listening to her praying so many years, I could repeat her prayer knowing what she was about to say next. I used to think that she has memorized her prayer and she was just repeating them over and over. My wife can tell you that about me. I can say that about my wife. I can even say that about some of the people we have been praying together. What is true about this is that we pray concerning what is very important to us and we can repeat ourselves over and over without knowing that we have been doing that.

Subjects Jesus was praying for at the last moment in his social life were very important to him. Let us pay great attention to these.

What did he pray for concerning his disciples?

I – KEEP THEM IN UNITY Verse 11

a) Unity KEPT THROUGH GOD'S NAME…" Verse 11

B) Jesus is going to go; they will be alone

- UNITY IS IMPORTANT – The world will believe (17:20-26)

II – KEEP THEM FROM THE EVIL ONE - Verse 15

KEEP THEM FROM SATAN - The first big enemy of all the disciples

SATAN IS THE KING OF THE WORLD

DISCIPLES ARE BRING CHRIST IN THE WORLD

   WHAT KIND OF PROTECTION DO WE NEED?

No temptation greater than the power which is in you I Cor. 10:13

NOTHING TO SEPARETE US FROM GOD'S GOD. Rom 8:35-39

GOD'S SPIRIT WILL ABIDE IN US

When we continue shining as the light of the world Matt. 5:14-16

When we remain BLAMELESS and PURE in a crocked world. Phil. 2:15

III – THE SANCTIFICATION OF THE DISCIPLES. Verse 17

-SANCTIFICATION – HAGIOS

– SET APART FOR HOLY PURPOSE.

QUESTION: WHAT IS THE ELEMENT OF SANCTIFICATION? THE WORD.

QUESTION: WHAT WILL HAPPEN IF SANTIFICATIEF?

– THE WORD WILL KEEP THEM UNIFIED

– THE WORD WILL KEEP THEM FROM EVIL ONE – Satan

IV- WHY WILL GOD GRANT THESE PETITIONS?

THE DISCIPLES ARE GODS GIFT HIS SON (verse 6)

THE DISCIPLES HAVE RECEIVED GOD'S WORD. (John 17:6b)

THE DISCIPLES BELONG TO THE FATHER AND THE SON.

THE DISCIPLES GLORIFY CHRIST. (John 17:10b)

THE DISCIPLES DON'T HAVE CHRIST BUT THE HOLY SPIRIT

THE DISCIPLES ARE HATED BY THE WORLD.

THEIR MISSION IS TO CHANGE THE WORLD.

THE DISCIPLES ARE SANCTIFIED BY THE WORD OF GOD

V- WHY THIS PRAYER IMPORTANT TO US TODAY?

JESUS STILL HAS THE SAME CONCERNS FOR US TODAY AS THEN.

WHAT WAS TRUE THEN IS STILL TRUE TODAY:

3) -SATANT IS STILL OUR ENEMY – WE ARE STILL IN THE WORD
4) -WE DON'T BELONG TO THE WORLD BUT WE ARE IN THE WORLD.
5) THE ONLY WAY WE CAN BE SANCTIFIED IS BY THE WORD.
6) OUR MISSION IS TO CHANGE THE WORLD FOR CHRIST
7) WE ARE JESUS' DISCIPLES.
8) WE ARE STILL TEMPTED.

CONCLUSION:

HAVE YOU RECEIVED THE WORD OF GOD?

ARE YOU HIS DISCIPLE?

SEEK YOUR PROTECTION BY THE SPIRIT AND THE WORD OF GOD.

BE SANCTIFY; BE BLAMELESS, BE HOLY AND BE PURE IN THE WORLD

KNOW THAT YOU ARE JESUS' DISCIPLE

LET US STAY UNITED THROUGH THE WORD.

JESUS IS PRAYING FOR US. Amen.

Machiasport Jan.27.2009

(40)

Text John 17: 20ss. My prayer is not for them alone. I pray also for those who will believe in me through their message. That they all may be one, Father, just as you are in me and I am in you....Father, I want those you have given me to be with me where I am, and to see my glory....I have made you known to them, and will continue to make you known in order that the love you have for me may be in them.

THEME: JESUS'PRAYER RESQUESTS FOR ALL BELIEVERS.
(1)They be one ;(2) they behold his glory ;(3) they be loved by his Father as He is loved.

INTRODUCTION:

1. In this "The Greatest Prayer ever prayed", we noted that...
   IN THIS PRAYER JESUS PRAYED FIRST:
   a. FOR HIMSELF ("Father...Glorify Your Son")
   - John 17:1-5 - HE HAS REAVELED HIS FATHER TO US

   IN THIS PRAYER, JESUS PRAYED SECOND:
   b. FOR HIS DISCIPLES ("I Pray For Them") - John 17:6-19

   IN THIS PRAYER, JESUS PRAYED THIRD:

c. FOR THOSE WHO WILL BELIEVE:

"Those who will believe through their word"...- John 17:20-26

This would include everyone who believes in Jesus NOW

CONCLUSION: THIS PRAYER IS FOR THE CHURCH OF CHRIST.\

THIS PRAYER IS FOR YOU TODAY IN MACHIASPORT

I- JESUS PRAYED THAT ALL THE BELIEVERS BE ONE.

(1) FATHER-SON-HOLY SPIRIT MODEL OF THAT UNITY.

-Just as you are in me and I am in you (John 17:20)

(2) THE UNITY SHOULD START WITH THEM

-May they also be in US. (BEING IN THEM)

WHAT WILL BE THE CONSEQUENCES OF THAT UNITY?

The world may believe that Jesus was sent

QUESTION: WHAT ABOUT IF THE WORLD DOESN'T BELIEVE?

1. THE SOURCE OF THAT UNITY: Jesus desires - John 17:21,23a

   a. As He and the Father are one

   b. Together with the Father and the Son.

2. THE PURPOSE OF THAT UNITY Jesus desires - John 17:21c, 23b

   a. That the world may believe the Father sent the Son

   b. That the world may know the Father, who sent Jesus,

and who loved them.

QUESTION: WHAT WILL BE THE RESULT OF THAT UNITY?

Jesus desires - John 17:22

ANSWER: THE GLORY OF THE FATHER IN JESUS CHRIST -

CONCLUSION:

1. If we have been all adopted by God through the blood
2. If we have the same Spirit
3. If we have the same model of UNITY – FATHER/SON/HOLY SPIRIT
4. If we have the same peace, joy, love –why not united?

II-JESUS HOPED THE BELIEVERS TO BEHOLD HIS GLORY

1. WHEN: END OF TIME: where He is - John 17:24a

   a. That is, in heaven, as He had mentioned earlier - John 14:3

   b. Using the futuristic present form of speech

2. That we behold His glory given to Him by the Father -

   a. The eternal glory He had with the Father before the world

   b. When the Father loved Him before the creation of the world.

CONCLUSION:

How will you feel standing in the presence of the Lord and seeing some Baptists, some Pentecostals, some Evangelists, some independents some, some, some and others you and I we have denied heavens here?

HOW COME THAT SOME STUDENTS WHO ATTENDED SCHOOLS LIKE Easport, Machias, Lubec, Lee Academy etc…be admitted in AVILIC COLLEGES

- -BELIEVE IN THE NAME OF JESUIS AND BE SAVED

The message of Peter the day of Pentecost is the only one.

Acts 2:38-40 Repent and be baptized every one of you, in the name of Jesus Christ for the forgiveness of your sins. And you will receive the gift of the Holy Spirit. The promise is for you and your children and for all who are far off – for all whom the Lord our God will call."

III- JESUS PRAYED THAT ALL BELIEVERS MAY BE LOVED

BY HIS FATHER AS HE HAS BEEN LOVED ON THIS BASIS: BECAUSE THEY HAVE KNOWN THROUGH JESUS AND JESUS WILL CONTINUE TO MAKE HIS FATHER KNOWN TO THEM.

1. The Father has loved us -

   a. Manifested by sending His Son - John 3:16

   b. Manifested by offering Him as a propitiation - 1 John 4:10

2. The Father will love us -

   a. With the same love He has for His Son!

THE CONDITION:\
ALL THOSE WHO KEEP HIS COMMANDMENTS THESE ARE:

that we be one; (2) That we behold his glory; and that (3) we be loved.
VERY IMPORTANT: HOW SHALL WE REACT TO THESE?

THERE IS A RELATIONSHIP BETWEEN –

   (1) BEING ONE

   (2) BEHOLDING JESUS' GLORY

   (3) BEING LOVED BY THE FATHER AS CHRIST HAS
       THE "OIDA "WE HAVE FROM GOD AND JESUS
       IF WHAT WE HAVE IS "GINOSKO" we will stay divided.
       "QUI S'ASSEMBLE, SE RESEEMBLENT"

IV. WHAT TO DO IN RESPONSES TO THESE REQUESTS: LET US:

(1) STAY MORE FOCUSED TO KNOW GOD AND HIS SON JESUS

(2) LET US WALK IN UNITY, IN SPIRIT....

    1. Preserving the unity of the Spirit – Eph. 4:3-6

        a. Keeping that which Jesus accomplished for us

        b. through doctrinal faithfulness to each of the seven 'ones'

    2. Attaining unity of mind and judgment - 1 Cor. 1:10-13

        a. In our dealings with one another as brethren

        By developing and displaying the mind of Christ

        That the world know God's loves by sending His Son

(3) LET US WALK BY FAITH...

    1. To remain steadfast to the end - He 3:12-14

        a. There is a real danger of developing a heart of unbelief

        b. We are partakers of Christ (and His glory) if we remain steadfast to the end

    2. To receive the crown of life – Rev. 2:10; 3:21-22

        a. We must remain faithful till death

        b. We must overcome if we are to sit with Him on His throne

    -- That we behold his glory in heaven for Eternity

(4) LET US WALK IN LOVE

    1. Love for God -

        a. The greatest commandment of the Old Law

        b. Demonstrated by keeping the commandments of the Lord

    2. Love for the children of God – Eph. 5:1-2; 1 John 5:2

        a. Imitating God who loved us

        b. Demonstrated by keeping the commandments of God

        That we might remain in His love

CONCLUSION

1. If we take Jesus' prayer seriously, we will do all we can to...

a. Walk in unity b. Walk in faith c. Walk in love

Are you doing your part to see that His prayer is answered?

Jesus taught us and his disciples how to know his Father and himself.

ARE HIS TEACHINGS FULFILLED IN US: TO BE ONE? TO BEHOLD HIS GLORY, TO BE LOVED AS HE WAS BY KEEPING HIS COMMANDMENTS?

KNOW THE FDATHER AND THE SON; WALK IN UNITY, IN FAITH, IN LOVE.

Amen.

(41)

John 17:1-3

THEME: DEFINITION OF ETERNAL LIFE: TO KNOW GOD AS THE ONLY GOD AND JESUS CHRIST HIS SON SENT BY HIM

After Jesus said this; he looked towards heavens and prayed: "Father, the time has come. Glorify your Son, that your Son may glorify you. For you granted him authority over all people that he might give ETERNAL LIFE to ALL THOSE you have given him. Now this is ETERNAL LIFE: THAT THEY MAY KNOW YOU, THE ONLY GOD, and JESUS CHRIST, whom you have sent.

INTRODUCTION: The principle goal of the Bible is to teach you and me to know GOD AND JESUS CHRIST.

Jesus teaches us today that: TO KNOW GOD AS THE ONLY GOD, AND TO KNOW

JESUS HIS SON AS THE ONE SENT BY HIM IS ETERNAL LIFE. IF YOU HAVE THAT DOUBLE KNOWLEDGE, YOU HAVE ETERNAL LIFE.

Would you say that you know God personally?

Do you know him BARELY? Do you know him CASUALLY? Do you know him INTIMATELY? Do you know him PERSONALLY?

I – WHAT DOES IT MEAN TO KNOW GOD?

There are two verbs about to know in GREEK LANGUAGE:

(1)- (OIDA (- INTIMACY, CONVICTION- DEEPT HIDDEN PARTS – SPIRITUAL RELATIONSHIP, FULL UNDERSTANDING - ACQUAINENCY,

(2)-(NOT GYNOSKO) INTELLECT - FACT - LETTER - HEAD

The knowledge Paul got when transported in heaven in II Cor. 12:2

That was the knowledge Herod has for John in Marc 6:20

FACTUAL KNOWLEDGE, INTIMACY KNOWLEDGE, UNDERSTANDING KNOWLEDGE, EXPERIENCING, ACQUAINTENCY, FAMILIARITY

QUESTION

HOW CAN WE COME TO KNOW GOD AND JESUS – ETERNAL LIFE?

1) - THIS KNOWLEDGE CANNOT BE TAUGHT-

2) - THE HOLY SPIRIT HAS TO BE IN ACTION IN YOU-
(I HOPE HE IS TOUCHING YOU RIGHT NOW)

3) - KNOWING GOD AND JESUS – LIVING BY HIS PRINCIPLES–

TEACHINGS.

THEY MUST BE REVEALED IN VERY PERSONAL WAYS RESULTS WHEN THIS KNOWLEDGE HAS BEEN AQUIRED:

I – KNOWING GOD CREATES A DESIRE TO BE LIKE HIM.

- THE MOST NATURAL THING: CHILDREN BECOME LIKE THEIR PARENTS

Do you ever remember saying that you weren't going to be like your parents?

I have heard me saying things my father used to say

IN ORDER TO BE LIKE THEM, WE MUST KNOW THEM BETTER, ACCEPT, BELIEVE THEIR WAYS AND START ACTING AS THEY DO RIGHT NOW.

IT S A GREAT DISADVANTAGE OF A CHILD TO GROW UP WITHOUT KNOW HIS PARENTS

QUESTION: DO YOU KNOW YOUR GOD AND HIS SON JESUS CHRIST?

II –KNOWING GOD REVEALS ALL THE TRUTH ABOUT ONESELF Isai. 6:1-5
ISAIAH IN THE TEMPLE:

(1) ONCE HE SAW GOD - Seraphim - Holy! Holy! Holy. And the posts of the door moved at the voice of him that cried, and the house was filled with smoke.

(2) HE SAID, Woe is me! for I am undone; because I am a man of unclean lips, and I dwell in the midst of a people of unclean lips: for mine eyes have seen the King, the LORD of hosts.

Isaiah said, "I am a man of unclean lips. As we learn about God we discover that He is holy and we're are unholy. It doesn't hurt to know that; it actually helps us.

ISAIAH KNEW HIMSELF IN THE PRESENCE OF GOD:
God is strong and we are weak.

God is patient and we're impatient.

God is impartial, yet we are prejudiced.

God is in control, we run in fear.

God is Holy, we are sinners

WHERE TO YOU LOOK FOR HELP?

WHERE DO YOU LOOK FOR PEACE?

WHERE DO YOU GO FOR LOVE?

WHERE ARE YOUR HOPE AND YOUR TOMORROWS?

DO YOU REALLY KNOW YOURSELF

III- KNOWING GOD HELPS US TO INTERPRET OUR WORLD GIVES US KNOWLEDGE THAT GOD IS IN CHARGE-

We should not panic because things are going certain way.

(2) WE CAN'T GIVE UP – THERE IS TOMORROW.

We have to be patient and WAIT FOR HIM

God's ways are past finding out.

(3) GOD STILL LOVES THE WORLD AND HIS CHURCH

God is strong and we are weak

Being confident of this very thing, that he which hath begun a good work in you will perform it until the day of Jesus Christ:

IV- KNOWING GOD GIVES US AN ETERNAL DIMENSION

(1) KNOW GOD INTRODUCE TO THE INVISIBLE WORLD – HIS KINGDOM

1 Corinthians 2:9-10 But as it is written, Eye hath not seen, nor ear heard, neither have entered into the heart of man, the things which God hath prepared for them that love him. But God hath revealed them unto us by his Spirit which searches all things, yea, and the deep things of God.

(2) Knowing God understands of UNDERSTANDING OF HIS WILL

(3) Knowing God's help TO UNDERSTAND THE MEANING OF THE CROSS.

(4) KNOWING TEACHING TO STAY AWAY FROM SIN AND LOVE HIM MORE

(5) KNOWING HELP ME TO PRAISE HIM, GLORIFY AND SERVE HIM ALWAYS.

Jesus Christ introduces us to an eternal dimension of living. He lifts our minds above the present. He gives us hope for the future.

CONCLUSION:

Knowing God vs. Knowing about God

Knowing God alters the way we make decisions, it changes our direction; it affects our attitude and knowing God affects the way we live.

We are no longer tossed to-and-fro with every wind of doctrine.

QUESTION: DO YOU KNOW YOUR GOD, THE ONE REVEALED BY JESUS?

> DO YOU KNOW JESUS CHRIST, THE ONE SENT BY HIS FATHER?
>
> IF "YES" KNOW AND NOW (OIDA) THAT YOU HAVE ETERNEL LIFE.
>
> IF YOUR ANSWER IS "NO" TODAY IS THE DAY TO KNOW HIM IN FULL.

THEME:

TO HAVE ETERNAL LIFE IS TO KNOW THE ONLY GOD REVEALED TO THE WORLD BY HIS SON, JESUS CHRIST. HAVE IT TODAY. Amen. 01.13.08

I- GYNOSKO (Genesco) (1) Matt. 12:33 – Recognize by its fruit –

> (2) Romans 1:21 Although they knew God (Intellect) they neither glorified him As God nor gave thanks to him
>
> (3) After Jesus healed the blind. He did not want his disciples to tell others about it and Matt. 9:30 Jesus warned them sternly " See that no one knows about this " (Yinosko) – intellect – fact
>
> (4) Luke 16:14-15. The Pharisees, who loved money, heard all this and were sneering at Jesus. He said to them, " You are the ones who

justify yourselves in the eyes of Men, but GOD KNOWS YOUR HEARTS "(Fact, intellect acquisition of Knowledge.)

II- OIDA – USED BY JOHN

INTIMACY: with a prostitute. I Cor.6:16 Do you not know that he who UNITES himself with a prostitute is one with her in body (OIDA)
CONVICTION: Her. 10: 30 For we know him who said " It is mine to avenge "

DEEP HIDDEN PARTS OF MAN. Matt. 9:4 knowing their thoughts, Jesus said "Why do you entertain evil thoughts in your hearts?" (OIDA) Paul speaking about his SPIRITUAL EXPERIENCE WITH GOD. He said II Cor. 12:1-6 I know a man in Christ who fourteen years ago was caught up to the third heaven. Whether it was in the body or out of the body I do not know – God knows. I know that this man –whether in the body or apart from the body I do not know, but God knows – was caught up to paradise. (OIDA)

OIDA – INTIMACY - ACQUAINTENCY - FULL UNDERSTANDING
- WHAT CALLS ALL THE ATTENTION – PROPOSFULL KNOWLEDGE -

(42)

Text. Exodus 33: 15-16 Then Moses said to him, "If your Presence does not go with us, do not send us from here. How will anyone know that you are pleased with me and with your people UNLESS YOU GO WITH US? WHAT ELSE WILL DISTINGUISH me and your people from all the other people on the face of the earth?

THEME: IS GOD'S PRESENCE WITH YOU ALL THE TIME?

INTRODUCTION: Moses was called by God to lead the children of Israel from slavery to the Promised Land. After dwelling for sometimes at Horeb, the Lord talked to Moses ordering him to leave the place and advance to the Promised Land with the people of Israel. But God said something to Moses he never said before. Verse 3. "GO UP TO THE LAND FLOWING WITH MILK AND HONEY. BUT I WILL NOT GO WITH YOU, BECAUSE YOU ARE A STIFF-NECKED PEOPLE AND I MIGHT DESTROY YOU ON THE WAY"

WHAT WAS THE REACTION OF THE PEOPLE –
-They began to MOURN; no one put on ornaments
WHAT WAS THE REACTION OF MOSES?
Moses said to the Lord, you have put me in charge of this people:
You have not given me who is going to be on my side

IF YOU ARE PLEASED WITH ME:

TEACH ME YOUR WAYS SO THAT I MAY KNOW YOU

WHAT WAS GOD'S REPLY:

MY PRESENCE WILL GO WITH YOU AND I WILL GIVE YOU REST.

I - WHAT WAS THE CONTENT OF MOSES' PRAYER TO GOD?

MOSES WANTED TO KNOW GOD MORE THAN HE KNEW HIM:

If you want to better worship, praise, honor, serve God.

You better know him more and more

MOSES WANTED TO SEE THE GLORY OF GOD

IN ORDER TO CHANGE THE STIFF-NECKED ISRAEL, MOSES WANTED

TO KNOW MORE AND SEE THE GLORY OF GOD.

IF MOSES BEIND CALLED, DESERVED TO KNOW GOD BETTER.

II – WHAT WAS THE CONTENT OF GOD'S ANSWER?

GOD WAS TELLING MOSES THAT:

"I will make all my goodness pass before you, - God's glory is his moral attitudes – his goodness, his mercies, his grace, and his love.

The attitude of the people and Moses moved God to change his mind.

GOD SAW THAT IT WAS IMPORTANT TO MAKE HIMSELF KNOWN TO MOSES AND TO THIS PEOPLE SO THAT THEY WILL CHANGE their stiff-neckness.

NOTA BENE:

(1) ONLY GOD'S PRESENCE IN US CAN MAKE US CHANGE AND HATE SIN:

(2) HAVING ALL THE MILK AND HONEY OF THE WORLD, WITHOUT GOD'S PRESENCE, DESTROIS US FOREVER.

REMARKS:

THE PRAYER OF MOSES WAS THE CAUSE OF GOD'S REVELATION TO HIM

IF WE KNOW THE IMPORTANCE OF GOD'S PRESENCE IN OUR MIDST, HE WILL CHANGE HIS MIND AND GO WITH US.

MOSES RECOGNIZED HIS CALL AND RESPONSIBILITIES

THE PEOPLE KNEW THAT - MILK AND HONEY ARE NOT ALL THAT THEY NEEDED, BUT THE PRESENCE OF THEIR SAVIOR AMONGST THEM.

GOD IS LOOKING FOR MORAL ATTITUDES WITHIN THE PEOPLE HE LEADS.

MOSES MADE TWO IMPORTANT STATEMENTS TO GOD.

IN VERSE 14 OF EXODUS 33:

(1) IF YOUR PRESENCE DOESN'T GO WITH US, DON'T LET US LEAVE HERE

(2) NONE WILL KNOW THAT YOU ARE PLEASED WITH ME AND YOUR PEOPLE IF YOU ARE NOT WITH US.

CONCLUSION: THE KEY, IN ORDER TO DISTINGUISH THE PEOPLE OF GOD AND ALL OTHER PEOPLE OF THIS EARTH IS GOD'S PRESENCE WITH HIS PEOPLE ALL THE TIME.

CONCLUSION: ARE YOU LIVING IN THE PRESENCE OF YOUR GOD ALL THE TIME? IF THE ANSWER IS YES, YOU ARE HIS PEOPLE. IF NOT, SEEK TO KNOW HIM BETTER AND SEE HIS GLORY IN YOUR LIFE.

III – WHAT DOES THE PRESENCE OF GOD REQUIRE?

HOLINESS AMONG HIS PEOPLE, PURITY, (3) GOODNESS, RIGHTEOUSNESS, (4) MERCIES, LOVE, JUSTICE - ATT GOD'S ATTRIBUTES

CONCLUSION:

Today is the first Sunday of the New Year 2008. God is calling us to go ahead and to possess the land and every blessing he has given us. Are we going alone without him, without his Presence, his values, his attributes in and with us?

So that God goes with us, DO WE TELL HIM THAT WE NEED HIM?

ARE WE WILLING TO KNOW HIM BETTER?

ARE WE LOOKING TO SEE HIS GLORY?

IF WE DO, BE CERTAIN THAT HE WILL GO WITH US BECAUSE HE PROMISED THAT HE WILL NEVER LEAVE US OR FORSAKE

Amen

Machiasport, January 6th, 2008

(43)

Scripture Reading: Galatians 3:1-1

Text: Gal.3:1-5 You foolish Galatians, who has bewitched you? Before your very eyes Jesus Christ was clearly portrayed as crucified? I would like to learn just one thing from you: Did you receive the Spirit by observing the law, or by believing what you heard? Are you so foolish? After beginning with the Spirit, are you now trying to attain your goal by human effort? Have you suffered so much for nothing -- if it really was for nothing? Does God give you his Spirit and works miracles among you because you observe the Law, or because you believe what you heard?

THEME: EVALUATE YOUR WALK WITH THE LORD.

INTRODUCTION: If you study the letter the apostle Paul wrote to Galatians, you will conclude that, he has a series of questions for the Galatians. HE WANTED THEM TO EVALUATE WHERE THEY WERE HEADING IN THEIR CHRISTIAN WALK THESE FIVE QUESTIONS ARE FOUND IN CHAPTER 3 verses 1-5:

Paul's opening remarks seem very harsh and abrupt. He addresses his friends, "You foolish Galatians!" He repeats the adjective in verse 3, asking, "Are you so foolish?"

The word "foolish" describes the error of the Galatians and it defines the underlying problem of their churches. It refers to the mind, the intellect, the reason. THE O.T. the word foolish " BASKAINO" is translated "without reason" (Prov 17:28; 15:21).

THE N.T. it describes lacking of understanding, of knowledge, of instruction.

The opposite of "foolish," of course, is "wise" (Rom 1:14; Luke 24:25).

4) A word (baskaino) which means "to be fascinated" "To be charmed"

The Galatians were foolish, without reason, in that they lacked understanding of the gospel and the promises of the Old Testament. They did not comprehend the difference between law keeping and faith. This is why Paul's tone is so harsh. They did not understand the enormity of their error and the damage it was doing to the gospel of freedom in Christ. This was the underlying problem in Galatia, and this is what Paul will spend the rest of his letter addressing.

The apostle asks five questions that deal with how the Galatians began their spiritual journey. He wants them to make a common-sense evaluation of their spiritual lives. Of course, these are excellent questions for all Christians to ask themselves.

I – THE FIRST QUESTION IS ABOUT THE PERSON WHO HAS FOOLED GALATIANS: " SATAN" HAS BLINDED THEM:

"WHO HAS BEWITCHED YOU? eyes Jesus Christ was publicly portrayed as crucified?" "Who has bewitched you to take your focus off of Christ?" He wondered if they had been "bewitched" – Gal. 3:1

2) - WHAT SATAN HAS DONE IS TO TEACH THEM TO TAKE THEIR FOCUS AWAY FROM JESUS CHRIST WHO WAS CRUCIFIED FOR THEM.

3)--FORGETTING THE WAY THEY GOT THEIR FAITH – PROCLAMATION OF THE CROSS is the question. The word "who" is singular in the text. Perhaps this is a reference to Satan, not to the false teachers who were troubling them. "Bewitch" means to cast a spell by what in those days was called the "evil eye." If this "evil eye" was detected in time, the effect of the spell could be averted by spitting. Some hold that this was the situation that Paul had in mind when he used the word "loathe," literally "spit out," in 4:14.

--- FORGETTING THAT THEY STARTED THEIR SPIRITUAL JOURNEY BY HEARING THE WORD OF GOD – THE GOSPEL OF SALVATION-\The Galatians had begun their walk of faith with the public proclamation of the cross, of "Christ and Him crucified."

4)--- BY FORGETTING WHERE OUR FREEDOM STARTS – AT THE CROSS

The principle is obvious: as Christians, we maintain freedom when our focus remains on Christ. Anything that blurs our focus on Christ as the center of our faith will result in our being deceived and will cause us to drift into error.

The cross, of course, is central to the Christian faith. Here is what Eugene Peterson wrote about the crucifixion:

B- WHAT HAPPENS IF WE DON'T FOCUS ON THE CROSS?

(1) YOU FALL INTO LEGALISM – WHAT A MAN CAN DO TO SAVE HIMSELF
(2) SATAN AND THE HUMAN PRINCIPLES TAKE OVER.
(3) WE TRY TO BE ACCEPTED BY PLEASING AND FINDING GOD

OUR FAITH SHOULD REMAIN CHRIST CENTERED SPIRITUALITY

<u>CONCLUSION</u>: JESUS IS THE LAMP OF OUR BODIES: Jesus said, "The lamp of the body is the eye; if therefore your eye is clear, your whole body will be full of light. But if your eye is bad, your whole body will be full of darkness" (Matt 6:22-23). We maintain Christian freedom when we keep our eyes clear and focused on Christ and him crucified.

<u>II/III SECOND QUESTION AND THIRD QUESTIONS: THE WAY THEY STARTED THEIR SPIRITUAL JOURNEY</u> -Galatians began their spiritual journey IN THE SPIRIT He asks (verse 2b): "did you receive the Spirit by the works of the Law, or by hearing with faith?"

(1) THEY STARTED BY THE WORK OF THE SPIRIT "How did you begin your Christian life," asks Paul, "by works of law or by hearing and believing?" The answer is obvious: they received the Spirit by faith. We maintain freedom when we remember our beginnings. Faith and faith alone is all that is required to receive the Spirit and begin living the Christian life. No works of law will help accomplish what only God can do. Paul describes his own story of salvation in these words in chapter 1: "when He who had set me apart, even from my mother's womb, and called me through His grace, was pleased to reveal His Son in me" (1:15-16).

God consented. God called. God set apart.

(2) THEY WERE NOT SAVED BY GOOD WORKS: Do you believe that good works saved you? Of course, not! God is the only one who saves through grace in Christ.

! That would be a foolish and ungodly thing to claim. Every person here has a wonderful story to tell of how God saved them and how they began their Christian life. Every one of you could tell how God orchestrated things to bring you to the place where you reached out to the Hand that had long been stretched out to you. It is almost an invariable rule that we come to Christ when we finally give up on our own efforts to satisfy the hunger of our hearts. No amount of works or achievements or good efforts could bring us what we wanted.

<u>**JOHN SCOTT**</u> <u>SAYS THIS ABOUT THE LAW AND THE GOSPEL</u>
<u>THE LAW SAYS - DO THIS" -</u>
THE GOSPEL SAYS " CHRIST HAS DONE IT ALL"
THE GOSPEL REQUIRES FAITH IN CHRIST'S ACHIEVEMENT. THE LAW REQUIRES OBEDIENCE TO RULES AND REGULATIONS
LUTHER SAID: THE ESTABLISHEMENT OF THE LAW IS THE ABOLITION OF THE GOSPEL

<u>ILLUSTRATION</u>: Many of us found that after years of frustration spent looking for the perfect mate, we finally give up. Then, when we had stopped looking, our future spouse appeared, seemingly out of nowhere, a totally unexpected gift. At once we experienced infatuation, joy, and unconditional acceptance. But then, very subtly, through years of marriage, this relationship, which began as a gift, changed to a law-based thing. We began to make demands, seeking to control our spouse in an effort to have our expectations met. <u>Healthy marriages, however, are maintained by remembering how the relationship began in the first place</u>. In the same way, we maintain our freedom in Christ when we remember that our journey began humbly, by faith and faith alone.

<u>IV- THE FOURTH QUESTION IS: HOW DO WE INTEND TO FINISH OUR SPIRITUAL WALK</u> He asks, "Are you so foolish? Having begun by the Spirit, are you now being perfected by the flesh?"
<u>THIS IS VERY IMPORTANT QUESTION</u>: This is Paul's most important question, the main thing he wants the Galatians to evaluate. How did they intend to complete the Christian life?
THEY BEGUN THE COURSE WITH THE SPIRIT THROUGH FAITH IN CHRIST CRUCIFIED. IT DOESN'T MAKE SENSE TO

François Kara Akoa-Mongo

FINISH THE COURSE IN THE FLESH. WE MAINTAIN OUR
CHRISTIAN FREEDOM BY CONSTANTLY BEING REMINDED
THAT THE FLESH WILL NOT HELP US NOT NOW, NOR AT
THE END CHRISTIAN EXPERIENCE BEGINS WITH FAITH
WITH THE SPIRIT-

IT IS AS WE SAY TO GOD: "Thanks a lot, God for the start, but now
I can get along quite nicely on my own."

THE FLESH COULD NOT SAVE US IN THE PAST, IT WILL NOT
IN THE FUTURE

Whatever the flesh accomplishes, no matter how good the result looks,
will not change or enhance our acceptability before God, because we are
accepted in Christ, in him alone.

UNDER LEGALISTIC LIFE NO MORE CONTROL OF THE HOLY
SPIRIT BUT THE FLESH -

The flesh can sing in the choir.

The flesh can lead people to Christ.

STANDARD ESTABLISHED, RULES OBSERVED

– THE CROSS HERE AND THERE –CHRISTIAN FREEDOM
IS MAINTAINED BY KEEPING WITH THE SPIRIT. IT REQUIRES
CONSTANT EVALUATION.- ONE CAN EASILY DRIFT OFF.

Now we come to Paul's fourth question. He asks: "Did you suffer so many
things in vain -- if indeed it was in vain?" The apostle is asking, "Have you
undergone a change in values?" When

CHRISTIANS KEEP SIGHT OF YOUR VALUES.

FALSE VALUES LEAD TO EMPTY LIVES.

What happened to our values?

To the times when we used to stay up all night and pray for someone to
come to Christ?

What happened to the times when we would refuse to compromise?

216

To the times when we faced rejection because we stood on the cross of Christ?

V-FIFTH QUESTION: DID GOD WHO HAS DONE ALL THESE MIRACLES IN YOUR LIFE DO THEM ACCORDING TO THE WORK OF THE FLESH?

"Does He then, who provides you with the Spirit and works miracles among you, do it by the works of the Law, or by hearing with faith?" In other words, was it works of law or hearing with faith that caused God to supply the Spirit and work miracles in your life?

A- GOD IS THE SOURCE OF LIFE: Christian freedom is maintained by remembering that God is the source of life and transformation, and that all of this comes to believers as a gift. Remembering this will help us to continue to live by faith and not resort to law.

(1) WHY ARE YOU ACTING THAT WAY? TO SAVE YOURSELVES OR TO THANK THE ONE WHO HAS SAVED US?

    1)- IF TO SAVE OURSELVES – WE ARE THEN BEWITCHED BY SATAN-

      thinking that we will be ACCEPTED BY GOD THROUGH OUR WORK

      - We perform religious activity –

      - FALSE MOTIVATIONS -- pleasing others, gaining prominence,

      - acquiring reputation.

    2)- IF WE DO WHAT WE DO TO THANK GOD FOR WHAT CHRIST HAS

      DONE FOR US-

      - GOD BECOMES THE SOURCE OF LIFE

      (a)- WE ARE THEN SAVED BY GRACE

      (b)- WE ARE THEN FREE FROM THE LAW

(c) - OUR ACTIONS ARE RESPONSES TO GOD'S LOVE

B- <u>WE ARE FREE FROM THE CONTROL OF THE FLESH</u>
  (1)- EVALUATE YOUR MOTIVATION
  (2)- FOCUS ON CHRIST AND HIS CROSS
  (3)- AS YOU STARTED WITH THE SPIRIT, FINSIH WITH THE SPIRIT
  (4)- DON'T TRY TO COMPLETE THE WORK OF YOUR SALVATION
  IN THE FLESH, ACCORDING TO THE LAW.

C- <u>SEE YOUR GOD AS A GRACIOUS GIVER, YOUR LIFE AS A LOVING RESPONSE</u>

<u>CONCLUSION:</u>
(1) I AM ASKING EACH ONE OF US TODAY TO EVALUATE THE WAY YOU STARTED YOUR SPIRITUAL WALK AND WHERE YOU STAND TODAY.
(2) ARE YOU SAVED THROUGH THE WORK OF THE SPIRIT, THROUGH FAITH IN THE ONE WHO DIED ON THE CROSS FOR YOU
(3)ARE YOU DOING WHAT YOU DO TO BE SAVED OR TO THANK HIM FOR
  WHAT HE DID FOR YOU ON THE CROSS?
(4) ARE YOUR ACTIONS RESPONSES TO GOD'S LOVE?
(5) YOU CAN'T FINISH THE WORK THE SPIRIT STARTED.
(6) LET THE SPIRIT FINISH THE WORK OF YOUR SALVATION. I INVITE YOU TO BETTER MAKE YOUR OWN EVALUATION.
  Amen. 12.30.07

(44)

Luke 1:57-80

THEME: JESUS, THE LIGHT IN DARKNESS.

INTRODUCTION: Zachariah has been silent for 9 months. We went to the inner holy chamber of the Temple as a High Priest. Angel Gabriel told him that his wife Elizabeth is going to have a child and he could believe it. Therefore, God muted him for 9 months.

The passage we just finished reading contains the first words spoken by Zachariah.

These are his conclusion of what the Lord is going to do.

AFTER ZACHARIAH HAS FINISHED PRAISING GOD AND GLORIFYING HIM, HE GIVES US A MESSAGE IN THESE POINTS:

(1) Verse 68; HE SPEAKS ABOUT THE MESSIAH.

Blessed by the Lord God of Israel, for he has visited and redeemed his People, and had raised up a horn of salvation for us in the house of his servant David

----that we should be saved from our enemies and from the hand of all that hated us

(2) Verse 67-75; HE GIVES THE PROPHECY ABOUT JESUS

And you, child shall be called the prophet of the Highest; for you shall be before the face of the Lord to prepare his ways. To give knowledge of salvation unto his people by the remission of their sins through the tender mercy of God

(3) Verses 78-79a; HE SAYS ABOUT THE DAYSPRING FROM GOD

To give light to them that sit in darkness and in the shadow of death, to guide our feed into the way of peace.

<u>THIS REFERENCE IS ABOUT OUR LORD JESUS CHRIST</u>
<u>THESE VERSES SPEAK ABOUT THE BEGINNING OF A SUNRISE</u>
<u>AND WHAT IT ACCOMPLISHES.</u>

THERE ARE THREE AREAS THE WARMTH OF THE SUNRISE AFFECT:

THAT SUNRISE IF JESUS: WHAT DOES JESUS BRING?

JESUS BRINGS WHAT TO US?

<u>I. HE BRINGS THE LIGHT OF LIBERTY TO DARKNESS</u>

(1) PEOPLE WERE BOUND IN SPIRITUAL DARKNESS.

– RELIGIOUS LEGALISM AND

Think of Matthew, Peter, Andrew, James and John. Remember Mary Magdalene, Mary His mother, Luke 1:46-47,

JESUS, THE RAY OF THE RAISING SUN, DELIVERED THEM.

<u>APPLICATION</u>: Was the world changed today?

Jesus is coming as a light of liberty from darkness.

(2) JESUS IS COMING TO BRING NEW LIFE – LIGHT TO WORLD.

II. HE BRINGS THE LIGHT OF LIFE TO THOSE UNDER DEATH

(1) WE WERE ALL DEAD BECAUSE OF SEPARATION FROM OUR FATHER.

B. However, we need not fear death! We must always remember that the Lord Jesus faced death for us, 2 Cor. 5:14-15, and that by rising from the dead, Matt. 28:1-6, He conquered death on our behalf. Therefore, we do not need to fear death, 1 Cor. 15:53-58! Death is nothing more than a doorway through which we pass from this world into the presence of the Lord in Heaven. It is no more to be feared than a shadow on the wall, Psa. 23:4.

(2) JESUS' DEATH HAS BECOME A BLESSING FOR THE BELIEVERS

(3) WE CAN UNDERSTAND DEATH TODAY THE WAY JESUS LOOKED AT IT:

(a) THE WAY HER DEALT THE DAUGHTER OF JAIRUS-

(b) THE SON OF THE WIDOW OF NAIN

(c) LAZARUS.

(d) HIS OWN BURIAL – HIS OWN DEATH

APPLICATION- WHERE IS THE LIGHT OF JESUS, DEATH FLEE AWAY.

Death has no claim on you! Jesus conquered death for you forever - John 11:25-26; John 5:24. We may lay down these temporary bodies, but something better is waiting for the other side, 2 Cor. 5:1-8.

III. THE LIGHT THAT BRING DIRECTION THOSE ARE WITHOUT

(1) JESUS IS COMING TO GUIDE ALL OF US – OUR TEACHER.

Left to ourselves and our own devices, we merely tend to wander farther away from God, Isa. 53:6. In fact, the Bible teaches us that following our own ways leads nowhere but to death, Pro. 16:25.

(2) <u>HE IS COMING TO BE OUR GUIDE</u>

(3) <u>HE IS COMING TO BE OUR HELPER.</u>

(4) He Gave Us a New Heart –

(5) He Gave Us The Holy Spirit - John 16:13. The Spirit of God, Who dwells in the heart of every believer, John 14:16-17, gives direction and leadership as we go through 3. (6) He Gave Us the Word of God –

<u>CONCLUSION</u>: NOW, WE DON'T HAVE TO WALK IN DARKNESS ANY LONGER. WE NEED TO WALK IN THE LIGHT WHICH IS JESUS. 1 John 1:7.
WHAT IS THE GOAL OF THE COMING OF THE LIGHT WHICH IS JESUS?
TO BRING LIBERTY TO THOSE WHO USED TO WALK IN DARNESS
TO BRING LIGHT TO THOSE WHO LIVE UNDER DEATH. SO THAT HIS DEATH WILL BECOME A BLESSING.
TO GIVE A NEW DIRECTION TO OUR LIVES BY BECOMING OUR GUIDE
OUR HELPER
GIVING US A NEW HEART
GIVING US A NEW HOLY SPIRIT
GIVING US THE WORD OF GOD
MAKING US A NEW CREATION

ZACHARIA IS TELLING YOU TODAY THAT YOU SHOULD
DOUBT THE PROMISE GOD HAVE MADE FOR YOU. – JESUS
IS THE LIGHT, RECEIVE HIM
AND YOU WILL WALK IN THE LIGHT OF GOD FOREVER.
Amen. 12.15.2007

(45)

Isaiah 9:6-7

Luke 1:26-33

"For to us a child is born, to us a son is given; and the government shall be upon his shoulder, and his name shall be called (1) Wonderful Counselor, (2) Mighty God, (3) Everlasting Father,(4) Prince of Peace. Of the increase of his government and of peace there will be no end, on the throne of David and over his kingdom, to establish it and to uphold it with justice and with righteousness from this time forth and forevermore. The zeal of the Lord of hosts will do this."

THEME: UNTO US A CHILD IS BORN; A SON IS GIVEN..

INTRODUCTION: THE ANNOUNCEMENTS:

(1) To the ten oppressed tribes of the northern kingdom of Israel who left Judah, as Isaiah was the prophet of the northern part was proclaiming: "For to us a child is born, to us a son is given…."

(2) To the whole world: In Luke, the archangel Gabriel declares a word that will find fulfillment, literally in Mary: "…You will conceive in your womb and bear a son…" (Luke 1:31). This morning, I want to ponder these prophetic words.

(3) In both of these birth announcements, we find that God doesn't do things the way we might expect. AN INFANT SAVIOR? To quote the words of a popular contemporary Christian song, "Now that's A Mighty Strange Way to Save the World!" And so,

(4) Today, I would like to speak about what Isaiah and Luke want us to know. He is bringing to us the good news through these unusual announcements. Messiah was the complete opposite of the expectations of that time, and perhaps of our own time as well.

I – PERSPECTIVES OF THESE TWO ANNOUNCEMENTS
(1) FOR ISAIAH'S PERSPECTIVE.

In the historical context. "For to us a child is born….and the government shall be upon his shoulder, and his name shall be called Wonderful Counselor, Mighty God, Everlasting Father, and Prince of Peace. Of the increase of his government and of peace there will be no end…from this time forth and forevermore."

The prophetic material found in the first 39 chapters of the book of Isaiah is directed primarily to the ten northern tribes of Israel. The book of 1 Kings narrates how these ten tribes split from the kingly line of David after the death of King Solomon (1 King. 12ff.)

Israel becomes divided with the ten tribes in the north becoming known collectively as Israel, and the remaining two southern tribes called Judah. Simply put, Judah remains faithful to David's line in keeping his descendants on the throne. Sure enough, Judah has problems and goes into captivity herself in Babylon 126 years after the fall of Samaria, the capital of the northern kingdom]. Meanwhile, Israel in the north openly rejects the hope in David's line (cf. 1 Kings. 12:16,

Therefore, Isaiah the prophet issues prophetic words to the northern tribes in a recurring series of oracles of judgment and hope.

FIRST: THE MESSAGE OF JUDGMENT: God is going to punish the nation by carrying them off into exile because of their continuing unfaithfulness. (Read 1 & 2 Kings to chart their collective rebellion. God was patient and just in his dealings with the northern kingdom!) In bringing judgment, God uses the Assyrian Empire to do his bidding, (cf. Isa. 10:5, "Ah, Assyria, the rod of my anger; the staff in their hands is my fury

APPLICATION: Where God pronounces judgment, hope is never far behind.

SECOND: THE MESSAGE OF HOPE: to the northern tribes is that through repentance, God will forgive them and bring salvation through a coming Messiah.

THE HOPE IN ISAIAH IS DESCRIBED AS:
IT WILL BE THROUGH - Isaiah 7:14
"Behold, the virgin shall conceive and bear a son, and shall call his name Immanuel."
Isaiah 11:1-2"There shall come forth a shoot from the stump of Jesse, and a branch from his roots shall bear fruit. And the Spirit of the Lord shall rest upon [this child]."

II-FOR LUKE'S PERSPECTIVE:
In the Christmas story from Luke 2, the long expected MESSAIAH doesn't come:
(1) In appropriate comfort and splendor of a royal palace; but in a stinking cave laying in a common feed of animals' manger. quite unlike the nice wooden cradles that adorn our nativity displays! According to
- THE ALMIGHTY WILL LEAVE HIS THRONE-

- HE WILL COME TO FEED THE HUNGRY

- HE WILL COME TO RAISE UP THE HUMBLE

- HE WILL COME AS A BABY TO BE ONE OF US –

- HE WILL COME, AND BE – THE GOD-MAN Luke 1:51-53).

Why? HE WILL NOT DESCEND FROM HEAVEN; HE WILL BE BORN FROM A VERGIN MARY.

III –WHAT IS OUR LESSON TODAY FROM ISAIAH AND LUKE? JUST AS ISAIAH CALLS THE MESSAIAH

Our Wonderful Counselor, a repository for unlimited wisdom; a confidant whispering "strategy" in the ear when the enemy looks invincible.

Our Everlasting Father, his eternal love comparable to the intensity of a dad's devotion to his own children, a point that shouldn't be lost on any parent or grandparent!

Our Mighty God, giving meaning to Immanuel by emphasizing that it is God who fights battles for us.

Our Prince of Peace, which means that his rule will never be toppled by political intrigue, enemy invasion or popular discontent and unrest.

APPLICATION: ASSYRIA WILL COME AND GOD-

      BABYLONE WILL COME AND GO

      EGYPT WILL COME AND GO

      ROMAN EMPIRE WILL COME AND GO

      RADICAL ISLAM WILL COME AND GO

      SATAN AND HIS AGENTS WILL COME AND GO

BUT THE MESSIAH GOVERNMENT WILL INCREASE AND HIS PEACE WILL BE WITHOUT END

THE MESSIAH IS CONTRASTED TO:

BABYLONE, TO ASSYRIA, TO EGYPT, TO ALL THE POWERS OF THIS WORLD INCLUDED SATAN AND HIS VICTORY IS CERTAIN.

THE COMING OF THE MESSIAH WILL NOT BE ANYTHING LIKE THE OPPRESSIVE REGIMES OF THIS WORLD. PRAISE THE LORD!

BE CERTAIN ABOUT WHY CHRIST IS COMING THIS WAY:

CONCLUSION:
(1) REMEMBER THAT THE MESSIAH IS COMING AS AN INFANT

YOUR Wonderful Counselor,

YOUR Everlasting Father,

Your Mighty God,

Your Prince of Peace,

HE IS COMING AS GOD-MAN.

HE IS COMING TO DEFEAT THE EVIL POWERS OF THIS WORD

HE IS COMING TO ESTABLISH A KINGDOM WITH WILL BE WITHOUT END.

FOR US, A CHILD IS BORN; UNTO US A SON IS GIVEN.

Amen. 12/09/09

(46)

THEME: WHAT HAPPENED TO ZACCAEUS, CAN ALSO HAPPEN TO YOU.

INTRODUCTION: Do you still remember this little song I truly believe that every Sunday School child all over the world should have learned. This song is about a man called Zacchaeus. It goes like this: Zacchaeus was a wee little man, and a wee little man was he, He climbed up in a sycamore tree, for the Lord he wanted to see.(bis). And as the Savior passed that way, He looked up in that tree. And He said "Zacchaeus, you come down! For I'm going to your house today!"

This song tells the whole story, Jesus is ready to enter the house of any sinner. Are you ready to let him in? Are you willing to let him in? Are you availing yourself to let him in? He was come to save the sinners. Oh, Zacchaeus met Jesus and Jesus called him down out of that tree, but that isn't the whole tale! Oh no! Far more happened that day!

THAT DAY, WHEN ZACCHAEUS WAS CLIMBING THE TREE, HE WAS A SINNER; BUT WHEN ZACCHAEUS WAS DESCENDING THE TREE HE WAS A CHILD OF GOD. LET US SEE HOW THIS TRANSFORMATION TOOK PLACE:

This is what has happened to each one of us who has received Jesus and made a commitment to him. Others,

THE QUESTION IS: HOW ZACCHAEUS WAS SAVED?

I -ZACCHAEUS EXPERIENCED A DIVINE CONFRONTATION GOD CONFRONTS SINNERS BEFORE THEY MEET HIM IN PERSON.

Verses 1-4 tell that story.

THE KIND OF PERSON WAS ZACCHAEUS – Verse 2 tells the story

(1)He was a publican, (2) a rich man, (3) an employee of the Roman government as tax collector notorious for overcharging the people. If Rome, for example, levied a 5% tax, the tax collectors could charge 10% or 15% or whatever they wished. (4) guilty of gross extortion of the people. (5) Known as worst of sinner.

2) - ZACCHAEUS' DEEPER AND HIDDEN DESIRE verse 3 tells the story-

The Bible is clear when it says that Zacchaeus was a rich man. He had grown that way on the backs of his fellow Jews. Still it would seem that his money wasn't able to quiet the turmoil within his soul. His position would have given him much power over peoples and properties. It may be that Zacchaeus had a "Napoleon Complex". He was short and perhaps he tried to compensate for this by throwing his power around. Yet, his power and position couldn't satisfy him. It seems that something in his life was missing! Then he heard that Jesus is passing that way and he wanted to see him.

3) - THE DECISION ZACCHAEUS MADE:

Verse 4 tells the story. Being a small man, unable to see the road for the crowds that have gathered to see Jesus as He passed by, Zacchaeus found a tree and climbed up into it to see Jesus. This rich man humbled himself like a little child to climb a tree

QUESTION WHY WAS ZACCHAEUS SO INTERESTED TO SEE JESUS? MAYBE:

(1) He has heard the story of the blind man named Bartimaeus Luke 18:35-43.
(2) About sick folks, casting out demons and even raising up the dead.
(3) Zacchaeus was a miserable, lonely man who knew something was missing from his life.

CONCLUSION: He wanted help, wanted peace but nothing he tried could give him either. When he heard that Jesus was passing through Jericho, he may have thought, "Surely this Man Who has done so much for others can do something for me. I've got to see Him for myself!" REMEMBER: It was no accident that Zacchaeus heard about Jesus! God was working ahead through His Spirit in the heart of this little lost man.

APPLICATION: People can seem happy, rich, accomplished in OUTSIDE. But in the INSIDE they may be in turmoil. - ARE YOU TOSSING FROM ONE SIDE TO THE OTHER OF YOUR BED? Are you happy in your life? Do you feel as something is missing? Is Christ in the center of your life? Do you see yourself in the picture we have here about Zacchaeus?

GOD IS WORKING WITHIN YOU. HE WANTS YOU.

PERHAPS TODAY IS THAT DAY JESUS IS PASSING BY. CLIMB THE TREE!

This is the way the Spirit of God always begins to point people in God's direction!

That is the essence of conviction! The Spirit of God confronts the lost sinner with the claims and demands of the Gospel, John 16:7-11. By the way, this is an essential component in the process called salvation.)

II. ZACCHAEUS EXPERIENCED A DIVINE CALL (verse 5 tells that story. (As Jesus passed the place where Zacchaeus was up the tree, Jesus stopped and began to speak to Zacchaeus. He issued a call to this little man. This call would result in an eternal change of life for the tax collector. Let's listen in.)

1) - THAT CALL WAS A PERSONAL CALL:

When Jesus spoke, he called Zacchaeus by his name, which means "Pure" by the way! I doubt many people called Zacchaeus by his name. Most probably had some nasty little names for him. I doubt many called him "Pure". But Jesus saw him, not as he was, but as he could become through the power of God!

I am sure Zacchaeus thought he would get up in that tree, watch Jesus go by, then climb down and go home. He never expected the Lord to stop and talk to him. When Jesus did stop and when He did speak to this man, Jesus called him by his name. The very One Who had been offended the most, was the One Who spoke to Him in love and compassion! Don't you think old Zacchaeus almost fell out of that tree when he heard Jesus call him by his name? All this does is showing us that the Lord began looking for Zacchaeus before Zacchaeus ever started looking for the Lord!

(Note: When the Lord calls a lost person to come to Him, He does not issue blanket calls. When He calls it is personal! When He began to call me, I found out that He knew my name. I also found out that He knew everything that I had ever done in my life. I also found out that this God, Whom I had so greatly offended, loved me with a love eternal and unspeakable, Jer. 31:3. Rom. 5:8. When He called me, it was a very personal call. If you are saved, you can testify to that fact as well! Notice the personal nature of God's salvation call - John 7:37.

2) THAT CALL WAS A PLAIN CALL - "Make haste and come down" - The Lord told Zacchaeus exactly what he was supposed to do! There would be no debating, there would be no need for second guessing. Jesus was clear and He was plain. (Note: When the Lord calls a lost sinner to Himself for salvation, He will leave no doubt about what he expects them to do! You see, people may not know how to pray when they get before the Lord, but they know what they need! They know they are pressed under a heavy weight of sin. They know they have offended a holy God. They know Jesus is their only hope and they know He is the key to getting that sin taken care of. They know that He has a plan and that following His plan in t heir only hope! He does have a plan! It is a simple plan. In fact, it is as easy as ABC.

(1) Acknowledge yourself to be a sinner - Rom. 3:23 "

(2) For all have sinned and come short to the glory of God".

(3) - Believe on the Lord Jesus Christ - Acts 16:31" Believe in the Lord Jesus Christ and you will be saved." "If you confess with your mouth that Jesus is your Lord and believe in your heart that God raised him from the dead you will be saved." ; Rom. 10:9-10. Consider yourself saved.

(That is His plan and it never fails!)

3) -<u>THAT CALL WAS A PROMISING CALL</u>- The words of Jesus promised much more than a casual meeting under a tree. Jesus said "I must abide at your house". "Zacchaeus, none of your neighbors will come home with you. No one in this town will have anything to do with you, but I want you to know that I, the Lord of Glory am coming to your house!" What a promise! (Note: I found when I got saved that my association with Jesus wasn't going to be confined to that altar or even to the church house. When I got saved, He went home with me, and He has never left! I also found out that He wasn't going to leave anything at my house like He found it. He was going to change everything to suit Him. Many of you can testify to that truth today! You see, a life cannot stay the same when Jesus moves in, 2 Cor 5:17. Neither can a marriage! Neither can a home. Neither can any relationship in life. When He comes in, He changes everything to suit Him! He makes everything different and He makes everything better! Zacchaeus is about to find that out too!)

III. ZACCHAEUS EXPERIENCED A DIVINE CONVERSION

Verses 6-10 tell that story

(Before he can set his feet back on the ground, Zacchaeus is a new man. Notice what happened in his life.)

1)- <u>V. 6 ZACCAHAEUS HEEDED TO THE CALL</u> - Zacchaeus did exactly what the Lord has told him to do. He made haste and he came down. But, the Scripture also says that he "received Him". The word "received" is a big word! In the original it means "to receive as guest; to receive beneath the surface; to take in". HE MADE THE COMMITMENT TO JESUS – HE RECEIVED HIM IN HIS HEART.(Note: What is salvation all about! The lost person hears the claims of the Gospel, they feel the call of the Spirit and they receive Jesus by faith. –

STEP ONE- ZACCHAEUS HEARD THE CALL;

STEP TWO, ZACCHAEUS ACCEPTED THE CALL;

STEP THREE, ZACCHAEUS RECEIVED JESUS- Commitment.

The Bible is crystal clear, faith is the only component that will bring you into a saving relationship with God, (John 3:16; Eph. 2:8-9; John 8:24.)

2) V. 8 ZACCAHEAUS DEMONSTRATED THAT A CHANGE HAS TAKEN PLACE IN HIM:- THE NEW ZACCHAEUS

stands and makes a bold promise to give away half of his fortune and to restore fourfold anyone he has taken anything from under false pretenses. I wonder if his ears were shocked to hear what his mouth was saying. All he is doing here Maccabaeus renounced publicly his OLD LIFE OF LIE, STEALING, SINNING, LYING, CHEATING, and EXTORTING PEOPLE in order to EMBRACE A NEW LIFE, AS HOLY LIFE OF FAITH IN JESUS. (Note: ONCE you meet Jesus, you will never be the same! Ill. Eze. 36:36; Gal. 6:15; Eph. 2:10!)

3) - 9-10 ZACCAHAEUS RECEIVED CONFIRMATION OF THAT CHANGE: -

He knew he was different, but it was confirmed by the words of the Savior. Jesus told Zacchaeus and anyone who was listening that this man was a saved man, that he was a new man in the Lord. (Note: Salvation always brings with the assurance that it is real. There is an inner witness, Rom. 8:16; 1 John 3:19-22; 1 John 5:10, and there is an outer witness, James 2:18; 2 Cor. 1:12. Do you have the inner witness of the Spirit to support your profession of faith? Do you have the outward witness of a changed life to support your profession of faith? If you have the faith and the witness of changed life, then rejoice, for this is a demonstration of the truth of what you claim to be. It is as if Jesus himself were saying about you what He said about Zacchaeus!)

<u>CONCLUSION</u>: Jesus closes His remarks with a clear mission statement. He says "For the Son of man is come to seek and to save that which was lost." It is as if Jesus was saying to anyone in that room that day, and to anyone who would ever read or hear these words, "What has happened to Zacchaeus can happen to you!" This is still true today! If your life lacks meaning, if there is no hope, if everything you have tried has left you defeated, discouraged, disillusioned and looking for more, then Jesus is your answer. You don't have to climb a tree to meet Him, all you have to do is to respond to His call and come to Him right now. If you will do that and if you will receive Him, He will save your soul! Are you saved? Would you like to be? Do what He is telling you today! Even if you are saved but out of God's will, you come. If you just want to bow at His feet and say "Thank you for stopping where I was that day and saving me.", you come

Amen. Machiasport, Nov. 25, 2007

(47)

THEME: **IF YOU REMEMBER TO GIVE THANKS,**
YOU WILL BE MORE BLESSED.

READING: Deuteronomy 8:7-18 and Luke 17:11-19

INTRODUCTION: One afternoon a shopper at the local mall felt the need for a coffee break. She bought herself a little bag of cookies and put them in her shopping bag. She then got in line for coffee, found a place to sit at one of the crowded tables, and then taking the lid off her coffee and taking out a magazine she began to sip her coffee and read. Across the table from her a man sat reading a newspaper.

After a minute or two she reached out and took a cookie. As she did, the man seated across the table reached out and took one too. This put her off, but she did not say anything.

A few moments later she took another cookie. Once again the man did so too. Now she was getting a bit upset, but still she did not say anything.

After having a couple of sips of coffee she once again took another cookie. So did the man. She was really upset by this - especially since now only one cookie was left. Apparently the man also realized that only one cookie was left. Before she could say anything he took it, broke it in half, offered half to her, and proceeded to eat the other half himself. Then he smiled at her and, putting the paper under his arm, rose and walked off.

–This is the way I treat God when he continually treats me well.

I –DO WE REALLY APPRECIATE AND REMEMBER WHERE ALL THESE GIFTS COME FROM?
MOSES, AFTER TELLING PEOPLE OF ISRAEL HOW THEY WILL PROSPER IN THE PROMISED LAND AFTER LEAVING THE LAND OF SLAVERY WARNED THEM

-WHEN YOU WILL EAT, HAVE FINE HOUSES, LARGE HERDS, HAVE SILVER AND GOLD, DO NOT SAY TO YOURSEL " MY POWER AND MY MIGHT, MY HAND HAVE GOTTEN ME THIS WEALTH"
" BUT REMEMBER THE LORD YOUR GOD, for it is He who gives you power to get wealth, so that he may confirm his covenant that he swore to your ancestors, and as he has swore to you today."

A – EVERYTHING WE HAVE IS A GIFT FROM GOD
  (1) WHO GAVE YOUR HANDS? - GOD!
  (b) WHO GAVE YOU THE STRENGTH? GOD – HIS OWN STENGTH.
  (c) WHO GAVE YOU THE KNOWLEDGE? GOD.
  (d) WHO GAVE THE HOUSE? GOD!
  (e) WHO GAVE YOU THE FOOD, THE MONEY, EVERYTHING YOU HAVE?

REMEMBER, REMEMBER, REMEMBER THIS ALL THE TIME!
MAGAZINE POLL ASKING PEOPLE IF THERE IS ONE WISH BE GRANTED:

"if you could be granted one wish that will come true right now - what would that be?"

There were some very interesting responses - but one response impressed the magazine's editors so much that they commented on. That response was this –

WISH I COULD BETTER APPRECIATE WHAT I HAVE.

IF EACH ONE OF US COULD APPRECIATE WHAT WE HAVE!

    - MY PARENTS - MY WIFE - MY FRIENDS

    - MY CHURCH - MY COUNTRY - MY CHILDREN.

    - MY,, MY, My, My, EVERYTHING and I will be THANKFUL!

II - ALL OF US LIKE TO BE APPRECIATED

    But we don't appreciate others

ALL OF US LIKE TO BE THANKED

    But we don't thank others.

EVEN I HAVE KNOWN PEOPLE WHO LIKE TO GIVE,

BUT THEY DON'T LIKE TO RECEIVE FROM OTHERS.

III - WE TEACH OUR CHILDREN THIS VERTUE

ILLUSTRATION: A little child who wanted his dollar back.

    - at our supper tables,

    - during birthday parties,

    - in the middle of visits from their grandparents,

    - and just about anytime that they are receiving something from someone or asking someone for something.

It is a great thing to teach our kids to say please and thank you, it helps them out in this world,

and it is a great thing to be appreciated, to be thanked;

but as we think with holy and prayerful minds today -

as we thank God in our worship service for the harvest we are all enjoying,

IV- WHERE IS YOUR SENSE, WHERE IS MY SENSE OF THANKFULNESS?

- HOW COMPLETE, HOW DEEP, HOW GREAT IS IT?

WHEN YOU SAY " THANKS" DO YOU REALLY MEAN IT?

DO YOU GIVE THANKS IN

ALL OCCASIONS?

ALL CIRCUMSTANCES?

TO ALL PEOPLE?

ALL THE TIME? I Thessal. 5:

> "Give thanks to God the Father at all times and for
> everything in the name of our Lord Jesus Christ." Eph.5:

V - WE NEED A THANKFUL LIVING- -

IT IS A DEMAND.

THIS IS VERY REWARDING!

OUR CULTURE DEMANDS IT

IT IS A RIGHT THING TO DO AS HUMAN AND SPIRITUAL, AND CULTIVATE PEOPLE.

-OUR GOD, OUR LORD, OUR SAVIOR REQUIRES IT.

CONCLUSION:

1) GIVING THANKS BLESSES THE THANKFUL.
2) GIVING THANKS TRANSFORMES HIME
3) NOT GIVING THANKS:
   - WHAT YOU HAVE LOOSES IT VALUE
   HARD THINGS GET HARDER.

OUR WANTS INCREASE MORE AND MORE.

-NO SATISFICTION -

4) GOD WANTS US TO BE THANKFULL TO HIM

5) GOD WANTS US TO CELEBRATE HIS LOVE - CELEBRATION

6) PEOPLE WHO GIVE WANT US TO KNOW THEY LOVE US.

7) GOD AND PEOPLE WANT US TO REMEMBER THEIR DEEDS REMEMBER, YOU HAD NOTHING BEFORE EVERYTHING WAS GIVEN.

    GIVE THANKS TO GOD, OUR LORD.

    SING PRAISES TO THE MOST HIGH

    GIVE THANKS FOR THE BLESSINGS YOU HAVE RECEIVED.

THEME " **IF YOU REMEMBER TO GIVE THANKS,
YOU WILL BE MORE BLESSED.**"

GIVE THANKS: Give thanks with a grateful heart Give thanks, to the Holy one

Give thanks, because he's given Jesus Christ, his Son.

(bis)

REFRAIN:

And now, let the weak say, "I am strong" Let the poor say, "I am rich "

Because of what the Lord has done for us (bis)Give thanks, Give thanks!

Give thanks!

Amen. Machiasport, Nov. 18th, 2007

(48)

Mark 14:1-9

Text. Mark 14:6,8. "Leave her alone", said Jesus," Why are you bothering her? She has done a beautiful thing to me...SHE DID WHAT SHE COULD.

THEME: SHE DID WHAT SHE COULD.
HAVE I DONE FOR JESUS WHAT I AM ABLE TO?
HAVE YOU DONE FOR HIM WHAT YOU ARE CAPABLE OF?

INTRODUCTION: "A Christian businessman was traveling in Korea. In a field by the side of the road was a young man pulling a rude plow while an old man held the handles. The businessman was amused and took a snapshot of the scene."' I suppose these people are very poor,' he said to the missionary who was interpreter and guide to the party.

"'Yes,' was the quiet reply, 'those two men happen to be Christians. When their church was being built, they were eager to give something toward it, but they had no money. So they decided to sell their one and only ox and give the proceeds to the church. This spring they are pulling the plow themselves.'

"The businessman was silent for some moments. Then he said, 'That must have been a real sacrifice.'"' They did not call it that,' said the missionary.' They thought themselves fortunate that they had an ox to sell!'

"When that businessman reached home, he took the picture to his pastor and told him all about it. Then he added, 'I want to double my giving to the church and do some plow work. Up until now I have never given God anything that involved real sacrifice."

IT WAS ABOUT THE KIND OF SACRIFICE THESE PEOPLE HAVE DONE:

EVERY SINGLE BELIEVER IN JESUS SHOULD MAKE SUCH A SACRIFICE: The sacrifice mentioned by Paul in Romans 12:1, "I beseech you therefore, brethren, by the mercies of God, that ye present your bodies a living sacrifice, holy, acceptable unto God, which is your reasonable service."

I - THE CONTEXT OF THIS STORY:
Jesus on his way to CALVARY.

    1) A woman expresses the depths of her love and devotion to Jesus.

    2) Her costly sacrifice is misunderstood by others,

    3) BUT SHE IS COMMENDED BY THE LORD.

    SHE HAS DONE WHAT SHE COULD.

    ASK YOURSELF: HAVE YOU DONE FOR JESUS AS YOU ARE ABLE TO?

II - JESUS KNOWS WHAT WE ARE CAPABLE OF:
I. V. 3-4 IN THE AREA OF SACRIFICE
1) THE KIND OF SACRIFICE SHE MADE:

A. She broke the bottle of ointment

    Valued to $15,000.00 – One year salary, her whole dowry.

    It was a rare perfume brought from Himalaya Mountain.

    It is believed that it was Mary of Magdalene, John 12,

B. She poured it all on Jesus. She gave it for Jesus' GLORY.

QUESTION: HAVE YOU GIVEN ANYTHING IN SUCH A WAY TO JESUS?

III – HOW DID JESUS LOOK AT THIS SACRIFICE?
  1) JESUS SAID, SHE DID WHAT SHE WAS ABE TO:
  2) JESUS SAID NO ONE SHOULD BOTHER HER.
  3) HE SAID WHEREVER THE GOOD NEWS WILL BE PROCLAIMED
      PEOPLE WILL KNOW ABOUT THIS ACT.

REMARK: JESUS HAS A HIGH INTEREST IN PEOPLE WHO MAKE SACRIFICE FOR HIS WORK. DO YOU REMIMBER THE WIDOW IN THE TEMPLE

IV- WHEN SHOULD WE MAKE SUCH SACRIFICE?

1) Whenever you have an opportunity, Mary took advantage of it and experienced a once in a lifetime blessing.

2) When the Spirit of God speaks to our hearts that is the time to step up and serve God. Too often, we miss out on those special moments of service to Jesus when we ignore the impulses and leadership of the Holy Spirit. That is why the Bible warns us to be careful lest we quench the Spirit of God, 1 Thes 5:19.

3) How many times have we ignored the impulses of the Spirit of God and missed opportunities to serve the Lord?

APPLICATION: JESUS IS LOOKING FOR THOSE WHO WILL TAKE ADVANTAGE OF HIS PRESENCE TO GIVE THE BEST OF THEMSELVES TO HIM. JESUS ON HIS WAY TO THE CROSS WAS MET BY MARY WHO GAVE.

V- THE SACRIFICE OF MARY WAS HER SURRENDERING TO JESUS. SHE GAVE IT ALL!

1. SHE KNELT TO WIPE JESUS' FEET
2. SHE GAVE WHAT WAS HER WHOLE FUTURE AND HOPE – DAWERY –
3. SHE MADE A GREAT STATEMENT ABOUT HER SURRENDING TO JESUS.
4. IT WAS AN EXPRESSION OF HER LOVE FOR JESUS
5. JESUS BECAME HER KING, HER HIGH PRIEST, AND HE LORD

What about you? Are you surrendered to the same level as Mary? Does the life you live show you kneeling before Him as absolute Lord and God? When Mary arrived at that place, truly she had done all that she could do. When we get there, we can go no farther with Jesus. At that point He will be everything and we will be nothing. We will find ourselves lost in His glory. Are you there yet, or are there pieces of your life that remain unsurrendered? Just as Mary broke the bottle of ointment so that every drop mind be extracted, let us break our lives on His altar so that He might extract the very last drop of glory from us. That is the price of surrender!

V DON'T WAIT THAT SOMEONE ELSE IS GOING TO DO IT: MAYBE, THERE IS NO ONE TO DO IT. – THE STORY OF FOUR BROTHERS AND THE PARTY THEY ORGANIZED.

There is a story from the Middle East of four brothers who decided to have a feast. As wine was rather expensive, they concluded that each should bring an equal quantity and add it to the common supply. However, one of the brothers, thinking to escape the expense of such a contribution decided to bring water instead of wine. "It won't be noticed," he reasoned.

But at the feast when the wine was poured out it wasn't wine at all. It was only water. Each of the four brothers had thought alike, "Let the others do it. Water is less expensive."

CONCLUSION:

SHE HAS DONE WHAT SHE COULD. HAVE I DONE AS I COULD?

WHAT HAVE YOU DONE AS YOU COULD FOR JESUS?

ILLUSTRATION: This story took place somewhere. A husband and his wife were crossing a railroad track some when his wife's foot slipped and became wedged between the rail and a wooden crosswalk. Frantically she tried to get loose as a train approached around the curve. Her husband desperately attempted to free her. AS THE EXPRESS CAME CLOSER, SEEIN THAT HIS EFFORTS WERE USELESS AND HE COULD NOT SAVE HIS WIFE, " MARY YELLED AT HER HUSBAND, "BILL, LEAVE ME, LEAVE ME, SAVE YOUR LIFE." BILL YELLED AT HER, BILL YELLED, I WILL STAY WITH YOU, MARY" BOTH WERE KILLED BY THE TRAIN.

THIS IS A GRAPHIC PICTURE OF THE KIND OF SACRICE JESUS EXPECT FROM YOU AND ME.

THEME: SHE DID WHAT SHE COULD.

HAVE I DONE FOR JESUS WHAT I AM ABLE TO?

HAVE YOU DONE FOR HIM WHAT YOU ARE CAPABLE OF?

Amen. Machiasport, Nov. 4, 2007

(49)

Scripture Reading Romans 6:1-23 and Titus 3:1-6

Text Rom. 6:22-23 But now having been FREED FROM SIN AND ENSLAVED TO GOD, you derived your benefit resulting in SANCTIFICATION, and THE OUTCOME, ETERNAL LIFE. For the wage of sin is death but THE FREE GIFT OF GOD IS ETERNAL LIFE IN CHRIST OUR LORD.

THEME: THE ROAD TOWARD ETERNAL LIFE. WHERE IT STARTS AND WHERE IT ENDS

INTRODUCTION

1. A familiar verse is that found at the end of Romans six...
   "For the wages of sin is death, but the gift of God is
   Eternal life in Christ Jesus our Lord." (Ro 6:23)

2. SOME BELIEVE THAT ONCE YOU BELIEVE IN JESUS, YOU HAVE ETERNAL LIFE. THEREFORE YOU DON'T HAVE TO DO ANYTHING BECAUSE
   "ONCE IN THE GRACE ALWAYS IN THE GRACE"
   a. It is a GIFT GIVEN
   b. No EFFORT REQUIRED FROM THE RECEIVERS

3. YES, ETERNAL LIFE IS A PRESENT POSSESSION ENJOYED BY THE BELIEVERS WHO LIVE IN GOOD RELATIONSHIP WITH THEIR FATHER –

As you have given him power over all flesh, that he should give eternal life to as many as you has given him. And this is eternal life that they might know you the only true God, and Jesus Christ whom you have sent. John 17:2-3 "abundant life"

NO! SALVATION IS NOT MERITED OR EARNED Ti 3:4-7

-----IT REQUIRES OBEDIENCE - Heh 5:9

4. THE ETERNAL LIFE IS WHAT WE TOTALLY RECEIVE AFTER LIVING A A HOLY LIFE IN CHRIST JESUS.

FOR THE WAGES OF SIN IS DEATH, BUT THE GIFT OF GOD IS ETERNAL LIFE THROUGH JESUS CHRIST OUR LORD. Ro 6:22

IMPORTANT QUESTION:

TO WHOM IS ETERNAL LIFE GIVEN?

TO PEOPLE WHO HAVE GONE THROUGH FOUR STAGES:

I.-TO THOSE WHO HAVE BEEN SET FREED FROM SIN:

A. BY DYING TO SIN... Paul begins chapter six by revealing:

1. Those who died to sin NO LONGER LIVE IN SIN - Ro 6:1-2

2. THOSE WHO DIED ARE FREED FROM SIN - Ro 6:7

B. OUR BAPTISM IS A SYMBOL OF OUR DEATH IN SIN...

1. WE ARE BAPTIZED IN CHRIST'S DEATH - Ro 6:3-4

2. OUR OLD MAN HAS CRUCIFIED WITH CHRIST - Ro

a. OUR SINS HAVE BEEN DONE AWAY

b. WE ARE NO LONGER SLAVES TO SIN AND SATAN.

II.- TO THOSE WHO HAVE BECOME SLAVES TO GOD FREED TO SIN AND SATAN, SLAVES TO GOD AND THE SPIRIT.

A. NO LONGER SLAVES OF SIN...

1. We have died to sin - Ro 6:1-2

2. We now live with Christ - Ro 6:8-11

3. SIN HAS NO LONGER DOMINION OVER US - Ro 6: 12,14

B. FOREVER SLAVES OF RIGHTEOUSNESS...
WHAT ARE THE DUTIES OF A CHRISTIAN TODAY?

1. TO BE ALIVE THROUGH CHRIST JESUS – Ro 6:13

2. BEING AND INSTRUMENTS OF RIGHTEOUSNESS - Ro 6:13

3. TO BE SLAVES OF GOD'S RIGHTEOUNESS THROUGH OUR OBEDIENCE – Ro 6:16-18

III. TO THOSE WHO PRODUCE FRUIT OF HOLINESS (WE ARE HERE TO DO THIS)
A. WE WERE IN THE PAST SLAVES OF SIN... Ro 6:19

1. NOW, WE ARE FREE TO RIGHTEOUSNESS - Ro 6:20

2. WE NO LONGER PRODUCE SHAMEFUL FRUIT OF DEATH - Ro 6:21

B. WE ARE NOW SLAVES OF RIGHTEOUSNESS...

1. THE PURPOSE OF OUR LIFE IS HOLINESS - Ro 6:19c

2. WE ARE CALLED TO PRODUCE FRUIT LEADING TO HOLINESS –

IV. AT THE END, IT WILL BE TOTALLY GIVEN TO:
THOSE WHO ARE AWAITING THE FULL RETURN OF CHRIST:
IT WILL BE TOTALLY GIVEN TO THOSE WHO:

1. THOSE WHO HAVE DIED TO SIN - Ro 6:22a, 1-11
2. THOSE WHO HAVE BECOME SLAVES TO GOD - Ro 6:22b,12-18
3. HAVE PRODUCED THE FRUIT OF HOLINESS - Ro 6:22c,19-21

CONCLUSION

1. ROMANS 6:22-23 TEACHES US THAT: ETERNAL LIFE IS:
   a. GIVEN TO THOSE WHO HAVE BEEN FREED FROM SIN.
      ARE YOU FREED FROM SIN – YOU HAVE ETERNAL LIFE.
   b. THOSE WHO HAVE BECOME SLAVES TO GOD
      ARE YOU SLAVE TO GOD? YOU HAVE IT.
   c. THOSE WHO LIVE THROUGH GOD'S RIGHTEOUSNESS.
      DO YOU LIVE THROUGH GOD'S RIGHTEOUSNESS? YOU HAVE IT.
   d. TO THOSE WHO WAIT THE RETURN OF CHRIST TO RECEIVE
      FULL THAT ETERNAL LIFE IN CHRIST JESUS.
      -AS A GIFT NOT SOMETHING THEY ACQUIRED.
      ARE YOU WAITING CHRIST RETURN THAT WAY? YOU WILL HAVE IT.

QUESTIONS:

1. DO YOU DESIRE TO RECEIVE GOD'S GIFT OF ETERNAL LIFE?

    1) BE FREE FROM SIN.

    2) BECOME SLAVE OF GOD THROUGH OBEDIENCE IN CHRIST.

    3) LIVE THROUGH GOD'S RIGHTEOUSNESS

    4) PRODUCE THE FRUIT OF HOLINESS.

    5) AWAIT THE FULL RECEPTION OF ETERNAL LIFE WHEN JESUS RETURNS. AMEN.

Machiasport Oct.28, 2007

(50)

Matthews 7:21-23

THEME: WHO WILL ENTER THE KINGDOM OF HEAVEN?

INTRODUCTION

1. Most people believe they will go to heaven when they die...
    a. Their hope is fostered by the comforting words of many preachers, priests, and rabbis
    b. Their hope is based upon the idea that heaven is for all believers, or for those whose good works outweigh the bad

2. But are such hopes well-founded?
    a. Will most people go to heaven when they die?
    b. Is salvation based upon good works? Is it based upon faith only?

3. In His sermon on the mount, Jesus gave some ominous warnings...
    a. Few, not many, would be saved - Mt 7:13-14
    b. Many religious people, including some believers in Jesus, will learn that they too will be lost! - Mt 7:21-23

4. With Mt 7:21-23 as the spring board for our study, I wish to address the question: "**Who will enter the kingdom of heaven?** "[Before

considering this question, perhaps this is good opportunity to answer another one first...

I. WHAT IS THE KINGDOM OF HEAVEN?

A. THE TERM "KINGDOM OF HEAVEN"...
1. Is synonymous with the "kingdom of God" - Mk 1:14-15
2. Refers to God's kingship, or rule, from heaven
    -- The kingdom of heaven is focused in the Person of Jesus Christ, and is especially manifested where He rules in the hearts of men - Luke 17:20-

B. IN BRIEF, THE "KINGDOM OF HEAVEN"...
1. Is spiritual in nature - John 18:36; Ro 14:17
2. It began when all authority (rule) was given to Jesus - Mt 28:18; Ac 2:36;
3. Today, it includes the Lord's church on earth (for those who submit to the Will of Christ are added to the kingdom) – Cor. 1: 13.
4. In the future, it will involve the "new heavens and new earth," where we will be with God and Jesus for eternity! Mt 13:40-43
    -- The kingdom of heaven was "inaugurated" on the Day of Pentecost, and will be "culminated" when Jesus returns to deliver it back to God - 1 Cor. 15:23-28

C. THE KINGDOM OF HEAVEN IN OUR TEXT...
1. Appears to have the future aspect of the kingdom in view
    a. Note that Jesus says "in that day..." - Mt 7:22
    b. An apparent reference to the day of judgment - 2 Ti 1:12
2. Thus Jesus is talking about who will enter the kingdom in its future aspect

a. Of which He spoke on other occasions - Mt 25:31-34

b. Of which Peter wrote in 2 Pet. 1:10-11

II. WHO WILL ENTER THE KINGDOM OF HEAVEN?

A. NOT EVERYONE WHO PROFESSES JESUS...

1. "Not everyone saying, 'Lord, Lord,' shall enter the kingdom of heaven"

2. Some believed in Jesus, but were not saved- John 12:42,43

   a. That salvation is by "faith only"

   b. Even though the only time "faith only" is found in the Scriptures, it says: "You see then that a man is justified by works, and not by faith only." - James 2:24

3. But there is such a thing as "an unsaved believer"...

   a. The demons believe, but are not saved - James 2:19

   b. There were some who believed in Jesus, but were not saved- John 12:42,43

   c. Jesus described a true disciple as one who not only believes in Him, but does what He says - John 8:30-32

Let no one think that just because they "believe" in Jesus, they have a free ticket into heaven!

B. NOT EVERYONE WHO DOES MANY GOOD WORKS...

1. "Many will say to Me in that day, 'Lord, Lord, have we not...'" – Mt 7:22

2. Some people believed Jesus and also believed that they had:

   a. Prophesied in His name!

   b. Cast out demons in His Name!

   c. Done many wonders in His Name!

These people thought they had been empowered to do such wonderful works!

3. Such good works certainly did not earn their way to heaven

    a. Indeed, salvation is by grace, not meritorious works -Ti 3:3-7

    b. Good works had not save Cornelius, he still needed to be told what to do to be saved Act. 10:1-5;11:14

4. Indeed, what we may think is a good work is without authority...

    a. Jesus condemns these as those "who practice lawlessness - Mt 7:23

    b. Literally, those who act without authority

        1) It was not that they did something condemned by Jesus

        2) It was that they did things for which they had no authority!

    -- We might be very religious, and do many things in the name of Jesus, yet He might still say: "I never knew you; depart from Me..."

C. ONLY THOSE WHO DO THE FATHER'S WILL...

1. As Jesus said, "...he who does the will of My Father in heaven." Mt 7:21

    a. Here is the dividing line: those who DO the Father's will!

    b. As James would write later, it is the "doer of the work" who is blessed in what he does - cf. James 1:22-25

2. Is this legalism?

    a. No! Legalism is salvation by perfect law-keeping, believing that one earns salvation by the merit of what they have done

    b. Salvation by grace does not preclude the necessity of obedience

        1) Our obedience does not earn or merit salvation

        2) When all is said and done, we are still unworthy! - Luke 17:10

3. What the Father requires for salvation by grace, is obedience!

    a. Those who obey from the heart will be delivered - Ro 6:17-18

    b. Christ is the author of salvation to all who obey Him- He 5:9

    c. Christ will judge those who obey not the gospel - 2 The 1:7-9

CONCLUSION

1. Who will enter the kingdom of heaven?

    a. Not those who profess to believe, but do not obey

    b. Work does not buy salvation

    c. Only those who do the Father's will!

2. What Jesus says must be taken seriously...

    a. "Seek first the kingdom of God and His righteousness..." Mt 6: 33

3. What is the Father's will? It begins with...

    a. Repentance faith in Jesus Christ are required - Ac 20:21

    b. Confessing Jesus as Lord - Ro 10:10

    c. Being baptized into Christ for the remission of sins - Ac 2:38

    -- When we follow Christ, faithfully confession our sins along the way -

Are you convinced that what you do is the real pure will of your Father in heaven? If so, be certain that you will enter his Kingdom/ Amen.

(51)

Matt. 9:32-38

Text. 9:37-38 Then, he said to his disciples," The harvest is plentiful, but the workers are few. Therefore beseech the Lord of the harvest to send out workers into his harvest

THEME: THERE IS A NEED FOR VISION
There is a need of those who take the initiative.

INTRODUCTION
1. Any successful endeavor requires a vision...
   a. The word "vision":
   1) Literally means the ability to see things that are visible
      a) We need reachable goals and Objectives (how it can be done)
      b) "Vision is the art of seeing things invisible"

2. The Lord's work, we desperately need an elevated vision.
   a. We need great reachable goals and greater Objectives (how it can be done)
   b. Jesus certainly had a great vision: the saving of souls! Mt 9:36-38.

I-QUESTION: WHAT CAN HELP US ELEVATE AND ENLARGE OUR VISION IN THE LORD'S WORK? **ANSWER:**

(1) TO SEE PEOPLE THROUGH THE EYES OF JESUS:

Jesus went through all the towns and villages, teaching in their synagogues, preaching the GOOD NEWS of the Kingdom and healing every diseases and sickness. WHEN HE SAW THE CROWDS, HE HAD COMPASSION ON THEM:

    a) They were HARASSED, or HELPLESS – NO GOD'S PEACE

    b) They Were LIKE SHEEP WITHOUT SHEPHERD - NO LEADER –

(2) TO FEEL THE COMPASSION OF GOD FOR PEOPLE

    a) Do you believe that PEOPLE SEPARATED FROM GOD ARE LOST?

    b) When you see people DO YOU LOOK AT THEIR HEARTS?

(3) TO PRAY FOR GOD TO SEND THE WORKERS:

There are more lost people than those who are saved

    a) GO ON YOUR KNEES AND PRAY.

(4) TO FEEL PASSIONATE FOR THE LOST SOULS:

DO YOU CARE FOR THE LOST SOULS -Psalm 142 says "No man cared for my soul

It was that passion which propelled on the RUGGED CROSS. Mark 10:45

II – WHO ARE THE WORKERS THE LORD IS GOING TO SEND?

ANSWER: **HIS DISCIPLES:**

JESUS TURNED TO HIS DISCIPLES - Every child of
God has a mission of COMPASSION FOR THE LOST.

Matt. 28:19-20 – Go all over the world and make all nations my
disciples.

III –WHAT SHOULD BE OUR VISION FOR THE WORLD?

1. IT SHOULD BE MODELED AFTER CHRIST HIMSELF...
   1. We may have the vision of "teaching as many people the gospel as possible"
   2. A noble vision on the surface, but we might by afflicted by the same shortcomings:
      a. We may think too small concerning what can be done
      b. We may think too generally about what we should be doing

2. IT SHOULD NOT BE TOO GENERAL...
   1. No dream has ever been achieved except by someone who dared to flesh it out in terms of the specifics necessary to make the dream a reality
   2. For example, it is fine to plan:
      a. To go to heaven
      b. To serve the Lord faithfully
      c. To do the work of evangelism
   3. But how do we do such things?
      a. By what means do we get those results?
      b. What specific, measurable actions will take us where we want to be?
      c. How much time, effort, and money will it take?
      -- We need to see our vision of the Lord's work in concrete terms of things we can actually do...and plan specifically how much of them we are going to do!

PROBLEMS ABOUT OUR VISION THAT IS TOO LITTLE...

1) When we convince ourselves that no one will come.

2) Telling ourselves that people are not interested

3) Just "keeping house for the Lord"

4) When we think that the PASTOR IS ALL THAT WE NEED.

IV. WHAT DOES OUR VISION NEED?

1. OUR VISION NEEDS SPECIFIC ACTION-STEPS...

1). To double in attendance every year:

2). Invite two people a week; by the end of the year you will likely have a least one attending regularly

3). Provide transportation to people who can't drive; is the value of a soul not worth what time or effort might be involved? - cf. Mt 16:26
-- If each person succeeded in getting one person to come regularly, the attendance would easily double

4). To spread the gospel to thousands in our community each year:

2. OUR VISION NEEDS FAITH IN THE LORD.

1). Faith in the power of the gospel

2). Faith to open doors Phil. 4:13

b. To produce souls that have been born again - 1 Pet 1:22-25

2. Faith in the power of the Lord

a. To open doors for His prepared servants -

3. OUR VISION NEEDS BOLDNESS...

1). A virtue displayed often by the early Christians - Ac 4:13;

2). A boldness based upon our hope in Christ - 2 Co 3:12

3. Faith to say what needs to be said, when it needs to be said, despite the circumstances - 1 Thessalonians 2:2

4. OUR VISION NEEDS PERSISTENCE...

   1. Not losing heart, for we shall reap in due time - Gal 6:9

   2. Always abounding, knowing that our labor is not in vain -

   -- Many visions are never realized because people give up too soon!

CONCLUSION

1. **THERE IS A NEED FOR PEOPLE WHO HAVE VISION.**
2. SEE PEOPLE THROUGH JESUS EYES
3. FEEL PASSION FOR THE LOST WORLD.
4. AS JESUS' DISCIPLE, YOUR CALL:TO SAVE THE LOST.
5. THERE ARE MORE LOST PEOPLE THAN THOSE WHO ARE SAVED.
6. BE SPECIFIC IN YOUR VISION – START SMALL
7. HAVE FAITH I
8. BE BOLD IN YOUR VISION.
9. DON'T STOP, PERSEVERE IN YOUR VISION.

Jesus says:" Behold, I say to you, lift up your eyes and look at the fields, for they are already white for harvest!" (John 4:35) Amen.

Machiasport, October 21, 2007

(52)

Text Mat. 4:10 And Jesus said to them," Follow me,
AND I WILL MAKE YOU FISHERS OF MEN. Follow me..

THEME: JESUS, THE TRANFORMING POWER ON THE RECEIVERS OF HIS CALL. IF CALLED, YOU WILL BE TRANSFORMED. BE CERTAIN!

INTRODUCTION

(1) MY UNCLE WAS A GOLDSMITH – I SAW HOW HE TRANSFORMED PIECE A SCRAPTED MATAL INTO USEFUL TOOLS.

(2) WHEN YOU GO TO BANGOR, STOP AT THE CROSSROAD WHEN COMING FROM THE BLACK WOOD ROAD. YOU WILL SEE ONE WHO OPERATES MIRACLES ON WOOD.

(3) LOOK AT THE PICTURE OF YOUR BULLETIN – SOME DO THAT EVERY DAY WITH SAND.

3. His ministry was not limited to preaching; it also involved "discipline"...

    a. In which He called select individuals to follow Him

    b. Creating His own group of "disciples"

4. We read of Jesus calling His first disciples in our text...
    a. The call of Peter and Andrew - Mt 4:18-20
    b. The call of James and John - Mt 4:21-22

5. Throughout His public ministry...
    a. Jesus called others to become His disciples - . Mt 9:9
    b. Jesus spent much time with His disciples
    c. Jesus ended His time on earth with a command for his disciples - Mt 28:19-20

I – WHO JESUS CALLED TO BE FISHERS OF MEN?

SIMON, called PETER

ANDREW HIS BROTHER (Both fishermen) - Professional

JAMES and his brother John, SONS of ZEBEDEE (Fishermen, professional)

MATTHEW – Tax Collector – Mat. 9:9

PHILIP, BARTHOLOLMEW, THOMAS, JAMES, son of Alphaeus, THADAEUS SIMON, the ZEALOT, And JUDAS ISCARIOT, the one who BETRAYED HIM.

II. WHAT DOES IT MEAN TO BECOME JESUS' DISCIPLE?

A. THE WORD "DISCIPLE"...
1. The word "disciple" literally means a learner
2. According to Vine's Expository Dictionary Of New Testament Words, it denotes "one who follows another's teaching"
3. But a disciple was not only a learner, he was also an adherent
4. For this reason disciples were spoken of as imitators of their teachers

-- When Jesus told Peter, Andrew, James, and John to "Follow Me" (Mt 4:19), it meant more than to just physically follow Him!

B. <u>THE GOAL OF JESUS CALL IS WHAT?</u> – GO FISHING
THE WORK OF A FISHERMAN IS TO GO AFTER THE FISH

1. "I will make you fishers of men "
   a. Just as they had worked in going after fish, now they will fish men!
   b. the Great Commission, to make more disciples - Mt 28:19
2. to be like their teacher
   a. Those trained will be like their teacher - Luke 6: 40
   b. Just as Christ sought to save men and make them disciples,

THE TASK OF THE DISCIPLES IS TO SAVE THE LOST

III. <u>HOW DOES ONE BECOME JESUS' DISCIPLE?</u>

A. <u>JESUS SAID "FOLLOW ME"</u>... HE KNOWS WHAT TO DO

1. This command He gave to His future disciples - Mt 4:19;
   a. They would spend three years following Jesus around Palestine
   b. TO BE ONE OF THE FUTURE WORKER – Mt 28:19-20
   c. TO BE THOSE WHO WILL CARRY ON THE WORK
   - Mt 28:19-20

B. <u>JESUS SAID "ABIDE IN MY WORD"</u>... ABIDE IN HIS WORD.

1. This He said to those who believed in Him - John 8:31
   a. By learning and observing what He taught, they would truly be His disciples
   b. As Jesus would say later, future disciples would be made as they were taught "to observe all things that I have commanded you" - Mt 28:20

c. It would begin with baptism, for He had just commanded His

2. To be a disciple of Jesus, then, requires that one:

a. Be baptized (having repented and confessed one's faith in Jesus)

b. Follow Jesus by doing what He taught His first disciples (the apostles)

-- By continuing steadfastly in the apostles' Ac 2:41-42

To follow Jesus by abiding in His word implies some degree of effort and cost. This leads to our next question...]

IV. WHAT DOES IT COST TO BECOME JESUS' DISCIPLE?

A. HIS FIRST DISCIPLES LEFT "ALL" TO FOLLOW JESUS... LEAVE ALL.

1. They left their business and family - Mt 4:20-22

2. As Peter would say later: "we have left all and followed You"- Mt 19:27

B. JESUS EXPECTED THE SAME OF OTHER DISCIPLES...

1. That He must come before family - Mt 10:3

2. That one must be willing to suffer hardship - Mt 10:38;

3. Simply put, to forsake all to follow Him - Like 14:33

C. JESUS EXPECTS THE SAME OF HIS DISCIPLES TODAY...

1. To seek first the kingdom of God - Mt 6:33

CONCLUSION:

1. ARE YOU A PROFESSIONAL? - JESUS WILL PERFECT YOU.

2. ARE YOU SOMEONE LIKE MATTHEW - Jesus will use your talent.

3. ARE YOU LIKE THOMAS – Doubtful, Jesus will affirm your faith.

4. DON'T BE LIKE JUDAS. JESUS IS WILLING TO TRANSFORM YOU.

5. HE HAS HIGH EXTECTATIONS THAT YOU WILL DO WHAT HE DID:

   -a) PREACHING HIS WORD ALL OVER.

   -b) HEALING THE SICK,

   -c) FEEDING THE HUNGRY,

   -d) THROWING OUT DEMONS, -e)- SAVING THE LOST

   -f) BRINGING HIS KINGDOM HERE ON EARTH.

DEAR BROTHER AND SISTER, FOLLOW JESUS TODAY, HEAD TO HIS CALL.

Amen. Machiasport, October 14, 2007

(53)

THEME: THE MARKS OF CHRISTIAN MATURITY

INTRODUCTION Co 1:28-29, we saw that Paul's primary goal in his labors was to "present every man perfect in Christ Jesus." That is, that they be "spiritually mature in Christ."

2. This being the case, we are not surprised to find Paul now writing to the Colossians of:
   a. His great concern for them - Co 2:1-3
   b. The reason for this concern - Co 2:4-5
   c. Some exhortations in light of his concern - Co 2:6-8

From these eight verses, there are a couple of things we can learn concerning the subject of "Spiritual Maturity In Christ"

I. INDICATIONS OF SPIRITUAL MATURITY (1-5)

1). A DEEP CONCERN FOR OTHER BROTHRS IN CHRIST (1)
   1. Remember that Paul is an example of spiritual maturity and thus worthy of our emulation - 1 Co 11:1
   2. We see that he had a concern for his brethren (even for those he had not seen!)

3. Epaphras likewise demonstrated this "mark" of maturity -
Co 4:12-13

QUESTION: Do we have such concern for your brothers in Christ?

2). HAVING A HEART WHICH IS READY TO COMFORT,
ENCOURAGED
It is the Will of God that we serve Him with hearts, be full of comfort
and encouragement

APPLICATION: Jesus was concerned for his disciples- Luke 21:34
Paul was praying for others - 2 Th 2:16-17
THIS IS NOT TROUBLED, ANXIETIOUS" BUT CONCERNED

3). A LOVING HEART FOR OTHER CHRISTIANS (2)
EXAMPLE: a love similar to that experienced by David and
Jonathan - 1 Sa 18:1

APPLICATION: Have we developed such hearts in Christian love?

4). A FULL ASSURANCE OF UNDERSTANDING
1. Do we have assurance of our own salvation as well as the salvation
of our brothers and sisters in Christ?
2. The kind of assurance which increases our understanding
Of who we are and what they have become in Christ?

THE WORD OF GOD HELPS US TO INCREASE THAT
UNDERSTANDING
BECAUSE OF OUR ASSURANCE IN Christ
Real sense of our MATURIRY AS CHRISTIANS.

5) A FULL KNOWLEDGE OF THE MYSTERY OF GOD

    1. We understand well the GOSPEL OF CHRIST which once was hidden, but has now been revealed - Rom. 16:25-26

APPLICATION: Knowledge of the gospel of Christ is essential to maturity in Christ

QUESTION: Are we increasing in this knowledge?

6) A MATURED CHRISTIAN HAS A GOOD STABILITY IN FAITH

    1. A matured Christian is one whose walk as a disciple is in proper line with what is expected

    The word "steadfastness" is a word which goes right along with this idea of marching in a straight line.

QUESTION: - Are we steadfast in our progress? Are we wavering constantly?

II. HERE ARE SOME STEPS TO SPIRITUAL MATURITY (6-8)
1). YOU MUST FIRST RECEIVE CHRIST AS YOUR LORD

    1. This the Colossians had done

    2. Many want Jesus as a "Savior," but not as "Lord" They profess to want to be saved but not to obey Him in what He commands.

    3. Yet God has made Him both! - cf. Ac 2:36

    4. Until we enthrone Christ as Lord in our lives, we cannot hope to become "perfect" (complete, mature) in Christ

2). WALK IN CHRIST (6-7)

    1. Having received Christ as Lord, we must now "walk" (or live) in Him

2. WALK IN CHRIST MEANS "ROOTED "
"THE FOUNDATION" – "THE SOURCE" SOURCE OF NUTRITION
In our lives (like tree depends upon its roots)
b. "built up in Him" - allowing ourselves to become the kind of building He would have us to be.
c. "established in the faith" " grounded in and living by the teachings of Christ.

3). A MATURED CHRISTIAN MUST BE AWARE.
1. To be aware of dangers which could hinder our spiritual growth.
2. To be careful with false doctrines which promise an easy route to heaven.
3. To fall into temptations.

CONCLUSION
LET'S ASK OURSELVES SOME HARD QUESTIONS:
Are you a mature Christen in your life?
Are you concerned about other believers, others brothers?
Do you have a heart ready to comfort and encourage?
Do you REALLY LOVE OTHER CHRISTIANS?
Do you fully understand what God has done in others?
Are your sure that others are saved like yourself?
Is Christ your LORD and SAVIOR?
ARE YOU WALKING, GROUNDED, ROOTED IN CHRIST?
ARE YOU AWARE OF THE DANGERS LURING YOU HERE AND THERE?

CONTINUE TO BEAR FRUIT EXPECTED FROM EVERY MATURE CHRISTIAN AS IN JOHN 15:1-2. I am the true vine, and my Father is the vinedresser. Every branch in me that does not bear fruit, He takes away and every branch that bears fruit; He prunes it so that it may bear more fruit. Amen.

(54)

THEME: SOME MARKS OF SPIRITUAL IMMATURITY.

INTRODUCTION

1. JUST BECAUSE ONE IS CHRISTIAN THAT DOESN'T MEAN HE IS MATURE. Many Years going to church, hearing sermons, singing hymns etc...does not make one a mature Christian.

2. THE LACK OF SPIRITRUAL GROWTH IS DANGEROUS.
   a. For there are blessings to enjoy in Christ that only the mature Christians can truly understand and appreciate.
   b. If one remains spiritually immature, they do not come to fully appreciate their standing and blessings that they have in Christ! Deprived of a greater understanding, they are more susceptible to Satan

3. THERE IS MUCH TO BE LEARNED TO REACH CHRISTIAN MATURITY.

QUESTIONS: Are you growing in your Christian faith?
-Are you repeating your first year in Christian life over and over again?

-How much do you get from reading the Bible, listening to a sermon, or signing songs?

From prayers, from the fellowship with other Christians, from Sunday School classes?

LET US LOOK ON SOME MARKS OF CHRISTIAN IMMATURITY

FIRST ONE: DULLNESDULNESS OF HEARING :
When we have much to say much to say
But it become HART TO EXPLAIN- Verse 11

INABILITY TO RECEIVE THE TEACHINGS SCRIPTURE:

(1) ENJOYMENT OF THE WORD NOW, THEN FORGOTTEN
(2) WHEN THERE IS EXCITEMENT FOR THE MOMENT
(3) WHEN THE PREACHER THINKS THAT WE HAVE REACHED CERTAIN LEVEL - BUT NO ONE IS THERE YET.
(4) WHEN THERE ARE TOO MANY UPS and DOWNS
(5) WHEN ATTENDANCE: varies between 35 and 15

QUESTIONS: ARE YOU "DULL OF HEARING?
  1. Ask yourself these HARD questions:
    a. IS YOUR BIBLE DULL
    b. IS THE BIBLE STUDY DULL
    c. ARE MY SERMONS DULL?
    d. IS OUR SINGING DULL? praying) dull?
    e. WILL TODAY'S SERVICE BE DULL TO YOU?

SECOND: THE INABILITY TO TEACH OTHERS (12a)

A. THE HEBREWS SHOULD HAVE BEEN ABLE TO TEACH OTHERS...

They had been Christians for some time (they ought to be Teachers now)

    a. HEY HAVE TIME TO LEARN.

    b. THEY HAVE TIME TO BE BEAR FRUIT

    c. THEY HAVE TIME TO TEACH OTHERS WHAT THEY HAVE LEARNED

    d. THEY HAVE TIME TO SHARE WHAT THEY HAVE HEARD

QUESTIONS: ARE YOU ABLE TO TEACH OTHERS?

ARE YOU ABLE TO TEACH OTHERS WHAT YOU HAVE LEARNED?

ARE YOU ABLE TO SHARE CHRIST WITH OTHERS.

WILL YOU BE ABLE TO TELL THIS MESSAGE TO SOMEONE ELSE THIS WEEK

    4. ARE YOU ABLE TO SHARE YOUR FAITH?

THIRD: ALWAYS IN NEED OF MILK AS A CHRISTIAN DIET" (12b, 13)

    A. NOW, A DIET OF "MILK" IS OFTEN NECESSARY...

        1. THIS IS FOR THE BABIES IN CHRIST

        2. FOR THOSE WHO HAVE REGRESSED AND HAVE TO START ANEW

QUESTIONS:

1)-ARE YOU STILL A BABY IN CHRIST, AS YOU HAVE BEEN FOR YEARS?

2) ARE YOU STILL ON THE ELEMENTARY PRINCIPLES OF CHRISTIAN FAITH Such AS A BABY IS ON MILK? He 6:1-3)

BUT OUR DIET MUST ONE DAY INCLUDE "SOLID FOOD"...

Just as a physical baby must graduate to solid food in order to grow to maturity

So a "babe in Christ" cannot mature unless the diet goes beyond the "first principles"

SOLID FOOD: LIVING AS THOSE WHO HAVE RECEIVED THE LORD WITNESSING TO OTHERS BEING SOLDIERS OF CHRIST IN THIS SOCIETY. BEING THE HOPE OF THE WORLD IN CHRIST.

<u>FOURTH</u>: THE INABILITY TO DISCERN BETWEEN GOD/EVIL (14)

   A. NORMAL SPIRITUAL GROWTH EXERCISES THE SENSES...

     a. DIFFERENCE BETWEEN RIGHT AND WRONG

     b. DISCERNMENT

     c. ABILITY TO DISTINGUISH BETWEEN GOOD AND EVIL

   B. SPIRITUAL IMMATURITY LACKS THIS ABILITY TO DISCERN...

     GOOD TEACHING, BAD TEACHING

     GOOD CONDUCT, BAD CONDUCT

QUESTIONS: DO YOU HAVE THE ABILITY TO DISCERN?

   (1) HAVE YOU CULTIVATED YOUR SENSES TO KNOW THE DIFFERENCE BETWEEN GOOD AND BAD?

   (2) IS THE SPIRIT OF GOD IN YOU HAS GIVEN YOU THE SENSE OF DISCERNMENT OF THE STARS OF SATAN?

   (3) ARE YOU CAPABLE NOW OF SUBMITTING YOURSELF TO GOD'S WILL?

CONCLUSION

1. There are certainly other indicators of spiritual immaturity...

   - BEHAVING IN A VERY CARNAL WAY-

   - BEING FULL OF ENVY, JEOLOUSY. 1 Co 3:1-4

OUR TEXT TEACHES US THE FOLLOWING SIGNS OF IMMATURITY:

1. DULLNESS OF HEARING
2. DULLNESS OF READING THE BIBLE (THE WORD OF GOD)
3. DULLNESS OF GETTING HIS TEACHING IN SERMONS
4. THE DESIRE TO HAVE MILK INSTEAD OF SOLID FOOD
5. INABILITY TO WITNESS TO OTHERS ABOUT CHRIST
6. INABILITY TO HAVE A SPIRIT OF DISCERNMENT
7. INABILITY TO HAVE CULTIUVATED SENES TO KNOW THE DIFFERENCE BETWEEN GOOD AND BAD.

BE MATURE IN YOUR CHRISTIAN WALK! Amen. Sept. 21. 2007

Are you growing in the grace and knowledge of our Lord?

(55)

THEME: GOD, I WANT TO HEAR YOUR VOICE! SPEAK. I LISTEN! WHAT IS YOUR WILL?

DAVID SAID TO GOD: Psal 143:10 "Teach me to do your will, for you are my God. Let your good spirit lead me on a level path.

JAMES GIVES US THIS ADVICE James 1_5-6: If any of you is lacking wisdom, ask God, who gives to all generously and ungrudgingly, and it will be given to you. But ask in faith, never doubting, for the one who doubts is like a wave of the sea, driven and tossed by the wind|}

YES, GOD IS WILLING TO REVEAL HIS WILL TO US.

I – QUESTION: WHY GOD IS WILLING TO REVEAL HIS WILL TO US?

GOD IS PERSONAL – HE HAS INTERESTS ON US
THEREFORE HE WANTS TO GIVE US PERSONAL DIRECTIONS.
When you believed in him, He revealed himself to you through Christ Jesus.

He sent his Holy Spirit to abide in you personally.

You have PUT YOUR TRUST IN HIM

You are WILLING TO OBEY HIM

YOU ARE SEEKING HIS WILL IN YOUR LIFE.

II – THINGS TO DO TO KNOW THE WILL OF GOD ARE:
THERE ARE CLEAR-CUT SITUATIONS WITH CLEAR
MEANINGS:

The 10 COMMANDMENTS. Exodus 20

No other gods before God your Savior No idol for yourself

Do not take the name of God in vain – no swearing

Remember the Sabbath day to keep in holy – SUNDAY

Honor your father and mother you shall not murder you shall not commit
adultery

You shall not steal you shall not bear false witness you shall not covet.

Love your God with all your heart, with all your soul, with all your
strength and love your neighbor as yourself

WHAT DOES THE BIBLE SAY ABOUT THESE THINGS?

You must read the HOLY BIBLE - STUDY IT

Go to Bible Studies - God to school – Seminars -Conferences

Listen to SERMONS PREACHED

HAVE THE MIND OF CHRIST – Philippians 2:1-11

BECOME THE LETTER WRITTEN BY CHRIST. II Cor 3:2-3

You will be able to do what is right in God's eyes not by your own will

<u>III – WHEN THE BIBLE GIVES NO ANSWER - DILEMA –BECAUSE</u>

(1) When you believed in him, He revealed himself to you through Christ Jesus.

(2) He sent his Holy Spirit to abide in you personally.

You have PUT YOUR TRUST IN HIM you are WILLING TO OBEY HIM

YOU ARE SEEKING HIS WILL IN YOUR LIFE.

YOU HAVE READ THE HOLY BIBLE - STUDY IT

YOU HAVE STUDIED - Gone to school – Seminars -Conferences

YOU HAVE LISTENED SERMONS PREACHED

HAVE THE MIND OF CHRIST – Philippians 2:1-11

BECOME THE LETTER WRITTEN BY CHRIST. II Cor 3:2-3

YOU WILL HAVE THE WISDOM TO ACT AS PAUL WHEN HE WAS WRITING ALL THESE 16 BOOKS OF THE BIBLE WE CALL EPISTLES

- YOUR LIFE WILL BECOME THE EPISTLE OF CHRIST –

YOU WILL HAVE THE WISDOM OF CHRIST IN YOU.

<u>IV – LAST WAYS TO KNOW AND ACT ACCORDING TO THE WILL OF GOD</u>

BE A PRAYER WARRIOR – GET ON YOUR KNEES FOR ANY SUBJECT. ASK GOD WHAT TO DO

SEEK THE COUNSEL OF A GODLY FRIEND – DO YOU HAVE ONE?

BE SURE THAT YOUR MOTIVATION IS LOVE
DO WHAT YOU REALLY BELIEVE THAT GOD WANTS YOU TO
DO
YOU ARE CALLED TO ACT ACCORDING TO THE WILL OF
GOD BECAUSE YOU BELONG TO HIM AND HE DOES HIS WILL
IN YOU.

Amen. Machiasport Sept. 9, 2009

(56)

THEME: WHERE IS YOUR TREASURE,
THERE YOUR HEART WILL BE ALSO.

MATERIALISM: TEMPTATION TO IDOLATRY Matt. 6:19-24In the first part of Jesus' teaching in chapter 6, he talks about true piety towards God:

INTRODUCTION: WAYS WE DESCRIBE A SUCCESS IN THIS LIFE.

-House - Money in the Bank, Expensive automobiles, respect, honor in the community, give to the community, street names

TRUE SUCCESS IN GOD IS NOT ON THE TEMPORAL REWARDS BUT ETERNAL JESUS IS LOOKING FOR OUR PURITY OF HEART TOWARDS GOD AS THE WAY TO WORSHIP HIM . In 6:19-24 INWARD PURITY IN THE MATTER OF MONEY STORING TREASURE IN HEAVEN,

I - STORING TREASURES. Matt. 6:19-24.
TREASURE IS WHERE WE GIVE ALL OUR TIME AND ENERGY TO

   - AMASSING THINGS

(1) IS IT BAD TO HAVE TREASURES? - The answer is "NO"

(2) JESUS IS GIVING US ADVICE ABOUT WHERE TO STORE OUR TREASURERS:

FIRST NEGATIVE:

NOT TO STORE TREASUERS FOR OURSELVES ON EARTH-WHY? –

(a) MOTH, (b) RUST = THEY DESTROY THEM

© THIEVES BREAK IN AND STEAL

ILLUSTRATION: Many people have lost everything they have had.

MAN'S LIVE DOES NOT CONSIST IN THE ABUNDANCE OF POSSESSIONS

And he told them this parable: "The ground of a certain rich man produced a good crop. He thought to himself, 'What shall I do? I have no place to store my crops.'

"Then he said, 'This is what I'll do. I will tear down my barns and build bigger ones, and there I will store all my grain and my goods. And I'll say to myself, "You have plenty of good things laid up for many years. Take life easy; eat, drink and be merry." '

"But God said to him, 'You fool! This very night your life will be demanded from you. Then who will get what you have prepared for yourself?'

"This is how it will be with anyone who stores up things for himself but is not rich toward God." (Luke 12:15-21) I see this parable as the missing context of Jesus' similar teaching in the Sermon on the Mount (6:19-24). It contains the same elements of greed and storing up.

STORING UP ITSELF IS NOT WRONG

Even the Temple had storerooms where the tithe of the people's produce was stored up to be distributed during the year to the priests and Levites whose families depended upon it (Malachi 3:10). Storing up for later use was wise and prudent. Jesus is not commanding against this kind of storing. "A rainy day,"

Money is deceptive. If we were to be rich, we imagine that we wouldn't have to be dependent upon the vicissitudes of poor harvests, or working for a living, or having to ask God for our daily bread.

THE THINKING OF SOME RICH PEOPLE: If they have more, they will find peace, find security, have easy life, and be marry.

II - JESUS CONTINUED TO GIVE US ADVICE:
POSITIVE WAY NOW
STORE TREASUERS FOR OURSELVES IN HEAVEN-
WHY? - (a) MOTH, (b) RUST = DO NOT DESTROY THEM
(b) THIEVES DO NOT BREAK IN AND STEAL
HOW DOES ONE BECOME RICH IN HEAVEN?
- GOD WILL REWARD YOU: Just previously, Jesus had taught about doing acts of piety "in secret" so that "your Father, who sees (YOUR FATHER WILL REWARD YOU" (6:4b). WHEN YOU GIVE TO NEEDY (6:20).

AS PAUL SAYS I Corinthians 3:8-15, "I have fought the good fight, I have finished the race, and I have kept the faith. Now there is in store for me the crown of righteousness, which the Lord, the righteous Judge, will award to me on that day--and not only to me, but also to all who have longed for his appearing." (2 Tim. 4:7-8)

III – YOUR HEART IS THE KEY OF YOUR STORAGE: Matt.6:21
THE INNER SELF - THE HEART AND THE SPIRIT – THAT IS YOU
"For where IS your treasure, there your heart will be also." (vs. 21)

IF YOU WOULD FIND OUT WHAT I REALLY LOVE, FIND WHERE MY HEART IS. WHERE IS YOUR HEART? – ARE YOU AT WAR BETWEEN THE TWO MASTERS OF OUR AGE: MONEY - WEALTH – POSSESSION, PROPERTY?

IV - STRUGGLE BETWEEN GOD AND MOMMON:

"If we have food and clothing, we will be content with that. People who want to get rich fall into temptation and a trap and into many foolish and harmful desires that plunge men into ruin and destruction. For the love of money is a root of all kinds of evil. Some people, eager for money, have wandered from the faith and pierced themselves with many grief's.... Command those who are rich in this present world not to be arrogant nor to put their hope in wealth, which is so uncertain, but to put their hope in God, who richly provides us with everything for our enjoyment." (1 Timothy 6:8-10, 17)

"Keep your lives free from the love of money and be content with what you have, because God has said, 'Never will I leave you; never will I forsake you.' "(Hebrews 13:5)

ILLUSTRATION: The farmer whose cow gave birth to TWIN CALVES. He came running to his wife to let her know that one of the calves is given to God. His wife asked which one, he said, we will talk about it later. Two weeks later, one of the calves died. He came to tell his wife the bad news. He said, God's calf has died. His wife said but we haven't decided which one belongs to God, he said, I decided longtime ago and the one I gave to God died.

WHEN IT COMES TO PAYING BILLS, AND WE GIVE WHAT WE HAVE LEFT, IT IS GOD'S CALF WHICH DIES FIRST- SOMEONE PUT THIS INSCRIPTION ON HIS TOMBSTONE

"WHAT I SPENT, I LOST;

WHAT I SAVED, I LEFT;

WHAT I GAVE, I HAVE."

As we invest in the Kingdom of God, we assure for ourselves an Eternal Reward.

YOU CANNOT SERVE TWO MASTERS:

WHO HAS ABSOLUTE AUTHORITY and CONTROL OVER YOU?

IF THE MONEY IS THE MOST IMPORTANT, IT IS YOUR GOD. IF GOD IS THE MOST IMPORTANT, HE IS REALLY YOUR GOD.

CALVIN SAID:

"Where riches hold the dominion of the heart, God has lost his authority"

MARTIN LUTHER SAID

"There are three conversations necessary:

The conversation of the heart, the mind and the purse."

WHERE IS YOUR HEART TODAY? GIVE YOUR HEART FIRST TO GOD AND YOUR POSSESSIONS WILL BELONG TO HIM TOO.

The question, then, becomes, Where is your heart? What is your real treasure? Do you find yourself in despair over money? Has Money become the center of your existence? Determine today to put God back squarely in first place. It's where he belongs -- and he will help you do just that if you ask him. Amen.

Machiasport September 2nd, 2007

(57)

THEME: WHY DO I CHERISH THE OLD RUGGED CROSS?

Galatians 6:14 But God forbid that I should boast except in the cross of our Lord Jesus Christ, by whom the world has been crucified to me, and I to the world.

INTRODUCTION:

1. The cross has become a Christian symbol ... a thing of beauty.

A. PEOPLE BUY THEM TO WEAR ... sterling silver, 14k gold, or crusted with diamonds and rubies. Jewelers can make them beautiful. But there was nothing beautiful, about the cross on which Jesus of Nazareth died. First century equivalent of an electric chair or gas chamber.

B. NO DEATH WAS MORE HUMILIATING. So inhumane, Roman law did not permit a citizen of the empire to die by crucifixion.

C. THE CROSS WAS AN OBSTACLE OF FAITH. Jesus dying by crucifixion was a great obstacle to the conversion of both the Jews and Gentiles.

1 Corinthians 1:22-25 22 For Jews request a sign, and Greeks seek after wisdom; 23 but we preach Christ crucified, to the Jews a stumbling block

and to the Greeks foolishness, 24 but to those who are called, both Jews and Greeks, Christ the power of God and the wisdom of God. 25 Because the foolishness of God is wiser than men, and the weakness of God is stronger than men.

D.YES, WE HAVE OTHER SYMBOLS: VIRGIN BIRTH, MIRACLES OF CHRIST, HIS SINLESS LIFE, HIS PREACHING, BUT THE CROSS- CENTRAL EVENT.

Galatians 6:14 But God forbid that I should boast except in the cross of our Lord Jesus Christ, by whom the world has been crucified to me, and I to the world.

E. THE DAY OF CRUCIFIXION, WAS THE GREATEST DAY IN HISTORY. The influence of the cross has become the mightiest power in all the world.

1 Corinthians 1:27-29 27 But God has chosen the foolish things of the world to put to shame the wise, and God has chosen the weak things of the world to put to shame the things which are mighty; 28 and the base things of the world and the things which are despised God has chosen, and the things which are not, to bring to nothing the things that are, 29 that no flesh should glory in His presence.

F. WE MUST FIND THE MEANING OF THE CROSS IN OUR HEARTS

I. THE UGLINESS OF MY SIN REVEALS THE BEAUTY OF THE CROSS

We think we know something of ugliness of sin.

Newborn baby left in toilet in Disney World.

2. The love of God is the only force that is stronger.

3. It is in the cross that one sees the forces of evil and the love of God clash.

II.JESUS' SUFFERING REVEALS THE BEAUTY OF THE CROSS.

A. The Biblical accounts of crucifixion told simply and in few words. "There they crucified him."

B- WHAT HAPPENED WHEN THEY CRUCIFIED HIM?

1. Jesus was beaten and spat on. 2. Mental torture.

John 19:1-3 1 So then Pilate took Jesus and scourged Him. 2 And the soldiers twisted a crown of thorns and put it on His head, and they put on Him a purple robe. 3 Then they said, "Hail, King of the Jews!" And they struck Him with their hands.

3. The March toward Golgotha.

Jo 19:17 And He, bearing His cross, went out to a place called the Place of a Skull, which is called in Hebrew, Golgotha,

Luke 23:26 Now as they led Him away, they laid hold of a certain man, Simon a Pyrenean, who was coming from the country, and on him they laid the cross that he might bear it after Jesus.

4. Disrespect of soldiers.

John 19:23-24 23 Then the soldiers, when they had crucified Jesus, took His garments and made four parts, to each soldier a part, and also the tunic. Now the tunic was without seam, woven from the top in one piece. 24 They said therefore among themselves, "Let us not tear it, but cast lots for it, whose it shall be," that the Scripture might be fulfilled which says: "They divided My garments among them, and for My clothing they cast lots." Therefore the soldiers did these things.

5. Mocked by people and high priest.

Mk 15:27-32 27 With Him they also crucified two robbers, one on His right and the other on His left. 28 So the Scripture was fulfilled which says, "And He was numbered with the transgressors." 29 And those who passed by blasphemed Him, wagging their heads and saying, "Aha! You who destroy the temple and build it in three days, 30 "save Yourself, and come down from the cross!" 31 Likewise the chief priests also, mocking among themselves with the scribes, said, "He saved others; Himself He cannot save. 32 "Let the Christ, the King of Israel, descend now from the cross that we may see and believe." Even those who were crucified with Him reviled Him.

6. He hung on the cross from 9 o'clock in the morning until 3 o'clock in the afternoon.

Mk 15:25 Now it was the third hour, and they crucified Him.

Mk 15:33-34 33 Now when the sixth hour had come, there was darkness over the whole land until the ninth hour. 34 And at the ninth hour Jesus cried out with a loud voice, saying, "Eloi, Eloi, lama sabachthani?" which is translated, "My God, My God, why have You forsaken Me?"

- In the midst of his thirst, pain and humiliation, Jesus was thinking of others rather than himself. Luke 23:34

III. THE ETERNAL LIFE I RECEIVE REVEALS THE BEAUTY OF THE CROSS-. 2 Corinthians 5:18-21 ..... we implore you on Christ's behalf, be reconciled to God. 21 For He made Him who knew no sin to be sin for us, that we might become the righteousness of God in Him.

God had not walked upon earth with man since the days of Eden.

I HAVE BEEN RECONCILED WITH GOD

1 Peter 2:24 who Himself bore our sins in His own body on the tree, that we, having died to sins, might live for righteousness-- by whose stripes you were healed. Romans 6:23.

2. His death became the PRICE OF OUR REDEMPTION.

C. THE BEAUTY OF THE CROSS IS CHRIST LOVE FOR US.

John 3:16 "For God so loved the world that He gave His only begotten Son, that whoever believes in Him should not perish but have everlasting life

I HAVE ACCEPTED CHRIST RIGHTEOUSNESS

1. SALVATION BEGINS AT THE CROSS

2.YOU MUST TRUST IN THE DEATH OF JESUS CHRIST.

CONCLUSION:

Faith, the biblical term which embraces the total response one makes to the grace of God.

1. YOU MUST ACCEPT THE DEATH OF CHRIST IN YOUR BEHALF

John 8:24 "Therefore I said to you that you will die in your sins; for if you do not believe that I am He, you will die in your sins."

2. YOU MUST CLAIM YOUR REDEMPTION IN HIS BLOOD. Romans 6:3-4 3

3. YOU MUST LIVE IN CHRIST AND CHRIST IN YOU. Galatians 2:20 "

THE BEAUTY OF THE CROSS IS ON THE FACT THAT JESUS CHRIST'S DEATH HAS OPENED THE PATH OF ETERNAL LIFE FOR ALL WHO BELIEVE IN HIM.

DO YOU PUT YOUR HOPE FOR SALVATION ON THE CROSS OF JESUS?

Machiasport, August 26, 2007

(58)

Text: Though the fig tree does not bud and there are no grapes on the vines, though the olive crop fails and the fields produce no food, though there are no sheep in the pen and no cattle in the stalls, yet I will rejoice in the LORD, I will be joyful in God my Savior. (Habakkuk 3:17-18)

THEME: TRUST IN GOD NO MATTER WHAT HAPPENS.

INTRODUCTION: There are certain things to do in order to exercise our faith in God even during the worst of times. One of them is TO WAIT PATIENTLY FOR THE LORD even when you are afraid. (verse 16) The second one is TO CHOOSE TO REJOICE IN GOD even when everything in life goes wrong. Look at verses 17-18:

These verses represent one of the strongest expressions of faith you will find in the whole Bible, as Habakkuk determines to rejoice in God even when everything else in life goes wrong. Habakkuk paints three scenarios here. Each scenario contains a matching couplet of images.

I - THE SOURCE OF OUR LIFE IS HOPE: HOPE FOR THE FUTURE, HOPE FOR THE PRESENT HOPE FOR THE PAST. WITHOUT HOPE WE ARE NOTHING.

From today's text , here are three symbols of those hopes we live by:

(1) HOPES FOR THE FUTURE: This verse 17a shows the way the prophet nullifies all the hopes of the future in his life::

"Though the fig tree does not bud and there are no grapes on the vines."

THINGS TRUSTED FOR THE DAYS TO COME. These flowers are the sign that the figs and the grapes are coming.

ILLUSTRATIONS: - Fig trees that do not bud, we know them- Application for a job, College Degree, - A Young man/woman you met the other day. Children you had; a new job you just got; - marriage today.

Do you have hopes and dreams for the future, but no visible signs that they will ever come to fruition? And Habakkuk would tell you, when you have nothing to hold on to for the future, hold on to God, and that will be enough.

(2) HOPES FOR THE PRESENT:

Though the olive crop fails and the fields produce no food."

THINGS TRUSTED FOR DAYS When the field produces no food. When there is nothing to count on right now. When we are filled with DECEPTION, DISAPPOINTMENT, FAILURES!

When you have planted, CULTIVATED, WORKED HARD, You have planted and cultivated the fields, you have worked hard, and the fields produce no food. It was all a deception. All that hard work, all that effort, and it all come to nothing. You get laid off after years of faithful service to the company. NO CURRENT SOURCES OF INCOME. ALL YOUR INVESTMENTS GONE you put years into a relationship with another person and now the relationship breaks apart.

What do you do when all that you are counting on in the present suddenly falls apart? What do you do when you suffer bitter disappointments in life?

Habakkuk says, trust God no matter what. "I will rejoice in the Lord. I will be joyful in God my Savior."

<u>(3) HOPES FROM OUR RESERVES</u>:
"Though there are no sheep in the pen and no cattle in the stalls."
THINGS TRUSTED FROM THE PAST, THE FOUNDATION OF OUR LIVES! When there is no reserve to FALL BACK ON. NO SHEEP ON THE PEN; NO CATTLE IN THE STALLS. NO MONEY IN THE BANK; NO EQUITY IN THE HOUSE. NO FRIEND, NO FAMILY, NO STRENGTH, NO CREDIT CARDS, NO WAY OUT
What do you do when you have nothing to fall back on? Habakkuk would tell you, fall back on God, and he will hold you up.
"YET I WILL REJOICE IN THE LORD; I WILL BE JOYFUL IN GOD MY SAVIOR."
<u>II - IT IS EASY TO TRUST IN GOD WHEN:</u>
<u>THE FUTURE, THE PRESENT, and THE PAST ARE WELL.</u>

When the fig tree is budding and there are grapes on the vines,
When the olive crop succeeds and the fields are producing food,
When you have plenty of sheep and cattle in reserve.

<u>VERY OFTEN, WE TRUST IN THE THINGS NOT IN GOD.</u>
THINK ABOUT JOB: Job showed his true colors when God removed the blessing, and Job continued to trust him no matter what. Habakkuk challenges us with the same question. Do you really trust God, or do you only trust him when you know his blessing on your life?

QUESTION: Which would make you feel more financially secure – having a million dollars in the bank or having a God who promises to meet your daily needs? Stop and think about that one for a moment. Be honest with yourself. If the answer is the million dollars in the bank, then you are not trusting. But if the answer is having a God who promises to meet your daily needs, then no matter what your situation, you can feel more secure than the person who has the million dollars in the bank! That's pretty good! That is trusting in God no matter what.

Habakkuk determined to rejoice in God despite visible circumstances, even if he did not see any visible signs of God's presence or favor

Habakkuk says, "Though you have no visible hope for the future, and what you were trusting in the present has let you down, and you have no reserves from the past to fall back on - still rejoice in the Lord, still be joyful in God."

III – WHY SHOULD WE ALWAYS REJOICE IN THE LORD NO MATTER WHAT?
BECAUSE GOD IS GOD, HE IS YOUR SAVIOR.
HE IS THE ONE WHO WILL DELIVER YOU IN HIS TIME.
HE WILL NOT LET THE RIGHTEOUS FALL.
LISTEN TO I THESSALONIANS 5:16-18

Be joyful always;

Pray continually;

Give thanks in all circumstances, for this is God's will for you in Christ Jesus.

CONCLUSION: How do you exercise faith during the worst of times? Choose to rejoice in God even when everything in life goes wrong. Trusting God No Matter What"

SING: WHY SHOULD I BE DISCOURAGED? #103

(59)

Text. I Peter 1:014-16 As obedient children do not conform to the evil desires you had when you lived in ignorance. But just as he who called you is holy, so be holy in all you do. For it is written: Be holy, because I am holy.

SERMON: HOW CAN I BE HOLY AS THE LORD IS HOLY?

INTRODUCTION:
THE IMPORTANCE OF SANCTIFICATION

Someone has put it like this: "Christ comes with a blessing in each hand – forgiveness in one and holiness in the other.

On the basis of what is true about us, we should now live our lives in this way. That's the gist of what Peter is now beginning to say in verse 13. In particular, he makes a three-fold application:

1. gird up the loins of your mind.
2) øbe self-controlled
3) øset your hope fully on the grace to be given you when Jesus Christ is revealed

It is interesting that Peter should be giving a lot of emphasis on the mind and the way we think. But not only that, but evil-desire which once governed our way of life is to do so no longer. And what Peter is getting is 'the holiness code" from Leviticus:

"Be holy, as I am holy" (v.16)

The specific way in which holiness manifests itself is, first of all, in the way we think.

Nothing is more important than our personal likeness to Jesus Christ. Nothing can prepare for difficulty more than conformity to our Savior. But, what does holiness mean?

- Freedom from any malice, or deceit, or hypocrisy, or envy, or slander (2:1).

Before we look at these in detail, which we'll do on another occasion

I THE HOLINESS OF GOD – THE GOD WE SERVE IS HOLY THE MOTIVATION " BE HOLY BECAUSE I AM HOLY.

ISAIAH 6: when the prophet saw the holiness of God in the temple area: the seraphim which continually cried, "Holy, holy, holy..."Think of how it affected Isaiah (and affect him it did for the rest of his life!). His favorite designation for God thereafter is "The Holy One." Whenever he thought about God or spoke about Him,

Holiness is both intimidating and attractive at the same time.

Our holiness ought to have similar characteristics.

That is the quality that Peter seems to be calling his readers to emulate.

II- JESUS'S GOSPEL INVITES US TO HOLINESS- HE DEATH

In verses 17-21, language and significance of redemption, redemption is the language of purchase by the shed blood of Jesus Christ.

(1 Peter 1:20). Do you see, Peter seems to be asking, that nothing less is required to make me holy. It took the coming of Jesus Christ into the world, and in this way, to make you holy!

When I survey the wondrous cross. On which the Prince of glory died. My richest gain I count but loss. And pour contempt on all my pride.. Jesus paid it all. All to him I owe; Sin hath left a crimson stain. He washed it white as snow.

III. WE ARE MEMBERS OF GOD'S FAMILY

In verse 22, Peter uses the language of rebirth, or regeneration. By being born again, we have been brought into a new family. "born-again" . The idea of regeneration or new birth was not limited to the Christian faith in the first century. We have come to share in the risen life and power of Jesus Christ, and have entered into vital fellowship with Him.

God's ultimate purpose is make us like His Son and the resurrection of Jesus, and our re-birth are parts of that great end.

But note v.13, where it is combined with the coming of Christ, the consummation, the glory, that grace that has been given to us! Peter thinks of the day of judgment—not with terror but with joy! It is that joy that evokes the longing to grow. We have an inheritance that is incorruptible, undefiled, cannot fade away (1 Pet. 1:4-5). It is non-perishable, non-spoilable, non-faceable.

IV-QUESTION: CAN I EVER CHANGE? WILL I EVER BE UNABLE TO SIN?

Spiritual rebirth through faith in Christ does not make us unable to sin. If sinning becomes an impossibility, there was no need for the writers of the New Testament epistles to call the readers not to entertain anger, jealousy, immorality, covetousness and the like. The recipients of these letters were actually believers, called to be saints (Rom 1:7; 1 Cor 1:2; Think of the condition of the Corinthian Christians! Sinless perfection is not at all promised during our earthly sojourn. On the other hand, the Scriptures emphatically state, "If we say we have no sin, we deceive ourselves," and "We all stumble in many things" (1 John 1:8)

Apostle Paul confessed, "Evil is present with me" (Rom 7:21). His Epistle to the Romans was the textbook of Protestant Reformation for Martin Luther (1483-1546). Luther was ruthlessly opposed for his preaching of salvation by faith. He told his close friends, "I more fear what is within me than what comes from without!" Three centuries later John Wesley (1703-1791) the Father of Methodism penned, "Worst of all my foes, I fear the enemy within!"

What we are given at rebirth is an obedient heart instead of our stony heart, and a new spirit instead of our rebellious spirit (Ezek 36:26).

V- THE DIFFERENCE BETWEEN PETER AND JUDAS

I am afraid that this teaching might be misunderstood. Apostle Paul who boldly expounded this subject had the same apprehension. He made a daring statement, "Where sin abounded, grace abounded much more!" (Rom 5:20b). Suddenly he realized that he might be grossly misunderstood. Therefore he asked and answered a corrective question: "Shall we continue in sin that grace may abound? Certainly not!" (Rom 6:1,2a). Here is no suggestion to excuse sin, but this is a persuasion to embrace and exalt grace.

Many Christians are living under "condemnation" because of repeated failures in their lives. The Bible asserts, "There is no condemnation for those who belong to Christ Jesus" (Rom 8:1). The Holy Spirit never "condemns" God's people. He just "convicts" them. Judas Iscariot accepted "condemnation" and that led to awful destruction. On the other hand, Simon Peter came under "conviction" which led to awesome restoration. Judas betrayed Christ only once whereas Peter denied Him thrice! Peter learnt the all-important lesson that only by patiently trying again and again one can grow in godliness. This he wrote in his second Epistle (2 Pet 1:6). He listed seven virtues for growing in fruitfulness and increasing in effectiveness in Christian life. Patience is mentioned fourth as the central one! Patience is to be added to the first three, and the last three to patience! (5-8).

-POTTER'S CLAY

Because God is patient towards us, especially in our failures, we must persevere in our efforts to live holy. It is the goodness of God, even His tolerance and patience that motivates us to keep on repenting (Rom 2:4). We fear God because He abundantly forgives (Psa 130:4). Christ is tirelessly interceding for us from the right hand of His Father and that's why we must resist temptation to sin (1 John 2:1). God is the Potter and we are the clay. We are still in the making. He has not finished with us yet. When God Himself is so patient with us in shaping our character, how can we become impatient with ourselves and quit trying? Patience strengthens the spirit, sweetens the temper, stifles anger and subdues pride.

VI - LEOPARD & SNAKES, CAN WE CHANGE?

Psychologists differ on whether or not temperaments and traits are genetic. Condemning the sins of Judah, God asked, "Can an Ethiopian change the color of his skin? Can a leopard take away its spots? Neither can you start doing good, for you always do evil!" (Jer 13:23). Jesus once rebuked the Pharisees, "You brood of snakes! How could evil men like you speak what is good and right?" (Mt 12:34). These analogies speak simply of the extent of ungodliness and the futility of mere human efforts to change hearts. Otherwise how can God hold a person responsible for his behavior which is not his by choice but his by just inheritance? There was a proverb in the land of Israel, "The parents have eaten sour grapes, but their children's mouths pucker at the taste!" But God commanded that this proverb be quoted no longer. He said, "This is My rule: The person who sins will be the one who dies!" (Ezek 18:1-4). Of course children do what they observe their parents do.

Unlearning any learnt behavior which is not Biblically sanctioned is the individual's responsibility. That's why at rebirth we are transplanted with a soft heart which is flexible and pliable. Unlearning no doubt takes longer time, but when we patiently work at it the Holy Spirit helps us strip off sins which easily hinder our progress (Heb 12:1). We are to proceed steadily with patience!

VII- FRIENDSHIP AND FELLOWSHIP

Imitation is a human instinct. "Bad company corrupts good character" (1 Cor 15:33). If we associate with the humble, we will imbibe the spirit of humility (Rom 12:16). Fellowship with saintly Christians will deepen our love for holiness (2 Tim 2:22). Company of those who have a grip on grace will make us graceful in our dealings with people. Even a brief stay with missionaries in remote places will drive away from us murmuring of all sorts. Working with the poorest of the poor fills us with a spirit of gratitude and thankfulness for God's manifold blessings in our lives (Dan 4:27).

VIII- BE PATIENT WITH YOURSELF

God sends difficulties and disappointments, and allows defeats and diseases in our lives to serve as a rod of correction. His punishments are not just an expression of anger. He has the end in view, even our transformation (Heb 12:10).

IX- TAKE TIME TO BE HOLY

Even though we learn from our failures, every time we yield to temptation we become weaker and weaker. It is by overcoming we grow strong. The first preparation to resist temptation is to be watchful in prayer (Mt 26:41). A "willing spirit"

In the kind of busy world we live, we at times do not become instantly aware of our failures. Unhurried time before God in self-examination is a must. This is what prompted William Longstaff (1822-1894) to compose the hymn—

Take time to be holy, the world rushes on;
Spend much time in secret with Jesus alone
By looking to Jesus, like Him thou shall be;
Thy friends in thy conduct His likeness shall see.

X – GOD CANNOT LIE

The promises of God are as bright as God Himself! His "exceedingly great and precious promises" are just to make us "partakers of the divine nature" (2 Pet 1:4).

By standing, all believers in Christ are already holy before God. The robe of Christ's righteousness is on us. However, by state, we are still filthy and being sanctified. Our standing and state will become one and the same when we would meet Christ face to face. Here's the assurance for this anticipation: "Whom God predestined, those He also called; whom He called, those He also justified; and whom He justified, those He also glorified!" (Rom 8:30

Therefore, beloved, don't allow men or Satan to condemn you whether you stand or fall (Rom 8:31-34; 14:4).

Faithful is He who has called you to be holy; He will also do it! God Himself shall sanctify you completely; and your whole spirit and soul and body will be kept blameless at the coming of our Lord Jesus Christ (1 Thess 5:23,24). Therefore, "be patient; take courage; for the coming of the Lord is near!" (James 5:8).

Machiasport, August 12, 2007

(60)

Second Scripture Reading: Matthew 22:22:34-40

Text.Matt.22: 37-39 & Micah 6:8. Love the Lord your God with all your heart and all your soul and with all your mind. This is the first and greatest commandment. And the second is like it. Love your neighbor as yourself.......O man, what is good. And what does the Lord require of you? To act justly and to love mercy and to walk humbly with your God.

SERMON: WHAT DOES GOD EXPECT FROM ME ?

INTRODUCTION: Expectations! We live from expectations. It is our hope, our future.

We expect some things from people we live with. All relationships are based on expectations. Wife, Husband, friend, children, bosses, employees, leaders, subjects.

As believers, we should not forget that God expects some things from us. I would like to deal with 5 things God expects from those who call themselves Christians.

THE BIBLE' TEACHINGS ARE BASED ON 5 EXPECTATIONS FROM THE LORD

(1) TO LOVE AND WORSHIP THE LORD
   TO LOVE OUR NEIGHBOR
   TO ESTEEM OURSELVES
   TO BE GOOD STEWARDS OF OUR RESOURCES
   TO GIVE AWAY OUR LIVES – BE SERVANTS -

I –TO LOVE AND WORSHIP THE LORD:
BEING OBEDIENT TO HIM manifests our love to God from the heart
When we WORSHIP we become PARTICIPANTS – GOD THE AUDIENCE.
A live of worship begins with the life of OBEDIENCE
TRUE WORSHIP IS – PRAISE, SUBMISSION, DEPENDENCE, GRATITUDE, AND THANKSGIVING.
   IT IS A RESPONSE OF WHAT GOD HAS DONE.

II – TO LOVE OUR NEIGHBOR AS WE HAVE BEEN LOVED.

LOVING THOSE IN NEED - Luke 10:25-37 – The GOOD SAMARITAIN.
These people always come across our lives – How do you deal with them?

LOVE OTHER CHRISTIANS: John 13: 34-35 By this all men will know that you are my disciples if you have love for one another

John 17:21 and by loving one another, the world may believe that you have sent me.

LOVING OUR FAMILY: A secret of a good relationship in the family is found in Ephesians 5:18-6:4 – MUTUAL SUBMISSION FILLED WITH THE SPIRIT.

Husband and wives

Parents and children,

Masters and slaves.

Loving, respect, honor, dignity and worth of one another.

HOW MANY CLOSE FRIENDS DO YOU HAVE?

HOW MANY PEOPLE YOU CAN SHARE DEEP FEELINGS WITH?

III – TO ESTEEN OURSELVES – YOU ARE WORTHY:

Many of us have a love/hate relationship with ourselves. We love ourselves by we are also full of INFERIORITY COMPLEX, INSECURITY, INADEQUACY.

Someone has said that at 20 we weary about what people think about us At 40 we don't care what people think about us. At 60, we find out that people haven't been thinking about us at all.

OUR SELF-IMAGE HAS A DRAMATIC IMPACT ON HOW WE ACT.

SEE YOURSELF AS GOD SEES YOU.

PURSUE THE IMAGE OF GOD WITHIN YOU

ENJOY WHAT GOD HAS GIVEN YOU

IV- BE A GOOD MANAGER OF YOUR RESOURCES

YOUR TIME - Your success and your failure depends on 5 words.

   "I DO NOT HAVE TIME "

YOUR TALENT " There is not little talent; exercise yours "

YOUR TREASURE

THE ROLE OF DISCIPLINE IN YOUR LIFE

The "3" D's" DESIRE, DEDICATION, DISCIPLINE – a Coach and a team.

DISCIPLINE IS TO BE CONSISTENT IN ALL PERSONAL MATTERS

STRIVE FOR MEANING

OUR NATURAL TENDENCY

OUR NEED TO SERVE

CONCLUSION: WHAT DOES GOD EXPECT FROM YOU, FROM ME?

TO ACT JUSTLY, TO LOVE MERCY, and TO WALK HUMBLY WITH HIM

BY

LOVING AND WORSHIPPING HIM

BY LOVING OUR NEIGHBOR

BY ESTEEMING WHO WE ARE AND HAVE

BY MANAGING WELL THE RESOURCES GIVEN TO US

BY GIVING OURSELVES – SERVING. Amen.

(61)

Text Gal. 1:24 AND THEY GLORIFIED GOD IN ME.

THEME: WHAT IS MY PLACE IN GOD'S PLAN?

INTRODUCTION: God has a plan when he created the world:
To create a man and give him the highest place among all his creators.
To live in fellowship with man forever
To be honored, trusted and obeyed by the man FOREVER.

BUT AFTER THE FALL OF MAN IN THE GARDEN:
A NEW PLAN: TO SAVE THE MAN – PLAN OF SALVATION.
THIS BECAME THE CENTRAL GOAL OF GOD.
NOW: WHAT IS MAN'S PLACE IN THE PLAN OF MAN'S SALVATION?
In other words: What does God expect from you once you have received Jesus?
(1) To have FAITH in Him - THE KEY TO RELATIONSHIP WITH GOD.
GOD'S STRATEGY IN DEVELOPING HIS RELATIONSHIP WITH MAN:

REVELATION: He reveals the TRUTH TO MAN.

FAITH: HE ASKS MAN TO HAVE FAITH IN HIM

HE BLESSES THE FAITHFUL Faithfulness means obedience and trust.

RESULT: BLESSINGS - quality of a SATIFYING LIVING.

REPRODUCTION: BRING OTHERS TO GOD BY EXAMPLES.

I - HOW THAT TOOK PLACE IN THE OLD TESTAMENT?

A - GOD REVEALED HIS TRUTH TO MAN - ISRAEL:

He wanted to trust him NO LABOR AND TRUST HIM. – In the wilderness.

To rest on the seventh Day and worship him.

To Give him 10 percent – tithes

To have the JUBILEE YEAR - after 7 years – forgive

GOD PROMISED BLESSINGS TO ALL WHO DO THAT:

WHAT WAS AND IS STILL MAN'S NATURAL INCLINATIONS?

TO PROTECT HIMSELF

TO SUPPLY FOR HIMSELF

DISOBEDIENCE IS THE RESULT OF NOT TRUSTING AND OBEYING GOD

WHICH IS OUR RELIANCE ON OUR NATURAL INCLINATIONS?

THAT BROUGHT   (1) COMDEMNATION –
                (2) JUDGEMENT – (3) REJECTION OF ISRAEL

II – WHAT TOOK PLACE IN THE NEW TESTAMENT?

GOD REVEALED HIMSELF TO US IN JESUS CHRIST

HE CREATED A SPIRITUAL KINGDOM.

HE REQUESTED FAITH, TRUST, OBEDIENCE AS IN THE O.T.

TODAY, MAN GOES BACK TO NATURAL INCLINATIONS.
We must live for the next world not for this world.
WE MUST HAVE FAITH IN HIM - Satisfying living.

- TRUST AND OBEY -
GOD HAS PROMISED BLESSING FOR ALL THE FAITHFUL
- WE WILL BE BLESSED AND PRODUCE THE FRUIT OF
THE SPIRIT:
LOVE, JOY, PEACE, PATIENCE, KINDNESS, GOODNESS,
FAITHFULNESS, GENTLENESS, SELF-CONTROL –
(Gal. 5:22-23
HAPPY LIFE, MEANINGFUL LIFE:
WE WILL BECOME REPRODUCTION:
WE BECOME THE SALT OF THE EARTH: - TRUTH OF GOD.
THE LIGHT OF THE WORD – KNOWLEDGE OF GOD.

CONSEQUENCES:

GOD WILL BE GLORIFIED
THE MAN WILL BE SATISFIED
OTHER WILL BE EVANGELIZED
WE HAVE A PLACE IN THE PLAN OF GOD: Once we are saved, we
honor God, be satisfied, be the salt and the light of the world, and bring
many to Christ.

IF ONLY EVERY CHRISTIAN COULD BRING ONE PERSON TO
CHRIST, THE GREAT COMMISSION WILL BE FULFILLED IN
LESS TIME.
MUST I GO EMPTY HANDED? MUST I GO EMPTY HANDED?

THIS IS THE WAY AND THE ONLY WAY WE CAN BE PART OF GOD'S PLAN.

BELIEVE IN THE FORGIVENESS OF YOUR SIN THROUGH JESUS

FAITH, TRUST IN GOD, OBEY HIM,

YOU WILL RECEIVE BLESSING – SPIRITUAL KING -LOVE, JOY, PEACE, PATIENCE, KINDNESS, GOODNESS, FAITHFULNESS, GENTLENESS, SELF-CONTROL - Gal. 5:22-23

THE WORLD WILL BE CONVERTED TO CHRIST BECAUSE OF YOU.

BE THE SALT AND THE LIGHT OF THE WORLD. Amen.

Machiasport July 1st, 2007

(62)

Text: 20 I have been crucified with Christ; and it is no longer I who live, but Christ lives in me; and the life which I live now in the flesh I live by faith in the Son of God,

WHO LOVED ME, AND GAVE HIMSELF FOR ME?
Father, I have sinned against heaven and against you; I no longer deserve to be called your son; treat me as one of the hired men.

SERMON "WHAT DOES GOD SAY WHEN LOOKING AT YOU.
Know Who You are and See Yourself as God Sees You

INTRODUCTION: THIS TEXT IS ABOUT TWO INDIVIDUAL PERSONS WHO ARE ALSO ONE: THE SINNER WHO IS DEAD BUT ALIVE - THAT SINNER ALIVE IS THE ONE WE CALL CHRISTIAN.

I - WHO AM I? THE PERSON GOD HAS MADE I N ME: DEFINITION
I have been crucified with Christ;
  - I AM DEAD IN CHRIST.
(2) and it is no longer I who live, but Christ who lives in me;
  - I AM ALIVE BECAUSE OF CHRIST AND IN CHRIST.

and the life which I live now in the flesh I live by faith in the Son of God.

THE BOND BETWEEN ME, SINNER, AND CHRIST IS FAITH.
FELLOWSHIP, FRIENDSHIP , LOVE, TRUST, <u>THE SPIRIT OF HEAVEN</u>
THE GOODWILL TO ALL MEN – Luke 2:14
THE DEATH OF THE FIRST ADAM AND THE CALL OF GOD
CHRIST'S LOVE FOR ME IS GREATER THAN MY LOVE FOR HIM.
THE PRICE HE PAID ON THE CROSS SAVED ME NOT MY WORK:

- who loved me, and delivered Himself us for me

II – BECAUSE OF ALL THIS, HOW THE FATHER SEES ME?
Father, I have sinned against heaven and against you; I no longer deserve to be called your son; treat me as one of the hired men.

III – BECAUSE OF ALL THIS, HOW SHOULD I LOOK AT MYSELF NOW?
NO LONGER A SINNER (2) NOW FORGIVEN
(3)ACCEPTED AS SON/DAUGHTER OF GOD (4) SINLESS

IV- BECAUSE OF THIS, HOW SHOULD I BEHAVE NOW? - THEREFORE:
NO MORE CONDEMNATION FROM MYSELF OR FROM ANYONE ELSE:
HATING SIN AND LOVING CHRIST WITH ALL MY BEING:
LIVE A LIFE WHICH HONORS MY FATHER WHO IS IN HEAVEN.

LIVE FOR JESUS AND FOR HIM ALONE.

ILLUSTRATIONS OF WHAT JESUS DID FOR US. (1) Charles Dickens, a famous writer, a hundred years ago, in England. He wrote a famous book, called The Tale of Two Cities. – The Man who exchanged his clothes with the one who was about to be killed in the BASTILLE – French Revolution - So did Christ Who came from Heaven to take our clothes and give us His clothes. He took our rags, our sins and He gives us the royal robe of sonship. And He makes us the children of God.

(2) THE MAN WHO PROTECTED QUEEN VICTORIA throwing himself on the way of the bullet aimed at the Queen. JESUS took the bullet of God's judgment in Himself. He died for us. "The Son of God loved me and gave Himself for me."

LIVING FOR JESUS IS MY GOAL, MY PURPOSE TO BE. Mark 1:9-11, Mat 17:1-10

Text. In Mark 1: 11 And a voice came from heaven: " You are my Son, whom I love, with you I am well pleased. " In Matthew 17:5 and 6 A bright cloud enveloped them, and a voice from the cloud said, " This is my Son, whom I love; with whom I am well pleased, LISTEN TO HIM ". Amen. June 24.07

(63)

SERMON <u>"</u> THE FRUITS OF THE FATHER'S VOICE "

INTRODUCTION:

Do you remember things your fathers REPEATLY SAID TO YOU?

BAD things said and how THOSE WORDS affected a child's life.

Do you remember GOOD THINGS, GOOD IDEAS, ENCOURAGEMENTS, TEACHINGS, ADVICES GIVEN TO YOU BY YOUR FATHER and HOW THOSE WORDS CHANGED YOUR LIFE?
PAUL WROTE MANY LETTERS IN THE BIBLE WE CALL TODAY EPISTLES:
He was thinking of all these people as his children.

Even to Timothy, he calls him MY SON. Paul was writing these letters to them in order to see POSITIVE CHANGES in those he considered his SPIRITUAL children.

I - THE TWO PASSAGES WE READ SPEAK ABOUT WHAT GOD THE FATHER SAID TO AND ABOUT HIS SON JESUS CHRIST, OUR SAVIOR:

(1) GOD SAID TO JESUS: YOU ARE MY SON, WHOM I LOVE: SOME FATHERS DON'T SAY "I LOVE YOU " TO THEIR CHILDREN

(2) GOD TOLD OTHERS: THIS IS MY SON, WHOM I LOVE. SOME FATHERS DON'T TELL OTHERS ABOUT LOVING THEIR CHILDREN

(3) GOD SAID HE WAS WELL PLEASED WITH HIS BELOVED SON

APPLICATION: YOUR SON AND OTHERS MUST HEAR FROM YOU.

II – WHAT SAID AFFECTS OUR CHILDREN'S LIVES.

LOOK AT JESUS' LIFE:

HE WAS ANXIOUS TO DO HIS FATHER'S WILL

HE SPOKE TO HIM IN PRAYER ALL THE TIME.

HE WAS PROUD OF HIS FATHER

HE TOUGHT US ABOUT HIS FATHER (He knew him well)

HIS MISSION WAS SUCCESSFUL

APPLICATION:OUR CHILDREN ARE OUR SELF-FULFILLING PROPHESY

III - WHAT COMES TO YOUR MIND WHEN YOU THINK OF
WHAT YOUR FATHER SAID TO YOU:
IS IT: (1) GO ASK YOUR MOTHER
YOU ARE NOTHING (3) I DON'T HAVE THE TIME.
GO TO YOUR ROOM (4) A SWEAR.
THE WAY YOUR LIFE HAS BEEN AFFECTED BY THESE
THINGS:

III - TODAY'S PARENTS, LET US FOLLOW THE EXAMPLE OF
GOD OUR FATHER WHO WAS A GOOD FATHER OF OUR
LORD JESUS.
TEACH LOVE TO YOUR CHILDREN
SELF RESPECT
RESPONSIBILITY
HONOR
COMMITMENT
GOOD RELATIONSHIP WITH GOD AND OTHERS
BE GOOD EXAMPLES TO THEM.
GIVE THE HOPE,
HAVE SOME EXPECTATIONS FROM THEM
1) ME GA SO AYI WO JAL: Before going hunting, your couch is from home.
2) WORDS OF THE FATHERS MAKE THE BED OF THEIR CHILDREN.
3) JESUS SUCCEEDED IN HIS MISSION FROM THE WORDS OF GOD.
4) FATHER, WHAT FRUITS WOULD YOU LIKE TO SEE FROM YOUR CHILDREN WHEN YOU SAY WHAT YOU SAY TO THEM? Amen. 6/17/07

(64)

Scripture Reading: Colossians 3:12-17

Text. Colossians 3:16 & Rom.12:1 Let the word of Christ dwell in you richly as you teach and admonish one another with wisdom, and as you sing psalms, hymns and spiritual songs with gratitude in your hearts to God.... I urge you, brothers, in view of God's mercy, to offer your bodies as living sacrifices, holy and pleasing to God – this is your spiritual act of worship.

SERMON " PUBLIC WORSHIP WHAT IT IS "

INTRODUCTION: RESUME OF WHAT WE HAVE COVERED:WE have study this word "Worship" during the last three weeks. We learned that –

(1) WORSHIP IS NOT SOMETHING YOU DO, IT IS WHAT YOU BECOME because you are the temple of the Holy Spirit you are the worshipper 24 hours a day, 7 days a week and 365 days a year. You can't separate your life with the worship

(2) CHRISTIANITY IS NOT A RELIGION, not CHRISTIANISM as Islamism, Buddhism, and all the ISM which are " , which are sets of rules,

regulations, formulations, doctrines, principals, forms, organizations, rites and rituals, CHRISTIANITY IS A RELATIONSHIP with the person of Christ, a person who is Christian is the one who HAS DIED IN HIMSELF/HERSELF BUT NOW LIVES FOR CHRIST as Galatians 2:20 says .Therefore, WE LIVE IN A LIFE OF PRIVATE WORSHIP ALL THE TIME

(3) Today learn about "PUBLIC WORSHIP. This is the moment ALL THE ACTIONS OF GOD IN THE LIVES OF TRANSFORMED INDIVIDUALS, ALL THE TEMPLES OF CHRIST, ALL THOSE WHO HAVE TRUE AND SINCERE RELATIONSHIPS WITH HIM, ALL THOSE WHO WORSHIP HIM IN SPIRIT COME TOGETHER. The assembly of true worshippers is what we call PUBLIC WORSHIP.

THIS MOMENT IS NOT THE SINGING.

THIS MOMENT IS NOT THE STYLE

THIS MOMENT IS A PRIVATE WORSHIP EXPENDED IN PUBLIC

Just as Phil 3:3 - "We are the true circumcision; those who worship God in spirit, and glory in Christ Jesus, and put no confidence in the flesh."
It is about that hour Jesus mentioned in John 4:23. "But the hour is coming, and now is, when the true worshippers will worship the Father in Spirit and in truth, for such the Father seeks to worship Him."

I - WHAT IS THE PURPOSE OF SUCH A PUBLIC WORSHIP ?
TOGETHER GROWTH IN GRACE in order to become a better worshipper
to become more DEEPENED WITH GOD'S FACINATION,
to become more PASSIONATELY COMMITTED to honoring Him,

to become more EXPERIENCED IN RELATIONSHIP with Him.

<u>TO PRESENT ONES BODY AS A LIVING SACRIFICE</u>

That is why we focused on the key text in the whole Bible on worship, Ro 12:1-2. Paul appeals to us on the basis of the Gospel "to present your bodies as a living sacrifice, holy and acceptable to God, which is your [rational worship]." "be transformed by the renewal of your mind, that you may prove what is the will of God, what is good and acceptable and perfect." So your private worship of God - that time when you consciously come into the presence of the Lord to pay Him honor –

A PUBLIC WORSHIP IS YOUR ENGINE OF YOUR SPIRITUAL GROWTH.

Confession, prayer, meditation, and the study of the Bible that fuels those disciplines, are all worship, and are all ordained for us to know God personally.

THERE IS NO WAY TO KNOW GOD, EXCEPT AS A WORSHIPPER.

IN PUBLIC WORSHIP, WE COME TO PAY FOR GOD'S HONOR AND LEARN HIS CHARACTER

Our text, Col 3:16, gives a description of public worship. Addressing the entire congregation, Paul says, Let the word of Christ dwell in you richly, teach and admonish one another in all wisdom, and sing psalms and hymns and spiritual songs with thankfulness in your hearts to God."

<u>II – WHAT HAPPENS WHEN WE COME TOGETHER?</u>

THE WORD OF GOD DWELLS IN US RICHLY

HIS TEACHING AND ADMONISHION GIVE US WISDOM

WE HIM (OUR GOD) SONGS, HYMNS AND SPIRITUAL SONGS WITH

THANKFULL HEARTS

III – WE COME TOGETHER, TO BE A PART OF THE SERVICE-

You should not come here for what you can "get out of the service." You must come for one purpose only:

COME HERE AND BE A PART OF THE GROUP TO PAY HONOR TO YOUR GOD.

We think we can hold back in a group and no one will notice.

WHAT CAN PREVENT US TO BE A PART OF PUBLIC WORSHIP?

IF YOU hang on to a HIDEN SIN, because you will fear exposure.

If you don't have private moments even at your home to worship the Lord.

If you always question the life and motives of other believers, judging them.

IV- SOME POSITIVE EFFECTS OF TRUE PUBLIC WORSHIP:

(1) THE CHURCH WILL HAVE HER PLACE IN THE LIVES OF INDIVIDUALS

(2) THE CHURCH WILL BRING BELIEVERS TOGETHER.

THE CHURCH WILL HONOR, PRAISE AND SERVE THE LORD.

WHAT GOD HATES IN PUBLIC WORSHIP"

SELF STYLES, SELF-EXCALTING STATEMENTS, SELF PRIDE PRETENSE, ALL PRIDE,

WHAT GOD LOVES IN PUBLIC WORSHIP:

WHEN ONE APPROACHES THE THRONE OF GRACE WITH REVERENCE,

WHEN OUR HEARTS ARE THANKFUL, HONORING GOD, READY FOR A RASNSFORMING POWER OF OUR LORD JESUS CHRIST.

FRUIT OF TRUE AND SINCERE PUBLIC WORSHIP.

(3) WHEN BELIEVERS WILL BE ENVIGORATED, WHEN PRIVATE WORSHIP BECOMES THE CENTER OUR LIVES WHEN GOD'S CHARCTERS AND WALK ARE BETTER REFLECTED IN THE CHARACTERS AND THE LIVES OF ALL BELIEVERS.

CONCLUSION:

(1) IF WE LET THE SPIRIT OF GOD BRING US TOGETHER IN PUBLIC WORSHIP AS THOSE WHO WORSHIP IN TRUTH AND IN SPIRIT.

(2) IF WE GATHER TOGETHER AS INDIVIDUAL TEMPLES OF PRIVATE TRUE AND SPIRIT FILLED WORSHIPPERS, THOSE WHO HAVE DIED AND NOW LIVE FOR HIM, THOSE WHO LIVE IN RELATIONSHIP WITH CHRIST IN A DAILY BASIS, OUR PUBLIC WORSHIP WILL BECOME A DEMONSTRATION OF OUR GENUINE FAITH IN CHRIST.

Col 3:16, OH, PUBLIC WORSHIPPERS, LET THE WORD OF CHRIST DWELL IN YOU RICHLY, TEACH AND ADMONISH YOU ONE ANOTHER IN ALL WISDOM, AND SING PSALMS AND HYMNS AND SPIRITUAL SONGS WITH THANKFULNESS IN YOUR HEARTS TO GOD. AMEN. June 10th, 2007

(65)

THEME: **ICABOD- THE GLORY OF THE LORD HAS DEPARTED**

1 Sam 4:1-22

INTRODUCTION:

Mothers spend time looking for names they will give to their children.

Names have significance. Do you know the meaning of your name?

Is your life a reflection of your name?

(4) TELL THE STORY OF PHENEA NAMING HER SON ICABOD.

I – BIBLICAL NAMES GIVEN BY MOTHERS:

(1) ADAM = adama, take from the earth

(2) EVE = AYA , the mother of life

(3) ABRAM, ABRAHAM

(4) MOSHE = Saved from Water

(5) JOSUAH = JESUS = SAVIOR

(6) MIKAEL = WHO IS LIKE GOD?

(7) DAVID = THE BELOVED , passive in love

(8) THOMAS, TWIN =

- THERE ARE CERTAIN EXPECTIONS IN NAMINGS:

WHEN A MOTHER GIVES A NAME, SHE WISHES SOMETHING.

-WHAT WERE YOUR WISHES WHEN YOU NAMED YOURS?

-DID THESE WISHES BECOME TRUE?

II-WHY DID A MOTHER NAME HER SON ICABOD?

BECAUSE GOD'S PEOPLE WERE LOOSING BATTLES v 1-3 & 10

The Question is, WHY ISRAEL LOST THE BATTLES?

BECAUSE THEY FOLLOWED THEIR OWN PLANS NOT GOD'S:

They decided to bring the Ark of the Lord to the battle field.

They brought the two sons of Eli.

ISRAEL WON MANY BATTLES BY WALKING WITH THE LORD.

His presence was among them and as long as they were obedient, they won victories over the enemy. But now the presence of God was against Israel because of their sin. The second reason why this lady thought the presence of God was gone included ---

The People were Making Decisions Without Seeking God's Guidance.

III - WHY DID A MOTHER NAME HER SON ICABOD? BECAUSE GOD'S PEOPLE WERE MAKING DECISIONS WITHOUT SEEKING THE LORD'S

YES, THEY UNDERSTOOD THAT THE LORD DEFEATED THEM/PHILISTINES

THEN, they made their own plans:

- Taking the Ark, Bring the two sons of Eli, expecting the Lord to fight for them.

IV- WHY DID A MOTHER NAME HER SON ICABOD? BECAUSE PEOPLE MISUSED HOLY THINGS OF GOD

They used the ARK AS AN IDOL

Explanation

In verse 4, Phinehas, the father of this child named Ichabod, was one of the leaders in abusing the Holy Ark of God. He helped in leading the people to desire the Ark just so they might win a battle. A holy purpose never entered their minds, just get God on our side like some king or magical genie. A very unholy purpose for the Ark of the Covenant. No wonder this mother thought the presence of God was gone from these people.

Illustration

In the book of Daniel the story is told of a king who took the holy temple vessels and used them in drunken feast. It wasn't long until he saw the handwriting on the wall and the judgment of God fell on him.

Application

A nation can not abuse the holy articles and things of God without receiving God's judgment. God's presence will not bless a nation or a people who do these things. God's name is holy! This mother knew the glory of God had departed from Israel --- Because Sinful men were overseeing the work of God.

V- WHY DID A MOTHER NAME HER SON ICABOD? BECAUSE SINFUL PEOPLE WERE OVERSEEING THE WORK OF GOD. I Sam.2:22-25, & 3:11-13

(1) Eli was very old; and he heard all that

(2) His sons were lying with the women who served at the doorway of the tent.

NOTHING WAS DONE AGAINST THEM. THEY DID NOT LISTEN TO THE VOICE OF THE LORD 1 Sam 3:11-13 And the LORD said to Samuel, "Behold, I am about to do a thing in Israel at which both ears of everyone who hears it will tingle. 12 "In that day I will carry out against Eli all that I have spoken concerning his house, from beginning to end. "For I have told him that I am about to judge his house forever for the iniquity which he knew, because his sons brought a curse on themselves and he did not rebuke them.

Explanation

A little research reveals that Eli, the grandfather of this boy named Ichabod, was not the godly man he should have been.. He was the High Priest but he had stopped rebuking the sins of his own sons and was not delivering the Word of God to the people. His sons were filthy sinners and yet they were allowed to serve in the temple. (I Sam. 2:17, 22-25;

Application

Are we godly? Do we have a desire to grow in Christ-likeness that is measurable by what we do and what we don't do? Is the use of time, talent and possession motivated by a desire to be godly and walk in the presence of God? This mother thought the presence of God was gone---Because the Enemy no longer respected God of His People.

VI. -WHY DID A MOTHER NAME HER SON ICABOD? BECAUSE THE ENEMY NO LONGER RESPECTED GOD AND HIS PEOPLE.

v 5-9

The Philistines, once they heard about the arrival of the Ark.

They REMEMBERED what God has done in the past.

First they were afraid, then they redoubled their strength

THEY RENEWED ALL THEIR COURAGE ," O Philistines, lest you become slaves to the Hebrews, as they have been slaves to you; therefore, be men and fight."

Explanation

The leadership of Israel caused the Philistines to no longer respect the Ark and fear the God of Israel. The enemy had heard of what God had accomplished in Egypt and in many other battles, BUT SATAN AND HIS FORCES KNOW THAT YOU CAN'T FIGHT TODAY'S BATTLES WITH YESTERDAY'S VICTORIES. The enemy doesn't respect the Children of God unless they walk in righteousness with their God. A Christian is powerful and protected as he walks in the presence of God. But if the enemy knows you're a Christian who doesn't live up to your faith, they don't have respect for you. In verse 11 the Philistines captured the Ark.

Illustration

In Acts 19:13-16, a story is told of some persons desiring to be exorcists. They commanded an evil spirit to leave a person and the demons answered, "I recognize Jesus and I know about Paul, but who are you?" You see, the evil forces had no respect for these men because they were not godly.

Application

A mother knew the glory of God had departed from Israel because the enemy had taken away one of their most precious and holy articles.

Today can you mothers see a disrespect for God, His name, His house, His day? Could you name a child Ichabod today?

VII.- WHY DID A MOTHER NAME HER SON ICABOD? BECAUSE GOD'S JUDGMENT FELL ON HIS PEOPLE. v 15-22

(1) - 4,000 + 3,000. people died in the battle filed

(2) - Phineah and Hophni, sons of Eli died

(3) - The Ark of the Lord was taken by the Philistines

(4) - Eli, the prophet died

(5) - The mother of the baby ICABOD also died.

BECAUSE, "The glory has departed from Israel, for the ark of God was taken."

Explanation

When the glory of God is present within his people's life, they are not judged harshly by God. They may suffer and experience unpleasantness, but it is because they are godly and in opposition to the world. BUT when God sends Judgment or allows an evil nation to be His source of Judgment, it is evident His presence and glory no longer rest with a people.

Application

Mothers, do you see God's judgment on the lives of those who are living ungodly lives? Is the glory of God gone? Could you name a child Ichabod?

CONCLUSION:

This mother named her son Ichabod.

But approximately 1200 years later a mother named her son JESUS. The name Jesus means Savior, Jehovah Saves, or Power to save.

WHAT WOULD THE NAME YOU WOULD GIVE YOUR CHILDREN IN THIS TIME OF HISTORY?

WHERE IS THE HOPE OF TODAY'S MOTHERS?

MOTHERS SHOULD BE ANXIOUS ABOUT WHERE THE WORLD IS GOING AND HAVE THE COURAGE TO TELL THE TRUTH TO THEIR CHILDREN. Amen.

May 13, 2007

(66)

2 Kings 2:6-14 and Luke 24:44-53:

Text: II Kings 2:5-8

And he took up the mantle of Elijah that had fallen from him, and went back and stood on the bank of the Jordan. Then he took the mantle of Elijah that had fallen from him, and struck the water, saying, "Where is the LORD, the God of Elijah?" And when he had struck the water, the water parted to one side and to the other; and Elisha passed through.

<u>THEME:</u> THE IMPORTANCE OF THE ASCENSION.
ELIJAH"S MANTLE: DO YOU WEAR ONE ?

IN THE CHRISTIAN CALENDAR:

On the Christian calendar, we celebrate Ascension Sunday. It is a time when the church focuses on the ascension of Jesus into heaven and its meaning.

<u>NEITHER MATTHEW NOR JOHN MENTION ASCENSION</u>
<u>MARK, LUKE AND THE ACTS OF THE APOSTLES</u>

Based on these facts, it might appear that the ascension of our Lord wasn't all that important.

WHAT ASCENSION TEACHES US:

(1) IT GIVES US HOPE FOR THE FUTURE – He is coming again.

(2) COMFORT – HE IS PRESENT – HE CONTINUES TO WORK IN US.

Jesus' work continues on earth today.

(3) REMINDER OF THE WORK OF THE CHURCH NOW.

Acts 1:11, "This same Jesus, who has been taken from you into heaven, will come back in the same way you have seen him go into heaven."

THE ASCENSION: COMPLETION OF GOD'S SAVING WORK IN CHRIST.

-The WORK GOD STARTED TO SAVE US WAS COMPLETED HERE

(2) FULFILLMENT OF HIS PROMISES – TO SAVE US – GENESIS.

(3) THE TIME FOR JESUS' EXHALTATION HAS BEGUN:

Philippians 2:9 tells us, "Therefore God exalted him to the highest place and gave him the name that is above every name,"

HIS EXALTATION IN HEAVEN:

Then comes a voice from the throne: "Victorious is the Lamb that was slain. Blessed is the One who turned not aside the bitter cup, but drank it to the dregs. The night of suffering is ended. Come, enter into my joy." At this, a sustained cheer resounds in heaven, and a great celebration begins. Music and dancing and feasting proclaim the return and exaltation of the humiliated One. The joy of reunion, the satisfaction of knowing the work of salvation is complete is enthusiastically proclaimed by angels and archangels as the celestial choir sings: "Worthy is the Lamb who was slain to receive glory and blessing and honor and dominion and power, now and forever!"

Make no doubt, the completion of the work of salvation and the ascension of our Lord was celebrated in heaven in ways we can't begin to imagine.

II -THE ASCENSION: CONFIRMATION OF HUMAN PARTICIPATION IN CHRIST'S RESURRECTION.

BECAUSE CHRIST AROSE, WE WILL ALSO ARISE - He was the first fruit.

1 Corinthians 15:20, "But Christ has indeed been raised from the dead, the first fruits of those who have fallen asleep."

1 Thessalonians 4:16, "For the Lord himself will come down from heaven, with a loud command, with the voice of the archangel and with the trumpet call of God, and the dead in Christ will rise first."

Can we imagine that day, when all the dead in Christ rise from their graves and meet the Lord in the air?

Colossians 1:18-20, (18) And he is the head of the body, the church; he is the beginning and the firstborn from among the dead, so that in everything he might have the supremacy.

For God was pleased to have all his fullness dwell in him, and through him to reconcile to himself all things, whether things on earth or things in heaven, by making peace through his blood, shed on the cross.

JESUS' ASCENSION BRINGS HOPE TO ALL CREATION – ITS RENEWAL:

Christ, ascending to glory takes the whole of creation with Him to heaven.

Along with Jesus, everything God has made is exalted.

Everything was intended to be good as before the fall, as God said before.

THE LORD ASCENSION IS A FORTESTE OF OURS
III -THE ASCENSION: TRANSITION BETWEEN THE LORD'S EARTHLY

AND HEAVENLY WORK.
On earth, our Lord worked for our salvation.

In heaven, He works for our sanctification, to make us holy.

He works as our high priest, interceding for us day and night.

Hebrews 4:14-16, Therefore, since we have a great high priest who has gone through the heavens, Jesus the Son of God, let us hold firmly to the faith we profess. For we do not have a high priest who is unable to sympathize with our weaknesses, but we have one who has been tempted in every way, just as we are--yet was without sin. Let us then approach the throne of grace with confidence, so that we may receive mercy and find grace to help us in our time of need.

The ascension of our Lord gives great strength and comfort as we struggle and suffer.

IV -THE ASCENSION: TRANSFER OF RESPONSIBILITY FROM JESUS TO THE CHURCH. Acts 1:1-2,
(1) In my former book, Theophilus, I wrote about all that Jesus began to do and to teach

(2) until the day he was taken up to heaven, after giving instructions through the Holy Spirit to the apostles he had chosen.

One of the most significant words in Acts is that little word "**began**" in verse one.

THE GOSPEL OF LUKE IS RECORDS WHAT JESUS BEGAN TO DO AND TEACH. THE BOOK OF ACTS RECORDS WHAT HIS BODY, THE CHURCH CONTINUED TO DO AND TO TEACH.

The ascension of our Lord was vital to the continuation of His work through the church.

<u>V – THE ASCENSION: TRANSFOR OF WORK – JESUS/THE CHURCH THE SAME AS ELIJAH/ELISHA</u>
(1) Elisha chosen to succeed Elijah.
(2) He was been taken around the country on a tour by ELIJAH
(3) He has been shown the GOD'S POWER WORK evidently related to his mantle,
(4) ELIJA, being taken into heaven by a chariot of fire, his mantle fell to the ground in front of Elisha.
(5) <u>ELISHA, PICTED UP THE MANTLE!</u> He parted the water of the Jordan with it to prove that he not only had Elijah's mission, but his power as well.

"<u>Taking up a mantle</u>," means passing responsibility from one generation to another. Those who went before us give us the task they had.
<u>IF YOU TAKE UP THE MANTLE, YOU WILL DISCOVER YOUR POWER.</u> Do that; You will find out you have power inside. Power you never knew you had.

<u>YOU CAN'T HAVE THAT POWER UNTIL YOU PICK UP THE MANTLE.</u>

VI - SIMILARITIES BETWEEN JESUSA AND ELIJAH.

(1) BOTH ASCENDED INTO HEAVEN.

(2) ELIJAH'S MANTLE FALLS ON THE GROUND and ELISHA picks it up.

(3) THE DISCIPLES, THE CHURCH, US = ELISHA

(4) BOTH HAVE THOSE CONTINUING THE WORK-ELISHA, THE CHURCH

(5) AS ELISHA COULDN.T DO ANYTHING WITHOUT THE MANTLE,

THE CHURCH CAN'T WITHOUT THE HOLY SPIRIT.

AS ELIJAH'S MANTLE FELL ON THE GROUND, THE HOLY SPIRIT CAME

Jesus tells His disciples in Luke 24, "but stay in the city until you have been clothed (like a mantle) with power from on high."

Ten days after the ascension, the Spirit of Jesus came upon the disciples, like a mantle, WE HAVE TO BE EMPOWERED BY THE HOLY SPIRIT

ELISHA, PICKED UP THE MANTLE!!

That is exactly what the apostles did.

They preached the Kingdom, they healed the sick, they cast out demons, they converted the nations and they formed a new community called the church.

When you take up a mantle, you do extraordinary things, things you never thought you would or could ever do.

Jesus is ascended into heaven.

But His Spirit is here, like a mantle, waiting for us to pick it up.

PUT CHRIST'S MANTLE ON AND YOU WILL DO WHAT HE DID.

THIS IS YOUR TURN. Amen. May 6, 2007

(67)

THEME: **JESUS AND THE COMING OF THE HOLY SPIRIT**

INTRODUCTION: Jesus has been resurrected. He has been with his disciples for 40 days. He is telling them what is going to happen. He will ascend in heaven and the Father will send the Holy Spirit. They have to know the benefits they will have with the Holy Spirit.

QUESTIONS: Do you know the work of the Holy Spirit in your life? Do you allow him to do his work in you? Have you notice the difference between you without the Holy Spirit and you filled with the Holy Spirit in your life?
If your answer is "Yes" you will understand and see your own picture in this message. If "No", brother and sister, seek the Holy Spirit from today.

I - BENEFICTS FOR US THAT CHRIST IS LEAVING:
(1) THE HOLY SPIRIT CAN'T COME UNTIL HE LEAVES
John 16:7

But I tell you the truth: It is for your good that I am going away. Unless I go away, the Counselor will not come to you; but if I go, I will send him to you.

(2) THE HOLY SPIRIT MUST DWELL IN OUR HEARTS
Galatians 4:6-7

Because you are sons, God sent the Spirit of his Son into our hearts, the Spirit who calls out, "Abba, Father." [7] So you are no longer a slave, but a son; and since you are a son, God has made you also an heir.

(3) WE MUST BE CONTROLLED BY THE HOLY SPIRIT – SINFUL NATURE

Romans 8:9 . You, however, are controlled not by the sinful nature but by the Spirit, if the Spirit of God lives in you. And if anyone does not have the Spirit of Christ, he does not belong to Christ.

(4) THE HOLY SPIRIT MUST ACT AS OUR ADVISOR
The Holy Spirit will be your personal spiritual advisor.

John 14:16 And I will ask the Father, and he will give you another Counselor to be with you forever-

TO TEACH US, TO REMIND US OF THE TEACHING OF CHRIST

John 14:26 . But the Counselor, the Holy Spirit, whom the Father will send in my name, will teach you all things and will remind you of everything I have said to you.

TO TESTIFY ABOUT CHRIST

John 15:26 "When the Counselor comes, whom I will send to you from the Father, the Spirit of truth who goes out from the Father, he will testify about me.

HE WILL BE SENT BY JESUS HIMSELF

John 16:7 .But I tell you the truth: It is for your good that I am going away. Unless I go away, the Counselor will not come to you; but if I go, I will send him to you.

II –INSIDE OUT CHANGES IN THE BELIEVERS **THE WORK OF THE HOLY SPIRIT IN THE BELIEVERS IS: TO CHANGE THEIR MINDS:**

John 14:16-17 And I will ask the Father, and he will give you another Counselor to be with you forever-- [17] the Spirit of truth. The world cannot accept him, because it neither sees him nor knows him. But you know him, for he lives with you and is in you.

TO CHANGE THEIR WILL: Phil. 2:13 for it is God who works in you to will and to act according to his good purpose. and TO CHANGE THEIR CONSCIENCE: Gal.5:16 so I say, live by the Spirit, and you will not gratify the desires of the sinful nature. Ephesians 5:17-18 therefore do not be foolish, but understand what the Lord's will is. Do not get drunk on wine, which leads to debauchery. Instead, be filled with the Spirit.

III – THE HOLY SPIRIT WILL CONVINCE AND CONVICT EVERY ONE:

OF GUILT IN REGARD TO SIN

OF RIGHTOUSNESS IN REGARD TO SIN

OF JUDGEMENT IN REGARD TO SIN.

John 16:8-11 When he comes, he will convict the world of guilt in regard to sin and righteousness and judgment: in regard to sin, because men do not believe in me; in regard to righteousness, because I am going to the Father, where you can see me no longer; and in regard to judgment, because the prince of this world now stands condemned.

IV -THE HOLY SPIRIT WILL INSTRUCT US

TEACH US ALL THINGS: John 14:26 . But the Counselor, the Holy Spirit, whom the Father will send in my name, will teach you all things and will remind you of everything I have said to you.

WILL GUIDE US AND SPEAK THROUGH US: John 16:12-14 "I have much more to say to you, more than you can now bear. [13] But when he, the Spirit of truth, comes, he will guide you into all truth. He will not speak on his own; he will speak only what he hears, and he will tell you what is yet to come. [14] He will bring glory to me by taking from what is mine and making it his.

V - THE HOLY SPIRIT WILL GIVE US POWER:

TO WITNESS IN THE NAME OF THE LORD: Acts 1:8 But you will receive power when the Holy Spirit comes on you; and you will be my witnesses in Jerusalem, and in all Judea and Samaria, and to the ends of the earth."

THE HOLY SPIRIT WILL STRENGHTEN US – INNER BEING Ephesians 3:16 . I pray that out of his glorious riches he may strengthen you with power through his Spirit in your inner being,

VI - THE HOLY SPIRIT WILL HELP US PRODUCE SPIRITUAL FRUIT Gal 5:16-25

1) WE WILL NO LONGER GRATIFY THE SINFUL NATURE
   So I say, live by the Spirit, and you will not gratify the desires of the sinful nature. For the sinful nature desires what is contrary to the Spirit, and the Spirit what is contrary to the sinful nature.

2) WE WILL NO LONGER LIVE ACCORDING TO THE SINFUL NATURE

The acts of the sinful nature are obvious: sexual immorality, impurity and debauchery; idolatry and witchcraft; hatred, discord, jealousy, fits of rage, selfish ambition, dissensions, factions, and envy; drunkenness, orgies, and the like. I warn you, as I did before, that those who live like this will not inherit the kingdom of God.

2) BUT WE WILL PRODUCE THE FRUIT OF THE SPIRIT:

But the fruit of the Spirit is love, joy, peace, patience, kindness, goodness, faithfulness, gentleness and self-control. Against such things there is no law. Those who belong to Christ Jesus have crucified the sinful nature with its passions and desires. Since we live by the Spirit, let us keep in step with the Spirit.

3) **CONCLUSION**: THERE IS ONLY ONE QUESTION YOU MUST ANSWER TODAY: HAVE YOU RECEIVED THE HOLY SPIRIT?

IS THE HOLY SPIRIT ABIDING IN YOU?

EVERYTHING YOU JUST LEARNED WILL HAPPEN TO YOU AS IT DID TO ALL THOSE WHO HAVE RECEIVED HIM.

ASK HI|M IN YOUR HEART TODAY. Amen.

(68)

THEME: LIVE BY FAITH NOT BY SIGHT:

INTRODUCTION: "Doubting Thomas." It is a common expression even in our modern English. It refers to one of the disciples of Jesus who is often associated with one word: doubting." Make one little mistake and you're labeled for life!" I've got no proof of this, but I suspect Thomas may have been the first to utter that line. Thomas was one of Jesus' inner circle of twelve disciples.

(1). "Lord we don't know where you are going and how can we know the way?" We have no doubt that he loved Jesus even enough to be willing to go to Jerusalem and die with him.

(2) Upon hearing that Lazarus was sick Jesus told his disciples they were going to Judea. Thomas said, "Let us also go, that we may die with him." If he were that gloomy before the death of Jesus by crucifixion, what would he be like upon Christ's death?

After the crucifixion of Jesus Thomas was a brokenhearted man who wanted to be left alone to suffer alone. Perhaps he can rightly be described as "belligerent in his pessimism." Every time we see Thomas it is a day of appalling gloom.

Those who loved Jesus on the earth had to learn to live without the physical appearance of Christ, the actual seeing, touching, and hearing him. There would be no more sitting at the table with him and filling the mind with his words, but now they would learn to walk by faith, not by sight.

Yes, he would walk with them, sit with them, eat with them, but in a more profound manner not limited by space and time. Here is a tremendous lesson for us to learn.

JESUS CHOSE THOMAS AS ONE OF HIS DISCIPLES:

All four of the Gospels have Thomas in the list of the apostles of Jesus. Matthew and Mark mention him only once (Matt. 10:3; Mk. 3:18). Luke lists him once in his Gospel and in Acts (Luke. 6:15; Acts 1:13). John gives us eight references to Thomas as a disciple of Jesus. He was chosen and appointed by the Lord Jesus to be one of His followers. Jesus said, "No longer do I call you servants . . . but I have called you friends."

(1) THOMAS WAS THERE WHEN JUSUS RAISED LARAZUS.
(John 11:16). After Jesus healed the blind man in the Temple the Pharisees and Sanhedrin sought to kill both of them (John 9). Jesus left Jerusalem and word reached him that his friend Lazarus of Bethany, a suburb of Jerusalem, was near death Thomas was with the disciples when Jesus told them that Lazarus was already dead (11:13-15). Upon hearing the news that Jesus will go to Bethany Thomas responded to his fellow disciples, "Let us go too, so that we may die with him" (v.16).

(2) THOMAS WANTED TO DIE FOR JESUS:. Thomas came to Jerusalem to die with Jesus and he witnessed the Master of death call the dead man back to life. Thomas was just as prepared as the other disciples to believe in the resurrection, but along with the others he never grasped that prediction of the resurrection of Jesus.

(3) THOMAS WAS PREPARED FOR JESUS' DEATH:

They celebrated the Passover meal together, and Jesus spent time preparing them for his death the very next day. That night in the upper room Thomas listened to the encouraging words of Jesus about heaven (14:1-3).

Thomas said, "Lord, we don't know where you are going. How can we know the way?" (14:5. Jesus replied, "I am the way, and the truth, and the life. No one comes to the Father except through me. If you have known me, you will know my Father too. And from now on you do know him and have seen him" (vv. 6-7). Before the end of the day Jesus will be crucified, and three days later will be raised from the dead.

II – THOMAS AND JESUS' RESURRECTION (JOHN 20:24).

Jesus appeared to the twelve – THOMAS ABSENT - THE PROBLEM OF BEING ABSENT: -MISS THE BLESSING

We are not given the reason for Thomas not being with the disciples when Jesus first appeared to them on the day of His resurrection from the dead (John 20:24). But he was to blame for refusing to accept the testimony of his friends when they assured him they had seen the risen Jesus. We do have Thomas' reaction to the testimony of the other disciples. "Now Thomas (called Didymium), one of the twelve, was not with them when Jesus came. The other disciples told him, 'We have seen the Lord!' But he replied, 'Unless I see the wounds from the nails in his hands, and put my finger into the wounds from the nails, and put my hand into his side, I will never believe it!'" (vv. 24-25). His words ring with a little obstinate tone in his unbelief.

Perhaps it was Thomas' emotional reaction to the outcome of his appalling agony and disappointment. Death was real to Thomas. No doubt he had stood where you have at the graveside and said his last good by to friends and loved ones. Thomas declared he would not believe any rumors until those very wounds demonstrated the identity of Jesus.

THOMAS DEMANDED MORE EVIDENCE:

How tragic when in our unbelief we take pride in demanding more evidence than that given by a group of credible veracious men. unbeliever who thrives on doubt; he likes it, enjoys it, sports it, and lives by it. agnostic views. honest doubter and "the evil heart of unbelief."

THOMAS MET THE RESURRECTD JESUS:

So far as we can tell it was solely to remove Thomas' doubts that our Lord appeared to the assembled disciples the following Sunday. The apostle John brings his Gospel to a climax with what happens next. "Eight days later the disciples were again together in the house, and Thomas was with them. Although the doors were locked, Jesus came and stood among them and said, 'Peace be with you!'" (v. 26)

We don't know if the disciples expected a fresh appearance of their Lord on this day. But it is not without significance that after an uneventful week that Jesus appeared the next Sunday. The situation before us is an exact duplicate of the one sketched in verse 19. Silently and suddenly as before, without warning, without opening of doors, Jesus appears exactly as he did a week ago. He is suddenly standing in the midst of his disciples and he greets them exactly the same, "Peace to you!"

Jesus simply repeated almost in the same words the hard, rude, bare, crude test Thomas had proposed to the other disciples.

His words breathe forgiveness and encouragement to Thomas' faith. He brings Thomas to assurance, just as He did the other disciples. Thomas' faith is deepened with the appearance of his risen Lord.

POWERFUL AND CLEAR CONFESSION BY THOMAS:

The beautiful thing about the method of Jesus with Thomas is he is offering to all eleven of the disciples "many infallible proofs" or "demonstrative evidence" of his resurrection. Acts 1:3 reads, "To the same apostles also, after his suffering, he presented himself alive with many convincing proofs. He was seen by them over a forty-day period and spoke about matters concerning the kingdom of God"

Jesus not only answered Thomas' doubt, but every Thomas in the future. All eleven disciples were "witnesses" of his resurrection (Acts 2:32; 3:15). Their testimony would stand as being unassailable in all future ages (1 John 1:1-3

My Lord and my God!

Thomas gave Jesus Christ "full acceptance of His deity and of the fact of His resurrection." Remember these words are those of a Jewish man. The two possessives "my" makes the two affirmations stand out independently. This is the strong climax to the whole gospel of John.

LESSONS WE CAN LEARN FROM THOMAS ARE:
   1) **DON'T LOOSE OPPORTUNITY TO FELLOWSHIP WITH CHRIST.**
   2) **JESUS IS PATIENT WORKING WITH THE THOMASES.**
   3) **BE AN INTELLECTUAL, PRAGMATIC DISCIPLE AS THOMAS.**
   4) **BE A COURAGEOUS MAN AS THOMAS.**

CONCLUSION:

The apostle Paul prayed,

-"that Christ may dwell in your hearts through faith" (Eph. 3:17). Jesus said, "If anyone loves me, he will obey my word, and my Father will love him, and we will come to him and will make our dwelling place with him." (John 14:23).

WALK BY FAITH AND NOT BY SIGHT. Amen. April 15, 2007

(69)

Text. I John 4 7-12 - The whole passage.

THEME: FACTS ABOUT THE LOVE OF GOD.

INTRODUCTION: There is nothing like the love of God! It is the most overwhelming thing I have ever encountered in my life. It is the greatest thing God ever did for any of us! The reason I can say that is this, because He loved us, He was moved to do everything else that He has done. Allow me to say today that John's epistle has four purposes.

THE FOUR PURPOSES JOHN WROTE THIS EPISTLE ARE:
(1) That the believers' joy might be complete. (1:4)
(2) That the believers' might not sin. (2:1)
(3) That the believers may love one another. (4:11)
(4) That the believers may know that they have eternal life. (5:13)
1 John is the great book of love. It is mentioned 46 times in 135 verses. It was written to combat a heresy known as Gnosticism. The Gnostic believed that knowledge was power. They felt that they had a special knowledge of God and His ways. John wants us to know about THE GREAT GOD with A GREAT LOVE for GREAT SINNERS. It's that GREAT LOVE of that Great God that I want to address. Let the Lord speak to your heart as we consider the thought,

I. LET US DESCRIBE THAT GREAT LOVE OF GOD:

1. THAT GREAT LOVE IS UNSPEAKABLE - I can't understand it, or why, but I know I have experienced it and I can never be separated from it - Rom. 8:38-39 I am convinced that neither death nor life, neither angels nor demons, neither the present nor the future, nor any powers, neither height nor depth, nor anything else in all creation, will be able to separate us from the love of God that is in Christ Jesus our Lord.

2. THAT GREAT LOVE IS UNENDING Jer. 31:3…I have loved you with an everlasting love! THAT LOVE IS ETERNAL

3. THAT LOVE IS UNSELFISH - Ill. It asks for nothing in return! However, it leads man to repent and turn to God in love –
1 John 4:19- We love him because He first loved us!

4. THAT LOVE IS UNMERITED- Cannot be earned or deserved!. (Ill. His love is based in His grace!) (Ill. Jesus and Jerusalem - Matt. 23:37.)

5. THAT LOVE IS UNCONDITIONAL- It is not based on what we can or cannot produce, it comes from the heart of God. MAN CAN NEVER REACH A PLACE WHEN HE WILL NOT BE LOVED BY GOD! God loved us first, He loved us anyway and He loves us eternally!

6. THAT LOVE IS SUPERNATURAL, IS SACRIFICIAL, - IS SATISFYING

II CALVARY IS THE WAY GOD DEMONSTRATED THAT LOVE -Verse 10 SENT HIS SON AS AN ATONING SACRIFICE FOR OUR SINS.

1. THAT LOVE IS FULLY SEEN AT THE CROSS.
2. JESUS STOOD IN THE GAP - 2 Cor. 5:21-
3. ESUS SAVED US FROM HELL. Eph. 1:7-

III. THAT LOVE IS VISIBLE IN THE LIFE OF EVERY REDEEEMED CHRISTIAN Verses 11-12 Dear friends, since God so loved us, we also ought to love one another.

   NO ONE HAS EVER SEEN GOD:

   but IF WE LOVE ONE ANOTHER, GOD LIVES IN US

CONCLUSION: AND HIS LOVE IS MADE COMPLETE IN US

IF YOU ARE POSSESSED BY THE HOLY SPIRIT BIBLICAL EXAMPLES OF THOSE POSSESSED BY THAT LOVE

(1) THAT LOVE WAS IN JOSEPH -Forgiving Love - Gen. 45:1-8......
lied about, sold as a slave, ripped from his home and father, falsely accused. put in prison, waiting, waiting, waiting all because of his jealous brothers!......YET HE STILL Forgave.

(2) THAT LOVE WAS IN HOSEA -Redeeming Love- - Hos. 3:1-3...........wife named Gamer.....a prostitute....yet!!....what redeeming love!

(3) THAT JESUS LOVED PETER Compassionate Love- PETER DENIED JESUS –.....lied about Him.....Yet Jesus still said........On this Rock I will build my church!

(4) Healing Love Me...............angry.....bitter......jealous........
burning with lust.........Yet Jesus still reached down and picked
me up out of the sewer!.........Psalm 103:1-4

IV- WHEN THE LOVE OF GOD IS IN A BELIEVER, THAT LOVE WILL BE VISIBLE IN 5 AREAS:

1. THE BELIEVER WILL LOVE THE LORD (John 14:15- If you love me keep my commandments!) (Ephesus - Rev. 2:4- you have left your first love!.........)

2. THE BELIEVER WILL LOVE THE SCRIPTURES .... (John 5:39) You diligently study the Scriptures because you think that by them you possess eternal life. These are the Scriptures that testify about me.

3. THE BELIEVER WILL LOVE THE SANCTUARY (Heb. 10:25)- not forsaking the assembling of ourselves together , as is the manner of some, but exhorting one another and so much more as you see the day approaching......)
Psalms 122:1- I WAS GLAD WHEN THEY SAID TO ME, LET US GO INTO THE HOUSE OF THE LORD!)

4. THE BELIEVER WILL LOVE THE SAINTS – OTHER BELIEVERS (1 John 4:20-21; 1 John 5:1-3) When the saints walk in love, then God will be seen!

5. THE BELIEVER WILL LOVE THE SINNERS -. Jesus had a heart for sinners - God's love is more than just being loved! It is opening our lives so that the Lord can love through us. So that He can reach a world for Himself.)

CONCLUSION: We ought to praise the Lord today for His overwhelming love! We can shout, we can run, we can turn flips and act like monkeys, but the best means we have of thanking Him for His love is by letting Him love through our lives and reach others for Jesus. I invite you to join me today as I ask the Lord to help me to love like Jesus. I thank Him for loving me, and I am sure you do too. Today let's show that love for God by doing His will and being what He would have us be, and by loving like He has loved us. By loving others exactly as we have been loved by God as Matt. 22:39 says

YOU SHALL LOVE YOUR NEIGHBOR AS YOURSELF. Amen!
Jan. 28.2009

(70)

READING: Ezekiel 22: 23-31 and John 6:32-40

Text. Ezek. 22: 30 and John 6:35 I looked for a man among them who would build up the wall and stand before me in the gap on behalf of the land so that I would not have to destroy it, but I found none. Jesus said to them, I am the bread of life; he who comes to me shall not hunger, and he who believes in me shall never thirst.

THEME: BRING CHRIST THE LIVING BREAD TO THE HUNGRY WORLD.

INTRODUCTION:

John announced the invisible God has come to be a part of our life. The Word has become flesh and lived among us. Not only that the Word has become flesh, the Spiritual has become PHYSICAL and more than that, HE has become the FOOD OF THAT FLESH.

JOHN PRESENTS JESUS CHRIST AS THE LIVING BREAD FROM HEAVEN that sustains and supports life.

THIS CHAPTER PRESENTING JESUS AS THE BREAD OF LIFE FOLLOWS THE MIRACLE OF FEEDING FIVE THOUSAND.

JESUS, DURING HIS MINISTRIES, MET PHYSICAL NEEDS OF THE PEOPLE.

JESUS CAME TO MEET THE NEED OF PEOPLE'S HEARTS AND SOULS

JESUS USED A FIGURATIVE LANGUAGE BY TALKING ABOUT MANNA GOD GAVE TO ISRAELITES IN THE WILDERNESS.

I – THERE ARE GREAT HUNGER IN THE WORLD TODAY:

A – THERE IS A GREAT PHYSICAL HUNGER

B- THERE IS A GREAT SPIRITUAL HUNGER IN THE WORLD TODAY:

1) HUNGER OF TRUTH, Jesus is the TRUTH
2) HUNGER OF ABOUNDANT LIFE, Jesus is the SOURCE of life
3) HUNGER OF LOVE, Through Jesus, GOD HAS SHOWN US HIS LOVE.
4) HUNGER OF FORGIVENESS
5) HUNGER OF PEACE AMONG PEOPLE
6) HUNGER OF PURPOSE IN LIFE,
7) HUNGER OF ETERNAL, ETERNITY, and JESUS IS THE GIVER OF….

II – PHYSICAL FOOD DOES NOT SATISFY THE HUNGER OF THE WORLD.

FOOD CAN'T SATISFY THE HUNGER OF THE SOUL.

Luke 12:13-21

PLEASURE WILL NOT

KNOWLEDGE CAN'T

POWER CAN'T

PREVILAGES AND SOCIAL POSITIONS CAN'T
MATERIAL POSSESSIONS

III – CHRIST IS THE LIVING BREAD SENT FROM HEAVEN:
HUMANITY IS HUNGRY FOR TWO PRIMARY REASONS:

SIN HAS MADE PEOPLE HUNGRY FOR GOD
GOD HAS CREATED US WITH A HUNGER FOR HIM (TRUE
GOD)

IV- CHRIST IS THE BREAD SENT FOR ALL PEOPLE:

JESUS IS THE BREAD AVAILABLE TO THE CHIEF SINNERS
JESUS IS THE BREAD AVAILABLE TO THE HUNGRIEST
JESUS IS THE BREAD AVAILABLE TO THE THIRSTIEST
JESUS IS THE BREAD AVAILABLE TO THE POOREST
JESUS IS THE BREAD AVAILABLE TO THE BEST OF THE BEST
JESUS IS THE BREAD AVAILABLE TO THE WORST PERSON
CHRIST IS THE BREAD OF LIFE THAT MAKES LIFE POSSIBLE.
CHRIST IS THE BREAD OF LIFE THAT STRENGHTENS AND
NOURISHES
CHRIST IS THE BREAD OF LIFE THAT LETS US GROW
SPIRITUALLY
CHRIST IS THE BREAD OF LIFE THAT SATISFIES PERFECTLY
CHRIST IS ADEQUATE TO MEET EVERY SPIRITUAL NEED IN
OUR LIVES.
AS WE CAN'T LIVE OUR NATURAL LIVES WITHOUT BREAD
WE CAN'T LIVE OUR SPIRITUAL LIVES WITHOUT CHRIST.

CONCLUSION:

THE WORLD IS HUNGRY TODAY AS IT NEVER HAS BEEN.

STAND ON THE GAP TO FEED THE WORLD:

SOME PEOPLE MUST BE THERE TO REPRESENT THE TRUTH,

LOVE, FORGIVENESS, PEACE, and PURPOSE OF LIFE and show

that

THE MATERIAL,

THE POWER,

THE PRIVILEGES AND POSITIONS

KNOWLEDGE AND SO ON

CAN'T REPLACE JESUS CHRIST.

WHAT WE NEED IS JESUS, THE TRUE BREAD OF LIFE. Amen

(71)

Scripture Readings: Genesis 6:1-15, 22 and Philippians 2:12-18

Text. Num. 14:6-9 Joshua son of Nun and Caleb son of Jephunneh, who were among those who had explored the land, tore their clothes and said to the entire Israelite assembly, " The land we passed through and explored is exceedingly good. IF THE LORD IS PLEASED WITH US, HE WILL LEAD US INTO THAT LAND, because we will swallow them up. Their protection is gone, BUT THE LORD IS WITH US. DO NOT BE AFRAID OF THEM.

THEME: WHEN TO BE A PART OF THE SOLUTION.

I – GOD BROUGHT THE CHILDREN OF ISRAEL FROM EGYPT His Goal was to bring them to the Promised Land and not to kill them in the wilderness.

II – GOD IS THE ONE WHO ASKED MOSES TO SEND SPIES-

III – MOSES TOLD THE 12 SPIES WHAT TO LOOK FOR – He never asked them to find out if they will be able to win in case of war.

III – WHAT MAKES SOME TO BE A PART OF THE PROBLEM:

1)- THESE PEOPLE FORGET THE PAST 13:1 The Lord asked Moses;
   The land is already given to them.

2) THESE PEOPLE ASSUME THE FUTURE 13:31-14:1-4
   They already knew what is going to happen.

3) THEY ASKED WRONG QUESTIONS:
   Even Moses put in their minds wrong questions 13:17-20

4) THEY DRAW WRONG CONCLUSIONS –

5) THEY NOT SEE BEYOND THEMSELVES 13:28
   (THEY DID NOT BELIEVE IN THEMSELVES)

6) THEY LISTEN TO THE MASSES 14:1-4

IV – WHAT HELPS US TO BE A PART OF SOLUTION
WHEN WE DON'T FORGET THE PAST
(DEVELOP A BETTER MEMORY -Deut 8:1-18)
SEE LIFE IN THE LIGHT OF THE PROMISE (Rom.8:28/30)

QUESTION YOUR OWN QUESTIONS – OR REPENT WHEN YOU KNOW THAT YOU HAVE WRONGED GOD
BE CAREFUL WITH THE MASSES (13:30; Matt 7:13-14)
LIVE HUMBLY BEFORE GOD (14:13-19

V – WE ALL ARE GOD'S SPIES -
HOW DO WE SEE WHAT HE HAS PROMISED US?

VI – WHERE DO YOU WANT TO GO,
BACK TO EGYPT OR TO THE PROMISED LAND?
IF TO EGYPT, YOU ARE A PART OF THE PROBLEM.
IF TO THE PROMISED LAND, YOU ARE PART OF THE SOLUTION.
PEOPLE WHO ARE PART OF THE SOLUTION:
TRUST THE PAST, REMEMBER THE PAST – WHAT GOD HAS DONE
THEY LEAVE THE FUTURE IN GOD'S HANDS – TRUST GOD
THEY DON'T ASK QUESTIONS – THEY ACT
THEY SEE EVERYTHING BEYOND THEMSELVES _ GOD IN ACTION.

VII – WHO WILL ENTER THE PROMISED LAND? Read Numbers 14: 36-38
JOSUAH and CALEB SURVIVED -They will also enter the promised land 14:28-30

CONCLUSION:
DON'T FORGET THE PAST AND WHAT GOD HAS DONE.
DON"T FORGET GOD'S PROMISES
TRUST GOD WHEN FACING HIS PROMISES –DON'T RELY ON YOURSELF.
BE CAREFUL WITH THE MASSES
BE HUMBLE BEFORE THE LORD AND HE WILL STRENGHTEN YOU
THE VICTORY IS THE LORD'S.
BE A PART OF THE SOLUTION NOT THE PROBLEM. Amen

(72)

Text Phil..2;12-13,15. As you have always obeyed – not only in my presence, but now much more in my absence –CONTINUE TO WORK OUT YOUR SALVATION with fear and trembling for it is God who works in you to WILL and to ACT according to his good purpose…..so that you may become BLAMELESS and PURE, children of God without fault in a CROOKED AND DEPRAVED GENERATION.

THEME: WHAT IS A CHRISTIAN'S CALLING TODAY?

INTRODUCTION: Paul has spent some time encouraging the Philippians church to be humble and submissive to the Father and to the Lord Jesus. Paul even appeals to the supreme example of humility, Jesus Himself. In these verses, there is a call given to this young church to carry out the instructions they have been given and to do the Lord's work in true humility. This is a message that we all need to take to heart today. I would like to spend this morning looking at these verses and talking to you about Paul's Call to New Testament and today's Christianity.

I – OUR PLACE IN THE WORLD IS WELL DESCRIBED IN VERSE 15 " SO THAT YOU MAY BECOME BLAMELESS AND PURE, CHILDREN OF GOD without fault IN A CROOKED AND

DEPRAVED GENERATION, IN WHICH YOU SHINE LIKE STARS IN THE UNIVERSE".

Blameless, Pure, Children of GOD in a CROOKED and DEPRAVED GENERATION –

We are compared to SHINING STARS IN THE UNIVERSE-

(1) Let us DISCRIBE WHERE WE LIVE TODAY – Divorce, adultery, homosexuality, idolatry, pornography, few go to church, children not knowing Jesus, abortion.

Europe has many empty churches transformed into housing complexes-

(2) What should we do in order to be – Blameless, pure, Children of God in a

DEPRAVED AND CROOKED GENERATION? Should we become violent, biscotti shops, hate those who do not do what we do and believe?

II - VERSE 12 IS OUR CHALLENGE

Paul says: WORK OUT YOUR SALVATION "THE KEY OF OUR SUCCESS"

(1) REMEMBER: These people were already saved - Phil. 1:1. Paul wrote that Letter "TO ALL THE SAINTS IN CHRIST JESUS AT PHILIPPI."

THE RECOMMANDATION IS TO WORK OUT:

Literally - "To bring to the fullest completion."

EXPRESSION USED IN MINING - To get every ounce ore out of a mine.

AND FARMING - To work the land to achieve the greatest possible harvest.

IV –SIX IMPORTANT ATTITUDES ARE REQUIRED

(1) TO LIVE CHRISTIAN LIFE AS IT SHOULD BE FOR GOD. (CHRISTIANS ARE SEEN HERE AS TRUSTED WITH TALENTS BY THE MASTER -Mt.25:14-30)

(2) TO BE ONESELF - God never called you to be a cheap imitation of any one else. We are reflecting Christ - Ill. Moon and sun! (Ill. You can display a reflection that no one else can duplicate.)

(3) WE SHOULD BE FULL OF "FEAR

(4) WE SHOULD BE FULL OF TREMBLING "– WHY?
God's business is serious business - Souls are at stake!
No one knows how much following Jesus is going to cost them, or where it will lead – (a) Paul - 2 Cor. 11:23-29. did not know what was waiting for him)
We do have His promise for eternal life- Luke 18: 28-30. Jesus said to his disciples that no one who has left home, or wife or brothers or children for the kingdom will be received because they will receive eternal life.
We will have to face God and give an account of our lives - Rom. 14:12;
Do everything without COMPLAINING or ARGUING.

That means: We are to carry out God's WORK and WILL empty of:

-Murmurings - Complaining - Secret disputes; and displeasure. This is carried out more privately than publicly!- Disputing – Arguing- Hesitation and doubt. This refers to doubting God's promises and hesitating at His commands.

BOTH PRIVATELY and PUBLICLY

CONCLUSION: Our lives MUST BE emptied of these symptoms

<u>IV-GOD MUST BECOME OUR PARTNER: WE CAN'T DO THIS BY OURSELVES</u>: For it is God who works in you TO WILL and TO ACT according to his GOOD PURPOSE. (Phil. 2:13)

1) WE WILL BE ENERGIZED BY GOD. This verse means that God gives us the energy TO WILL AND TO DO. (Ill. We do not have to do it alone!)

2) GOD WORKS WITH US AND IN US IN TWO WAYS.
   (1) To Will - God reveals His will unto us, make to adopt His will as our own.
   (2) To Do - Not only are energized to know His will, but we are empowered to do His will as well. (Ill. The Holy Spirit is the key - John 14:6) (Ill. God works in, so the we can work out!) -

OUR WORKING OUT IS THE RESULT OF GOD WORKING IN US, TRANSFORMING US, RENEWING US AND STRENGTHENING US.

<u>CONCLUSION</u>. God doesn't just save us and leave us to sort out His will. He moves in our lives and brings us into His work, being Spirit-filled –(Eph. 5:18)

THEREFORE WE" Eph.5:18 MUST NOT GET DRUNK ON WINE, WHICH LEADS TO DEBAUCHERY, INSTEAD, BE FILLED WITH SPIRIT.

VI –CONSEQUENCES OF SUCH A LIVE - VERSES 15-16 CHOOSE SOME

CONSEQUENCES: So that you may become
- BLAMELESS
- and PURE, CHILDREN OF GOD
-WITHOUT FAULT in the CROOKED and DEPRAVED GENERATION, in WHICH YOU SHINE LIKE STARS IN THE UNIVERSE AS YOU HOLD OUT THE WORD OF LIFE – in order that I may boast on the day of Christ that I did not run or labor for nothing.

When we let PREVAIL God's ideal in Christianity, there will be some POSITIVE

CONSEQUENCES IN OUR LIVES. WE WIL STAND OUT- The true Christian is and will ever be different and distinct from the world. We will be seen as: Blameless - No one can point a finger at us. Harmless - Lit. "unmixed" Not diluted by the world, but full strength for the Lord! (Harmless to the Kingdom are those around us.)

CONCLUSION:
As we start a new year, we should remember that we live in a very different world. That our society is changing too much and too fast. The question is what is our place as a group of people who believe in Jesus as our Savior and Redeemer today in this world, in our society, in our area? What can be our role and how can we play that role here now?

Should we go on the road to denounce, and protest, and fight, and become violent? Should we seek coalition and go to courts and force people to follow us?

Philippians 2 gives us a solution:

BECAUSE WE ARE SAVED - WHAT WE ARE GOING TO DO DOESN'T HAVE ANYTHING TO DO WITH OUR SALVATION. WORK OUT YOUR SALVATION – LIVE IN FULL OUR CHRISTIAN LIFE.

LET US BE OURSELVES

LET GOD TAKE OVER OUR LIVES AND STRENGTHEN US

LET US BE FULL OF THE FEAR AND TREMBLING OF THE LORD

LET US DO THAT WITHOUT MURMURE OR DISPUTE

THERE WILL BE SOME POSITIVE CONSEQUENCES IN THE SOCIETY:

WE WILL STAND OUT IN THIS GENERATION

WE WILL BE BLAMELESS, HARMLESS, WITHOUT REBUKE

WE WILL SHINE OUT

GOD WILL BE GLORIFIED.

GO AND LIVE ACCORDING TO THE WORD OF GOD. Amen. Jan.07.07

(73)

New Testament Lesson: Acts 20:22-24; II Corinthians. 5:11-21

THEME: WE WERE MADE FOR A MISSION.

Text Acts 20: 24...I consider my life worth nothing to me, if only I may finish the race and complete the task the Lord Jesus has given to me – the task of testifying to the gospel of God's grace.

INTRODUCTION:

God is at work in the WORLD. He can't come from heaven and make his will be done on earth as in heaven – REMEMBER WHAT WE SAY IN THE LORD'S PRAYER. "May thy WILL be done on earth as in heaven." Have you imagined HOW GOD CAN DO THAT? –

GOD WANTS TO REACH OUT – unbelievers.

GOD HAS SENT YOU AS HIS MISSIONARY IN THE WORLD. Go has reconciled himself to us and has given us the MISSION of reconciliation 2 Cor.5:18

I – WHAT IS THE IMPORTANCE OF OUR MISSION?
   (1) A CONTINUATION OF JESUS' MISSION ON EARTH
   (2) YOUR MISSION IS A WONDERFUL PREVILEGE YOU
       HAVE

-Christ REPRESENTATIVES

-TELLING OTHERS HOW THEY CAN BE SAVED

YOUR MISSION GIVES YOUR LIFE A MEANING.

II – <u>HOW CAN YOU FULFILL THAT MISSION?</u>

SHARE YOUR MESSAGE LIFE – Each one of us has a message to tell

YOUR EXPERIENCE, YOUR TESTIMONIES

What my life was before I met Jesus, How I realized I needed Jesus.

How I committed my life to Jesus. The difference Jesus has made in my life.

<u>YOUR LIFE LESSONS</u> – What is the most important lesson God has taught you in your years in Christianity? Psalm 119:33 Teach me, O Lord, to follow your degrees; then I will keep them to the end.

<u>WHAT HAS GOD TAUGHT YOU</u> – from failure, money – illness – disappointments –family – church – relationship – etc…

<u>SHARING YOUR GODLY PASSIONS</u>

III – <u>THINK OF THE GREAT COMMISSION</u> –

When you sing, "WHEN WE ALL GET TO HEAVEN. (# 123) and when you read I Thess. 4:17 Then WE…shall be caught up together with the Lord…and so shall WE ever be with the Lord.

Will this mean only members of the First Congregational Church of Machiasport Only Congregationalist, Baptists, Lutherans, Episcopalians, Presbyterians, Methodists, Anglicans, Catholics, Conservatives, Liberals – WHO ARE WE? The answer is THOSE WHO BELIEVE IN JESUS CHRIST, THE LAMB OF GOD WHO CAME TO SAVE THE WORLD FROM SIN.

WHOEVER BELIEVES IN THE NAME OF THE LORD SHALL BE SAVED.

A MISIONARY OF JESUS CHRIST THINKS BEYOND – Local church – the community – The region – the State, the Country, - the Continent but the WORLD AS A WHOLE - BECOME A WORLD CLASS-CHRISTIAN.

NO MORE SELF-CENTERED You will tell everyone about me in Jerusalem, in Judea, in Samaria, and everywhere in the world. Acts 1:8

THINK ABOUT ETERNITY Fix you eyes not on what is SEEN, but on WHAT IS UNSEEN. What is seen is temporary, but what is unseen is ETERNAL. 2 Cor. 4 :18

CONCLUSION: GOD HAS CREATED YOU FOR FIVE PURPOSES. THIS WILL GIVE YOU A BALANCED LIFE –

PURPOSE ONE – Love God will ALL your life – PLEASE HIM ALL THE TIME

PURPOSE TWO- BE A MEMBER OF THE FAMILY OF GOD – Born again–

PURPOSE THREE- Teach everyone – CREATED TO BE LIKE JESUS

PURPOSE FOUR - WE WERE SHAPED FOR SERVING OTHERS

PURPOSE FIVE – YOU WERE MADE FOR MISSION. Bring others to Jesus.

LIVE WITH PURPOSE:

FOUR ADVICES

(1) Give a DIRECTION TO YOUR LIFE – (CENTER OF YOUR LIFE)

(2) KNOW YOUR ROLE (THE CHARACTER OF YOUR LIFE)

(3) FIND THE CONTRIBUTION OF YOUR LIFE.

(4) KNOW THAT GOD WANTS TO USE YOU FOR HIS PURPOSES.

Amen.

(74)

II CORINTHIANS 12:1-10"

Text. II Cor. 12:7-9a It was given to me a thorn in my flesh, a messenger of Satan, to torment me. Three times I pleaded with the Lord to trace it away from me. But he said to me, "my grace is sufficient for you, for my power is made perfect in weakness."

THEME: DO YOU HAVE A THORN IN THE FLESH? PRAY AND GET AN ANSWER FROM THE LORD.

INTRODUCTION

1. In 2 Co 12:7-10, Paul talks about "a thorn in his flesh" which greatly bothered him...
   WHAT DID HE DO? He prayed the Lord to remove from him
   WHAT DID THE LORD DO? The Lord did not do so, but gave Paul an answer that greatly encouraged him

2. Do we have to know exactly what the "thorn" was?
   OUR TODAY'S LESSON WILL BE ON FOUR POINTS:
   1). Why did God give this "thorn" to Paul?
   2). Why did God give a thorn to Paul?
   3). What was Paul's reaction to this "thorn"?

368

4). What was Paul's reaction to the answer given to him by the Lord?

In this study we shall consider each of these things, starting with

I. WHAT WAS PAUL'S "THORN IN THE FLESH"?
A. SEVERAL POSSIBILITIES HAVE BEEN PROPOSED..

1. A pain in the ear or head (Tertullian)
2. Unruly fleshly lusts (medieval commentators)
3. Staggering speech, 4. Malarial fever (Ramsay)
5. Acute eye problems (Farrar and others)

Such as a severe inflammation of the eyeball. Possibly brought on initially by the blinding vision on the Damascus road

B. I BELIEVE IT WAS THE "INFIRMITIES" PAUL SUFFERED...

1- the persecutions he as an apostle of Christ

2- "And so by the "messenger of Satan," he means...those who contended with and fought against him, those that cast him into a prison, those that beat him, that led him away to death); for they did Satan's business

IN THE O.T. adversaries are sometimes referred to as "thorns in your sides" (Num 33:55; Judge 2:3); there is no metaphorical use of "thorn" for illness or temptation.

a. The term "messenger" in Paul's writings always refer to a person

b. The basic topic of 2 Co 10-13 is Paul's opponents, those who were troubling the Corinthians and Paul himself.

c. Paul parallels the "thorn" with a "weakness" (or infirmity)in which he will glory; in the context of 2 Co 10-13 he connects his infirmities or weakness with persecution -2 Co 11:30-33.

369

SOME PEOPLE CONCLUDE THAT the "thorn" was "the opponents who dogged Paul's tracks throughout his mission, confusing churches every time he left one church to plant another."

II. WHY DID GOD GIVE A "THORN" TO PAUL?

    A. LEST PAUL BE "EXALTED ABOVE MEASURE" (2 Co 12:7)

  1. Paul had been blessed to receive many revelations...

    (1). On the road to Damascus - Ac 9:3-6

    (2). In Jerusalem - Ac 22:17-21

    (3). At Troas - Ac 16:8-10

    (4). In Corinth - Ac 18:9-11

    (5). In Jerusalem again - Ac 23:11

    (6). On his way to Rome - Ac 27:22-25

    (7). The vision of Paradise - 2 Co 12:1-6

  2. It would have been quite easy...

    (1). For Paul to be filled with pride over these revelations

    (2) For the church to exalt him too highly

  3. The THORN " TO STRIKE PAUL DOWN " (2 Co 12:7).

  4. TO KEEP PAUL UNDER CONTROL – I Cor. 9:27

  5. TO KEEP PAUL HUMBLE

SOME PRACTICAL LESSONS RELATED TO HUMILITY...

1. Humility is a necessary trait for God's people - Luke 18:13-14.

2. SOMETIME, WE NEED OUTSIDE HELP TO KEEP US IN LINE.

III. WHAT WAS PAUL'S REACTION TO THE "THORN"?

A. BEING HUMAN, HE WANTED TO GET RID OF IT! 2 Co. 12:8

1. He pleaded with the Lord three times to remove it

2. Just as the Lord Himself prayed in the garden at Gethsemane - Luke 22:39-43

3. INTERSTING SIMILARITIES between Paul and the Lord...

    a. Both prayed three times.

    b. Both did not receive the answer for which they prayed

    c. But they both received answers that were sufficient

        (1) An angel came to minister to Christ

        (2) The Lord told Paul:

            a) "My grace is sufficient for you"

            b) "My strength is made perfect in weakness"

THIS SHOULD REMIND US OF CERTAIN PRINCIPLES OF PRAYER...

1. We are to pray with persistence - Luke 18:1-8

2. We are to pray in earnest - Mt 7:7

3. We are to pray specifically (as Paul did)

CONCLUSION: Bring your THORON TO THE LORD, PRAY!

-THE LORRD KNOWS YOUR NEEDS. WAIT FOR THE ANSWER

IV. WHAT WAS PAUL'S REACTION TO THE LORD'S ANSWER?

A. TAKE A CLOSER LOOK AT HIS ANSWER (2 Co 12:9a)...

1. "My grace is sufficient for you"

    a. The Lord gave Paul what he "needed"

    b. Not necessarily what he "wanted"!

2. "My strength is made perfect in weakness"

Application: it is in times of weakness and hardship that the Lord's strength can be experienced most completely!

-For in such times we really come to depend upon the Lord, and not upon our own strength or wisdom!

B. LET US CONSIDER PAUL'S REACTION...THE WAY YOU SHOULD REACT ABOUT YOUR THORN: THESE REACTIONS SHOULD BE LESSONS LEARNED FROM INFIRMITIES

LESSONS:

1. "We should boast in our infirmities" - 2 Co 12:9b
2. Let us GLORIFY THE LORD in those circumstances,
3. Let us USE our INFIRMITIES as opportunities to experience the power of Christ in our lives.
4. Let us say as Paul "I take pleasure in infirmities...for Christ's sake. For when WE ARE WEAK THAT WE ARE STRONG - 2 Co 12:10
5. Let us REJOICE IN OUR Infirmities - Ro 5:3a
6. LET US USE INFIRMITIES as OPPORTUNITIES TO DEVELOP CHRISTIAN CHARACTER - James 1:2-4

CONCLUSION

1. It may be impossible to determine exactly the nature of "Paul's Thorn In The Flesh"
   a. This ambiguity was by design
   b. Those with different "infirmities" may think the spiritual lessons are not for them

2. WHAT TO DO WHEN YOU HAVE AN INFIRMITY?
   a. In time of infirmity, pray!

b. Don't be surprised if the answer to your prayers are similar to those given to Paul

God has and answer for those who pray him to remover their infirmities:

(1) "My grace is sufficient for you"

(2) "My strength is made perfect in weakness"

(3) The Lord may choose not to remove the infirmity...

(4) The Lord will choose to give you the strength to endure it

WHAT SHOULD BE YOUR REACTION WHEN THE LORD HAS ANSWERED?

Rejoice that the power of Christ rests upon you!

THE GRACE OF THE LORD IS SUFFICIENT FOR YOU - Ti 3:4-7

Amen.

(75)

THEME: SOME EXCUSES FOR NOT TO BE THANKFUL.

Text. Luke 17:15-19 One of them, when he saw that he was healed, came back, praising God in a loud voice loud. He threw himself at Jesus' feet and thanked him – and he was a Samaritan. Jesus asked, " WERE **THERE NOT TEN CLEANSED? WHERE ARE THE OTHER NINE?** Was no one found to return and give praise to God, except this foreigner? Then, he said to him, " Arise and go; your faith has made you whole.

Readings: Psalm 66; Luke 17:11-19

INTRODUCTION: Of all the Thanksgiving texts, perhaps the best known is Luke's account of the ten lepers. As the song goes 'one returned to give God thanks, but nine went away.' We often focus on the one who, when he saw that he was healed, turned back, praising God with a loud voice and he prostrated himself at Jesus' feet and thanked him. Jesus said, "Get up and go on your way; your faith has made you well." This Samaritan was able to link the head and the heart, the gratitude with the healing, the gift and the giver.

The other nine went out to celebrate their new found freedom

Those who were given healing but missed out on the wholeness

It is hard to imagine the devastation of leprosy. Because it was thought that leprosy was contagious, those with this illness were alienated from their families, ostracized from their communities and forced to live in caves and dwellings far from civilization. The book of Leviticus records the following

The person who has the leprous disease shall wear torn clothes and let the hair of his head be disheveled; and he shall cover his upper lip and cry out, "Unclean, unclean." He shall remain unclean as long as he has the disease; he is unclean. He shall live alone; his dwelling shall be outside the camp. Truly, this was a death sentence. These lepers knew the law and they acted out their part. When they saw Jesus passing by on the border between Galilee and Nazareth, they cried out to him as they cried out to all passers-by, 'Jesus, Master, have mercy on us.'

Perhaps they had heard of Jesus, for his three years of ministry had truly touched and changed the lives of thousands, or perhaps they wanted from Jesus the same as they wanted from others who passed down that busy byway ... food, clothing, money, anything that would help them survive. Yet what they got was so much more.

Luke writes, 'When Jesus saw them, he said to them, "Go and show yourselves to the priests." And as they went, they were made clean.' Sure they still had to go to the priest for verification and validation but they knew, beyond a shadow of a doubt, that they were healed, cleaned.

They were made new. One returned to give thank, and nine didn't.

I -WHY DID NOT ALL TEN RETURN TO JESUS?

Would not all of them have been thankful? What prohibited some from showing that thanksgiving? Now, I hope you will allow me plenty of licenses as I postulate on what might have been going through the minds of the other nine on that day when Jesus touched them.

What were their excuses for not being thankful? What are ours?

(1), Perhaps one was not thankful for no one told him to be! The two MAGIC WORDS TO TEACH OUR CHILDREN: "Thank you and Please Nowhere in the New Testament that Jesus asked for thanks. He just reached out and healed.
THANKSGIVING SHOULD BE TOUGHT - IT SHOULD BE A RESPONSE TO A GESTURE OF GRATITUDE, ACKNOWLEDGEMENT OF BLESSINGS.

(2)Perhaps it was BECAUSE JESUS WAS ONE OF THEIR OWN. "The MAJORITY OF THOSE HEALED WERE JEWS AS JESUS. The ONE WHO RETURNED TO GIVE THANKS WAS A SAMARITAIN

We will smile at a person we don't know, and make a grim face to our relative.
We will hold a door open for a stranger but tell our loved ones to get it themselves. There is an old country western song that says 'We only hurt the ones we love.' The other TOOK JESUS FOR GRANTED.

(3)Perhaps, one said to the others, 'He told us to go to the priest.'
Two little children received gifts from their grandmother. The oldest went first to his grandmother, received a gift and said to his grandmother, "THANK YOU GRAMMY!" And the grandmother said, "DON'T MENTION". The second went and also received his gift and proceed to rejoin his older brother. His mother said, "Jim, what do you say to grandma. Say the magic word I taught you; say thank you to Grandma". The boy looks at his mother and also at his grandma and said, "She said to Jim, don't mention it. Therefore I did not have to say anything."

(4) PERHAPS THERE WAS ONE WHO JUST WANTED TO GO HOME AND SEE HIS FAMILY. Go back to his community, simply to take back life. Such is strong motivation and sometimes it takes real concentration to embrace the gift and acknowledge the giver. Yet this acknowledgement is that wholeness of which Jesus spoke and in that, there is healing.

(5) PERHAPS, ONE WANTED TO DO THAT LATER,
-HE WANTED TO FINDF AN APPROPRIATE TIME. I hate this – TOMORROW. Another day - It feels too late! Missed opportunities because we live under the illusion that we are too busy to say thank you. Missed chances for wholeness!

(6) PERHAPS THERE WAS ONE WHO DID NOT KNOW WHAT TO SAY: events or surroundings. The lepers must have felt that way.

YOU DON'T HAVE TO SAY MUCH – JUST A GESTURE. The one who came did what? Luke writes that he fell on his face and thanked Jesus. No big words, flattery cards, grandiose motions were necessary to impress Jesus.

(7) PERHAPS ONE DID NOT EVEN THINK ABOUT GOING. WE MUST FIND THE TIME TO GIVE THANKS AFTER WE HAVE RECEIVED.

(8)PERHAPS ONE WASN'T SURE THAT HE WAS HEALED.
- When I was a young boy, I USED TO LIKE BEING SICK for two reasons even three: (1) I will stay in my mother's bed; (2) I will receive a special treatment from everybody in the family, and (3) I will stay home and not go to school.

LEPROSY HAS CERTAIN ADVANTAGES –

IF MADE WELL, SOCIAL EXPECTATIONS WILL INCREASE.

Thankfulness can be tempered by fear.

Now for those of you who are counting, you will be pleased to know that the sermon is almost over for I have finally reached leper number nine and the final excuse ... WHAT IS YOUIR EXCUSE. WHAT DOES PREVENT YOU FROM GIVING THANKS TO GOD AND TO OTHERS?

--IS IT ONE OF THE FIRST 8 PREVIOUS MENTIONED EXCUSES?

(1) NO ONE TOLD YOU TO GIVE THANKS.

(2) ARE YOU TOO FAMILIAR WITH JESUS ?

(3) ARE YOU WITHING ANYTHING TO BE THANKFUL ?

(4) ARE YOU JUST TOO BUSY?

(5) ARE YOU JUST POSPONING TO SAY THANKS?

(6) ARE YOU TELLING ME THAT YOU DON'T KNOW WHAT TO SAY?

(7) HAVE YOU NEVER THOUGHT ABOUT THAT?

(8) ARE YOU SAYING THERE IS NOTHING TO BE THANKFUL?

BE THANKSFULL FOR?

(1) ARE THERE SOME INTERNAL PROBLEMS – tensions

(2) Perhaps busyness ARE YOU JUST TOO BUSY - to time to

(3) HAS SOMETHING HAPPENED AND YOU CAN'T GO THEREFORE THIS THANKSGIVING WEEKEND:

(1) Take the time for gratitude. Think of the excuses,

(2) Think back to those whom we have sometimes forgetting along the way, in our busyness to get things done.

(3) Be grateful for the bounty of this season, food upon our table, warmth, shelter, love.

Give thanks for everything which has been possible

(4) Lift up in prayer and action those who do not and cannot share this blessing.

(5) May Thanksgiving be every day deliberate celebration in your life

Like the Psalmist, open yourselves to the blessings of God, the wonder of Creation, the strength of faith. Take time this weekend, at the feet of Jesus, for, the labor of our hands, the gratitude of our hearts, the reflections of our minds, and the strength of our spirit. Let THESE come together, and ACCEPT WHAT JESUS SAYS TO YOU, "now get up and go on your way, for your faith, your thanksgiving has made you whole." Amen.

(76)

THEME: CHOOSE THIS DAY, WHOM YOU WILL SERVE.

INTRODUCTION:

Life has been defined as the SUM TOTAL OF ALL A PERSON'S CHOICES. From the cradle to the grave, we are faced with many important decisions - Friends, Professions, Schools, ideologies, Churches, Cloths, Houses, cars, food, Husband, wife.

WE MAKE OUR CHOICES then OUR CHOICES MAKE US. OUR CHOICES PRODUCE ACTS WHICH PRODUCE OUR CHARACTERS= WHO WE BECOME -

YOU BECOME YOUR CHOICES. YOU ARE YOUR CHOICES TODAY.

I - THE BIBLE IS FULL OF OPPORTUNITIES GIVEN TO PEOPLE TO CHOOSE:

(1) -MOSES COMING DOWN FROM MOUNT SINAI – Golden Calf.
"WHO IS ON THE LORD'S SIDE, LET HIM COME INTO ME "

(2) -**ELIJAH**, ISRAEL WORSHIPING BALL ON MOUNT CARMEL. The prophet said this to the children of ISAEL:

"HOW LONG WILL YOU DANGLE BETWEEN TWO OPINIONS:

"If the Lord be God, follow him, BUT IF BAAL, follow him "

(3) -THIS IS THE THIRD TIME SUCH A CALL WAS MADE TO ISAEL.

JESUS SAID Matt. 6: 24 "NO MAN CAN SERVE TWO MASTERS, for either he will hate one and love the other. THE CHOICE IS YOURS TODAY.

TODAY IS YOUR SICHEM.

MAKE UP YOUR MIND, MAKE UP YOUR LIFE.

II - JOSHUA LET HISTORY SPEAK TO THE CHILDREN OF ISAEL:

Joshua 24: 2 to 10 speaks about what GOD HAS DONE TO ISAEL:

The choice of ABRAHAM from UR IN CHALDEA.

His Trip to Canaan, the descendants he GAVE HIM, the land he

PROMISED TO HIS GENERATIONS, the birth is Isaac, Jacob,

Egypt, deliverance from oppression, the wilderness:

I BROUGHT, I GAVE, I DESTROYED, AND I DELIVERED YOU.

I SENT, I GAVE YOU THE LAND CITIES YOU NEVER BUILT, VINEYARDS YOU NEVER PLANT.

APPLICATION:

God never asked anything from anyone if he hasn't done something first to that one.

LOOK AT YOUR LIFE, WHAT GOD HAS DONE TO YOU.

III – <u>NOW FEAR THE LORD, AND SERVE HIM WITH FAITHFULNESS.</u>
<u>SERVING THE LORD MUST BE FAITHFUL.</u>
-NOT SERVING HIM WITH OTHER gods on the side.
-THE LORD IS HOLY - THE LORD IS JEALOUS

IV - **IF** <u>YOU CHOOSE TO SERVE THE LORD, YOU MAKE YOURSELVES A WITNESS OF YOUR CHOICE. YOU WILL CONDEMN YOURSELVES IF YOU DON'T WORSHIP HIM FAITHFULLY.</u>

V – <u>LET US MAKE A COVENANT TODAY TO SERVE THE LORD</u>.
Josh. 24:25 ON THAT DAY JOSHUA MADE A COVENANT FOR THE PEOPLE.

VI - <u>CHOOSE THIS DAY WHOM YOU WILL SERVE.</u>

VII – <u>I HAVE MADE MY CHOICE, I WILL SERVE THE LORD.</u>

<u>CONCLUSION</u>:
SATAN WAS LOOKING FOR A MESSENGER WHO WILL COME ON EART DESTROY GOD'S WORK.

The First one …..I WILL TELL THEM THAT THERE IS NO HEAVEN.

The second……..I WILL TELL THEM THAT THERE IS NO GOD – Conscience

The third……….I WILL TELL THEM THAT SATAN IS POWERFUL… lie.

The Fourth one .. I WILL TELL THEM THAT THEY SHOULD BE IN A HURRY.

Satan said, YES, YOU ARE THE RIGHT MESSENGER.

IF YOU DELAY TO CHOOSE JESUS TODAY, YOU HAVE CHOSEN SATAN. AND FULFILL HIS GOAL WHICH IS TO DELAY THIS IMPORTANT CHOICE .

Amen ! August 07.2005

(77)

Text. 1:29-31,38-39. Here is the Lamb of God who takes away the sin of the world! This is he of whom I said, "After me comes a man who ranks ahead of me because he was before me. I myself did not know him; but I came baptizing with water for this reason, that he might be revealed to Israel."....Turning around, Jesus saw them following and asked, "What do you want?" They said, "Rabbi, where are you staying?" "Come and you will see "

THEME: JESUS, THE LAMB OF GOD: COME AND SEE.

INTRODUCTION: People feel good when it is known that one of their friends or relatives is a celebrity. But in this passage, even though Jesus should have been considered as celebrity, he has to be discovered and the Epistle of I John shows us here. I John makes it clear that without some extra divine help, no one could have picked Jesus out of a crowd as the Son of God. Even John the Baptist admits that if God hadn't let him see the Spirit descending onto Jesus like a dove, he himself wouldn't have known who Jesus was.

In verses 29-34 John declares some amazing things about Jesus. Yet the very next day it looks as though Jesus is still wandering around as just another face in the crowd. Verse 35 tells us that the day after John saw the Spirit descend on Jesus, John is chatting with a couple of his own disciples.

Suddenly John notices that Jesus is passing by and so he says to his friends, "Well now, look over there: it's the Lamb of God!"

Imagine you and a friend were sitting at Bangor Mall sipping a cup of coffee while you watched your fellow shoppers walk past. Then you perceive **George Bush** mixed into the crowd but with no entourage surrounding him, no one paying any attention to him--he's just another face in a rather large crowd of shoppers. "Well there's something you don't see every day," you might quietly say to your coffee-drinking companion, **"there goes George Bush, the President of the United States!"**

"The world was made through him," the apostle John wrote earlier in this chapter, "but when he was in the world, it didn't recognize him." Indeed, it didn't. Jesus existed as just another face in the crowd. Even his own cousin, John the Baptist, almost missed recognizing him. **And yet hidden inside that one man was all the power of God.** Somewhere under those modest outer trappings shined the light of the world, the light that just is the truest Life of everyone of us, if indeed we have true Life at all.

REMARK: But it took a specially designated person like John to point him out to the world. Verse 32 tells us that John gave a testimony about Jesus. **He's like a witness in a courtroom who testifies to something in front of a jury. That's all John the Baptist could do: proffer a testimony, bear witness, and tell what he believed was the truth. And so as in any courtroom trial, it is up to others to believe him or not.**

CONCLUSION: Do you find John a credible witness? Can you believe him? All we have to go on are his words. And what words they are!

II - SEE WHAT A GOOD TESTIMONY CAN DO: Did you catch how striking John's testimony is? Probably not. I doubt that many of you batted an eye a few minutes ago when you heard the phrase **"the lamb of God."** You've heard and sung that phrase countless times before. It is one of the most famous pieces of Christian jargon. But did you know that **John 1 is**

the *only* place in the entire Bible where it is used? No Old Testament prophet ever referred to God's Messiah as "the lamb of God" before John 1 and no New Testament writer will repeat it after John 1, either. Even in the Book of Revelation, where the apostle John often mentions the image of the Lamb, the exact phrase "the lamb of God" is not repeated.

In the Old Testament, the best known reference is Isaiah 53's where a lamb is being led silently to the slaughter. But how likely would it have been that John the Baptist would generate a whole new title for God's Messiah based on one little obscure verse? And so the discussions and debates go on.

If, as appears to be the case, this phrase was a novelty, perhaps coined by John the Baptist himself, then how did it strike those around him? **The people had long been looking for the Messiah, but in the form of a king, a warrior, a hero.** So calling Jesus a lamb would hardly have conjured up the idea of the Messiah. It maybe seemed downright queer or even cruel.

John calls Jesus "a lamb," which could have been perceived a couple of different ways. Lambs are often a symbol **of gentleness, meekness, and vulnerability**. In this sense, calling Jesus a lamb could have been a nice thing to say, but it would hardly be the type of description that would fit the Messiah. But, of course, in Jesus' day, because there was that long history in **Israel of using lambs as sacrifices**, there was another sense in which hearing Jesus called "a lamb" might have struck some people as cruel

III – AFTER YOU HEAR SUCH A TESTIMONY: "WHAT DO YOU WANT? What are you seeking? What do you want," Jesus asks. A simple question, unless the one asking it is the Son of God, the Lamb of God who is here to take away the sin of the world!

Today imagine you are one of these two men and Jesus asks you, "What do you want?" Now imagine the *answer* you'd give Jesus. Jesus asks. Their reply? "We want to know where you're staying."

I don't know about you, but at first blush this looks like a blown opportunity! You've got the Son of the living God, the lamb of God, writing you a blank check, giving you the chance of a lifetime to tell him what you want, and all you can come up with is,

The fact is, these two disciples didn't blow it. They didn't give a bad answer. "What do you want?" Jesus asked. In a way their reply was, "We want *you*!" What's that line from that old African-American spiritual? "You can have this entire world, but give me *Jesus*!"

THESE DISCIPLES KNEW WHAT THEY WANTED: **JESUS.** They wanted to be where he was, wherever that was. They wanted to follow where he led, even though John's words about a lamb who takes away sin probably tipped them off was this Jesus. This was the Jesus they wanted. THESE DISCIPLES DID NOT JUST WANT TO SEE JESUS, .THEY WANTED MORE. **THEY WANTED TO STAY WITH HIM.** LISTEN TO THEIR QUESTION TO JESUS: "Where are you staying?"

WITH YOUR TESTIMONY – MANY WILL WANT JESUS.
WITH YOUR TESTIMONY – MANY WILL WANT TO SEE AND STAY WITH HIM
LISTEN TO JESUS' ANSWER TO THESE DISCIPLES:

"Come and you will see," He didn't issue a bunch of pre-requisites, didn't make them jump through some moral hoops before letting them take what were quite literally their first steps of discipleship. Jesus didn't say, "First know my faith and only then may you come along with me."

Come and join our church. after we're sure you've got your spiritual and moral vision clear. Jesus says, "Come, then you will see." So they did.

And I don't know just what those two saw that first evening. BUT WE KNOW ONE THING, ANDREW WANTED HIS BROTHER SIMON TO BE WHERE HE WAS, TO SEE WHAT HE SAW.

LISTEN TO WHAT ANDREW TOLD HIS BROTHER:

"We've found the Messiah" Andrew impossibly claimed. And so Andrew brought his brother to the Lord. Jesus liked this Simon fellow from the first, which is why he immediately gave him a new nickname, one that would stick forever. "Simon," Jesus said, "I'm going to call you 'Rocky!'" Because even though Jesus could see that this Simon was an impetuous, tempestuous bundle of nerves and energy, this man also had a solid core of love and faithfulness that would make him the Rock on which Jesus could one day build his church.

SO BEGAN THE GOSPEL, SO BEGAN THE CHURCH.

So began that little clutch of disciples whose devotion to their master would, against all odds, go on to change the whole world. Somehow it all began when two disciples answered the ultimate question, "What do you want?" with the simply profound and profoundly simple answer, "We want *you*, Jesus."

What do you want? That's not a question from a long-ago day addressed to people we've never met. That's this morning's question, January 16, 2005. What do you want, First Congregational Church of Machiasport? What do you want, Alice, Kathy, Bart, Barbara?

John the Baptist wants to arrest our attention with a phrase to which we've grown altogether too accustomed: **the lamb of God who takes away the sin of the world.** He doesn't look like much more than a face in the crowd. He's not glamorous and so plenty of people then and since have missed noticing him.

"What do you want?" OUR ANSWER SHOULD BE: **WE WANT YOU, JESUS. WE WANT TO STAY WITH YOU FOREVER. WE WANT TO ABIDE WITH YOU. WE WANT TO BE YOUR DISCIPLES.**

It's been Jesus we've been looking for all along, whether we knew it or not. The good news is that he's here.

CONCLUSION: PEOPLE OF GOD, BEHOLD, THE LAMB OF GOD, WHO TAKES AWAY THE SIN OF THE WORLD. COME AND SEE! COME AND STAY WITH HIM. Amen. 01/16/05

(78)

Jesus Reading of the Scripture: John 11:17-27, 38-44 & 1 Corinthians 15:12-20

Text: John 11:25-26 "Jesus said unto her, I am the resurrection, and the life: he, who believes in me, will live, even though he dies, and whosoever lives and believes in me will never die. Do you believe this?

THEME: **THE SEVEN" BECAUSE "OF CHRIST RESURRECTION:**

There is a resurrection- Our preaching is true–Our Testimony about God is true- Our faith is not in vain - The dead will raise Rejoicing –We are the most joyful people

INTRODUCTION: FOR WHAT REASON?

How do you answer a question starting by: FOR WHAT REASON?

For what reason you are Christian? For what reason you are here today.

ANSWER: RESURRECTION IS THE MOST CENTRAL DOCTRINE

-John's statement: John 19:35 "The man who saw has given testimony, and his testimony is true: and he knows that he tells the truth, that you also may believe."

1. THE WORK JESUS CAME TO DO:
    1) TO BRING HOPE

2) <u>TO Bring Life</u>

    a) He brought new life to Lazarus.

    b). He brings new life if you trust in Him.

3) <u>TO FULFILL THE PROMISE OF SALVATION</u>

APPLICATION: HE ASKED MARTHA: - DO YOU BELIEVE THIS?

HE ASKS YOU TODAY: - DO YOU BELIEVE?

<u>THE SIX BENEFITS OF THE RESURRECTION: THE SIX REASONS THE</u>

RESURRECTION OF JESUS GIVES ME IN THIS LIFE ARE

(1) THE RESURRECTION, REASON *TO PREACH CHRIST.*

    1. Verse 14: "If Christ has not been raised,

    Then our preaching is in vain.

    "But **since Christ has been raised, our preaching is not in vain.**

    APPLICATION: - I REJOICE TODAY BECAUSE MY MESSAGES ARE NOT IN VAIN.

(2) <u>THE RESURRECTION, REASON TO HAVE FAITH</u>

    2. V 14: and your faith is in vain." But since Christ being raised, our faith is not in vain.

<u>APPLICATION:</u>

    1. OUR FAITH IS WELL FOUNDED

    2. WE HAVE SOMEONE WE CAN COUNT ON IN HEAVEN

    3. THE DEATH OF JESUS HAS PROVIDED US HOPE.

    4. NOW WE CAN SAY THAT WE LIVE FOR CHRIST

    "The life I live I live by faith in the Son of God who loved me and Gave himself for me" (Gal. 2:20).

(3) **RESURRECTION, REASON TO GIVE TESTIMONY**

    1. OUR WITNESSING IS NOT FALSE –

    2. OUR TEACHING IS NOT A LIE

    3. WE KNOW THE ABSOLUTE TRUTH IN JESUS

(4) RESURRECTION, TO BELIEVE FORGIVENESS OF SINS

    1. I HAVE REASON TO BELIEVE IN JESUS

    2. I HAVE REASON TO BELIEVE THAT I AM FORGIVEN

    3. TO BELIEVE THAT MY SINS ARE NO LONGER THERE

(5) RESURRECTION, REASON TO BELIEVE THAT *THEY WILL BE ALIVE*. LIFE DOESN'T END HERE

    1. THOSE THAT HAVE DIED WILL BE ALIVE.

    2. MY FATHER, MOTHER, TED KENNEDY WILL LIVE

    3. I WILL LIVE. Verse 18: If Christ has not been raised, then

(6) RESURRECTION, REASON **TO REJOICE IN THIS LIFE**

    6. Verse 19: If Christ has not been raised, then "we are of all men most to be pitied." But since Christ has been raised, we are not to be pitied.

    1. NOW MY SOUL IS SATISFIED

    2. NOW MY GOD IS GLORIFIED

    3. NOW MY SAVIOR IS IN HEAVEN

    4. NOW I AM FULLY JUSTIFIED

    5. NOW MY JOY IS COMPLETE, TOTAL, PERFECT

CONCLUSION:

The greatest news in the entire world is that God and his Son are most glorified in you when you are most satisfied in them. And to make that true, God raised his Son Jesus from the dead.

IN RAISING CHRIST FROM THE DEAD:

1) GOD GAVE US FORGIVENESS THROUGH CHRIST'S SACRIFICE.

2) GOD GAVE US A FRIEND TO COUNT ON, JESUS CHRIST - Faith

3) WE ARE FORGIVEN THROUGH CHRIST'S SACRIFICE A FOUNDATION FOR OUR LIFE.

4) GOD GAVE US A FRIEND TO COUNT ON, JESUS CHRIST

5) GOD GAVE US GUIDANCE, THE FULL KNOWLEDGE OF TRUTH, AND THE FOUNDATION FOUR OUR LIFE.

Brother, sister, LIFT UP YOUR HEARTS AND SAY WITH HEAVENLY ANGELS: Worthy is the Lamb that was slain and hath redeemed us to God by his blood to receive power and riches and wisdom and strength and honor and glory. Amen. 8/30/09

SEVEN POSITIVE STATEMENTS CONCERNINTING THE RESURRECTION

FROM CORITHIANS 15:13-19

If we remove the IFS of these 7 verses, here is the way these would be read 13 But <u>if</u> there be no resurrection of the dead then Christ is not risen:

<u>BECAUSE CHRIST WAS RISEN</u>, THERE IS RESURRECTION <u>And if Christ be not risen,</u> then our preaching is in vain, and your faith also is vain.

<u>BECAUSE HE WAS RISEN</u>: OUR PREACHING IS TRUE

Yea, <u>and we are found false witnesses of God</u>; because we have testified of God that he raised up Christ: whom he raised not up, that be so, the dead rise not.

<u>BECAUSE HE WAS RISEN</u> OUR TESTIMONY ABOUT GOD IS TRUE

(Witnessing)

For if the dead rise not, then Christ is not raised:
> BECAUSE HE WAS RISEN ,THE DEAD WILL ALSO RISE.

And if Christ be not raised, your faith is in vain; you are yet in your sins.
> BECAUSE HE WAS RISEN,OUR FAITH IS NOT IN VAIN

Then they also which are fallen asleep in Christ are perished.
> **YES,** BECAUSE HE WAS RISEN THOSE WHO ARE DEAD WILL ALSO RISE

If in this life we only have hope in Christ, we are of all men most miserable
> BECAUSE CHRIST WAS RISEN FROM THE DEAD.

WE ARE THE MOST JOYFUL PEOPLE IN THE WORLD Amen.
July 2009

(79)

Scripture Readings: John 10:1-18; Psalm 23

Text: John 10:11, 14 I am the good shepherd. The good shepherd lays down his life for the sheep…I know my sheep and my sheep know me.

THEME: JESUS IS THE GOOD SHEPHERD: ARE YOU ONE OF HIS SHEEP?

INTRODUCTION:

What I would like to talk about today is some characteristics of Jesus' sheep. Characteristics of Christ's Sheep. What is particular about the sheep Jesus is calling his own in this passage.

Jesus is the good shepherd; a good shepherd who gives his life for his sheep; which ones?

When we read the Scripture, we learn that all human races are divided into SHEEP and GOATS. Sheep can never become GOATS and GOATS can never become SHEEP.

People called sheep are those who will receive eternal life. And those called goats are those who are going to Hell.

THE FIRST QUESTION IS: ARE YOU A GOAT OR A SHEEP.

Matthew tells us what will happen when Jesus returns at the end time. Mat. 25:3133 "When the Son of man shall come in his glory, and all the holy angels with him, then shall he sit upon the throne of his glory: And before him shall be gathered all nations: and he shall separate them one from another, as a shepherd divides his sheep from the goats: And he shall set the sheep on his right hand, but the goats on the left."

That day that the distinction will be clear.

CHARACTERISTICS OF JESUS' SHEEP:
I. ALL THOSE SHEEP BELONG TO JESUS CHRIST:
(1) THEY HAVE BEEN CHOSEN BY HIM

John 15:16 "You have not chosen me, but I have chosen you, and ordained you, that you should go and bring forth fruit, and that your fruit should remain: that whatsoever ye shall ask of the Father in my name, he may give it you."

QUESTION 2: DO YOU BELONG TO JESUS?

II. ALL THOSE SHEEP HAVE GONE ASTRAY IN THE PAST:
You have to know who you were before Jesus chose you.

(1) THEY WERE DEAD IN THEIR SINS. Eph. 2:1-3

> **Is 53:6** "All we like sheep have gone astray; we have turned every one to his own way; and the LORD hath laid on him the iniquity of us all."

(2) THE SPIRIT OF GOD HAS CHANGED THEM

(3) THEY LIVE NOW UNDER THE GRACE OF GOD

QUESTION 3: HAVE YOU GONE ASTRAY?

III. ALL THE LORD'S SHEEP HAVE BEEN REDEEMED.
(1)-JESUS HAS GIVEN HIS LIFE FOR THEM.

(2)- THE BLOOD OF JESUS HAS WASHED AWAY THEIR SINS

The good shepherd has given his life for them John 10:11, 15

QUESTION 4: HAVE YOU BEEN REDEEMED BY JESUS' BLOOD?

IV. ALL THESE SHEEP HAVE BEEN CALLED
    (1) THE SHEPHERD HAS SOUGHT THEM
    (2) THE SHEPHERD HAS CALLED THEM
    (3) THE SHEPHERD CALLED THEIR NAMES
    (4) THE SHEPHERD - HIS OWN HAVE HEARD HIS VOICE.
    (5) THE SHEPHERD JESUS LED EACH OF HIS SHEEP
QUESTION 5: HAVE YOU BEEN CALLED BY JESUS?

V. ALL THESE SHEEP KNOW THE GOOD SHEPHERD

John 10:27 "My sheep hear my voice ...., and they follow me:"

    (1) THE GOOD SHEPHERD KNOWS THEM
    (2) THE SHEEP KNOW HIS VOICE
      a) HE KNOW THEM ETERNALLY
      b) HE KNOWS THEM DISTINCTIVELY (Matt. 7:23)
      c) HE KNOWS THEM UNIVERSALLY.
      d) HE KNOWS THEM AS THE SAVED ONES.

QUESTION 6: DO YOU KNOW YOUR SHEPHERD WELL?

VI. ALL THESE SHEEP ARE KNOWN:
    (1) THE GOOD SHEPHERD KNOWS THEM John 10:14
    (2) THEY KNOW THE GOOD SHEPHERD
    (3) THESE SHEEP FOLLOW HIM
- JESUS loves them

- JESUS takes care of them.

- HIS SHEEP ARE DEAR TO HIM

QUESTION 6: ARE YOU KNOWN BY YOUR SHEPHERD?

CONCLUSION:

BEING JESUS' SHEEP, THESE ARE THE 6 AFFIRMATIONS
   YOU STAND ON:

(1) GOD 'S PURPOSE FOR YOU IS REAL – YOU ARE SAVED

(2) JESUS' BLOOD HAS BEEN SHED, CAN BE WASHED AWAY

(3) YOU'RE SEALED BY THE HOLY SPIRIT.

(4) YOU'RE UNDER GOD'S GRACE; NONE TO ALTER IT.

(5) YOU'RE UNDER GOD'S POWER, NONE TO DEFEAT IT

(5) YOU ARE UNDER GOD'S WILL. NONE TO CHANGE IT.

   LET US ALL SAY THE PSALM 23

"The LORD is my shepherd;

I shall not want.

   He makes me to lie down in green pastures:

   He leads me beside the still waters.

   He restores my soul:

He leads me in the paths of righteousness for his name's sake.

Yea, though I walk through the valley of the shadow of death,

   I will fear no evil: for you are with me;

   Your rod and your staff they comfort me.

   You prepare a table before me in the presence of mine enemies:

   You anoint my head with oil; my cup runs over.

   Surely goodness and mercy shall follow me all the days of my life:

   and I will dwell in the house of the LORD for ever."

Machiasport, Aug.23, 2009

(80)

Reading John 1:1-5, 8:3-12

Text. John 8:12 When Jesus spoke *again* to the people, he said," I AM THE LIGHT OF THE WORLD. WHOEVER FOLLOWS ME will never walk in darkness, but will have THE LIGHT OF LIFE".

THEME: JESUS, THE LIGHT OF LIFE: WALK IN IT.

INTRODUCTION:

(1) Jesus claimed to be the eternal "**I AM**" (Exodus 3:13, 14).

(2) He also claimed to be the Bread (John 6:35) to give life and satisfy

(3) He claimed to be the Light (John 8:12) knowledge and , eternal life.

(4) He claimed to be the Door (John 10:9) the way to abundant life,

(5) He claimed to be the Good Shepherd, to care and protect,

(6) He claimed to be the Resurrection the promised life hereafter,

(7) He claimed to be the Way (John 14:6) to lead to God our Father.

(8) He claimed to be the Vine (John 15:1) to enjoy a personal and productive relationship with God.

THE CONTEXT OF THIS STORY: THE ADULTEROUS LADY

Jesus, John 8:11, had just exposed the hidden sins of the Pharisees by saying "**IF ANY ONE OF YOU IS WITHOUT SIN, LET HIM BE**

THE FIRST TO THROW A STONE AT THIS LADY " (verse.7). At that moment his "<u>light</u>" shined into the Pharisees' hearts and exposed their "<u>INVISIBLE SINS</u>".

Jesus called these people in Mat. 23:27 *"whited sepulchers"* white outside, but stinking bones inside.

This is typical of **RELIGIONISTS** of many of us, **HYPOCRITES**, calling ourselves Christians.

<u>TODAY'S LESSON IS THIS</u>: IT IS ONLY WHEN CHRIST, THE LIGHT COMES INTO OUR LIVES THAT WE SEE "<u>The hidden parts of our deceitful hearts.</u>

(Jeremiah 17:9) **The heart is deceitful above all things and beyond cure. Who can understand it?**

<u>I – THERE IS STILL DARKNESS IN THE WORLD TODAY</u>

1. Just watch the NEWS - wars - killing - terrorism.
2. Listen what is said in the MEDIA: sexual abuse, filthy language, pornography
3. Look how PEOPLE LIVE: adultery, greed, alienation,
4. Look at what PEOPLE'S GOD - WORSHIP: False religions

<u>II – JESUS IS THE LIGHT OF THE WORLD</u>**:**
THE SUN IS THE LIGHT OF THE PHYSICAL WORLD
CHRIST IS THE SPIRITUAL OF THE WORLD

1. We have to have Jesus Christ to know WHO CREATED US.
2. We have to have him to know WHO MADE THE WORLD.
3. We have to have him to know our SINFULNESS
4. We have to have him to accept GOD'S PROVISION FOR OUR SINS: Christ
5. We have to have him in order to know the real LIFE'S DANGER (spiritual death)

JESUS IS THE LIGHT TO: (The meaning of Jesus being the light)

1. BE PRESENT IN OUR LIVES - Fellowship - Personal relationship
2. TO PROTECT US, - obedience, submission, humility
3. TO GUIDE US IN THIS DARK WORLD - let God

III – MAN HAS INVENTED OTHER LIGHT.

1. PHILOSOPHY - head - reason
2. SCIENCE - knowledge
3. MAN HIMSELF - justice, morality, humanism
4. NON-CHRISTIAN RELIGIONS – half revelations half-truths

AS GOD WALKED IN A PILLAR OF FIRE WITH ISRAEL IN THE WILDERNESS <u>FOR FORTY YEARS</u> TO GUIDE THEM, SO JESUS HAS COME TO WALK TO BE OUR LIGHT SO THAT WE WILL NOT BE LOST

<u>JESUS IS THE PILLAR OF CLOUD IN OUR DARK WORLD TODAY</u>

1. He is not just for the JEWS; he is for the GENTILE too
2. He is not LOCAL, TEMPORAL, but GENERAL and ETERNAL
3. He is the light that brings the FATHER TO US" (John 14:6).
4. He is the light UNTO OUR FEET (Psa 119:105)
5. He is the light of THE WORLD - every human being can walk in it
6. He is the light OF LIFE – THAT GIVES LIFE - abundant life he gives
7. He is the light that SHOWS OUR SINFULNESS - slaves to Satan
8. He is the light that ENGULFES DARKNESS AND HELL (Jude 13)
9. HE IS THE EVERLASTING LIFE OF HEAVEN (Rev.22:5)

IV – WHAT TO DO TO LIVE IN THAT LIGHT HERE

1. LEARN YOUR SCRIPTURE- (Luke 2:46). Read, meditate, memorize
2. SEEK GOD AND MEN' FAVOR IN YOUR LIFE (Luke 2:52) – service
3. RESIST TEMPTATIONS USING THE WORD OF GOD (Mat 4:4, 7, 10)
4. SEE EVERY HUMAN BEING AS GOD'S PRECIOUS CREATURE (Mar5:42)
5. LIVE SIMPLY, BE HUMBLE IN YOUR LIFE (Mat 13:55, 8:20)
6. BE PRAYERFUL (Luke 5:16, 6:12) Spending time with the Lord, listening
7. BE FULL OF THE HOLY SPIRIT (Luke 4:1, 14)
8. WALK IN THE LIGHT OF YOUR GOD, JESUS. (No more darkness in you)

He that followed me shall not walk in darkness:

CONCLUSION: **IF WE TRUST AND LIVE ACCORDING TO JESUS' LIGHT:**

1. WE WILL NEVER WALK IN THE DARKNESS OF THIS WORLD
2. OUR DEEDS WILL PROVE THAT WE LIVE IN HIS LIGHT (John 3:20).
3. WE WILL ENJOY THE ABUNDANT LIFE PROMISED BY GOD TO EVERY CHRISTIAN WHO TRULY BELIEVES WE WILL COME TO THE FATHER

INVITATION: WALK IN THAT LIGHT, JESUS FROM TODAY. Amen.

Machiasport, August 10, 2009

(81)

Scripture Reading: John 10:1-11

Text: John 10:6-7 Jesus used the **FIGURE OF SPEECH**, but they did not understand what he was telling them. Therefore Jesus said to them, I tell you the truth, I AM THE GATE FOR THE SHEEP.

THEME: JESUS IS THE GATE: COME AND ENTER IN.
Understand this Figure of Speech today.

INTRODUCTION: Imagine yourself having been invited in an important reception. When you arrive, the door is locked up and people are dancing, eating, drinking, and having good time inside. Imagine yourself standing outside of your home when it is cool, snowing because you lost your key of the door! Imagine yourself that you went in the wood alone. After traveling in your car some 300 miles away and you lock the door of the car with your blanket, your phone, your shoes and everything inside and it is January in the night!

- The man who is locked out at the invitation needs one thing, the key to enter the door and share the joy of the invitation.
- The man standing outside of his home under the snow in winter time needs one thing to enter his door: the key and he will be warmed up.

403

- The man lost in the wood far away from home during January winter month about to die even though he has all that he needs in the car is missing one thing: the key to open the door of his car and be saved.

Jesus says, "I AM THE DOOR, I AM THE GATE FOR THE SHEEP".

I –THE DOOR IS AN ILLUSTRATION OF WHO JESUS IS:

(1) **THE DOOR TO GET TO HEAVEN, TO GET TO GOD OUR FATHER.**

(2) **THERE IS ONLY ONE GATE, ONE DOOR TO GET THERE:** I love the Bible. I truly believe that the Bible is the **Word of God**, being the only way we can know the will of God; the only way God could have been revealed to us was and is in Jesus Christ. What Jesus said and taught us is found in the Bible. And that the only way we can know the truth. When Jesus said "I AM THE GATE; I AM THE DOOR "we don't have to search and look for another GATE, another DOOR to get to heaven, to get to God.

JUDAISM IS NOT THAT DOOR.

ISLAM IS NOT THAT DOOR.

INDUISM IS NOT THAT DOOR.

YOUR OWN RIGHTEOUSNESS AND GOODNESS IS NOT THAT DOOR.

PAGANISM, HUMANISM or OTHER ISMS ARE NOT THAT DOOR. –

NOTHING, NO ONE ELSE CAN LEAD TO THE SALVATION!

CHRISTIANITY - NOT CHRISTIANISM

THE QUESTION IS: "HAVE YOU EVER BEEN THROUGH THAT DOOR?"

II – THIS DOOR IS A PROPOSAL, AN INVITATION TO ALL:

(1) THAT DOOR INVITES ALL SINNERS " any man "

There is a hope, John 3:16 For God so loved the world that he gave his one and only Son, that WHOEVER BELIEVES IN HIM SHALL NOT PERISH, but HAVE ETERNAL LIFE.

(2) THAT DOOR LEADS US TO HEAVEN, TO GOD, TO ETERNAL LIFE:

III – THAT DOOR THAT GATE SERVES TWO PURPOSES:

(1) AS A BARRIER – TO KEEP SOMETHINGS OUT...

– The lost, the world, Satan, everything which is not of GOD.

– The flesh, our selfishness, self-centerness –sin –

(2) AS AN OPENING TO LIBERATE SOME PEOPLE:

A) Those who come in are WITHOUT PENALTY OF THEIR SINS. Rom.6:23

For the wages of sin is death, but the gift of God is eternal life in Jesus Christ.

(3) ONCE LIBERATED, HERE ARE THE CONSEQUENCES:

A) DEATH IS REMOVED AND WE ARE SET FREE FROM GOD' WRATH.

Rom.5:9 Since we have now been justified by his blood, how much more shall we be saved by God's wrath through him! (That is Jesus).

B) YOU ARE NO LONGER SLAVE TO THE POWER OF SIN Rom.6:14

For sin shall not be your master, because you are not under law but under grace.

C) YOU LIVE NO LONGER IN THE PRESENCE OF SIN I Cor. 15:54 When the perishable has been clothed with the imperishable, and the mortal with immortality, then the saying that is written will come true, "Death has been swallowed up in victory," Where O death, is your victory?

Where, O death is your sting?"

III – <u>THE BLESSED LIFE WHICH IS BEHIND THAT DOOR.</u>

A <u>PARDONED LIFE</u>:
The cross of Calvary stands between sinful man and the HOLY GOD
Eph.2:12-17

B. <u>A PROSPEROUS LIFE</u> John 10:10
John 10: 10 THEY WILL HAVE LIFE IN FULL.

C. <u>A PERPETUAL LIFE</u>:
John 10:28 I give them eternal life and they shall never perish.

D. <u>A TRUE WORSHIPING LIFE.</u>
They will be in the presence of God and worship him forever

E. <u>AN ETERNAL RESTFUL LIFE</u>
- Rest from the suffering of this world.
- Rest from the attacks of Satan.
- Rest form the FIGHTS WE HAVE WITH OURSELVES – Flesh

<u>CONCLUSION:</u>
JESUS CALLED HIMSELF THE DOOR AS AN ILLUSTRATION
<u>THE ONLY WAY WE CAN GET TO HEAVEN, TO OUR FATHER GOD.</u>

QUESTION: HAVE YOU ENTERED THAT DOOR? IF YOU HAVE:

1)– YOU HAVE BE <u>FORGIVEN</u> FROM ALL YOUR SINS

2)–YOU HAVE A <u>PROSPEROUS LIFE NOW</u>.

3)–YOU WILL <u>LIVE FOREVER</u>

4)–YOU <u>WILL BE WORSHIPING YOUR GOD FOREVER</u>

5)–YOU WILL HAVE <u>REST FOR YOUR SOUL</u>.

6)–<u>ALL THE FIGHTS YOU HAVE KNOWN WILL BE NO MORE</u>.

COME TODAY AND ENTER THAT DOOR. JESUS IS THAT DOOR. Amen.

Machiasport, Aug. 2, 2009

(82)

Scripture reading: Romans 8:7-1

THEME: **DO YOU KNOW WHO YOU ARE, CHRISTIAN?**
YOU HAVE THE SPIRIT OF CHRIST IN YOU.

INTRODUCTION: People living in this world are divided into two groups: (1) Those who live according to the flesh, and (2) those who live according to the Spirit of Christ which lives in them. Those who live according to the flesh are not Christians; but those who live according to the Spirit are called Christians. This passage of Romans chapter 8:7 to 11 gives us a true description of those called Christians and non-Christians:

(1) NON-CHRISTIANS: (verse 8)

    1)- Their mind are set on the flesh

    2)-They're hostile toward God; for they are not subject to the law of God.

    3)-Those who are in the flesh cannot please God.

    4)-Non-Christians don't have the Spirit of Christ.

(2)FOR THE CHRISTIANS: (verse 9

    (1) Christians are not in the flesh but in the Spirit,

    (2)- The Spirit of God dwells in you.

    (3)- They have the Spirit of Christ,

    (4)-They belong to Christ.

(5)-Christ is in them (verse 10)

(6)-, though their body is dead because of sin, yet their spirit is alive because of Jesus' righteousness.

(7)-The Spirit of Him (God) who raised Jesus dwells in them.

(8)-God will raise them as he raised Christ Jesus from the dead

(9)-God will also give life to their mortal bodies through His Spirit

Therefore, you and I we should know the differences which are between us Christians and the Non-Christians. These differences set you apart from non-Christians of vv 7-8 Paul deals with two kinds of human beings that Paul is dealing with. People whose minds are set "**in the flesh**" and those whose minds are on the "**things of the Spirit** ".

The Question **I am inviting you today to answer is which group are you? We all should know that Christians are DISSIMILAR to Non-Christians in FIVE WAYS:**

I. THE SPIRIT OF GOD DWELLS IN THE CHRISTIANS:

(1) The presence of the Spirit in the life of a believer makes a great difference of who you are. **The Spirit of God DWELLS,**

Christians are the HOME (OIKOS), the temple, the doweling of the Holy Spirit.

(1) They are not a renting room,

(2) They are not a hotel room

(3) They are not a camping area - a vocational home 24 hours, 7 days a week, and 365 days a year the Holy Spirit is in you. APPLICATION: If someone makes your house their home, they will be near you a lot. They will become familiar with you and you with them. And they will have **an influence** on you and the way you live. Christians: the Spirit of God dwells – makes his home – in you. There must be a communication, a familiarity, an influence, an assistance within the HOUSEHOLD. Don't ignore him; don't grieve the Holy Spirit; don't resist the Holy Spirit who is in you.

- YOU HAVE THE SPIRIT OF CHRIST –
- YOU HAVE CHRIST IN YOU

THREE IN ONE: (1) "Spirit of God," (2) "Spirit of Christ," (3) "Christ"–

Jesus himself promised in. John 14:16-18, "I will ask the Father, and He will give you another Helper, that He may be with you forever; (17) that is the Spirit of truth, whom the world cannot receive, because it does not see Him or know Him, but you know Him because He abides with you and will be in you. (18) I will not leave you as orphans; I will come to you."

THE FIRST DIFFERENCE BETWEEN CHRISITANS AND NON-CHRISTIANS

The Spirit of God dwells in the Christians.

The Spirit of Christ is in the Christians.

Christ is in the Christians:

BECAUSE CHRISTIANS' MINDS ARE SET IN THE SPIRIT.

II. CHRISTIANS ARE IN THE SPIRIT

9: "You are in the Spirit." Note this carefully. This is not saying, "The Spirit is in you," but, "**You are in the Spirit**." And this is what distinguishes you from those who are in the flesh. Verse 9a: "However, you are not in the flesh but [you are] in the Spirit."

WHAT IT MEANS TO BE IN THE SPIRIT?

(1) YOU ARE UNDER THE POWER OF THE SPIRIT-

(2) YOU ARE UNDER THE INFLUENCE OF THE SPIRIT IN YOUR LIFE

(1) NOT THE INFLUENCE OF DARKNESS

(2) NOT UNDER THE INFLUENCE OF THE FLESH

-CHRISTIANS' HEARTS, CHRISTIANS' MINDS, CHRISTIANS' NATURE HAVE BEEN CHANGED (METAMORPHOSE) –

- THEY ARE NOW CONFORMED TO THE MIND OF CHRIST

Phil.12:2 Then make my joy complete by being like-minded, having the same love, being one in spirit and PURPOSE....Your attitude should be the same as that of Christ Jesus:

CHRISTIANS ARE DWELT BY THE SPIRIT OF GOD, OF CHRIST, CHRIST AND THEY HAVE THEIR HEARTS, MINDS, NATURE METAMORPHOSED, TRANSFORMED IN SUCH A WAY THAT THEY HAVE THE MIND OF CHRIST.

III- CHRISTIANS BELONG TO CHRIST:

    (1) WE DON'T BELONG **TO THE LAW**

    (2) WE ARE **CHRIST'S POSSESSION** – NOT OUR OWN.

    (3) THEY DON'T BELONG TO THE WORLD.

    (4) THEY DON'T BELONG TO SATAN and the Power of DARKNESS.

THEIR BODIES ARE THE TEMPLE OF THE HOLY SPIRIT

    1 Cor. 6:19- Do you not know that your body is a temple of the Holy Spirit.

IV- CHRISTIANS ARE DEAD IN THE FLESH, YET ALIVE IN THE SPIRIT:

WHAT DOES TO BE DEAD IN THE FLESH MEAN?

    (1) NON ACTIVE – We call a person who is dead a CORPS OF....

    (2) USELESS - What do we do with dead bodies? Bury them.

    (3) WE TALK ABOUT THEM IN THE PAST.

    (4) THEY ARE NOT PART OF THE HUMAN CENSUS.

APPLICATION: Make your body inactive; Useless, thing of the past, not important- KILL IT DAILY; ALL YOUR BODY'S DESIRES. And BE ALIVE IN THE SPIRIT:

WHAT DOES IN MEAN TO BE ALIVE IN THE SPIRIT?

(1) **GIVING** YOURSELF TO CHRIST.

(2) **ACTING** YOUR SALVATION

(3) **LIVING** IN THE PRESENCE OF CHRIST ALL THE TIME

(4) **FLEE** FROM SATAN AND THIS WORLD AND THE FLESH.

(5) **LETTING** THE SPIRIT TAKE OVER YOUR LIFE.

1) The Spirit dwells in you;

2) You are in the sway of the Spirit;

3) You belong to Christ;

4) Your spirit is alive because of the righteousness and the presence of Christ;

V – A CHRISTIANS' MORTAL BODY WILL RAISE FROM THE DEAD:

If you die and your living spirit is separated from your mortal body for a time, that separation will not last forever. Verse 11: "But if the Spirit of Him who raised Jesus from the dead dwells in you, He who raised Christ Jesus from the dead will also give life to your mortal bodies through His Spirit who dwells in you."

(1) CHRISTIANS' RESURRECTION IS CERTAIN AS CHRIST'S.

a) WE MAY BE WEAK, SICK, DEAD, OLD, POOR IN THE FLESH

- BUT OUR PRESENT BODY WILL BE RAISED THE LAST DAY.

- RESPECT, APPRECIATE, LOVE, PROTECT THAT BODY.

CONCLUSION: CHRISTIAN, DO YOU REALLY KNOW WHO YOU ARE?

1) YOU ARE THE HOUSE OF GOD & CHRIST'S SPIRIT, of the HOLY SPIRIT 2) YOU ARE IN THE SPIRIT - Heart, Mind, and Nature's influence – Born again. 3) YOU BELONG to Christ. Not to yourself, not to the world, not to Satan. 4 You are DEAD in the Flesh BUT ALIVE IN THE SPIRIT. 5) YOUR BODY WILL RISE FROM THE DEAD AS CHRIST AROSE. THEREFORE KNOW WHO YOU ARE AND LIVE ACCORDING TO THE SPIRIT OF GOD WHICH LIVES IN YOU. Amen.

Machiasport 14, 2009

(83)

Scripture Reading. Romans 8:1-17

Text. Rom.8:9-10 you, however, are controlled not by the sinful nature but by the Spirit, if the Spirit of God lives in you. And if anyone doesn't have the Spirit of Christ, he doesn't belong to Christ. But if Christ is in you, your body is dead because of sin, YET your spirit is alive because of the righteousness. And if the Spirit of him who raised Jesus from the dead is living in you, he who raised Christ from the dead will also give life to your mortal bodies through his Spirit, who lives in you.

THEME: CHRISTIANS' NEW LIFE IN THE SPIRIT.

INTRODUCTION: Many people, included Dr. Chafer in his seven-volume of Systematic Theology, have called Romans 8 "the consummating Scripture." the place certain key doctrines of the New Testament find their ultimate expressions. That chapter develops themes as: (1) There is no condemnation for those who are in Christ; (2) Nothing can separate us from Christ; (3) there is no defeat for the believers.

For me, there are two primary doctrines found in Romans 8.

(1) THE DOCTRINE OF CHRISTIAN ASSURANCE.

(2) THE DOCTRINE OF THE HOLY SPIRIT. No other chapter
mentions the Holy Spirit as much as Romans 8. In this chapter,

we have all important things the Bible says about THE WORK OF THE HOLY SPIRIT IN THE BELIEVER.

OUR LESSON TODAY IS ABOUT A BELIEVER'S LIFE IN THE SPIRIT. We need to know this as Christians.

I-WRONG WAYS TO LIVE OUR CHRISTIAN LIFE: (There are Three)
A. TO LIVE BY THE RULES:
Many of us Christians live according to the verb "DO" "Do this, don't do that." "Do this, this and this, but don't do this or this or that." A Christian's life is not an accomplishment of things according to a list going from A to Z. Once that list covered you put your hand on your forehead and pat yourself on your chest and say, "I AM A GOOD CHRISTIAN".

Living by rules leads to legalism. That is to believe that by doing this and that and not doing this or that, you are PLEASING GOD. God looks at you at moment in your life and he says, "WONDERFUL! WONDERFUL! WONDERFUL."

There is nothing we can do to please God. Everything we do is colored, dirty, and unacceptable to God. There is no time in our lives when we should believe that by our own will and action we can be RIGHT, we can do "WHAT IS RIGHT IN GOD'S SIGHT". It is because of Jesus' righteousness that God looks at us as Saints, and holy people. RULES AND REGULATIONS cannot make us Christians.

B. TO LIVE BY FORMULA:
When you pray, close your eyes. When you start first hymn during worship service, stand up; the Pastor must raise his hand when he prays; you must leave the church in silent; candles must be lit; the Pastor must wear pastoral gown when he preaches. Every member of the church should give

10%. You can't be member of the church if you haven't learned the 105 Questions of the Catechism.

You know all these little rites practiced in the Anglican, Catholic, Lutheran, Episcopal, Evangelical, Pentecostal, Congregational, and Presbyterian, Assembly of God, God's Church etc…churches.

Many people have chosen or stopped to go to certain churches; many have changed religions, many refuse to go to church because of these rites, these formula and many believe that BECAUSE OF THESE FORMULA, they are Christians. These have produced in us, MECHANICAL CHRISTIANS.

C. TO LIVE BY EXPERIENCE:

This third form has made some to spend all their lives SEEKING EXPERIENCE. Thinking that if they never went to church and see what ISAIAH SAW in Isaiah 6:1-8, if they haven't spoken in tongues, if they haven't heard a voice coming from heaven as Paul on his road to Damascus; if they never had the same dream Jacob had when he saw Angels going up and down in Peniel; if they can't make the lamb walk, the sick pick up their beds; IF THERE IS NO MIRACLE, THERE IS NOTHING,

No life-changing, No earth-shattering, No emotional experience with God, NOTHING!

REMEMBER, EXPERIENCE DOESN'T LAST: If you would like to live by the experience, you may have it, but it will not last forever. We have seen many having those experiences after they have gone to a conference, after they have heard a wonderful message preached. Even we have seen those experiences after reading a book. The experience doesn't last. If you are a Christian who is looking and living a Christian life based on experience, you should know that will be for a short time before you go back and be the same person you were before.

Examine yourself very well. Are you Christian because you have a list of "DO" and DON'T"? Do you consider yourself Christian because you follow certain formula? Or are you a Christian whose faith is based on certain experience(s). A true Christian life should not be based on these WRONG WAYS TO LIVE A CHRISTIAN LIFE

II – HOW DOES THE HOLY SPIRIT WORK IN A TRUE BELIEVER?

I AM GOING TO GIVE YOU AN ILLUSTRATION ABOUT THE WAY THE HOLY SAPIRIT WORKS IN THE LIFE OF A BELIEVER: - Think of a Car and Electrical Train. These two are used for transportation. If one uses a car, he will run as long as there is a gas in the tank. A car runs on the principal of storage. You are constantly running and stopping, running and stopping, filling and refilling. But an electric train runs on the contact principle. You have the two rails on the outside and the electrified third rail in the middle. What is keeping the electric train going? **As long as the train stays in contact with that third rail in the middle, it will go and go it never stops.**

Walking with the Holy Spirit is NOT LIKE riding in a car. You DON'T HAVE to get filled with the Holy Spirit and then run down and you get filled up again and you get run down. That's not the Christian life of the New Testament.

The Holy Spirit ALWAYS BEING WITH THE CHRISTAN BELIEVER, HE STAYS IN CONSTANT CONTACT WITH HIM AS AN ELECTRIC TRAIN – TGV. How do we know that? Because the believer who has the Holy Spirit receives **GIFTS:**

A. A BELIEVER MUST HAVE A NEW MIND: 5-8

"Those who live according to the sinful nature have their minds set on what that nature desires; BUT THOSE WHO LIVE IN ACCORDANCE TO THE SPIRIT HAVE THEIR MINDS SET ON THAT THE SPIRIT DESIRES. .

(1)-The mind of sinful man is death,

(2)-but the mind controlled by the Spirit is life and peace;

(3)-The sinful mind is hostile to God. Not submit to God's law.

(4)-The mind of his sinful nature cannot please God."

TWO WAYS TO LIVE IN THIS WORLD:

(1) LIVE ACCORDING TO THE FLESH LEADING TO DEATH

(2) LIVE ACCORDING TO THE SPIRIT LEADING TO LIFE.

You should know that God has given you a new mind so that you might develop a Christian way of thinking. What preoccupies your mind? What kind of subjects you spend time when you are with your friends, your neighbors, your colleagues, alone or with your family? Do you talk about how much you have known the love of God or do you share that love with others? But remember what Jesus said. The first and greatest commandment is to love God with all your heart, with all your soul, with your entire mind, and with all your strength (Mark 12:28-30).

Do you let your mind to be CONTINUALLY TRANSFORMED as Romans 12:2 says, **"Do not be conformed to this world, but be transformed by the renewing of your mind."** The word in Greek is a form of the word **metamorphoses**—the change of shape that takes place within a cocoon whereby a caterpillar becomes a butterfly. Let a "mental metamorphoses" take place in your mind. Let the very shape of your thinking be changed by the renewing of your mind.

This is what the Holy Spirit continually does in the life of a believer: SETTING HIS MIND TO THE THINGS ABOVE...

THE SPIRITUAL METAMORPHOSES taking place carefully, intentionally, repeatedly, deliberately, daily through the studying of the Word of God

THAT METAMORPHOSES TAKING PLACE THROUGH SERVICE:

If you know Jesus Christ, you must make a difference in every area of life.

(1) The way you speak, (2) - the way you talk, (3) - the way you write,

(4) The way you relate and yes, the way you make decisions in the public arena.

THERE IN NO PRIVATE FAITH, NOT PRIVATE CHRISTIAN – ALL or NOTHING

YOU WERE GIVEN A NEW MIND TO MAKE A DIFFERENCE FOR GOD.

God gave you a new mind so you could be a difference-maker for the kingdom of God.

B. A BELIEVER MUST HAVE A NEW NATURE: ROMAINS 8:9-11 "You, however, ARE CONTROLLED NOT BY THE SINFUL NATURE, BUT BY THE SPIRIT, IF THE SPIRIT OF GOD LIVES IN YOU. And if anyone does not have the Spirit of Christ, he does not belong to Christ.

But if Christ is in you,

(1)-your body is dead because of sin,

(2)- Yet your spirit is alive because of righteousness.

And if the Spirit of him who raised Jesus from the dead is living in you,

(3)-he who raised Christ from the dead will also give life to your mortal bodies

THROUGH HIS SPIRIT, WHO LIVES IN YOU".

<u>TRUE DEFINITION OF WHAT IS TO BE CHRISTIAN</u>:

(2)-To become the HOUSE OF THE HOLY SPIRIT"

(2)-To have a transformed "**metamorphosed**" mind;

(3)-To be DEAD in his NATURAL BEING and ALIVE in his SPIRITUAL BEING IN CHRIST.

<u>WE CAN NOW CONCLUDE THAT</u>:

(1) THE HOLY SPIRIT GIVES TO THE BELIEVER <u>A NEW NATURE</u>: - LIFE.

(2) THE BELIEVER HAS <u>THE PROMISE OF THE RESURRECTION</u>. (v.11)

(3) THE BELIEVER HAS NOW <u>A NEW IDENTITY</u>
ROM 8:14-17

"Because those who are led by the Spirit of God are sons of God. For you did not receive a Spirit that makes you a slave again to fear, but you received the Spirit of sonship. And by him we cry, 'Abba, Father.' The Spirit himself testifies with our spirit that we are God's children. Now if we are children, then we are heirs—heirs of God and co-heirs with Christ, if indeed we share in his sufferings in order that we may also share in his glory."

WE ARE <u>NO LONGER</u> SONS OF SATAN BUT OF GOD:

(1) No longer in the flesh; but in the Spirit.

(2) No longer live according to the world; but according to God's Word.

III- <u>THE FIVE PRIVILEGES OF A BELIEVER'S LIFE IN SPIRIT</u>:

1. THE HOLY SPIRIT IS **HIS GUIDE.** Verse 14

   He is led by the Spirit – "TAKE MY HAND PRECIOUS LORD "SHOW ME THE WAY ".

2. A BELIEVER IS **FREE FROM FEAR.** ROM. 8:15a. "HE **IS THE SON** "
   .

3. THE BELIEVER HAS **THE RIGHT TO CALL GOD** "FATHER "15b

   God is his, "Daddy," He knows your voice as you know his. voice.

   THE BELIEVER HAS AN <u>INWORD ASSURANCE</u>. ROM 8: 16

   John Calvin called this "**witness of the Spirit**"; inner assurance.

   This brings that "**peace that passes all understanding.**"

   THE BELIEVER IS <u>THE HEIR IN GOD'S FAMILY</u>. ROM.8: 17.

IV-. <u>THE BELIEVER ONLY ONE OBLIGATION</u> ROM. 8: 12-13

"Therefore, brothers, we have an obligation—but it is not to the sinful nature, to live according to it. FOR IF YOU LIVE ACCORDING TO THE SINFUL NATURE, YOU WILL DIE, BUT IF BY THE SPIRIT YOU PUT TO DEATH THE MISDEEDS OF THE BODY, YOU WILL LIVE."

1. A BELIEVER OWES NOTHING TO THE FLESH. Verse 12

   HE IS NO LONGER IN THE FLESH" but "IN THE SPIRIT "THE FLESH, NO GOOD FOR HIM"

2. <u>A BELIEVER OWES EVERYTHING TO THE SPIRIT</u>: Verse. 13

   (1) His mind has been set for the things above.

   (2) He has been dead in the flesh

   (3) He has been transformed "METAMORPHOSED"

   (4) He has now a new NATURE.

   (5) HE IS AWAITING FOR HIS RESURRECTION

(6) HE IS THE SON AND HEIR OF THE FAMILY OF GOD.

<u>CONCLUSION</u>: The Life of a believer is not based on rules, formula or experience. The believer lives in Spirit. He has the Spirit of God, and lives in permanent constant relationship's life in the HOLY SPIRIT.

• He is just as an ELECTRIC TRAIN: GUIDED, FILLED, PROTECTED, RENEWED, TRANSFORMED, METAMORPHOSED, ALL THE RIGHTS OF THE SON, THE HEIR, THE RESURRECTION AND HIMSELF BEING DEAD IN THE FLESH BUT ALIVE IN THE SPIRIT NOW AND FOREVER.

Do you see yourself in the picture here? Are you living as the one who has received that power, walks with that power, speaks through that power, lives by that power, and has his future in that power? If until this moment, you don't see yourself in this picture that you are lived by the Holy Spirit, ask him today to come to your heart and he will come and dwell in you and change you into a new person from today. Amen

Machiasport, June 6, 2009

(84)

Readings, Job 1:1-22; Romans 3:21-26

Text. Job 1:21-22 Naked I came from my mother's womb, and naked I will depart. The Lord gave and the Lord has taken away, may the name of the Lord be praised. In all this, Job did not sin by charging God with wrongdoing.

THEME: WHY DOES GOD ALLOW BAD THINGS TO HAPPEN TO GOOD PEOPLE?

INTRODUCTION: We have a series of questions people often ask. I am certain that you have asked similar ones on your own sometimes concerning your own life or the lives of some loved ones.

(1) Why does God allow bad things to happen to good people?

(2) Why does God allow birth defects?

(3) Why does God allow natural disasters: earthquake, hurricanes, and tsunamis?

(4) Where is God? Does God really exist?

(5) Where is God when all this happens to men?

(6) Is it wrong to ask these questions of God?

6 ASSUMTIONS THESE KINDS OF QUESTIONS LEAD US TO STATE:

(1) THAT, we know that what good things and what we call bad things are.

(2) THAT, we know those who good people are.

(3) THAT, We also know who are bad people

(4) THAT, We BELIEVE THAT good people deserve good things.

(5) THAT, We BELIEVE THAT bad people deserve bad things.

(6) THAT, We also BELIEVE THAT God is the one who causes all that happens.

I – THERE ARE CERTAIN THINGS WHICH ARE TRUE:

1 - GOD IS GOD; HE IS THE MASTER OF THE WORLD AND HISTORY:

God is omnipotent (He does everything); Omniscience (He knows everything) Omnipresent (He is everywhere). Therefore, nothing happens without his permission, his plan, his goodness, and his will. – HE IS IN CONTROL OF EVERYTHING. -

HE IS GOD and THE ONLY GOD.

QUESTION: Why does the omnipotent, the omniscience, the God and only God who is in control of everything let bad things to happen to good people?

2- GOD IS THE CREATOR AND HE WILL BE WHO HE IS: He is the one who created everything. He is the one who owns everything. He is the one who will determine when everything will end.

3- GOD WANTS MAN TO BE FREE TO CHOOSE: If he wants us to be ROBOTS, he will never let man eat the fruit of KNOWLEDGE. He does want man just to say, "YES" without being free to believe that he is GOD AND THERE IS NO OTHER.

Genesis 3:22 And the Lord God said, "The man has NOW become like one of us, knowing good and evil. He must not be allowed to reach out his hand and take also from the tree of life and eat and live forever.

FREEDOM TO CHOOSE; WE ARE FREE.

4- WHAT GOD EXPECTS IS THAT MAN HAS FAITH IN HIM:

-THE CONERSTONE OF BELIEF IS FAITH IS GOD

-OUR TOTAL ABANDONMENT,

-OUR TRUSTING AND FAITHFULNESS IN HIM - FIDELITY, OBEDIENCE

- RELINQUISHING ALL CONTROL INTO HIS HANDS.

QUESTION: Why does God allow bad things to happen to good people?

II – QUESTION: WHO IS A BAD OR GOOD PERSON? (PEOPLE)
The biblical answer is there are no "good" people. The Bible makes it abundantly clear that all of us are tainted by and infected with sin.

Romans 3:9-18what shall we conclude then? Are we any better? NOT AT ALL! We have already made the charge that Jews and Gentiles alike are under SIN. As it is written: There is none who is righteous even one; there is no one who understands, no one who seeks God. All have turned away; they have together become worthless; there is no one who does good, not even one. Their throats are open graves; their tongues practice deceit. The poison of vipers is on their lips. Their mouths are full of cursing and bitterness. Their feet are swift to shed blood; ruin and misery mark their ways, and the way of peace they do not know. There is no fear of God before their eyes.

Romans 6:23 for all have sinned and fall short of the glory of God.

QUESTION: WHO IS GOOD? When you and I formulate this question asking God why does he allow bad this to happen to good people? According to the Bible, every human being, even the baby who is still in the womb of mother is a sinner. Every person who has died in an earthquake, in a tsunami, in a hurricane or any natural disaster; every child born with birth defects; every one who has died at sea, in a plane crash, in a car accident, by a gun shot; everything which has happened to people we believe should not deserve what happened to them are SINNERS!

-THEY HAVE FALLEN SHORT OF THE GLORY OF GOD-
THERE IN NO GOOD PERSON, WE ARE ALL SINNERS!

III – THE REAL QUESTIONS WE SHOULD ASK TODAY ARE:
1- ASK YOURSELF: WHY NOT ME? WHY NOT ME?
2- SAY TO YOURSELF) I AM THE ONE WHO SHOULD HAVE DIED THAT WAY NOT THEY. -
3-SAY TO YOURSELF: I HAVE SINNED AGAINST GOD –
4- SAY TO YOURSELF: I DESERVE DEATH, NOT THEY.
5- ASK YOURSELF THIS QUESTION:

IV WHY AM I STILL HERE NOT THEY? If they have died and I deserve to die_like them but I am still here as God is the Master, the Creator, the one in control, why hasn't he let this happen to me?

HERE ARE THE ANSWERS TO THESE QUESTIONS:
YOU ARE HERE BECAUSE:

(1) GOD HAS NOT FINISHED WITH YOU: Maybe you are not yet convinced about his love. He wants you to learn more about it.

YOU ARE STILL HERE BECAUSE:

(2) GOD WANTS YOU TO LEARN THAT YOUR TIME IS COMING: It happened in Haiti few weeks ago, it might happen here soon. This is the time to be prepared. GET READY! GET READY! IT IS COMING!

YOU ARE STILL HERE BECAUSE

(3) GOD WANTS YOU TO SERVE HIM NOW: Many people have turned their hearts to God by seeing what happens to others: Martin Luther became a monk when a lightning next to him killed his best friend. You know Martin Luther as the Reformer of the Church from 1513. God may have a plan, and this may be the way he is calling you to serve him. YOU ARE STILL HERE, AND ALL THIS NOT TOUCHING YOU BECAUSE:

(4) YOU PRAISE HIM IN ALL CIRCUMSTANCES AS JOB DID: You are nothing; I am nothing. Everything we have in this world will pass away. JOB SAID:

Naked I came from my mother's womb, and naked I will depart.

The Lord gave and the Lord has taken away,
MAY THE NAME OF THE LORD BE PRAISED?

CONCLUSION: Ask the right question, which is: WHEN BAD THINGS Happen to people, why don't they happen to me, too?

(1) We all are sinner – there is no good person in this world.
(2) ASK YOURSELF A REAL QUESTION: WHY NOT ME?

Franćois Kara Akoa-Mongo

(3) IF YOU ARE STILL HERE:

(a) GOD WANTS YOU TO LEARN THAT YOUR TIME IS COMING.

(b) GOD HAS NOT FINISHED WITH YOU.

(c) He wants you to serve him. This is your calling.

(d) PRAISE GOD in all circumstances because because nothing And nobody is more important than him. Amen. 01. 24.2010

SUMMARY: The question we will try to answer today is the one for generations, people, even Christians have been asking. Why God does allow bad things to happen to good people. By asking this question, we mean that (1) we know that God is the master of history. Everything which happens is under his control; (2) we also assume that we know what is good and what is bad; (3) we also assume that we know who is good and who is bad; (4) We also assume that people who are good deserve what is good and people who are bad deserve what is bad coming from God.

But we should know that (1) God is God the creator, the master the omnipotent God and the only one; (2) that we are free to believe that he is God and the Master of the history. (3) We should not forget that every humans being is a sinner. There is no way we can please God. Therefore, asking God why things happen the way they happen is not the question we should ask. Every human being deserves one thing: death. But if other human being suffers and die in the way we don't, the real question we should ask ourselves is: WHY NOT ME? Them and I we are alike. Why this is happening to them but not me?

Four answers can be given to this reasonable question a true believer, a person who knows who is God should askL1) God is giving you more time to know how much he loves you. Perhaps you haven't reached that level yet. (2) Know that your time is coming. Be prepared ;(3) He is calling you to serve him. Now is the time ;(4) Give him praise; you are created to praise him and know that this world is nothing, but God. Amen.

(85)

Readings: Genesis 3:17-24; Luke 13:1-9

Text. Luke 13:1-3 now there were some present at that time that told Jesus about the Galileans whose blood Pilate mixed with their sacrifice. Jesus answered, « Do you think that these Galileans were worse sinners than all the other Galileans because they suffered this way? I tell you, NO! BUT UNLESS YOU REPENT, YOU TOO WILL ALL PERISH. »

SEROMON: WHY SUFFERING IN THE WORLD?

INTRODUCTION: Last week, we asked the same question Christians as well as non-Christians have been asking for generations, « WHY DOES GOD ALLOW BAD THINGS TO HAPPEN TO GOOD PEOPLE? We reached certain conclusions I wish to remind us of today, before we continue.

We said that:

1) God is God. He is the one who created everything and he is in charge of all things

2) Nothing happens without God's permission. He has a plan for everything.

3) God has given us freedom to choose. We can choose him or Satan.

4) What God expects from us is TO HAVE FAITH IN HIM.

We also learned that:

1) We are all sinners. There is no good one. We all deserve death

2) The question we should ask is « WHY NOT ME? »Then, we covered the 4 reasons God doesn't allow bad things to happen to you now:

1) God hasn't finished with you. - He still wants to make you like Christ like.

2) Your time is coming. He is still patient with you.

3) He is calling you for a special mission in his church.

4) Now is the time to praise the Lord in your life. PRAISE HIM!

Today, our question is, WHY SUFFERING IN THE WORLD?

HERE ARE THE SIX (6) REASONS GOD ALLOWS SUFFERING:

I – IT IS BECAUSE THE WAY THINGS ARE TODAY:

We learned in the book of Genesis that, after man made his choice to sin, to disobey God, he came to know what is good and what is bad. All of us we don't have to go to school to learn what is good and what is bad. Our society has made certain choices eliminating what for generations people have called sins: I don't have to name

(1) what we see on television, (2) what we find in magazines, (3) what we read in books, (4) what we watch in movies and television, (5) what we hear on radio, (6) songs we sing every day, (7) the way people live in cities, - Hollywood, - celebrities, - rich people. – (8) What money does in the world - drugs - sex - killing - devil –?

(9) You know what happens with food, drugs, alcohol, tobacco - ABUSE! The question is: Are you praying? Are we learning? No difference.

But we know that when God created everything, he called all « GOOD » My brother, my sister, nothing will change until the day Jesus will return.

We are made our choices; we suffer because of these:

1- we know that eating too much food is not good; what do we do?

2- we know that smoking is not good; what do we do?

3- we know that pollution is not good; what do we do?

4- we know that speeding is not good; what do we do?

5- we know that stealing is not good; what do we do?

6- we know that divorce is not good; what do we do?

7- we know that killing is not good. But WHAT DO WE DO?

We pray and will pray for our actions here and over there

II – SUFFERING IS OUR DIRECT PUNISHMENT:

WE ARE BRINGING PUNISHMENT TO OURSELVES: Remember the time of Noah. When the sins of man increased so much, God let the flood come and annihilate the whole world. Noah, his family and the animals he took with him in his ark were saved. God did not care about the number of people who had to perish that time. He let them all die because of their sins. What happened in the past is happening now and will happen, when Christ returns, on a much large scale.

Romans 6:23 says « FORTHE WAGES OF SIN IS DEATH,

BUT THE GIFT OF GOD IS ETERNAL LIFE. »

GOD WILL NOT WAIT FOREVER! GOD PUNISHES SIN!

Some people said that 911 was God's punishment for us. Some have even said that the earthquake in Haiti is also their punishment.

Some have even said that the earthquake in Haiti is also their punishment.

ARE WE BETTER THAN THESE HAITIANS WHO DIED IN THE EARTHQUAKE?ARE WE BETTER THAN PEOPLE WHO DIED IN THE TSUNAMI?ARE WE BETTER THAN PEOPLE WHO GET HURT OR KILLED?ARE WE BETTER THAN THOSE WHO SUFFER FROM FLOODS?THE ANSWER IS « NO! »YOUR TIME HAS NOT YET COME

III- SUFFERING TO SHOW US THE WICKEDNESS OF SIN=RESULT.

Tsunamis the result of what water can do;

Tornadoes the result of what the wind can do.

Avalanches the result of what the snow can do.

Death is the result of what sin can do.

Jail time in prison is the result of what speeding with your car can do.

Physical and Spiritual death is what sin can do.

Any act, any thought, any decision people make and keep on making can be measured by results: for example:

(1) The assassination in 1914 of the heir Prince FRANK FERDINAND and his wife in SARAJEVO had a consequence WORLD WAR ONE. DO WE REALLY THINK OF THE CONSEQUENCES OF WHAT WE DO? ABOUT WHAT WILL HAPPEN NEXT TO OUR SOCIETY?

ILLUSTRATION: Last week, it was raining in California, and I saw a house built on the cliff. The owner of that house was investing to build a strong foundation around it hoping that the foundation will hold against mudslide coming from the bare hilltop behind the house. Everybody around this man's home was moving their stuff trying to salvage what they could. But this guy was hoping against the odds that his house would hold. Even the Policemen came at his door and told him that he should leave because there was no hope. He was just standing there as if he did not hear them.

DO WE REALLY THING THAT THE END RESULT WILL BE DIFFERENT?

IV – SUFFERING FOR FRIAGILITY; WE ARE NOTHING

I still have images of people being crushed under the rubble, walls, and concrete. I still see corpses lying on the streets, I still see these trucks dumping bodies in a hole and caterpillars filling up the hole.

I still see people carrying their little dead ones crying.

I still see hospital beds full of people with broken arms, legs and hands not attended. These are people who look just like you and me.

These are people who walked, talked, lived and were just like us.

Now, they don't have names, they don't have homes, they don't have husbands and wives, they don't have children, money in the bank, country – NOTHING!-

TODAY	TOMORROW
Today we are born	Tomorrow we die
Today we are young	Tomorrow we are old
Today we are rich	Tomorrow we are poor
Today we have	Tomorrow we have nothing.
Today we are happy	tomorrow we cry.
Today we are healthy	Tomorrow we are sick/

WE ARE NOTHING!

V- SUFFERING IS WHAT WE DESERVE: Luke 13:1

If there is only one thing you and I deserve in this World: suffering.

God loves us so much that we have his grace and merci through his Son Jesus Christ

TURN YOUR EYES TO THE GRACE OF GOD
TURN YOUR EYES ON THE MERCY OF GOD.
WE REJOICE BECAUSE OF HIS GRACE AND MERCY.
YOU KNOW LOVE BECAUSE OF HIS GRACE AND MERCY.

VI- THE WAY OUT OF SUFFERING IS REPENTANCE:
SUFFERING INVITES US TO REPENT:
   TO REPENT FROM OUR SINS.

THE ONLY THING, TO SATISFY HUNGER, IS FOOD.

THE ONLY THING WHICH CAN SATISFY THRIST IS DRINK

THE ONLY THING WHICH CAN SATISFY SIN IS SUFFERING

THE ONLY THING, WHICH CAN SATISFY SUFFERING, IS REPENTANCE.

THE ONLY THING TO SATISFY DEATH IS ETERNAL LIFE

THE ONLY THING TO SATISFY CONDAMNATION, IS THE CROSS

THE ONLY THING TO SATISFY BELIEVERS IS JESUS

TO HAVE PEACE, REST, WE ARE CALLED TO REPENT

ASK GOD FORGIVENESS OF YOUR SINS, THE SINS OF YOUR FAMILY, YOU'RE RACE, YOUR NATION, THE SINS OF OUR MODERN SOCIETY, THE SINS OF THE WORLD.

LET US REPENT TODAY, AND RIGHT NOW, FROM OUR SINS!

CONCLUSION : These are the six (6) reasons we suffer as we do :

1. WE SUFFER BECAUSE THE WAY WE LIVE TODAY – OUR CULTURE
2. WE SUFFER BECAUSE WE HAVE CHOSEN THAT WAY, PUNISHMENT
3. WE SUFFER BECAUSE SUFFERING IS A CONSEQUENCE OF OUR ACTS
4. SUFFERENCE SHOWS US OUR FRAGILITY – WE ARE NOTHING.
5. WE SUFFER BECAUSE IT IS WHAT WE DESERVE. Not grace, not mercy.
6. WE SUFFER BECAUSE WE HAVEN'T YET REPENTED FROM OUR SINS. Amen.

Machiasport Jan.31, 2010

(86)

Scripture Readings: Luke 26-43

Text. Luke 23:34 Then said Jesus, Father, forgive them; for they know not what they do.

THEME: THE WORD OF FORGIVENESS

INTRODUCTION: Christianity has some important CHARACTERISTICS which are difficult to apply in our daily life. These CHARACTERISTICS define what the true foundation of CHRISTIANITY IS.

Last week, we talked about LOVE. How human love differs from divine love, which Jesus invites us to have and practice in our lives. The kind of love, which feeds others, sustains, others. Keeps others alive, forgetting oneself and putting others first doing everything not expecting anything in return.

TODAY, we will learn about "FORGIVENESS"

The first word Jesus said on the cross after man has done all the worst things he could, Jesus prayed to his Father saying, Father, Forgive them.

I –FORGIVENESS ACCORDING TO CHRISTIAN FAITH:

What is forgiveness according to Jesus?

1- PUTTING AWAY – the hurt another person did to you.

2- MAKING DISAPPEAR the hurt.

3- LETTING EVERYTHING BE AS IT WAS BEFORE.
   SOME EXAMPLES OF FORGIVENESS:

4- Resist not evil but whosoever smite on your right cheek turn the other also.

5- Peter asked Jesus," Lord, how many times shall I forgive my brother when he sins against me? Up to seven times? Jesus answered," I tell you, not seven times, but seventy-seven times.

II – WHO WAS PRAYING TO HIS FATHER FOR FORGIVENESS?

Each one of us have committed all kinds of sins. The worst one was when we crucified the one who came to save us, our Lord Jesus Christ

(1) The one who came and be born as a human being;

(2) The one who emptied himself, his glory and honor to become like us

(3) Resurrected the dead, fed the hungry, defended the widows

(4) preached the word of Salvation to those who lived in darkness.

(5) The one at his birth there was no room for Him in the inn,
    Which foreshadowed treatment to receive from the hands of men

(6) The one Herod sought to slay as a little child, and this intimated the hostility his Person evoked and forecast the cross as the climax of man's enmity.

(7) The one who was condemned by a mock trial.

(8) The one judges found no fault in him,

(9) The one the judges yielded to the insistence of those who hated him as they cried again and again "Crucify him".

AFTER WE HAD COMMITTED THE WORST SIN, Jesus said.

(Luke 23:34)., Father, forgives them; for they know not what they do.

II– FOR WHOM WAS JESUS PRAYING TO HIS FATHER?

(1) <u>THE INN KEER</u>, who let him be born in the manger.

If the Inn Keeper knew that the baby Mary was about to give birth to was Jesus, he would have done everything to find a place for him. Because he did not, Jesus on the cross asked for his forgiveness.

2-**THE CROWD,** that received him as a King, at the trial, yelled crucify him. If this crowd knew, they would never say," Crucify him"

3-**JUDAS ISCARIOT,** who sold his Master for 30 pieces of silver. If Judas Iscariot knew that Jesus has come to die for his sin, he would never have sold him for 30 pieces of silver

4-PILATE, who let the crowds will dominate during the trial. If Herod knew that Jesus did not come to take his throne, his kingdom was not on earth, he would never give him to the crowd.

5- THE JUDGES who, even though they found Jesus innocent, let him die. If the judges knew that Jesus was the Son of God and he was the one who will render the final right judgment, they wouldn't have done what they did.

6- THOSE WHO MOCKED HIM, SPAT ON HIM, THOSE WHO STRUCK ON HIM

People who spat on Jesus, if they knew they would never do that.

7- THE CHIEF PRIESTS, They would have been those who did not praise him.

8-THE DISCIPLES, who abandoned him.

9-The Soldiers who crucified him and gambled for his tunic. The Soldiers wouldn't do anything like that if they knew – ignorance!

10-YOU AND I haven't received Jesus as our true Savior. It is pitiful today that, with all the KNOWLEDGE we have today, we still sin against Jesus. But you should know that he is praying to his Father even at this hour on our behalf today saying,

FATHER FORGIVE them because THEY DON'T Know what they are doing.

III – WHY DID THEY DO ALL THESE THINGS TO JESUS?

ANSWER: THEY DIDN'T KNOW = IGNORANCE.

Being DARKENED in their understanding,

Being ALIENATED from the life of God,

because of the ignorance that is in them,

because of HAVING HARDENED HEARTS." Ephesians 4:18

IV -WHY SHOULD WE FORGIVE AS JESUS DID ON THE CROSS?

"Then said Jesus, Father, forgive them; for they know not what they do."

1- FORGIVENESS IS A DIVINE PREROGATIVE.

-- Christianity starts with love and ends with forgiveness The Jewish scribes were right when they reasoned "Who can forgive sins but God only?" (Mark 2:7)... And when the Lord Jesus cried "Father, forgive them"

2) GOD WILL NOT FORGIVE THOSE WHO DON'T FORGIVE. Matt 6:14-15 for if you forgive men when they sin against you, your heavenly Father will also forgive you. But if you don't forgive men their sins, your heavenly Father will not forgive your sins.

3)- FORGIVENESS IS THE FIRST STEP TOWARD RESTORATION Matt. 5:32

4) TRUE FORGIVESS LEADS TO CHANGE: John 8:11. The adulterous woman.. Jesus said to her, I do not condemn you, Jesus declared, GO NOW, LEAVE YOUR LIFE OF SIN".

5)- WE SHOULD FORGIVE BECAUSE CHRIST TAUGHT US TO FORGIVE EXAMPLIFICATION OF HIS TEACHING

In the Sermon on the Mount our Lord taught his disciples, "Love your enemies, bless them that curse you, do good to them that hate you, and pray for them which despitefully use you and persecute you" Mat. 5:44

6. RIMARY NEED OF MAN Every human being needs forgiveness. We are sinners. Our joy, our peace, our hope, our being to become what it should be when we know that we have been forgiven.

7. FORGIVENESS IS THE TRIUMPH OF THE REDEEMING LOVE When the sin of man has reached the highest level against the heart of God, then comes the most unexpected word, " Father. Forgive them"

Jesus, Father, forgive them. When man has dared to crucify the Lord of glory. "Father, forgive them". That was the triumph of redeeming love. "Love suffers long, and is kind . . . bears all things . . . endures all things" (1 Cor. 13). "Then Jesus, Father asked for their forgiveness.

CONCLUSION:

1)- Forgiveness is putting away the hurt someone has afflicted on you

2) Forgiveness is to let everything be the way it was before the hurts.

3) Everything a human being including you and I have done to God, today Jesus let you know that you and I are forgiven.

4.) What we have done as human beings, it was true IGNORANCE.

5.) Forgiveness is divine – you have to have God in you to forgive

6) We should forgive others so that God also forgives us – FATHER FORGIVE them because they don't know what they are doing.

7.) Forgiveness is the first step toward RESTORATION – NORMALITY.

8.) THE ONLY WAY WE CAN CHANGE IS THROUGH FORGIVENESS.

9.) Jesus taught and was the EXAMPLE OF FORGIVENESS.

10.)EVERY HUMAN BEING NEEDS FORGIVENESS.

11.)THE WORK OF REDEMPTION IS BASED ON FORGIVENESS.

QUESTIONS: HAVE YOU ACCEPTED GOD'S FORGIVENESS? HAVE YOU FORGIVEN THOSE WHO HAVE OFFENED YOU? Jesus said, "Father, Forgive them, because they don't know what they are doing"

A PRAYER OF FORGIVENESS:
Dear God, I choose as an act of my will, regardless of my feelings, to forgive the persons who have wronged me. I release them, and I set myself free to your healing. With Your help, I will no longer dwell on the situation or continue to talk about it. I thank you for forgiving me as I have forgiven them. I thank you for releasing me. I ask this in Jesus' name. Amen.

Machiasport, February 20, 2010

(87)

THEME: FORMULA FOR A FELLOWSHIP WITH GOD.

Intro: The word fellowship means "things held in common." It implies

1- **God desires to have a close, personal relationship with you, where you and God stand together on common ground."** John doesn't think so! In fact, he tells us exactly how this can take place. He shows how close communion and intimate fellowship with the Father can be the normal Christian experience, instead of some mystical thing we only hear about, or see in the lives of others.

When a Christian sins, he breaks fellowship with God. But, praise God, there is a formula for restoring and then maintaining that fellowship day by day.

I share with you how you can experience this "fullness of joy"

That John refers to in verse 4. From these verses, you can

Draw near to God, and remain in sweet, wonderful fellowship with him.

FORMULA FOR FELLOWSHIP

I. v. 8, 10 WE MUST RECOGNIZE OUR SINS

If we say that we have fellowship with Him and YET walk in darkness

We lie and do not practice the truth.

TRUE FELLOWSHIP WITH GOD HINGS ON OUR ABILITY TO ADMIT OUR

SIN: (God forgives sin, but it must be admitted before receiving forgiveness)

IT IS AN ACCIDENT IN THE LIFE OF A BELIEVER. (Ill. This is BEFORE SIN CAN BE FORGIVEN, IT MUST BE SEEN AS AN AFFRONT TO GOD.

(An Attack to God -)

- SIN IS NOT A MISTAKE OR SICKNESS, SIN IS AN ATTACK A SINNER MAKES TO GOD- Matt. 19:16-22)

D. Here is the world's viewpoint concerning dealing with sin:

1. EDUCATION - Man can be taught to live without sin.
2. SCIENCE - Solve the problems and mysteries of nature and man and SET MAN FREE FROM SIN
3. SOCIOLOGY - Sin is the by-product of the environment.
4. PSYCHOLOGY - Talk about yourself long enough, focus on what you need, and eventually you can eliminate your own guilt.
5. RELIGION - Learn the doctrines, practice the rituals and do good things and feel better about yourself and God will accept you.

II. V.9 WE MUST REPENT OF OUR SIN

If we walk in the Light as He Himself is in the Light,

We have Fellowship with one another,

And the Blood of Jesus his Son cleanses us from all sin.

A. If we will recognize our sin, confess it to God, and truly repent of that sin, He will forgive us and cleanse our lives - Heb. 8:12.

B. WHAT IS REPENTENCE?

- TOTAL CHANGE OF HEART AND MIND

- CHANGE OF DIRECTION AND ACTION.

- CHANGE OF RELATIONSHIP WITH GOD/ NEIGHBOR.

REMOVED, AND REPLACED BY PEACE AND JOY..

III. v.7 WE MUST REVEAL OUR SINS If we say that we have no sin, We are deceiving ourselves and the truth is not in us.

ADAM AND EVE IN THE GARDEN

MANY BELIEVERS ARE TEMPTED TO HIDE THEIR SINS.

They have sinned and they act as if everything is all right. They are lying. They lie to themselves, they lie to others, and they lie to God. And begin to believe the lie themselves. At that point, they deny their sin and call God a liar.

NO PROSPERITY IN THIS LIFE WITH HIDDEN SIN

Pro. 28:13. SIN MUST BE BROUGHT OUT INTO THE OPEN

C. Light - Reveals error! This is why many people do not attend church regularly.

Because their sin is exposed to the light of the Word of God, the

THE HOLY SPIRIT SHOULD CONVICT US OF OUR SINS

- SIN IS AN ABOMINATION TO GOD.

IV. v.9 WE MUST RELATE OUR SINS

A. WHAT IS CONFESSION? Simply naming your sin to God, specifically, and agreeing with Him concerning the nature of that sin. (Present Tense!) Sin ought to be confessed immediately. (Ill. You wouldn't wait all day to get an eyelash out of your eye. Would you?) (Ill. A good prayer!)

B. A true Spirit filled life is not only sinless, it is also lived in close fellowship with God. (The Spiritual Rollercoaster) If we would learn the principle of instant confession, we would live more consistent lives. (People with mountains of unconfessed sin, lying like heaps of dirty laundry in the corners of their hearts.)

V. v.9   WE MUST REST IN THE LORD

IF WE CONFESS OUR SIN He is faithful and righteous to forgive us our sins and cleanse us from ALL unrighteousness. I John 1:9

THE BEST NEWS IN THE WORLD FOR THE CHRISTIANS IS THERE IS A PLACE WHERE WE CAN DEAL WITH OUR SINS, WHERE OUR GUILT CAN BE EXCHANGED WITH PEACE; JESUS OFFERS THAT PLACE FREELY THROUGH HIS BLOOD.

JESUS IS THE ANSWER:

CONCLUSION: The first step toward fellowship with God

(1) ADMIT YOUR SIN - You cannot cleanse yourself.

(2) ASK FORGIVENESS. - Jesus is faithful to forgiver and cleanse you.
Be received, forgiven, cleansed and in fellowship with him.
You have wandered far and you are carrying a load of guilt..

(3) JESUS IS WAITING FOR THE SINNERS, YOU ARE A SINNER RECEIVE GOD'S PEACE AND JOY

(4) BE IN FELLOWSHIP WITH GOD AND YOUR NEIGHBOR FROM TODAY.

Amen. Machiasport, 16, 2007

(88)

1 Corinthians.15:1-28

Text. I Cor.15:3 For what I received, I passed on to you AS OF FIRST IMPORTANCE that Christ died for our sins according to the scriptures, that he was buried, that he was raised on the third day according to the scriptures, and that he appeared to Peter and then to the twelve.

THEME: CHRIST IS RISEN FOR YOUR GOOD.

INTRODUCTION. How can you summarize your life? If I ask you to tell me in few words who you are? What will you say? If I ask you to summarize this congregation, what will you say? What about if I ask you to give me a summary of today's worship service, what will be the content of those few words I am asking you. :

DEFINITION OF A SUMMARY OR A RESUME IS A SHORT STATEMENT PRESENTING THE MAIN POINTS: SAYING IN FEW WORDS WHAT COULD HAVE BEEN SAID IN LENGTH: AN EVENT, A BOOK, AND THE LIFE OF A PERSON TELLING A STORY.

The life of Jesus can be summarized. Christianity can be summarized. In today's reading of, chapter 15 of I Corinthians we just finished reading;

we have a real summary, THE FOUNDATION OF OUR CHRISTIAN
FAITH AND BELIEF: WE CALL THAT THE GOSPEL:
I- WHAT IS THE GOSPEL? WHAT IS GOOD NEWS?
(1) CHRIST LIVED; (2) CHRIST DIED;
(3)CHRIST WAS BURIED (4) HE ROSE FROM THE DEAD,
(5) HEIS ALIVE FOREVER, (6) CHRIST IS COMING AGAIN.
ALL THISE HAPPENED ACCORDING TO THE SCRIPTURES
I Cor.15:3-8

II – THE GREATNESS OF THE RESURRESTION FROM THE
DEATH OF OUR SAVIOR JESUS CHRIST

There are certain facts which make the Resurrection among so many other
facts the greatest. Yes, the birth of Jesus is great fact; his life on earth is a
great fact; his death on the cross is a great fact; his ascension going back to
where he was in eternity is a great fact; but is resurrection from the dead is
the greatest fact for us in particular. We will demonstrate the greatness of
the resurrection: in three ways: History, promise, and hope.

1.   THE RESURRECTION IS THE GREATEST FACT IN HISTORY
(1) The Old Testament predicted the Resurrection
(2) PEOPLE AS ACTORS are named in these documents:
Adam, Eve, Abraham, David, Isaiah, Messiah, Mary, Joseph, Judas,
The 12 disciples, James, 500 followers, (I Cor.15:3-8)
Mary Magdalena, Peter, Matthew, John, Paul etc…
(3) Places where events took place are still: found in Palestine.
Jerusalem, Bethlehem, Golgotha, Gethsemane, the tomb, Mount
Olive, Nazareth
(4) Dates: His birth, of his death, of his resurrection, of his
ascension.

2. THE RESURRECTION: PROMISE MADE TO MEN

    (1) Many sinned in Adam and Even, Genesis 3:15 tells about the promise

    (2) God covenants with Israel, the promise of the Messiah in Isaiah

    (3) That promise lasted more than 6,000 years

    (4) It was made BEFORE THE CREATION OF THE WORLD.

    (5) IT IS MADE FOR EVERYONE WHO LIVED, LIVES AND WILL LIVE.

3. THE RESURRECTION: THE GREATEST HOPE TO MEN:

That those who believe in Jesus WILL LIVE AGAIN

That the IS LIFE AFTER DEATH, LIFE DOESN'T END HERE

That there is a place where we will be forever rejoicing.

That death is a passage all these make the resurrection

the cornerstone of life.

ALL THESE MAKES THE RESURRECTION THE CORNERSTONE OF LIFE:

III – WHAT IS CHRISTIANITY, OUR FAITH?

    A - WHAT CHRISTIANITY IS NOT:

    (1) CHRISTIANITY IS NOT A PHILOSOPHY.

    (2). CHRISTIANITY IS NOT IDEAS OR CREEDS

    (3) CHRISTIANITY NOT RULES AND REGULATIONS

    B- WHAT CHRISTIANITY DEFINED AS A LIFE:

A NEW LIFE IN THE BELIEVERS; THE LIFE CHRISTIN THE LIFE OF THE BELIEVERS OF HIS DEATH AND RESUREECTION THE THIRD DAY.

    (1). HE BRINGS TO THEM SALVATION

    (2) HE BRINGS FORGIVENES TO THE SINNERS

    (3) HE BRINGS THEM RECONCILIATION

(4) HE BRINGS TO THEM PEACE

(5). HE BEINGS HOPE THROUGH HIS SACRIFICE.

(6) HE BRINGS TO THEM VICTORY OVER DEATH

(7). HE BRINGSTO THEM HOPE FOR THE FUTURE

(8). HE BRINGS ETERNAL LIFE FOREVER

ALL THIS TOOK PLACE ACCORDING TO THE SCRIPTURES

B- IF THERE IS NO RESURRECTION, WHERE WILL WE BE? IF CHRIST WAS NOT RAISED FROM THE DEAD?

I Corinthians spells out who we will be without Jesus Resurrection:

(1) OUR PREACHING IS USELESS (Verse 14)

(2) OUR FAITH IS USELESS (Verse 14)

(3) WE ARE FALSE WITNESSES (Verse 15)

(4) WE ARE STILL LIVING IN OUR SINS (Verse 17)

(5) THOSE WHO HAVE DIED ARE LOST (Verse18)

(6) WE ARE THE MOST PITIED PEOPLE IN THE WORLD (Verse 19)

CONCLUSION:

WE ARE PROCLAIMING TO YOU THE GOOD NEWS:

CHRIST WHO DIED IS RISEN!

THAT GOOD NEWS IS THE GREATEST YOU NEVER HEARD:

HISTORY CONFIRMS IT

IT IS THE GREATEST PROMISE MADE TO MANKIND

IT IS THE GREATEST HOPE WE MUST HAVE AND LIVE BY

3) BECAUSE CHRIST WAS RAISED FROM THE DEAD:

(1) YOU HAVE SALVATION

(2) YOU HAVE BEEN RECONCILED WITH GOD

(3) YOU HAVE PEACE AND HOPE FOR THE FUTURE

(4) YOU HAVE VICTORY OVER DEATH

(5) ETERNAL LIFE IS YOURS NOW AND FOREVER.

QUESTIONS:

    (1)- ARE YOU STILL DOUBTING THAT CHRIST WAS RAISED FROM DEATH?

    (2)- ARE YOU STILL LIVING IN YOUR SINS?

    (3)- ARE YOU STILL LOST AND SEPARATE FROM GOD.

REJOICE WITH ALL THE BELIEVERS BECAUSE CHRIST WAS RAISED AND YOU WILL ALSO BE RAISED AND LIVE WITH HIM FOREVER. Amen

Machiasport, Easter, April 12, 2009

(89)

Readings. John 4:7-26 and 19:28-30;

Text. 129:28 Later, knowing that all was now COMPLETED, and so that the Scripture be fulfilled, Jesus said, « I AM THIRSTY «

THEME : JESUS IS THIRSTY.

INTRODUCTION- I AM THIRSTY. THIRSTY: I was born in the equatorial region, of Africa, and working under the sun makes you perspire all day long. You must drink a lot of water. After working, and working, once you sit down to rest, the first thing you will need is some fresh water to quench your thirst.

In this passage, Jesus seems to express that emptiness, that strong desire, that urge nothing can stop when it comes into our lives, except to have something in the form **of LIQUID** - It must be something running, not solid. For some, it will be water; for some, it will be wine, for some it will be soda, for some it would be whiskey, or Gin, or Vodka, Spirits. Jesus desired something, which will stop his thirst. That thirst was not physical, it was spiritual. Eternal.

The text speaks about the timing of that saying, « I AM THIRSTY ». Later, knowing that all was now completed. The question is, what had been completed before Jesus said, » I AM THIRSTY »

I – HERE ARE THE THINGS THAT TOOK PLACE AT THAT HOUR:

A – THE FORGIVENESS OF ALL SINNERS WAS COMPLETED

Jesus, before saying, « I AM THISTY, » he had already said that, FATHER, FORGIVE THEM, FOR THEY DON'T KNOW WHAT THEY DO »

(1) Forgiveness of sins committed against the person of Jesus.

(2) Forgiveness for every child born from ADAM, descendant of Adam

(3) Forgiveness for all Jews

(4) Forgiveness for all gentile

(5) Forgiveness for YOU and FOR ME present in this church today.

(6) The Criminal on the cross, said to Jesus, » Remember me when You get to your kingdom. Jesus said to him,"Today you will be with me in Paradise

B – THE ASSURANCE OF OUR PLACE IN HEAVEN WAS COMPLETED.THE DOOR WAS OPENED FOR ALL WHO REPENT FROM SIN.

You can be with Jesus, you can belong to Jesus this minute.

THIS CONDITION BECAME COMPLETED AT THAT HOUR JESUS LOOKED AT HIS MOTHER AND SAID,

Mother, here is your son, Son, and here is your mother.

C - THE PLACE TO EXPRESS OUR BROTHERLY LOVE AS AN

expression of the love we have for Jesus was complete

OF THE LOVE WE HAVE FOR JESUS WAS COMPLETE. You can't say today that you don't know how or to whom you can express the love you have for Jesus. You have your fellow believer who is a man or

a woman. THIS IS A FACT ALREADY COMPLETED. - LOVE OF NEIGHBOR.

JESUS SAID, MY GOD, MY GOD, WHY ....FORSAKEN ME?

Jesus already carries all the sins of the world, and now he has availed to all his RIGHTEOUSNESS. What is required for each one now is to receive it.

D- THE EXCHANGE OF OUR SINS WITH CHRIST'S JUSTIFICATION ON THE CROSS WAS COMPLETED AT THAT MOMENT.

II - THINGS HUMAN BEINGS SEEK TO SATISFY THEIR THIRST :

1–PEOPLE SEEK WEALTH - to be rich, to have more and more.

2–PEOPLE SEEK HONOR – that everyone bows before you

3–PEOPLE SEEK HAPPINESS THROUGH

Drugs - smoking, given themselves shots, Sex, Money, The anger, - killing,

hurting, breaking things, breaking promises, Drinking - Alcohol

PLEASURES – THE PURSUE OF HAPPINESS« Who will reach the end of it ? – Salomon said. Ecc.1 :1-11 Everything Is Meaningless

1- The words of the Teacher, Son of David, King of Jerusalem:

2- "Meaningless! Meaningless!" says the Teacher.

"Utterly meaningless! Everything is meaningless."

3- What does man gain from all his labor?

4- Generations come and generations go, but the earth remains...

5- The sun rises and the sun sets, and hurries back to where it rises.

6- The wind blows to the southland turns to the north; round and round it goes, ever returning on its course.

7- All streams flow into the sea, yet the sea is never full. to the place the streams come from, there they return again.

8- All things are wearisome, more than one can say., the eye never has enough of seeing, nor the ear its fill of hearing.

9- What has been will be again, what has been done will be done again; there is nothing new under the sun.

10- Is there anything of which one can say,

"Look! This is something new"? It was here already, long ago; it was here before our time. 11There is no remembrance of men of old, and those who follow will not remember even those who are yet to come.

III – THINGS THAT SATISFY SPIRITUAL THIRST. WHAT CHRISTIANS SHOULD BE SEEKING FOR ON THIS EARTH :

1- THE KINGDOM OF GOD. Matt 6 :33 But seek first his kingdom and his righteousness, and all these things will be given to you as well

2)- THE HOLY SPIRIT, THE SPIRIT OF GOD

3)- THE PEACE OF GOD John 14 :27 Peace I leave with you, my peace I give to you. I

do not give to you as the world does

4)- The love of God. Zeph 3:17 The Lord your God is with you.

5)- The living water – God's Word - - Psalm 119 :105 Your word is a lamp to my feet and a light for my path READ IT –

6)- MEMORIZE IT BE GUIDED BY IT - LOVE IT - DESIRE IT

IV – WHAT WILL SATISFY JESUS THIRST?
THINGS YOU AND I SHOULD DO TO SATISFY CHRIST'S THIRST:

1) That all the sinners be saved .– Rom.5 :8 when we were sinners

2)- That he changes our human nature /SPIRIT TO DOMINATE.

3)- ALL ACCEPT HIS FORGIVENESS AND RECEIVE HIM.

4)- THAT ALL HUMAN BEINGS WILL GO TO HEAVEN.

For this is good and acceptable in the sight of God our Savior: Who will have all men to be saved, and to come unto the knowledge of the truth. For there is one God, and one mediator between God and men, the man Christ Jesus.—I Timothy 2:3-5

CONCLUSION: JESUS SAID ON THE CROSS, « I am thirsty »

1)- WHAT IS YOUR GREAT DESIRE? How can you satisfy it?

2)- THINGS OF THIS WORLD WILL NEVER SATISFY YOU

3- SEEK FIRST THE KINGDOM OF GOD – and all will be yours and ours.

4- JESUS HAS OPENED ALL DOORS FOR YOUR SATISFICTION

5- The Kingdom of God – The peace of God, - The Love of God – The Living

Look! Jesus is on the Cross. He already forgave you; open thaw door of heaven for you to enter in once you have received him, and accepted him as your Redeemer. He already taught you about loving him by loving your fellow person, living the love he has loved you. Now, he is thirsty. How are you going to quench his thirst? He is waiting that you go to the cross, where he is crucified, and quench his thirst. (1) Be member of his kingdom by seeking it first; (2) by living by the peace he gives to those who follow him; (3) live

according to the Spirit, which lives in you; (4) May the Bible be your guide and counselor. (5) Be among those Jesus will present to his Father the Day of Judgment, those who will inherit the Kingdom of heaven with him forever. JESUS IS THIRSTY, SATISFY HIS THIRST TODAY. Amen
March 20/2010

(90)

Text: Readings. Deuteronomy 8:7-18; Luke 17:11-19

Text Deut. 8:18 & I Thess. 5:16-18 You shall remember(all the time) the Lord your God, for it is he who Gives you power to get wealth; that he may confirm his covenant which he swore to your fathers. ..."Rejoice always; pray without ceasing; in everything give thanks; for this is God's will for you in Christ Jesus"

THEME: LET US CELEBRATE OUR THANKS LIVING.

INTRODUCTION: This week, some of us will eat TURKEY at least twice.

We call that celebration held in the United States in November, Thanksgiving.

I - QUESTION: WHO ARE WE THANKING THIS YEAR?

SOMEONE MUST RECEIVE THANKS: - WHO IS HE/SHE/IT?

(1) TO GOD WHO BROUGHT US INTO THIS COUNTRY

(2) TO GOD WHO HAS BLESSED US BEYOND MEASURE.

(3) TO GOD WHO HAS GIVEN YOU EVERYTHING YOU HAVE.

　- **QUESTION:** What did you bring into this life
and what will you go away with when you depart from this world?

II- WHY DO WE HAVE A HARD TIME WITH EXPRESSING THANKFULNESS

Why THE NINE DID NOT RETURN TO THANK JESUS

Here follow some nine suggestions

1   The first one: to wait and see if the cure was real

2   The second: He wanted to see if the cure will last.

3   The Third was healed but he wanted to SEE JESUS LATER.

The Fourth: He thought that he never had leprosy. (He was not sick)

The Fifth: He thought that he would have gotten well anyway.

The Sixth: He gave glory and honor to the priest and not to Jesus.

The Seventh: He thought that Jesus didn't REALLY DO ANYTHING.

The Eighth: Thought that ANY RABBI COULD HAVE DONE IT.

The Ninth said that" HE WAS ALREADY MUCH IMPROVED.

QUESTION: ARE WE TOO DIFFERENT FROM THESE 9?

OUR REASONS:

(1) Myself, I went to school.

(2) Myself, I worked and did this and that and whatever.

(3) I never met God on the road or received anything from Him.

(4) If I don't, nobody else will.

QUESTIONS: Our country and Canada are the only ones who have an official "Thanksgiving Day". Now that we don't want to speak about God, WHOM ARE WE THANKING? ARE WE THANKING?

(1) Our own successes? (2) Our intelligence; (3) our technology;

(2) OURSELVES MAYBE.

III- <u>WHAT IS OUR CALLING, WHAT KIND OF LIFE SHOULD BE OURS?</u>
<u>THREE THINGS FOR OUR SPIRITUAL DISCIPLINE:</u>
I Thessalonians gives us these:
1) REJOICING ALWAYS
2) PRAYING WITHOUT CEASING
3) GIVING THANKS IN EVERYTHING

One of the most difficult things for all of us Christians, children of God, to do is to observe this command made by Paul in I Thessalonians chapter 5:16-18. It reads "Rejoice always; pray without ceasing; in everything give thanks; for this is God's will for you in Christ Jesus" These three attitudes are God's will for us:
REJOICING ALWAYS
PRAYING WITHOUT CEASING
GIVING THANKS IN EVERYTHING.

I don't know about you, I see myself falling short on all three items for Christians recommended as daily attitudes: We should always rejoice; we should always pray; we should always give thanks. According to Paul, anyone who is a true Christian is well described in these attitudes:
JOYFUL, PRAYERFUL, AND THANKFUL HEART.

A book by Ben Patterson called "He Has Made Me Glad "Would you know who the greatest saint in the world is? It is not he who prays most or fasts most, it is not he who gives most alms or is most eminent for temperance, chastity, or justice; but it is he who is always thankful to God,
(1) IF THANKFUL TO GOD, YOU WILL DO HIS WILL
(2) YOU WILL RECEIVE EVERYTHING AS AN EXPRESSION OF GOD'S GOODNESS.
(3) YOUR HEART WILL ALWAYS BE READY TO PRAISE HIM AND TURN THAT INTO HAPPINESS.

-THIS IS A DESCRIPTION OF A CHRISTIAN LIFE
-GRATEFULNESS IS A SPIRITUAL DISCIPLINE,
GRATEFULNESS IS A MATTER OF FAITH,
GRATEFULNESS IS A MATTER OF CHOICE.

CONCLUSION:

I INVITE YOU TODAY TO LIVE A THANKS LIVING LIFE
WHICH HAS THESE THREE IMPORTANT ASPECTS:

(1) ALWAYS REJOICE IN THE LORD WHO LOVES YOU.

(2) PRAY ALWAYS COUNTING HIS BLESSINGS.

(3) DISCIPLINE YOURSELF IN THANKSLIVING LIFE

-This will lead to do the Lord's will – Doing his will.

-This will be a matter of an expression of our faith in God.

-This will be an expression that we belong to the Lord.

When you leave this place today, don't celebrate thanksgiving only
in November, go and live a thanks living life for the rest of your
life thanking God your Lord

Amen. 11.21.09-

(91)

Readings: Matt.1:18-15 and Philippians 1:5-11

Text: Matt.1:20-21 but as he considered this, behold, an Angel of the Lord appeared to him in a dream, saying, "Joseph son of David, do not fear to Mary your wife, for the THAT WHICH IS CONCEIVED IN HER is of the Holy Spirit. She will bear a son and YOU SHALL CALL HIS NAME JESUS, FOR HE WILL SAVE HIS PEOPLE FROM THEIR SINS

THEME: JESUS WAS MORE THAN A PROPHET.

INTRODUCTION:

(1) WE HAVE LEARNED THAT for our salvation, we needed a Savior. When we sinned through our parents Adam and Eve in the Garden of Eden, God promised a SAVIOR, the son of a woman.

(2) WE HAVE LEARNED THAT God gave the law to the children of Israel in Sinai around 1,400 before Christ. Man could not please God and fulfill his will in order to save himself. The law became a mean to convince us from our sin. From about 750 before Christ through the prophet Isaiah, God let us know that our salvation will depend on the MESSIAH, the One he will send. We covered that part when we learned about the MESSIANIC PROPHECIES. Prophets were given the Spirit of God in order to see in advance HOW THINGS WILL EXACTLY HAPPEN.

(3) TODAY, WE WILL LEARN WHY CHRIST WAS MORE THAT A PROPHET.

CHRIST WAS MORE THAN MOHAMED, ZORUA, CHANTO, BUDDA and other founders of NON-CHRISTIAN RELIGIONS. Why can we say that.

I – CONSIDER WHAT HIS NAME WAS: Jesus was given a name. Joseph or Mary did not give him a mane as his terrestrial parents. But God, through the Angel Gabriel, recommended Joseph to give him a name. Matthew says the angel said to Joseph "YOU MUST GIVE HIM THE NAME JESUS".

(1) THE NAME JESUS in English in Hebrew language is YESHUA means "GOD IS OUR SALVATION". Matt.1:21. The Angel continues by giving the reason of that name, "BECAUSE HE WILL SAVE HIS PEOPLE FROM THEIR SINS"

(2) THE NAME CHRIST: which is a translation of Hebrew name MESSIAH means the anointed (I Kings 19:16). Jesus is our Priest (Exod.29:7) He was elected to come and take away our sins. Jesus was chosen as that descendant of DAVID SPOKEN BY THE PROPHET DANIEL in 9:25.

II – CONSIDER HIS BIRTH; THE WAY HE WAS BORN:
Luke 1:26-38

(1) Jesus was born from the Virgin Mary. Man did not take part in his birth. "The Holy Spirit will come UPON YOU and the power of the MOST HIGH WILL OVERSHADOW YOU".
Some people have questioned this birth. Was Jesus conceived in wedlock? is the man the BEARER OF SIN AND NOT THE WOMAN.

(2) Jesus was born by the POWER OF THE MOST HIGH

(3) Jesus was the SON OF GOD BY BIRTH

III – CONSIDER JESUS' DIVINITY:

(1)- ELOHIM - (GODS – in the Creation). Jesus was the one who spoke and created everything. When you read the Old Testament and God acts under names like:

(2)- ANGEL OF THE LORD APPEARED –

Abraham, - Jacob fight, to Moses in the burning bush

(3)- Not any other could save us. We couldn't do anything to save us. John 3:16 says, GOD GAVE HIS ONLY SON TO SAVE US.

(4) LOOK AT WHAT JESUS DID WHEN HE WAS HERE:

He raised the dead - he healed the sick , the lame, the blind, the deaf, the dumb, the lepers - He cast out demons, the fed the hungry, he turned water into wine, walked on water, multiplied a few pieces of bread and fish to feed the multitudes,

HIMSELF ROSE FROM THE DEAD AND HE ASCENDED BODILY TO HEAVEN.

IV – THE QUR'AN CONFIRMS THAT:

1. Jesus was born of a virgin (Sure 19:16-35)
2. He was the Messiah (Sure 4:171)
3. He was a Spirit from God (Sure 4:171)
4. He was the Word of God (Sure 4:171)
5. He was Sinless (Sure 19:19)
6. He could give life to the dead (Sure 3:49)
7. He was taken into heaven by God (Sura4:158)
8. He will come back as a sign of the Hour of Judgment (Sure 43:61)

V- CONSIDER WHAT HIS DISCIPLES SAID ABOUT HIM:

(1) OHN SAYS in John 1:1-3, and 10-12

a) In the beginning was the Word, the Word was with God and ….

b) All things were made through Him (that is the Word –Jesus)

c) Verse 12 All those who received him, who believed in his name he gave the power to become the children of God

(2) <u>PAUL IN COLOSSIANS</u> 1:15-20

a)JESUS IS THE IMAGE OF THE INVISIBLE GOD

b)He is the FIRST BORN OF ALL CREATION

c)HE IS BEFORE ALL THINGS

d) HE IS THE HEAD OF THE BODY

e) IN HIM IS THE FULNESS OF GOD.

(3) <u>PHILIPPIANS</u> 2:5-11

a) At the incarnation though in the form of God…emptied himself, taking a form of a servant, being born in the likeness of men, and being found in the human form, humbled himself and became obedient unto death

VI – <u>LET US CONSIDER HIS OWN WORDS</u> . JESUS SAID:.

(1) John 20:27-29 when THOMAS was convinced that Jesus really was raised from the dead and Thomas said "MY LORD AND MY GOD" Jesus did not deny that he was the Lord and he was God

(2) John 20:24-33 Jesus said, "I AND THE FATHER ARE ONE "

(3) When Jesus walked on the water and calmed the storm, those who were with him in the boat said to him "Truly you are the Son of God" Matt. 14:33

(4) Simon Peter made this confession about him: YOU ARE THE CHRIST, THE SON OF THE LIVING GOD" Jesus said to him "Blessed are you, Simon son of Jonah for this was not revealed to you by man, but by my Father in heaven. Matt.16:16-17.

Isaiah 9:6 gives us Jesus' names:

He will be called WONDERFUL, COUNSELOR, MIGHTY GOD, EVERLASTING FATHER, PRINCE OF PEACE.

CONCLUSION:

The one who is coming; the one who is coming to be born our Savior, our Messiah, and our Redeemer is the one who was promised. He is greater than all the prophets of the Old Testament; He is greater than all MUHAMED, BUDDA, CHANTO, ZORUA, and any other Non-Christian religion in the world.

(1) HIS NAMES JUSTIFY THAT: Jesus, the Savior, Christ the Anointed, the priest

(2) HIS BIRTH JUSTIFIES IT: The power of God conceived him; He was born from a virgin; He was the Son of God

(3) HIS DIVINITY JUSTIFIES IT: He is part of the Trinity; He was before the creation of the world. He was God. God gave his Son to be our Savior and Lord.

(4) The QUR'AN CONFIRMS IT-

(5) HIS DISCIPLES JUSTIFY IT: He was the Son of the living God

(6) HIMSELF SAID THAT: He was one with his Father.

QUESTION: DO YOU BELIEVE WHOLE HEARTLY THAT JESUS IS YOUR LORD AND THE ONLY ONE WHO CAN SAVE YOU FROM YOUR SINS? Amen

November 29, 2009.

(92)

Romans 5:1-21.

THEME: CONSEQUENCES OF OUR JUSTIFICATION.

I – THE FRUITS OF OUR JUSTIFICATION ARE

(1) We have peace with God;

(2) We have gained access to the grace of God;

(3) We rejoice in the hope of the glory of God.

IT IS BECAUSE, WE HAVE PEACE WITH GOD, THAT WE HAVE GAINED ACCESS TO HIS GRACE, AND THAT WE REJOICE IN THE HOPE OF GOD'S GLORY.

II – THE FRUITS OF OUR STAND IN GRACE NOW ARE:

(1) Sufferings; (2) Perseverance; (3) Christian Character; and (4) Hope

1-OUR POSITION AS BELIEVERS

A. Our Position Declared - Paul says that we who have believed have been "justified". This is a word that many do not fully understand. Basically, it means "to count someone righteous." It means "to reckon, to account, to judge, to treat, or to look upon as righteous." It does not mean to make righteous! It does mean that we are treated like we were righteous.

B. Our Position Described - How did this great miraculous and fantastic justification come about in your life and mine? By faith! We didn't earn it! We didn't deserve it! All we did was take God at His Word concerning the Person and Work of the Lord Jesus and God justified us by faith!
I. Our Position As Believers

II. V. 1b-2 OUR POSSESSIONS AS BELIEVERS:
A. V. 1b We Possess Acceptance - According to Paul, salvation brings with it peace with God! This is a truth that can hardly be understood by our mortal minds! You see, every lost person is the enemy of God, Rom. 8:7. But, when that lost person turns to Jesus Christ by faith, God declares an end to the hostilities! God declares peace. He then brings that person into a right relationship with Himself. When Jesus is trusted by faith, that person enjoys immediate peace with God. What does this mean?
1. God's wrath is turned away - Rom. 5:9.
2. Heaven is satisfied - 1 John 2:2
3. Old enemies have been reconciled - 2 Cor. 5:18
Colossians 1:20, "And, having made peace through the blood of his cross, by him to reconcile all things unto himself; by him, I say, whether they be things in earth, or things in heaven.")
B. V. 2a We Possess Access - This verse teaches us the truth that through Jesus Christ, we have direct access to God Himself. The word "access" means "to enter the presence of the king." Through Jesus, we have the right to enter into the very presence of the God of Heaven without fear! We have access to the Heavenly Father!
have no trouble entering the presence of the Father!)
C. V. 2b We Possess Assurance - Not only is there peace with God and access into God presence, but the believer also enjoys blessed, deep-settled assurance of salvation. Notice that the assurance we have is two-fold.

<u>1. Assurance Here - Notice the phrase</u>, "grace wherein we now stand." The word "stand" carries the idea of permanence, of being firmly fixed and immovable. Basically, this verse teaches us that we are absolutely secure in the Lord Jesus Christ. In other words, this verse is all about our eternal security as believers.

(The eternal security of the believer is a doctrine that many do not hold to this evening. Many people prefer to believe that a person can be saved and then, somehow, they can lose their salvation and need to be saved all over again. These folks laugh at us Bible believers who affirm the security of the believer. And, one of the main problems they express with the doctrine is that it leads to loose living among many who profess to be eternally saved. Sadly, they are right! Many use the eternal security of the believer as a license to commit sin. However, the person who lives such a life neither understands eternal security, nor does he understand salvation! Our security in Christ leads the genuine believer to live a clean, holy life. A life of gratitude to the One Who paid the ultimate price to provide salvation in the first place.)

<u>NOTE:</u> Romans 8:31-34. These verses tell us that the highest court in the universe has declared the believer to be justified. Where is the court that can over turn that verdict?)

There is always someone who wants to ask what if this or what if that. Well, regardless of the if, the child of God is still secure in Jesus! Notice the following:

1. What if I deny Him? - 2 Tim. 2:13

2. What if I cannot hold out? - Phil. 1:6; Jude 24; Gal. 3:3

3. What if I sin after I am saved? - Col. 2:13-14; Rom. 5:20; 1 John 1:9

4. What if it is you that are wrong? - John 6:37

III. V. 3-5 OUR PRIVILEGES AS BELIEVERS

We are saved and we are secure, but right now, we live in a world of trials and tribulations. We need help tonight in these areas as well. Notice some of the great privileges that are ours as believers in Jesus Christ.)

A. V.3a The Ability To Rejoice In Trouble - Paul says that the Christian can rejoice in the bad times of life. Why is this true? Because of the little word "knowing". When the trials of life descend, the true believer knows that God is working out His will in our lives and is attempting to produce in us a state of Christ likeness. God is trying to make us like Jesus.

(We can rejoice in trouble if we will remember that every trial is a blessing from the very hand of God, Rom. 8:28. That it will produce in us more of the image of Jesus. That when we have been chosen to suffer for Him, He is merely helping us become more like Him. With that in mind, it is easier to endure the difficult days.)

B. V. 3b-5a The Ability To Recognize Our Troubles - In this section, Paul tells us all about the benefits derived from the "pressures" of life. Note the progression mentioned in these verses.

1. Tribulation - Pressure
2. Patience - Endurance
3. Experience - Proven Character or Maturity
4. Hope - The confident expectation that we will not be disappointed. The road to maturity is paved with struggle!"

Just as any growing saint of God.

1. ASK ABRAHAM and he will point to Mt. Moriah.
2. ASK JACOB and he will point to a pillow of stone.
3. ASK JOSEPH and he will point to a Egyptian prison.
4. ASK MOSES and he will point to the backside of the desert.
5. ASK HEBREWS children and they will point to a fiery furnace. MT. SINAI and 40 YEARS IN THE DESERT

6. ASK DANIEL and he will point to a DEN OF LIONS.

7. ASK PETER and he will point to HIS THREE DENIALS

8. ASK JOHN and he will point to Patmos.

9. ASK ALL THE BELIEVERS WHO HAVE RECEIVED JESUS, THEY will tell you that "God's blessings are poured from a bitter cup!" - THE CROSS, "YOU WILL KEEP IN PERFECT PEACE HIM WHOSE MIND IS STEADFAST, BECAUSE HE TRUSTS IN YOU.", Isa. 26:3.)

CONCLUSION: ARE YOU SAVED? DO YOU TRULY BELIEVE THAT THERE IS NO MORE CONDEMNATION FOR YOU? IF YES.

BE IN PEACE WITH YOUR GOD.

KNOW THAT YOU HAVE GAINED ACCESS TO HIS GRACE

THAT YOU REJOICE IN THE HOPE OF THE GLORY OF GOD TO COME THEREFORE:

1) YOU SHOULD REJOICE IN YOUR TURBILATION

2) BEING PERSEVERANT

3) CULTIVATING A CHRISTIAN CHARACTER

4) LIVING IN GOD'S ETERNAL HOPE – YOU WILL NEVER BE DISAPPOINTED.

Machiasport Oct. 5, 2008

(93)

John 21:15-17

"So when they had finished breakfast, Jesus said to Simon Peter, "Simon, son of John, do you love me more than these?" He said to Him, "Yes, Lord; you know that I love you." He said to him, "Tend My lambs." 16 He said to him again a second time, "Simon, son of John, do you love me?" He said to Him, "Yes, Lord; you know that I love you." He said to him, "Shepherd My sheep." 17 He said to him the third time, "Simon, son of John, do you love me?" Peter was grieved because He said to him the third time, "Do you love me?" And he said to Him, "Lord, You know all things; you know that I love you." Jesus *said to him, "Tend My sheep."

THEME: DO YOU LOVE JESUS? DO I LOVE JESUS?

Introduction: This important Question Jesus asked Peter, after 2,000 years, is still asked to everyone who is called to be a Peter in his community. This question is yours this morning and tries to answer it personally.

In Greek in the Bible, there are three words for love: Eros, pile, and agapao

Eros is generally known as physical love

Phileo is brotherly love

Agape is generally known as divine love

Three times Jesus commissioned Peter to care for the flock:

Feed My lambs; (v. 15); Boske ta arnion mou

Take care of My sheep (v. 16); poimane ta probata mou

Feed My sheep (v. 17). Boske ta probata mou

In Jesus' three questions of love (agapas, agapas, and phileis).

Perhaps the most important of all questions: "Do you love me?".

I - JESUS USED TWO KINDS OF WORDS FOR LOVE:

1st time "AGAPAS ME PLEON TOUTOWN? Verse 15

    PETER ANSWERED USING FILO SE (I love you)

2nd time "AGAPAS ME. (Do you love me) Verse 16 Do you love me?

3rd time FELEIS ME (Do you love me?) Verse 17

PANTA SU OIDAS, SU GINOSKEIS OTI FILO SE. GINOSKO= perceive, find out, realize, notice, understand, comprehend,, come to the point to know someone.

OIDAS = VIDEO knowledge. Everything you know that

II – WHAT IS PARTICULAR ABOUT THIS QUESTION:

THIS QUESTION IS PERSONAL:

Jesus is asking Peter in a personal level IF HE LOVES HIM.

Not Thomas, Not the world, No John and Matthew.

Jesus wanted to know HOW MUCH PETER LOVED HIM

He simply asked Peter, "Do you love me?" "Do I love Jesus Christ?"

The love that your family, friends, or church has for Him will.

IT IS NOT ABOUT THIS WORSHIP, THIS CHURCH, THAT PERSON. IT IS ABOUT HIM. DO YOU LOVE HIM?

THIS QUESTION IS CENTRAL

He did not ask ABOUT PETER CONFESSION

HE DID NOT ASK ABOUT WHY HE DENIED HIM.

Christ might have asked, "Simon, Son of Jonah, have you had any extraordinary supernatural experiences?"

Peter could have responded, "Of course, I have walked on the sea, cast out devils, etc.

A hypocrite may have a good profession of faith, have been baptized, hold a church office, and a myriad of other external privileges.

THE NATURE OF THIS QUESTION IS ACTIVE:

NOT JUST THE PROFESSION OF FAITH merely a profession of Peter's

NOT JUST THE STANDING IN THE GROUP OF DISCIPLES, ONE OF Peter's love: "Peter, if you love me, feed my sheep."

BUT BEING ACTIVE NOT AND THEN:

Matt. 22:37-40, "And He said to him, "'You shall love the Lord your God with all your heart, and with all your soul, and with all your mind.' 38 "This is the great and foremost commandment. 39 "The second is like it, 'You shall love your neighbor as yourself.' 40 "On these two commandments depend the whole Law and the Prophets."

HE IS LOOKING FOR THE FRUIT: Gal. 5:22-23, "But the fruit of the Spirit is love, joy, peace, patience, kindness, goodness, faithfulness, 23 gentleness, self-control; against such things there is no law."

God is love and the Christian is to show Love.... But first... you must love Jesus.

You cannot truly love your brother or sister if you do not truly love Jesus. He died for you and freed you from sin. He showed his love for you by dying for you.

Do you love Jesus?

How is it manifested in your life?

III- WHAT LOVE QUESTION REQUIRES OF US:
LOVING JESUS REQUIRES RESPONSE:
- WE LOVE HIM BECAUSE HE FIRST LOVED US. I John 4:19
- OUR LOVE IS BASED ON HIS LOVE WHICH IS APAPE, NOT FILEO 2 Cor.5:14-15

1) LOVING JESUS REQUIRES BELIEVING
2) LOVING AND BELIEVING SHOULD GO HAND IN HAND. WE LOVE HIM THOUGH WE HAVE NOT SEEN HIM. I Peter 1:7
3) LOVING JESUS REQUIRES SINCERITY. Eph. 6:24 BE SINCERE IN YOUR LOVE. II Cor. 8:8.
4) LOVING JESUS MAKES HIM SUPREME Mat.10:37

   He who loves his father or mother more than me is not worthy of me; and he that loves his son or daughter more than me is not worthy of me.

   -CHRIST MUST BE THE FIRST IN OUR LOVE. Col. 1:18
5) OVING JESUS REQUIRES OBEDIENCE. John 14:15

   If you love me KEEP MY COMMANDMENTS.
6) LOVING JESUS REQUIRES HUMINITY:
7) LOVING JESUS REQUIRES FAITHFULLNESS:

   Jesus was looking for a faithful Peter who is going to continue his ministry of FEEDING HIS, AND CARING FOR HIS SHEEP

CONCLUSION

IF WE LOVE JESUS, LET US DEMONSTRATE THAT LOVE
(1) RESPONSIBLY, (2) BELIEVINGLY, (3) SINCERELY, (4) SUPREMLY,
(5) OBEDIENTLY, (6) HUMBLY, (7) and FAITHFULLY.
QUESTION: DO YOU LOVE JESUS, TAKE CARE AND FEED HIS
SHEEP.

Machiasport, 4, 20, 2008

(94)

Reading: Psalm 100:1-5 Hymns:341 " Come Thou Almighty King"
#343 "Sing Praise to God Who Reigns Above"; 495 " It Is Well with my
Soul"

THEME: WHAT TO BRING TO CHURCH.

INTRODUCTION: Today, people bring many things in their worship
services:
   (1) Some bring snack, (2) candy and toys toys to entertain the kids(3)
books to read for boring sermons (4) some file their nails, (5) some bring
                    Bibles they never open.
PSALM 100 TELLS US WHAT THE TRUE WORSHIPPER HERE
ON EARTH AND IN HEAVEN SHOULD BRING– THE KIND OF
WORSHIP THE SAINTS WILL WHEN THE LORD JESUS WILL
COME BACK.

IT WILL BE THE GLORIOUS DAY WHEN THE TRUE CHURCH
WILL WORSHIP THE LORD OF LORDS AND KING OF KINGS...
Heb. 10:25. With that in mind, let it be said that this Psalm tells us exactly
what everyone ought to bring to church when they come. Let's look at that
together this morning.

LET US LEARN TODAY, WHAT EACH ONE SHOULD BRING TO CHURCH:

I. V. 1-2 BRING THE RIGHT SPIRIT. Verses 1-2

A. V. 1 A Shouting Spirit –

We are told to "Make a joyful noise unto the LORD."

WHAT THAT MEANS TO MAKE A JOYFUL NOISE?

(1) SING TO THE LORD

(2). "Joyful". - SING TO THE LORD WITH JOY.

(3) TELL GOD WHO HE IS FOR YOU- LET HIM KNOW

(4) "Noise". – RAISE YOUR VOICE – CRY TO THE LORD

CONCLUSION: PARTICIPATE IN WORSHIP SRRVICE

(Ill. Psa. 40:1-3

B. V. 2a SERVE THE LORD – HAVE A SERVING SPIRIT-

(1) BE IN BONDAGE WITH THE LORD

(2) FEEL TO BE CALLED TO BE HERE.

- THE WORSHIP IS THE TIME YOU BRING YOUR GIFT TO HIM WITH GLADNESS

II. V. 3 BRING THE RIGHT SUBMISSION

A. SUBMIT TO THE PERSON OF GOD

(1) KNOW THAT THE LORD IS GOD-

(a) HE IS HERE - HE IS HOLY - HE IS OMNIPOTENT

HE IS PRESENT HERE –

HE IS THE ONLY ONE YOU WORSHIP HERE.

B. BE SUBMISSIVE TO HIS PURPOSE – GOD MADE US

"Made" "to take some material and fashion something new out of it!"

WE WERE MADE ANEW IN JESUS CHRIST

1 Cor. 15:10; John 15:5 .

- GOD SAVED US IN JESUS CHRIST FOR A PURPOSE
THAT WE SERVE HIM AND HIM ALONE, Eph. 2:10;
James 2:18 . He has a plan for your life.
HE WANTED TO USE YOU; THAT'S WHY HE SAVED YOU
AND ME.

C. BE SUBMIVIVE TO HIS PROMISE –
WE ARE THE SHEEP OF HIS PASTURE Psa. 23. "The LORD is my Shepherd."
HE IS OUR GOD - HE LOVES US VERY MUCH.

III. V. 4-5 BRING THE RIGHT SACRIFICE
Heb. 9:7. Thank God, we do not have to offer a blood sacrifice this morning!
Jesus Christ has already taken care of that forever, Heb. 10:10-14.
THERE IS STILL A SACRIFICE EACH ONE OF US SHOULD BRING-

- NOT MONEY - your tithes and offerings!
- NOT ATTENDANCE! Yes, many people is good
- THAT SACRIFICE IS YOURSELF:
- A PRAISING HEART TO THE LORD - "praise.")
"Enter into His gates with thanksgiving and into His courts with praise: Be thankful unto Him and bless His Name."

1. GOD'S HOUSE IS A PLACE OF THANKSGIVING
2. GOD'S HOUSE IS A PLACE OF PRAISES
    (a) HE INVITE US TO COME TO HIS PRESENCE
    (b) HE CALLS US TO ENTER HIS "GATES"
    © WE ARE FREE TO ENTER HIS COURTS.

ONE CONDITION: IT SHOULD BE WITH PRAISES:
THE PSALMIST IS CHALLENGING US TO BE THANKFUL TO
THE LORD.

LET US BRING THE RIGHT SACRIFICE TO THE LORD
TODAY!

6. Verse 5 - THREE REASONS TO PRAISES GOD FOR:

A. <u>PRAISE HIM FOR HIS GOODNESS</u> – HE IS "good, pleasant, beautiful, delightful, glad, joyful, precious, correct and righteous." Everything God does is an expression of His goodness! We can praise our God because He is good! No matter what happens in our life, God is always good to us! No matter how things turn out, God is still good! THEREFOR PRAISE HIM FOR HIS GOODNESS

B. <u>PRAISE HIM FOR HIS GRACE</u> –

Next we are told that God's "mercy is everlasting."

- DO NOT FORGET WHAT YOU DESERVE" - DEATH!

C. <u>PRAISE HIM FOR HIS GUARANTEE TO YOU</u> –

- HIS TRUTH IS FOR ALL GENERATIONS

"Truth endured to all generations."

WHAT HE HAS PROMISED, HE WILL ACCOMPLISH IT

CONCLUSION:

- WHAT ARE YOU BRINGING TO CHURCH TODAY?

DO YOU KNOW NOW WHAT YOU SHOULD ALWAS BRING TO
CHURCH?

1) BRING A RIGHT SPIRIT.

2) BE PART OF THE WORSHIPPERS SINGING TO GOD.

3) KNOWING THE ONE YOU WORSHIP – THE LORD YOUR
GOD.

4) BE SUBMISSIVE TO HIS PURPOSE

5) BE SUBMISSIVE TO HIS PROMISE – TO YOUR SHEPHERD

6) BRING THE RIGHT SACRIFICE TO HIM

7) PRAISE HIM:

    (1) FOR HIS GOODNESS TO YOU

    (2) PRAISE HIM FOR HIS GRACE TO YOU

    (3) PRAISE HIM FOR THE GUARANTEE HE HAS GIVEN

    - HIS TRUTH IS FOR ALL GENERATIONS.   Amen.

Machiasport, Sept. 7th, 2008

(95)

Reading: Romans 5:1-11

Text. Rom.5:6-8 YOU SEE, AT JUST THE RIGHT TIME, when we were STILL POWERLESS, CHRIST DIED FOR THE UNGODLY. Very rarely will anyone die for a righteous man, though for a good man someone might possibly dare to die. BUT DEMONSTRATES HIS OWN LOVE FOR US IN THIS: WHILE WE WERE STILL SINNERS, CHRIST DIED FOR US .

THEME: YES! ALL THIS WAS DONE JUST FOR ME, THE SINNER.

INTRODUCTION This passage of Scripture joins others like Isaiah 53 ; Psalm 23; Hebrews 11 ; Philippians 4 ; and John 3 in being among the greatest in the Word of God. All these passages that I have mentioned, as well as others, have long brought comfort to the hearts of men.

In this passage, we hear about the BENEFITS THE NEW BORN IN CHRIST, HAS FROM GOD; PREVILAGES, THE GREAT PROVISIONS WHICH HAVE COME TO US THROUGH THE DEATH OF JESUS ON THE CROSS HERE IS WHAT PAUL SAYS IN ROMAN 5:8

BUT DEMONSTRATED HIS OWN LOVE FOR US IN THIS: WHILE WE WERE STILL SINNERS, CHRIST DIED FOR US .

REMEMBER:

EVERYTHING CHRIST DID WAS FOR US, SINNERS.

I – HOW DOES THE BIBLE DEFINE SINNERS? WHO IS A SINNER ACCORDING TO THE BIBLE?

1) - V. 6-10 ANY PERSON LIVING IN A HOPELESS CONDITION PAUL QUALIFIES THAT CONDITION WITH FOUR WORDS:

1) WITHOUTH STRENGHT, Verse 6, -

    (a) HE IS WEAK, (b) POWERLESS, (c) HELPLESS

2) UNGODLY, Verse 6.

    (a) WITHOUT THE FEAR OF GOD

    (b) LIVING AS GOD DOESN'T EXISTS

3) SINNER Verse 8.

    (a) ALWAYS MISSING THE MARK,

    (b) DOING WRONG THINGS

4) ENEMIES. Verse 10.

    (a) ADVERSARIES, (b) LIARS

CONCLUSION:

    THIS IS WHO WE ARE WITHOUT JESUS IN US.

    THIS IS WHAT MAN IS WITHOUT GOD IN HIM

II. V. 6-8 HOW DID JESUS REACT IN HIS MISERY, WITH THE SINFUL, THE WEAKED, THE UNGODLY? WHAT DOES THE BIBLE SAY?

A- HE BECAME COMPASSIONATE: - VERSES 6 and 7 .

YOU SEE, AT JUST THE RIGHT TIME, WHEN WE WERE STILL POWERLESS, CHRIST DIED FOR THE UNGODLY. Very rarely will anyone die for a righteous man, though for a good man someone might possibly dare to die.

(1) HIS COMPASSION EXCEEDED THE LOVE OF MAN:

No one in this world would do what Christ did for us.

ILLUSTRATION: Two miners were trapped in a cave-in mine. They had two oxygen masks, but one was damaged. Only one of these men would be able to get out alive. One of the miners, a single man, handed the good mask to the other miner and said, "Here, you take it. You've got a wife and children. I don't have anybody. I can go. You've got to stay."

JESUS MADE A COURAGEOUS SACRIFICE FOR US. Human love has its limits; THANK GOD! HIS LOVE IS LIMITLESS.

(2) V. 8 HIS COMPASSION DEMONTRATED GOD'S LOVE FOR US:

1) FOR WHAT REASON JESUS LEFT HEAVEN?

2) FOR WHAT REASON DID HE LIVE ON EARTH FOR 33?

3) FOR WHAT REASON DID HE DIE ON THE CROSS?

4) FOR WHAT OTHER REASON DID HE SEND THE HOLY SPIRIT?

5) FOR WHAT REASON DID HE LOVE HIS CHURCH AND THE BIBLE?

6) FOR WHAT REASON IS HE AT THE RIGHT HAND OF GOD NOW?

7) FOR WHAT REASON IS HE COMING AGAIN?

JUST BECAUSE HE LOVES THE SINNER, YOU and I.

III. V. 9-11 OUR MATCHLESS PERFECTION AFTER GOD HAS LOVED US SO MUCH, AFTER CHRIST HAS VDONE WHAT HE HAS DONE FOR US, WQHAT IS OUR MATCHLESS CONDITION NOW? WHO ARE YOU NOW?

IN THESE VERSES (9-11), PAUL TELLS US WHO WE HAVE BECOME THROUGH THE SACRIFICE OF JESUS CHRIST.

1). V. 9a WE ARE JUSTIFIED –SINNER, YOU ARE NOT GUILTY!

2). V. 9b WE ARE PROTECTED:
SINNER YOU ARE SAVED FROM GOD'S WRATH!
Read John 3:36 . and Eph. 2:3.

3). V. 10a WE HAVE PEACE WITHIN US AND WITH GOD:
SINNER, YOU ARE RECONCILED WITH YOUR GOD!
Read, Heb. 13:5

4). V. 10b WE ARE PRESERVED:
SINNER, YOU HAVE ETERNAL LIFE!

5). WE ARE DEFENDED:
SINNER YOU HAVE AN ADVOCATE IN HEAVEN!
Jesus INTERCEEDS FOR YOU NOW. Heb. 7:25 -

6) V. 11a NOW WE LIVE IN THE TIME OF CELEBRATION
SINNERS, LET US REJOICE THROUGH OUR LOVED JESUS CHRIST, BY WHOM WE HAVE RECEIVED ATONEMENT!

7). 11b WE LIVE A LIFE OF GREAT PREVILEGE: -
SINNER, YOU HAVE BEEN ATONED.
YOUR SINS HAVE BEEN FORGIVEN,
YOU LIVE NOW CLOSER TO GOD THAN EVER BEFORE!

CONCLUSION: GOD DID ALL THIS FOR YOU, THE SINNER

1) **HOW FAR DO YOU STILL FEEL TO BE FROM GOD?**
2) ARE YOU STILL FEELING GUILTY?
3) **GOD'S LOVE HAS SURPASSED HUMAN'S LOVE.**
4) JUST ACCEPT WHAT CHRIST DID FOR YOU.
5) FIND PEACE AND REJOICE IN HIM.

HE DID ALL THIS FOR YOU. FIND PEACE. YOU ARE HIS CHILD.

Amen.

(96)

John 15:1-11

Text: John 15:1-2 "I am the true vine, and my Father is the gardener. HE CUTS OFF EVERY BRANCH IN ME THAT BEARS NO FRUIT, WHILE EVERY BRANCH THAT DOES BEAR FRUIT, HE PRUNES SO THAT IT WILL BE EVEN MORE FRUITFUL."

Listen to what the Father does to ALL THE BRANCHES:

(1)-Every branch in Jesus that does not bear fruit God cut it off
        WHILE, at the same time he cuts this one off

(2)-Every branch that bears fruit = GOD, THE OWNWER prunes it

    WHY DOES HE PRUNE THOSE WHO BEAR FRUIT?

    ANSWER: SO THAT THEY WILL BEAR MORE FRUITFUL

THEME: JESUS, THE TRUE VINE; WE ARE THE BRANCHES.

INTRODUCTION: Jesus loved using illustrations or figures of speech in order to make sense to everyone who listens to him.

(1) When speaking to shepherds, he uses sheep, goats, and shepherds

(2) When speaking to the construction builders, he uses, cornerstone, houses.

(3) Speaking to the Pharisees and Sadducees, he uses law, cleanliness', sin, justice, judge.

(4) When speaking to the farmers, he uses seed, fields, harvests, weeds, wheat, good soil and bad soil. In this text: Vine, branches, Gardener,

I am sure that even though we are not farmers here in Downeast, we know what a vine, a fruit, a branch, the gardener, and good fruit are because we all have little gardens during summer and we use fertilizers.

I – THE KINGDOM OF GOD , THE CHURCH OF JESUS

A. Jesus came to die for us on the cross in order to create a new race, a new kingdom we call the Church. All the believers from over the years and from all generations and the entire world from the day of PENTECOST are members of that Church.

(1) JESUS IS THE VINE –Jesus said "I AM THE VINE "

(2) MEMBERS OF THE CHURCH ARE THE BRANCHES.

Jesus said –"YOU ARE THE BRANCHES". Who are "YOU?" Jesus is talking about all those who have, who are and who will believe in him as their Savior and Redeemer. He was referring to the believers of all time, all generations, and all churches who claim to be saved by the work he did on the cross.

First Question: IS JESUS YOUR SAVIOR? If your answer is "YES"
Question 2: ARE YOU ATTACHED AS A BRANCH TO JESUS?

II – THE RELATIONSHIP =THE VINE AND THE BRANCH:

1. <u>DEPENDENCY:</u> A branch no life if not attached to the vine
No Attachment to the Vine = NO LIFE.

Believers should know deep down in their hearts that a minute the thought of separation," freedom from the vine" leads to their death.

<u>QUESTIONS</u>: Do you really depend on Jesus this way?
Do you really understand that no Christ, no life?
Do we really know that living without Christ is a dead life?

2. <u>ABIDING IN CHRIST AND CHRIST IN US</u>: Christianity is not a religion because there in no separation between the worshipper and the one who is worshipped. Christ is in us and we are in Christ. We are not Christ and Christ ABIDES IN US. He is IN US; he is WITH US. The blood or the Spirit of Christ IN US.

- A NEW LIFE IN JESUS: Jesus has come to give us life.

He has come to RESTORE THE LIFE WE LOST

HE IS THE SOURCE OF LIFE IN US.
WE HAVE PASSED FROM DEATH TO LIFE IN HIM...

III THERE IS AN EXPECTATION FROM EACH BRANCH:

A-HERE IS WHERE WE SEE SOMEONE ELSE, THE GARDENER

The job done by Jesus was not for nothing. The Salvation you received is not for nothing. God is expecting something from you: glorification The branch must BEAR FRUIT. God is glorified through our fruit...

ILLUSTRATION: I have been disappointed because it rained a lot this summer. Those who planted gardens, myself with my flowers are disappointed. Nothing is doing well. In Africa , I know some cocoa farmers who will start borrowing money from buyers because they believe that their plantations are going to produce good crops. They can tell you that by looking at the leaves,

They can tell you so by looking at the buds;
They can tell you that just by looking at the color of the plants

EXPECTATIONS FROM YOUR MASTER.
THERE IS AN EXPECTATION FROM YOUR REDEEMER.
THAT IS BEARING FRUIT:
B-WHAT FRUIT IS EXPECTED FROM US? THE FRUIT OF THE SPIRIT:

Love, joy, peace, patience, kindness, goodness, faithfulness, gentleness, self-control…" Our relationship with Jesus produces such fruit.

Fruit is good, tasty, and flavorful. The same is true with those nine virtues of the spirit; the fruit of the spirit sweetens life.

ALL CHRISTIANS FROM ALL GENERATIONS AND IN ALL CHURCHES MUST PRODUCE THE FOLLOWING FRUIT:

ILLUSTRATION:
If I say Orange , Apple, Pineapple, Banana, - Can you call apple " banana?"
Is it possible that you can call orange "tangerine?" - Love is love; Goodness is goodness,

Faithfulness is faithfulness; self-control is self-control. These are what God is expecting from you and me. This is what rejoices our Father who is in heaven.

(1) GOOD WORKS-
- DON'T SAVE BUT SHOW THAT YOU ARE SAVED
- FAITH WITHOUT WORK IS DEAD" (2: 18, 26, ESV).
- SOMETHING WILL HAPPEN IF THERE IS NO FRUIT:
Jesus says every branch which doesn't produce fruit will be cut off
(2) That branch will be BURNED (15: 1, 6).

C- THAT EXPECTATION IS MEASURED BY WHAT YOU DO
IF YOU PRODUCE LESS, HE WILL PRUNE YOU.
(1) IF YOU DON'T PRODUCE FRUIT –
The Master of the vine, the Lord God will CUT YOU OFF.
(2) IF YOU DON'T PRODUCE ENOUGH –
The Master, the Vineyard, the Lord God will prune you.

D- DISCIPLINE IS GOD'S PRUNING
-Hebrews "discipline"
-The Church disciplines those who are not producing fruit

Fruit of the Spirit; from Good work.

The Church is called to PRUNE even those who produce so that they will PRODUCE MUCH. –
LESSON HERE: God is expecting you to do more and more and more and more until the day you will see him. Don't stop and do more of whatever you do to glorify the Lord in your life.

IV – REMEMBER, SOMEONE IS GLORIFIED IN YOU:

GOD TAKES GLORY FROM WHOM PRODUCES FRUIT.

WE ARE CREATED TO GLORIFY THE LORD ALL OUR LIFE.

CONCLUSION:

(1) GOD THE SON IS THE VINE

(2) YOU ARE THE BRANCH – THE CHURCH OF JESUS-

(3) GOD THE FATHER IS THE VINEYARD – THE GARDENER.

QUESTIONS:

(1) DO YOU DEPEND, IN RELATIONSHIP WITH THE VINE?

(2) ARE YOU ALIVE OR DEAD IN YOUR RELATIONSHIP ?

(3) ARE YOU CUT OFF FROM THE VINE? IF " NO ".

(4) ARE YOU PRODUCING MORE AND MORE FRUIT?

IS YOUR FATHER GLORIFIED WITH YOUR FRUIT?

Machiasport, Aug. 16, 2009

(97)

Reading of the Scripture John 6:22-40

Text. John 6:26, 35.Jesus answered, "I tell you the truth, you are looking for me, not because you saw miraculous signs but because you ate the loaves and had your fill. Do not work for food that spoils, but for food that endures unto eternal life, which the Son of Man will give you....Then Jesus declared, "I am the bread of life. He who comes to me will never hunger, and he who believes in me will never be thirsty.

THEME: JESUS IS THE BREAD OF LIFE: WHAT IS YOUR FOOD?

INTRODUCTION: Tell me what will happen if a baby is born and is not fed? No living thing can go without FOOD AND DRINK.
The question I want you to answer this morning is what is your food and drink

I -THE CONTEXT OF THIS TEXT: Jesus fed the people the day before. The next day they were looking for him and many followed him taking some boats from Tiberias to Capernaum searching for Jesus. When he saw them, Jesus said, "I tell you the truth, you are looking for me, not because you saw miraculous signs but because you ate the loaves and had your fill.

Do not work for food that spoils, but for food that endures to eternal life, which the Son of Man will give you."

II - SIGNIFICANCE OF BREAD – Bread is associated:

WITH LIFE - WITH HEALTH, WITH NOURISHMENT, and WITH PROSPERITY

You and I we live for LIFE, for Health, for our Nourishment and for Prosperity.

III –WHAT WE SHOULD NOT WORK FOR:

Each one of us now or later spends all his or her life working. Some leave their home early in the morning; some by night; some late or the afternoon. All of us we have to have what we call SOURCE OF INCOME. Some have money in the banks, some have invested. YOU HAVE TO HAVE MONEY. YOU HAVE TO HAVE WORK. If you don't work as in Africa and many underdeveloped countries, you have to do something in order to make a living.

A – WHY DO PEOPLE WORK? What are you working for?
1) To put money in the bank
2) To have a beautiful home
3) To drink and do drugs.
4) To gamble
5) To EAT

B- WHAT JESUS SAYS ABOUT THAT WORK.
1) That food DOESN'T LAST - it spoils

Application: Tell me whether any of these will last forever.

IV – WHO IS JESUS IN THIS TEXT?

1) Verse 27 - He gives the MEAT THAT LEADS TO ETERNAL LIFE
2) _____ GOD SENDS
3) Verse 29 THE ONE YOU MUST BELIEVE
4) Verse 32 THE TRUE BREAD
5) Verse 33 THE BREAD WHICH CAME FROM HEAVEN
6) Verse 33 THE BREAD THAT GIVES LIFE TO THE WORLD
7) _____ 35 HE WILL END HUNGER and THIRST

V- JESUS' RECOMMANDATION TO US TODAY:

1) LABOR FOR THE MEAT THAT NEVER PERISHES (V. 27)

2) LABOR FOR THE SPIRITUAL MEAT.

Lay not up for yourselves TREASURES upon earth, where moth and rust do corrupt, and where thieves break through and steal: BUT LAY UP FOR YOURSELVES TREASURES IN HEAVEN, where neither moth nor rust corrupt, and where thieves do not break through nor steal: FOR WHERE YOUR TREASURE IS, THERE WILL YOUR HEART BE ALSO." Mat.6:19

-James says "WHAT WILL PROFIT MY BROTHER, THOUGH MANY SAY HE HAS FAITH, AND HAS NO WORK?

3) WORK FOR YOUR SALVATION
4) HAVE AN ABIDING FAITH IN JESUS
5) EAT HIS BREAD – LEARNING FROM JESUS.

CONCLUSION:

1) I PLACE BEFORE YOU TODAY THE BREAD OF LIFE: JESUS

2) DON'T WORK FOR THE BREAD THAT SPOILS

3) CHRISTIAN – CONTINUE WORKING FOR THAT BREAD

4) IF YOU HAVE FALLEN AWAY, RETURN TO GOD TODAY

5) QUESTION: What will you do with this bread this morning?

6) QUESTION: WILL YOU PARTAKE OF THIS BREAD THIS MORNING? Believe with all your heart, repent from your sins, and confess Jesus today as your bread and your bread of life coming from heaven. Amen. July 26, 2009

(98)

Scripture readings: John 7:1-18 and James 1:1-8 , 12-18

Text. James 1:5 , John 7:17 But if any of you lacks wisdom, let him ask of God, who gives to all generously and without reproach, and it will be given to him. … If anyone is willing to do His will, he will know of the teaching, whether it is of God or whether I speak for myself.

THEME: HOW TO KNOW THAT WE ARE DOING GOD'S WILL

Or WE HAVE RECEIVED WISDOM FROM GOD?

INTRODUCTION: How can we know the will of God in our lives? How can I know that what I am doing is according to the will of God? How can anyone say that he or she has received wisdom from God?

I never received a letter from God, nor saw a sign in heaven from Him.

ILLUSTRATION: A farmer wanted to know the WILL OF GOD IN HIS LIFE. When he was plowing his field, he looked in the sky and saw that the clouds had formed two big letters "P and C " He thought and thought and thought about these two letters. Then he said, "YES, I KNOW WHAT THEY MEAN. God is telling me to PREACH CHRIST." He left his tractor in the field, run to see his pastor and told him the story. He said; please let me preach this coming Sunday. The pastor agreed. He came prepared to preach on Sunday and he did. He went home, came back to see his pastor on Monday. The farmer asked what the pastor thought about his calling. The pastor said to him. The sign you saw in the sky was telling you to PLANT CORN not to PREACH CHRIST. Go home and plant your corn well.

Have you heard someone telling you that "GOD TOLD ME THIS or THAT?" I have. A person who has never had a DRAMATIC EXPERIENCE TO HEAR GOD like me will wander, what is wrong with me? Why God doesn't speak to me as to ADAM and EVE, ABRAHAM, MOSES, ISAIAH, JEREMIAH, PAUL in his way to DAMASCUS , CORNELIUS in his upper room, and John in the island of Patmos ?

What a joy that will be that I see him speaking directly to me when I have some important decisions to make as:

(1) Who to marry (2) What job to accept and to refuse? (3) Which home to sell or to buy, (4) should I leave my country Cameroon to come to the United States with my whole family, (5) should I stay in this TROUBLED MARRIAGE with my wife? (6) Should I leave the First Congregational church of Machiasport or not?

GOD, I WANT TO HEAR YOUR VOICE! SPEAK I LISTEN!
 WHAT IS YOUR WILL?
(1)DAVID SAID TO GOD:
 Psal 143:10"Teach me to do your will, for you are my God".

Let your good spirit lead me on a level path.

(2) <u>JAMES GIVES US THIS ADVICE</u> James 1 _5-6: If any of you is lacking wisdom, ask God, who gives to all generously and ungrudgingly, and it will be given to you. But ask in faith, never doubting, for the one who doubts is like a wave of the sea, driven and tossed by the wind.

YES, GOD IS WILLING TO REVEAL HIS WILL TO US.

I – <u>WHY IS GOD WILLING TO REVEAL HIS WILL TO US?</u>

<u>GOD IS PERSONAL – HE INTERESTS IN EACH ONE OF US. THEREFORE HE WANTS TO GIVE US PERSONAL DIRECTIONS.</u>

When you believed in him, He revealed himself to you through Christ. He sent his Holy Spirit to abide in you personally.
You have <u>PUT YOUR TRUST IN HIM</u>
You are <u>WILLING TO OBEY HIM</u>

<u>YOU ARE SEEKING HIS WILL IN YOUR LIFE.</u>

<u>II – THINGS EACH CHRISTAN SHOULD DO TO KNOW THE WILL OF GOD IN THEIR LIVES ARE:</u>

<u>THERE ARE CLEAR-CUT SITUATIONS WITH CLEAR MEANINGS:</u>

(1) No other gods before God your Savior
(2) No idol for yourself
(3) do not take the name of God in vain – no swearing
(4) Remember the Sabbath day to keep in holy – SUNDAY

(5) Honor your father and mother

(6) You shall not murder

(7) You shall not commit adultery

(8) You shall not steal

(9) You shall not bear false witness

(10) You shall not covet.

(11) Love your God with all your heart, with all your soul, with all your strength and love your neighbor as yourself Matt 22:27

B- WHAT DOES THE BIBLE SAY ABOUT THESE THINGS?

You must read the HOLY BIBLE - STUDY IT

Go to Bible Studies - Go to school – Seminars -Conferences

C- LISTEN TO SERMONS PREACHED

D- HAVE THE MIND OF CHRIST – Philippians 2:1-11

E- BECOME THE LETTER WRITTEN BY CHRIST. II Cor 3:2-3

You will be able to do what is RIGHT IN GOD'S EYES NOT YOUR OWN.

III – WHEN THE BIBLE GIVES NO ANSWER - DILEMMA –

BECAUSE –

(1) When you believed in him, He revealed himself to you through Christ Jesus.

(2) He sent his Holy Spirit to abide in you personally.

You have PUT YOUR TRUST IN HIM

You are WILLING TO OBEY HIM

YOU ARE SEEKING HIS WILL IN YOUR LIFE.

YOU HAVE READ THE HOLY BIBLE - STUDY IT

YOU HAVE STUDIED - Gone to school – Seminars -Conferences

YOU HAVE LISTENED TO SERMONS PREACHED

HAVE THE MIND OF CHRIST – Philippians 2:1-11

BECOME THE LETTER WRITTEN BY CHRIST. II Cor 3:2-3

YOU WILL HAVE THE WISDOM TO ACT AS PAUL WHEN HE WAS WRITING

ALL THESE 16 BOOKS OF THE BIBLE WE CALL EPISTLES

YOUR LIFE WILL BECOME THE EPISTLE OF CHRIST –

YOU WILL HAVE THE WISDOM OF CHRIST IN YOU.

IV- WAYS TO ACT ACCORDING TO THE WILL OF GOD

(1) BE A PRAYER WARRIOR – Get on your knees for all subjects.

(2) ASK GOD WHAT TO DO

(3) SPEAK TO A GODLY FRIEND – DO YOU HAVE ONE?

(4) BE SURE THAT YOUR MOTIVATION IS LOVE

(5) DO WHAT YOUR BELIEVE TO BE THE WILL OF GOD

(6) ACT ACCORDING TO THE WILL OF GOD BECAUSE

(7) YOU BELONG TO HIM AND HIS WILL IS DONE IN YOU.

Amen. Machiasport Sept. 9, 2007

(99)

Readings Psalm 22 :1-11 and Matthew 27 :45-54

Text. Mat.2746 Eloi, Eloi, Lama Sabachthani which means, « My God! My God, why have you forsaken me?

THEME : MY GOD! MY GOD! WHY HAVE YOU FORSAKEN ME? JESUS, THE HUMAN SUFFERED FOR YOU AND ME.

INTRODUCTION : All Christianity speaks about seven (7) words Jesus pronounced at the cross. All Gospels don't have them in the same order. For Matthew, the today's' message was the last he pronounced and after that he gave up his spirit. When the Christians classify these words, « My God! My God! Why have you forsaken me? » the third. This morning, we will learn what the Spirit wants us to know about these words.

I – JESUS 100% MAN CAME TO SAVE US ON THE CROSS

We should never forget that Jesus was 100% a man and 100% God. The cry we have as the text and message today is not coming from the Jesus Christ « GOD » but from the Jesus Christ, « THE MAN ».

A- JESUS 100% GOD ON THE CROSS COULD NOT SAVE US:

If on the Cross the Jesus man had not been there, we would be saved.

(1) the price would never had been paid.

(2) Jesus on the cross was someone IDENTICAL a 100% man who could die as substitute for us. He was one of us to redeem us

(3) He was someone who was born but without sin who could save us.

(4) He was someone who could suffer the pain who could save us.

(5) That person must have dies on the cross , that person may have been capable yelling:

« MY GOD! MY GOD! WHY HAST THOU FORSAKEN ME? »

B- SOME PEOPLE HAVE SAID THAT JESUS WAS NOT

GOD because of this sentence he pronounced of the cross.

They question how God can abandon himself? If Jesus was God, how could he say that God has abandoned him? Why God can forget his Son?

1)-The Jesus who said these words was THE JESUS MAN

2)-The Jesus who said these words was the incarnated one.

3)-The Jesus who said this words was the one who became sin.

he who never knew sin., became a sinner at that hour .

4)- HE INCARNATED ALL THE SINNERS AT THAT HOUR!

5)-GOD COULDN'T LOOK AT HIM BECAUSE OF YOU, ME!

C- JESUS WHO SAID THESE WORDS WAS FULFILLING THE WHOLE O.T

1) at that moment on the Cross, Genesis 3 :15, "He will crush your head" and he will strike his heel. Was getting accomplished.

2)-Psalm 22 written 1,000 years before the birth of Jesus was getting fulfilled.

II – SUPPOSE JESUS DID NOT SAY THESE WORDS »

1) He was not a man - The cross was just a seemingly place of suffering

2) The price was not paid – The price to be paid for sin is death.

3) JESUS DIDN'T DIE AT ALL.

Only a man could die, Our Savior must have been a man.

4)-WE ARE STILL LIVING IN OUR SINS TODAY.

5) We are not justified by Jesus' death on the cross .

III – JESUS SUFFERED ON THE CROSS : - IT IS TRUE!

1) THE BURDEN OF OUR SINS WAS VERY HEAVY.

2) GOD COULDN'T LOOK AT HIM BECAUSE OF OUR SINS.

3) THE PRICE WAS PAID IN FULL.

4) WE ARE FORGIVEN, REDEEMED, AND JUSTIFIED

IV- THE FOUNDATION OF OUR CHRISTIAN BELIEF

1)-GOD GAVE US HIS ONLY BEGOTTEN SON –

He came and suffered on our behalf.

2) JESUS GAVE HIS LIFEON THE CROSS-FOR US.

He took on the punishment we deserved

3) JESUS TRULY WAS FORSAKENBY THE FATHER ON OUR BEHALF

because he carried the sins of all mankind

4) THE VICTORY HAS BEEN WON ON THE CROSS ONCE AND FOR ALL.

Now, we belong to the Father forever.

CONCLUSION:

THE CRY OF JESUS ON THE CROSS,

» MY GOD! MY GOD! WHY HAVE YOU FORSAKEN ME? »

IS A DEMONSTRATION THAT

1) The person on the cross suffered. He was the lamb of God who takes away the sin of the world
2) Being human, he was the one who could save us from our sins.
3) Jesus fulfilled all the Old Testament, all the promises God made to us
4) If Jesus had not pronounced these words, that would have meant

   (1) HE DID NOT SUFFER - The Cross was there for his suffering!

   (2) HE DID NOT PAY THE PRICE

   (3) WE HAD NOT BEEN FORGIVEN and we would still be living in sins.

BUT REMEMBER :

   (1) GOD GAVE his only begotten Son to come and save SINNERS

   (2) JESUS GAVE HIMSELF FOR YOU ON THE CROSS

   (3) JESUS WAS TRULY FORSAKEN BECAUSE OF YOUR SINS

   (4) THE VICTORY HAS BEEN WON – YOU BELONG TO GOD

   MY GOD! MY GOD! WHY HAVE YOU FORSAKEN ME?

   Amen

(100)

John 19:26-27

THEME: THE LOVE OF GOD THROUGH THE FELLOW MAN "DEAR WOMAN, HERE IS YOUR SON"

INTRODUCTION: This We continue in our series on the seven sayings from the cross.

THE THIRD SAYING FROM THE CROSS IS FOUND IN (JOHN 19:26-27).

Last week, we preached on the second word Jesus said on the Cross. Today, you will be with me in Paradise. The week before was the first word he said on the cross. Father forgive them because they don't know what they are doing. »

Today, we will preach on the third word. « Woman, this is your son, this is your mother. » John 19 :26-27.

Last week it was Jesus and two criminals. Today it is Jesus and his mother and beloved friend. Mary and John were with Jesus all the way to the cross. They followed everything people said, or did to Jesus from the place he left Pilate to the place of his crucifixion. They were hopeless. Nothing they could do to save Jesus.

Jesus has forgiven everyone who has taken part at this odious act. Jesus has promised eternal life to the criminal of the cross. His mother and the friend he loved have witnessed all this. What about them?

When Jesus addressed her mother, « WOMAN, » it was not because he didn't know who she was. It was not because he didn't care who she was, it was to show that she has stood for something and she is strong.

I –YOUR ATTITUDE IN SUPPERING CAN SHOW YOUR STRENGTH :

When Jesus called his mother « WOMAN » he saw in her the strong person. Someone who has endured difficult circumstances :

1- The Angel of the Lord – She has met in her life

2- Elizabeth and her pregnancy 3- the wise men4- The Shepherds

5- Anna in the Temple6- the death of the 8- Cana' an at the wedding

QUESTION : WHAT WILL MAKE YOU STRONG?\

WHEN WILL YOU STAND YOUR GROUND

WHEN WILL PEOPLE KNOW THAT YOU CAN?

Jesus looking at his mother, he knew that she has qualified as a WOMAN.

B- JESUS AND JOHN, THE DISCIPLE HE LOVED.

Jesus remembered that John has been with him for 3 years.

1. They have been at the mount TRANSFIGURATION
2. 2. UPPER ROOM
3. JUDAS LEAVING THEM TO BETRAY HIS MASTER
4. At the Garden where he prayed
5. The ARRESTATION
6. THE JUDGMENT
7. THE CROWD
8. THE CRUCIFICTION

II – WHEN JESUS WAS ON THE CROSS, HER MOTHER STOOD BY:

THESE TWO STOOD THERE

(1) THE SUFFERING

(2) THE LOVE

Can you imagine Mary's horror as she looked up at her son who was suffering and near death? Those of you who are parents – especially those of you who have lost a child – can fully understand what Mary was going through.

III - WHERE WILL COME THE COMFORT ?

MOTHER – COMFORT YOUR SON

SON, COMFORT YOUR MOTHER

III - IMPORTANT IT IS TO HONOR OUR PARENTS.

As a boy, Jesus clearly honored and obeyed His parents. I think of the words of Scripture in (Luke 2:51) where we are told that Jesus "went down to Nazareth with (His parents) and was obedient to them."

Jesus respected His parents and was always obedient to them. Even on the cross Jesus showed Himself to be perfectly obedient…specifically to the fifth commandment, which teaches to honor your father and mother.

With His words from the cross, Jesus demonstrated how children of all ages are to treat their parents. In essence, Jesus asked John to provide for His mother's present and future needs. To give her shelter, food, clothing, protection, and love. Jesus arranged to have all that provided for His mother.

As Christians, we have a responsibility to provide for our parents. We must provide our parents with food, shelter, clothing, protection and love.

SECOND, JESUS TEACHES US THAT WHILE WE ARE GOING THROUGH DIFFICULT TIMES, WE CAN STILL BE CONCERNED ABOUT THE NEEDS OF OTHERS.

Even though Jesus was suffering on the cross, He was still concerned about others.

At times, when we are struggling with difficult situations, we become self-focused. We become so absorbed with our own struggles that we neglect those around us.

But Jesus shows us that when we suffer, we should not only be concerned with our own welfare, but also with the welfare of others.

EVEN THOUGH WE SUFFER – LET SET ASIDE OUR PROBLEM ANS SHOW CONCERN FOR OTHERS.

ILLUSTRATION:

Brethren, no matter what kind of trial we may be experiencing, we should still be concerned for others. We need to set aside our problems and help comfort people with their problems. We should do what that caring little child did in the story I just read…recognize a need…climb into someone's lap…and cry with them.

CONCLUSION:

In closing, we have learned several lessons from Jesus' third saying from the cross.

We have learned how important it is to honor our parents.

We have learned that even when we suffer…we should still be concerned about the needs of others.

An important lesson we have learned today is that, some of us say" I love God". Nobody sees God. We see our brothers and sisters in Christ. These are the John; we are our sisters in Christ, these are "the mother of Jesus Mary". If you don't show love you want to show to Jesus to these, you don't love Jesus you don't see.

Go and practice the love of Jesus in the people you know. Amen.

(101)

Luke 23:26-43

Text Luke 23 :40-43 « don't you fear God, » he said « …we are punished justly, for we are getting what our deeds deserve. But this man has done nothing wrong.…Jesus remember me when you come into your kingdom. » Jesus answered him, « Amen! Amen, today you will be with me in Paradise. »

THEME : WHAT IT TAKES TO GO TO PARADISE.

INTRODUCTION: It was Friday in Jerusalem. They just crucified three people; one thief on the left, and the other on the right; Jesus in the middle. The one in the middle was pronounced innocent by Pilate, the judge. Those on both sides of Jesus were criminals. They knew it, people standing around knew it, and God in heaven knew it. Judas, the chief priests, the crowd, the soldiers, even the disciples have abandoned their Jesus. Except the ladies who followed him. They were standing at the foot of the cross. Only one disciple was mentioned being there. It was John. An innocent man was on the cross with two criminals.

I – THE SIMILARITIES BETWEEN THESE TWO CRIMINALS

1) both were criminals sentenced to death.
2) Both were crucified as Jesus was also crucified on the mount Golgotha that day.
3) Both heard Jesus saying, "Father, forgive them because they do not know what they are doing."
4)Both were crucified near Jesus, one on the left, one on the right
5) Both were dying.
6) Both needed help, they didn't want to die.

BUT THEY WERE ALSO DIFFERENT. DIFFERENT THE WAY THY LOOKED AT THE MAN CRUCIFIED IN THE MIDDLE, JESUS.
THE WAY THEY THOUGHT ABOUT HIM
-THE THINGS THEY WANTED FROM HIM
-One agreed with the crowds and the world, the other disagreed with the crowds. As it was then, the crowds of the world still rejects Jesus even today as then. They didn't need the redemption from the Cross as today. People seek redemption outside the cross.

II -WHAT DID THE MAN WHO REJECTED JESUS SAY?

1-HE INSULTED JESUS: Verse 39.Aren't you the Christ? Save yourself and us. He mocked Jesus. What kind of Christ are you? What kind of Savior are you when yourself are dying with us? You are not different from us. PROVE THAT RIGHT NOW!

III- AND THE REDEMABLE CRIMINAL? HE FEARED GOD:
Verse 40"Don't you fear God?

THE REDEEMABLE CRIMINAL FEARS GOD. He was a sinner, but the fear of the Lord was still in his heart. When the fear of God, the guilt are no longer there; when the heart doesn't feel pain, when the behavior becomes similar to an animal; when cruelty, and the blood become normal things and when conscience becomes silent, the person who is qualified those ways can never be redeemed. This was the condition of the first criminal. But the second criminal on the cross was full of the fear of God. His conscience was still alive; he could still know the difference. He could still point finger at himself.

IV-THE REDEEMABLE CRIMINAL AKNOWLEDGES HIS FALSE/ CRIME
Verse 41 we are punished justly for we are getting what our deed deserves

(1) The second criminal acknowledged that he has sinned.
(2) He acknowledged that he deserved to be punished;
(3) He acknowledged that the punishment of death on the cross was what he deserved because not any other punishment could be equal to his deed

APPLICATION :
(1) A sinner who acknowledges that he is a sinner,
(2) Who acknowledges that he deserves punishment,
(3) And who acknowledges that the punishment that any sin deserves is death is on his way to Paradise. This man on the cross looked at himself differently that the other criminal. He looked at Jesus as the kind of person he wanted to be like. He knew that he deserved to die on the cross not the innocent man who was Jesus.

He knew that he deserved DEATH AS PUNISHMENT- HE SINNED.

APPLICATION : The attitude of this criminal was unheard of and is still unheard of. Someone who can say, « Yes, I deserve to die because of the sin I committed ». I know what most of us would say and could have said, « I DON'T DESERVE TO DIE. » But this man said, « YES, I DESRVE TO DIE, I AM A SINNER.

V-THE REDEEMABLE CRIMINAL ACKNOWLEDGES WHO IS JESUS
1) THE INNOCENT ONE CRUCIFIED FOR NO REASON
2) THE RIGHTEOUS MAN WHO IS DYING FOR THE UNRIGHTEOUS

Verse 41-42 But this man has done nothing wrong.

There is no possibility of redemption if a sinner doesn't acknowledge who Jesus is.

THE LAMB OF GOD WHO TAKES AWAY THE SINS OF THE WORLD.

The difference between Jesus and any other person who has lived, who lives or will live is that he died on the cross for our sins. This man at that point knew that Jesus was there on the cross not because of his own sins, but because of his. He looked at Jesus as the one who didn't deserve to die but is going to die because of him. REDEMPTION BELONGS TO PEOPLE WHO SEE THEMSELVES AT THE CROSS AND NOT JESUS.. That criminal saw himself at the cross

Look at the cross; do you see yourself there? Do you see your sins covering the innocent person who died there?

IF YES, YOU ARE ON YOUR WAY TO PARADISE.

VI-THE REDEEMABLE SINNER PLEADED FOR HELP :

JESUS, REMEMBER ME WHEN YOU COME IN YOUR KINGDOM.

THE PENITENT THIEF :

(1) FEARED GOD

(2) HE ACCEPTED JUSTICE

(3) HE ACKNOWLEDGEED THE GOODNESS AND THE POWER OF JESUS

(4) HE PLEADED FOR HELP

(5) "Jesus, remember when you come into your kingdom."

-JESUS IS ALWAYS READY TO FORGIVEWHOEVER CONFESSES HIS SIN

-JESUS IS ALWAYS READY TO RECEIVEWHOEVER NEEDS SALVATION

THE KINGDOM OF HEAVEN BELONGSTO THE PENITENT SINNERS.

LISTEN TO JESUS,

AMEN! AMEN,! TODAY YOU WILL BE WITH ME IN PARADISE.

I – SALVATION BELONGS TO THOSE WHO REPENT:

(1) SALVATION DOESN'T KNOW ANY DELAY. It is today

(2) WHERE IS PARADISE. II Cor. 12:3Paul says, "I know a man in Christ, who fourteen years ago was caught up to the third heaven— whether in the body or out of the body, I do not know; God knows. And I know that this man was caught up into Paradise.

PARADISE, IS BEING WITH THE LORD FOREVER. We believe that we are members of the Kingdom of God here on earth and when we die, when believers die, they go right to be with the Lord. Jesus promised to be with this penitent sinner, criminal in Paradise the day and hour of their death.

There were three crosses on mount Golgotha that Friday.

(1) The Cross of the criminal who condemned Jesus as the world

(2) The cross of Jesus, the innocent, the righteous and the redeemer

(3) The cross of the repentant who feared God, acknowledged Jesus as innocent and repented.- With whom do you associate yourself today?

QUESTIONS **FOR YOU TO CONCLUDE THIS MESSAGE ARE:**

(1) DO YOU FEAR GOD?

(2) DO YOU ACKNOWLEDGE YOUR SIN?

(3) DO YOU KNOW THAT WHAT YOU DESERVE AS A SINNER IS DEATH?

(4) DO YOU ACKNOWLEDGE THE GOODNESS AND POWER OF JESUS?

(5) DO YOU REPENT FROM SIN AND NEED JESUS' HELP? TODAY, YOU AND JESUS WILL BE IN PARADISE. Amen. Feb. 28. 2010

(102)

Readings Peter 1:1-8; James 1:1-12

Text. James 1:12 blessed is the man who endures temptation: for when he is tried, he shall receive the crown of life, which the Lord had promised to them that love him.

THEME: WHY DO CHRISTIANS SUFFER?

INTRODUCTION: Today, God has sent us a message. I hope that by the time you leave this church today, God would have finished with you. By that time, you will have a different look of your headache, conflicts you have with yourself, your neighbor who may be your wife, your husband, your child, your relative. YOU WILL LOOK A ALL YOUR SUFFERINGS, the death of your friend, the accident of someone dear to you, anything which may have been a THORN in you preventing you to live IN FULL the new life Christ
AS A BLESSINGS FDROM GOD.
Now, I will like to give you some moment to bring to mind THE MOST HORRIBLE THING WHICH CAN HAPPEN TO YOU, CAPABLE TO TURN YOUR LIFE UPSIDE DOWN. HAVE THAT IN MIND AS WE GO ALONG THROUGH THIS MESSAGE. God is going to

talk to you about HOW YOU SHOULD DEAL, LOOK AND USE THAT CIRCUMTANCE IN YOUR LIFE.

The question we will try to answer today is: WHY DO CHRISTIANS SUFFER?

I - SUPPOSE CHRISTIANS DO NOT SUFFER IN THIS WORLD!

(1) Churches would be full every Sunday.

(2) Christianity would be the only religion in the world.

(3) Suffering would disappear forever – no sickness, no cancer, no death,

(4) People would continue living as we live today assured that they will not suffer.

(5) None would believe that there are Hell, Satan, Devil and Punishment.

(6) SALVATION AND ETERNAL LIFE would be taken for granted

(7) WE WOULD NOT BE NEED OF HOPE.

II – WHO ARE THOSE PETER CALLS CHRISTIANS? PETER IN I PETER gives us a true definition of the kind of people we should call Christians and the life of those people vis-à-vis suffering in the world.

Christians should not think that because they are loved by God, God should not let them suffer. Sometimes, our prayers give me the impression that most Christians think that they shouldn't suffer. LISTEN TO OUR PRAYERS! Lord, heal my child, my mother, my friend, myself and so on and so forth. IT IS US SAYING TO GOD, WE DON'T DESERVE TO SFUFFER WHEN WE HAVE YOU AS OUR GOD!

I Peter says" I Peter 1:1 Peter, an apostle of Jesus Christ, TO….(he is addressing this letter to people he is going to define here) : WHO ARE CHRISTIANS; TRUE

CHRISTIANS; THOSE JESUS DIED FOR:

1) – Strangers scattered – Christians, strangers living in this world
2) – The elected according to their foreknowledge of God.
3) - Sanctified – Sanctification of the Holy Spirit,
4) - Obedience and sprinkling of the blood of Jesus Christ

Therefore, we are not talking about just any person who lives in this world. We are not talking about anyone who calls himself or herself Christian;

1) -Christians are strangers here on earth.
2) -They have chosen Jesus as their Savior and Redeemer.
3) -They are in the world but not of the world;
4) -They are the elect from eternity by God the Father;
5) -They are sanctified by the Holy Spirit abiding in them;
6) -And they have pledged allegiance obedience to their Lord.

THESE PEOPLE WHO ARE ALREADY IN THESE CONDITIONS HAVE A DIFFERENT LOOK AT THE SUFFERING = GOOD THING.WHY MUST RUE CHRISTIANS SUFFER?(7) Complete

HOW DO YOU SPELL SUFFERING: T. R. I. U. M. P. H

T =Training ion obedience

R =Refinement of their character.

I = Intimacy with compassionate God

U =Understanding of the hurts of others

M =Maturity for ministering to others

P = Perseverance in difficult times

H= Hope for the future

(I)- SUFFERING,TRAININGSCHOOL FOR THE CHRISTIANS

(1) LOOK AT JESUS, THE ONE CHRISTIANS MODEL THEMSELVES AFTER: Hebrews 5:8 says "Even though Jesus was God's Son, He learned obedience from the things He suffered" (Hebrews 5:8).

-Jesus never sinned –but he suffered to be obedient to his Father.

-Jesus ENDURED HARDSHIP on behalf of you and me = SALVATION

(2) Suffering is the way to TEACH US OBEDIENCE and refusal to sin.

The Puritan Thomas Watson wrote,

"A sickbed often teaches more than a sermon,"

(3) Suffering brings man to the end of himself. The psalmist 119:7

"Before I was afflicted I went astray, but now I obey your word"

Hebrews explains, "The Lord disciplines those He loves, and He punishes everyone He accepts as a son

CONCLUSION: WHERE ELSE CAN YOU BETTER LEARN OBEDIENCE THAN THROUGH SUFFERING – SUFFERING IS NECESSARY FOR OUR OBEDIENCE.

(II)- SUFFERING PRODUCES REFINEMENT=PURIFICATION

Christians are purified through suffering.

(1) It is necessary in this life to have OPPOSITION; to have adversaries; to feel pressure; to know that you can lose. How can anyone slow down on the road if there is no (2) DANGER? LOOK AT OUR CHILDREN, NO (3) DISCIPLINE, And THEN WHAT – The TV. NANNY. Look at the situations that lady fixes in less time. SUFFERING IS THERE (4) TO PURIFY US.

SUFFERING IS THERE (5) TO BUILD OUR CHARACTER,

SUFFERING IS THERE (6) TO MAKE US BECOME MEN AND WOMEN –

MASSA CULTURE: If a boy has not killed a lion, or stolen someone else's cow or performed a heroic act, he can't go through the rite of MANHOOD.

LISTEN TO JOB IN 23:10"[God] knows the way that I take; when He has tested me, will come forth as gold"(Job 23:10,).

CONCLUSION: CHRISTIANS ARE REFINED, PURIFIED, TRANSFORMED THROUGH SUFFERING – REFINEMENT – BEFORE CRUDE, AFTER PURE

(III) - SUFFERING PRODUCES INTIMACY WITH GOD/SAVIOR

1)- I don't know if there is no one here who doesn't know the DEEP, TRUE, COMPLETE MEANING OF THIS WORD "INTIMACY" If you have been in love in your whole life, this part of THE WAY A CHRISTIAN BECOMES WITHIN HIS/HER RELATIONS WITH GOD WILL BE WELL UNDERSTOOD.
Job told God, (Job 42:5) "I had heard about You before, but now I have seen You with my own eyes"

2) ASK TRUE CHRISTIANS, who have been sick, have cancer, death, gone through certain situations, many others become broken, destroyed and finished. You would hear them saying, "I am so glad I have cancer. It caused my faith to become strong, and my relationship with Christ to really become intimate.

CONCLUSION: The more A TRUE CHRISTIAN goes through adversity with God, the more he/she will learn about how faithful God is to help him/her in time of need.
Our suffering produces intimacy with the Savior.

(IV)- SUFFERING PRODUCES UNDERSTANDING OF HURTS

1)- Suffering produces those MOMENTS ONE OPENS THE EYES. I have heard people say; now I know who my best friends are. Now, I know what being poor is. Now I know how precious being married is, having a wife, having a roof over my head. Now I now what life is all about. I have heard people saying, IF I GET THROUGH THIS, I WILL LIVE DIFFERENTLY.

2)- SACRATES SAID " La souffrance est un meilleur educateur "

– Suffering is the best teacher

If you see someone, after suffering of something, go back to doing something bad, it is true is that he/she will never learn anything from that.

(2) SUFFERING GIVES US WHAT WE CALL: EXPERIENCE-WHAT SOMEONE LIVES ACCORDING TO THE EXPERIENCE, WE CALL (4)THAT WISDOM: IS THE UNDERSTANDING OF HOW THINGS WORK:

UNDERSTAND WHAT TO AVOID.

UNDERSTAND WHAT TO DO

UNDERSTAND WHERE TO GO

UNDERSTAND WHO IS WHO

UNDERSTAND WHAT IS WHAT.

Understand, when, why, for what reason etc.

How can someone acquire UNDERSTANDING without suffering?

IT is through suffering that we understand words like:

Love, Grace, Mercy, fidelity, choice, death, life, health, sickness, HURT, sympathy, apathy, hatred, sin, forgiveness, make sense

CONCLUSION: IF YOU ARE LOOKING FOR THE WAY TO UNDERSTAND AND MASTER EVERYTHING, LET SUFFERING TAKE YOU THERE.

<u>(v)- SUFFERING PRODUCES MATURITY IN CHRIST</u> when we have just received Jesus, we are not different from a little baby. But the longer we stay in relationship with him, the more we grow and become mature in faith and belief. Another important product of suffering is that it makes us mature very fast.

<u>EXAMPLE</u>: When I was thirteen, I left my mother's home in order to go to school. My father used to give me some money so that I could take care of myself for at least 30 days. Let's say I spent all that money before he came back to give me more, I would live all that time without money. Because of that experience in my life, I don't remember anytime I have been without money. Some people even think that I have a lot of money, but I will never spend all my money. That's the way I am
.Some older girls or boys have become mothers and fathers when they still were children themselves. They had to raise their siblings. Some people have even aged physically because of some experiences they have gone through in their lives. It is the same with our relationship with Christ.

WE NEED SUFFERING in order to take in our his nature.
- PRAYING - READING THE BIBLE - UNDERSTANDING HIS GRACE AND LOVE – HEARING AND SEEING HIM – TRUSTING HIM - LOVING HIM – SERVING HIM - BELIEVING - HOPING KNOWING THAT EVERYTHING IS GOING TO BE FINE BECAUSE HE IS THERE FOR YOU.
How can you trust God is you never reach maturity?
Being a model to other Christians is suffering. (1 Thess. 1:6-8)
trials, temptations, suffering, hurts, produces maturity.

CONCLUSION: Do you want to know if you have REACHED YOUR MATURITY IN CHRIST? LOOK AT THE WAY YOU HANDLE Adversity, suffering, hurts, and death, in your life.

If you always praise God, trust God, believe in God, pray to God, give your burden to him, feel peace and stay hopeful through those moments, feel closer to your Savior, be certain that you have MATURED IN CHRIST JESUS.

(VI) -SUFFERING PRODUCES PERSEVERANCE:

Listen to James' advice to Christians:

"Dear brothers, is your life full of difficulties and temptations? Then be happy, for when the way is rough, your patience has a chance to grow" (James 1:2, 3)

IN ROUGH ROADS, YOUR PATIENCE HAS A CHANCE TO GROW

Do you want to be TOUGH, STRONG, COMPETITIVE, SUCCESSFUL, FIRST? DO YOU WANT TO WIN? DO YOU WANT TO BUILD MUSCLES? DO YOU WANT TO LAST UNTIL GOD CALLS YOU HOME?

ILLUSTRATION: SURVIVORS: They have much competition. Most of their competitions are on ENDURANCE, PERSEVERANCE

Standing on a pole,

  _ Pulling something for a longer period of time

  _ carrying something heavy

ENDURANCE, PERSEVERANCE, PATIENCE, WAITING ON GOD, IS IN SUFFERING.

God often uses adversity to MAKE YOU TOUGH, SALID in your resolves

(VIII)- SUFFERING PRODUCES HOPE = FUTURE GLORY:

HOPE IS THE ABILITY:

(1)The ability to see life through to death

(2) The ability to see light being in darkness

(3) Capacity to laugh when crying

(4) The ability to hope inside DESPERATION.

(5) The ability to be alive when dying

(6) the ability to have when poor, empty handed, depraved,

(7) the will to win when about to lose everything

(8) It is that capacity to see life at the end of the tunnel

- VICTORY IS COMING!

- GLORY IS AHEAD!

- PROMISES WILL BE FULFILLED!

- PEACE WILL ENDURE FOREVER!

CHRISTIANITY IS NOTHING BUT HOPE, A LOOK AHEAD.

We know and know and know that God is going to win!

WE know and know and know that the Kingdom is coming!

We know and know and know that NOTHING WILL BE ABLE TO SEPARATE US FROM THE LOVE OF CHRIST. Shall trouble or hardship or persecution or famine or nakedness or danger or sword, separate us from the love of Christ? No, in all these things we are more than conquerors through Him who loved us" (Romans 8:35, 37,)

WHAT IS YOUR WAR AT THIS MOMENT?

1) IS IT YOU HEALTH?

2) YOUR HUSBAND, YOUR WIFE, YOUR CHILD?

3) IS IT ABOUT FINANCE,

4) PROBLEMS IN THE FAMILY?

5) SOME KIND OF PERSECUTION,

6) EMOTIONAL, MENTAL, WORRIES?

7) YOUR FAITH IN GOD?

WHAT IS YOUR PROBLEM, YOUR WAR, YOUR SUFFERING NOW?

LOOK AHEAD, HAVE HOPE IN GOD. REMEMBER PROMISES.

WE KNOW HOW TO SPELL SUFFERING = TRIUMPH

T= TRAINING\

R= REFINEMENT

I= INTIMACY

U = UNDERSTANDING

M= MATURITY

P = PERSEVERANCE

H = HOPE

Amen. Machiasport Feb. 7, 2010

(103)

Rom.1:8-15

THEME: SOME CHARACTERISTICS OF A TRUE CHRISTIAN
LIVING. WHAT EVERY CHRISTIAN SHOULD BE

INTRODUCTION: Have you known in your life some Christians who
have made an impression on you, have convinced you that a sinner can
live a life modeled after Jesus? Have you known men or women of whom
you truly believe that they have lived the message they heard and read
from the book we call the Bible? Do you know, either now or in the past
some honest, trustworthy, faithful Christians you are sure that if Christ
returns today, they will count amount those who will inherit eternal life?
These are the people to whom the book of Romans addressed. These are the
people, who, in their past, were sinners like you and me, but by the grace of
God, through his JUSTIFICATION AND SANCTIFICATION now are
called the saints. This book speaks about that process which can be active
in your life as well as in mine. The book speaks about the process which
can help us to live with certain Christians values now. PAUL who wrote
this book was the best living example to us all of what a genuine Christian
should be. In the first 7 verses of this chapter, Paul introduces himself to
the believers in Rome. He tells them about himself, the messenger, and
about his message, the Gospel of grace. Now, Paul turns the spotlight

upon himself in a very real way. He shares with these people, whom he has never met, the motives behind the letter he was sending to them. In these 8 verses, the Apostle Paul reveals 8 traits of genuine Christian characters that tell us what every Christian should be.

I. THE FAITH OF EVERY CHRISTIAN'S SHOULD BE KNOWN: Verse 1:8I thank my God through Jesus Christ for all of you, because YOUR FAITH IS PROCLAIMED THROUGHOUT THE WORLD. Every Christian's faith should be known wherever he or she lives. Jesus said, " You are the salt of the world. You are the light of the world. You are a city built on the hill. The lamp is lit to shine and dissipate all darkness around". It doesn't matter how thick is the darkness, how deep is the hole. Wherever a Christian is, he or she is there to witness, to proclaim the Good News, to tell the dying world that there is a

possibility to go from death to life in Jesus. Paul, who was far away from the saints, who lived in Rome, heard about how their faith was radiant in those regions

IS THERE SOMEWHERE IN THE WHOLE WORLD SOMEONE TODAY WHO WOULD TESTIFY ABOUT OUR FAITH THIS WAY? ARE MEMBERS OF YOUR FAMILY, OF YOUR CHURCH, of whichever group you are known, would someone say what Paul was saying here about the Saints who lived in Rome? Have you made a difference in someone's life because of your faith? The first characteristic of a faithful believer is that his or her faith's "ECHO"

REACHES FAR FROM WHERE HE OR SHE LIVES. Paul teaches something else here to all of us. When we hear that people speak about the faith of our fellow Christian, instead of being jealous, what should we do? BE THANKFUL! PRAISE THE LORD! PRAY FOR THAT PERSON or THOSE PEOPLE. Recognize that the Word of God is at work. God wants His children to be the light of the world, to be a thankful people. In fact, I know that a thankful spirit is with this church and we will continue to encourage others to shine in our community

II. EVERY CHRISTIAN SHOULD ANNOUNCE THE GOSPEL.

Verse1: 9. For God whom I serve with my spirit by announcing the Gospel. This phrase: FOR GOD WHOM I SERVE – DOING WHAT? - BY ANNOUNCING THE GOSPEL.

EVERY BELIEVER MUST KNOW WHOM HE OR SHE SERVES: Paul was the servant of God. He knew deep down in his heart that the person to whom he has given all his life and the one he is working for is the Lord. In no time in his life could he ignores who was his master, his boss.

This doesn't mean that Paul was working in God's shop, or was teaching in God's school, or was working in God's bank. But that whatever Paul was doing alone, with other people or for others, he was serving the Lord. No separation between the time he prayed, and the time he was making his tents for a living.

This is the Christian Concept of life. To live for Jesus. To see Jesus' face in other people. To feel Jesus' call wherever there is a need of deed, participation, action, mercy, input.

ILLUSTRATION: Someone fell on the railroad in a subway tracks in New York. A bystander jumped on the track in front of an incoming train, rescued the man, and till had enough time to leave before the second train came. People asked him after this why he did what he did. He said he felt pushed and called to do what he did. They asked him. After showing him the video, they asked him if he would do that again. He said, after looking at the video; he wouldn't have the courage to do it. But if the same feeling, push, and call he had before would come to him, he will do that again. This is the LIFE OF A CHRISTIAN: to respond to the call wherever he is. He is on duty all the time. His Master is in charge of his life. He does what He requires of him or her.

III – CHRISTIAN'S SERVICE IS FOR THE GOSPE :We do what we must do to announce the Good News to the world. There is only one purpose everything a Christian person does: to tell the world that God loves the sinners and he is looking for his salvation. We may not be preaching when we cook public supper. But our message we transmit is so doing is " Jesus loves you; believe in him". When we send money to the mission, when you do what you do, everything is for Christ.

ILLUSTRATION: A young guy took a bus but knew only the name of the town he was supposed to get off. He told the bus driver his dilemma. The bus driver promised to let him off at that town. When they arrived there, the boy was sleeping and the bus driver forgot. After a long distance, the boy went to see the bus driver asking if they haven't arrived yet. The bus driver said, " I am sorry; we passed that town longtime ago." The boy did not know what to do. As he was going back to his seat, someone in the bus said to him," I will help you to get back to your place when we get to town." The guy went back and sat for a while. Then he came back and touched that man on his shoulder and asked," Are you a Christian?" What a wonderful way to discover that you are a Christian by your deed, by your word, by your look, by the way you dress, by whatever good message the world can get from you! The purpose we are here is to PROCLAIM THE GOSPEL IN ANY FORM. This is your calling this is the witnessing without ceasing.

IV- CHRISTIANS MUST SHARE THEIR SPIRITUAL GIFTS IN ORDER TO STRENGTHEN EACH OTHER.

A. Paul now tells the Romans that he is totally committed to the Lord. Every word he uttered, every thing he wrote, everywhere he went, and Paul was a living witness to total surrender. This certainly explains the reason behind Paul's great success. When nothing else matters in your life but what matters to the Lord, His work will get done! B. I don't know where this message finds you, but I know that this is an area where I can always find room to work. Notice the word "serve". It is the same word that is translated "worship" in other parts of the New Testament. It is my opinion that there is no greater form of worship that can be rendered unto the Lord than pure; heart felt service and devotion to the Lord.

QUESTION: Is your life committed? It should be - Rom. 12:1-2!

V. EVERY CHRISTIAN MUST BE PRAYERFUL

Verse 1:9bWITHOUT CEASING, I REMEMBER YOU ALWAYS IN MY PRAYER The Apostle's ministry was primarily that of preaching the Gospel, v. 9a. However, he had a secondary ministry that was just as vital as the first. Paul had a ministry of prayer. That is, he made prayer a priority and the Roman believers were never taken off Paul's prayer list. HERE ARE SOME SUBJECTS WE FIND IN PAUL PRAYERS:
Eph. 3:14-19

1)- That God will strengthen the inner beings of the believers by the Holy Spirit's power

2)- To comprehend the breadth, the length, the height, and the depth of the love of Christ Phil. 1:9-11

3)- That their love may overflow more and more with the knowledge and full insight

4) That they be pure and blameless, having produced the harvest of righteousness0

5)- and they come through Jesus Christ for the glory and the praise of God Col. 1:9-11.

6)- To be filled with the knowledge of God's will, spiritual wisdom and understanding.

7)- That they may lead lives worthy of the Lord, fully pleasing him

8)- That they be made strong with all the strength that comes from his glorious power. God wants His children to be under a prayer burden for others, Gal. 6:2, Rom. 15:1. God would have you and me involved in a prayer ministry touching the lives of others.

APPLICATION: How would you describe your prayer life today? Who is the main topic of your prayer life? What is the content of your prayers for others? This is an area where we can all improve!

VI.EVERY REAL CHRISTIAN MUST BE SURRENDERED TO GOD:

Verse 1:10:Asking that by God's will I may somehow succeed at last to come to you.

Be there all the time waiting to hear from God. Being ready to go and do whatever He wants you to do. This is a life surrendered to the Lord. Not living for you but for Christ. Not having a personal agenda, but following God's agenda Having a heart that knows no higher goal than pleasing the Father at all times, John 4:34; John 8:29. Imagine what the Lord could do with a church filled with people who were totally sold on the will of God ahead of everything!

VII. EVERY CHRISTIAN MUST BE FRUITFUL Verse 1:13: I have intended to come to you…in order that I may reap some harvest among you as I have among the rest of the Gentiles. Each one of us is called to bear fruit. Can you imagine this if before you leave this world, you bring one, two or three people to Christ, and each one of these people brings, one, two or three people to Christ, and so on and so forth, do you have any idea where Christianity influence and faith would be in the world in one hundred years? Our calling as Christians is to bear fruit. To make others the Disciples of Christ as we ourselves have become his.

OUR ATTITUDES SHOULD DRAW PEOPLE TO CHRIST
Gal. 5:22-23.

WE SHOULD BE INVOLVED IN CERTAIN ACTIVITIES. When a believer lives for the Lord, there would be activity in his life and fruit would be produced for the glory of the Lord. PEOPLE MUST SEE A HOLY PERSON LIVING IN YOU - Rom. 6:22 2.)

THEY MUST SEE A PRAISING LIFE IN YOU - Heb. 13:15 3.

THE SPIRIT OF GOD WILL WORK THROUGH YOU) -

VIII. V. 15 EVERY CHRISTIAN SHOULD BE EAGER Verse 15: HENCE MY EAGERNESS TO PROCLAIM THE GOSPEL TO YOU, ALSO THOSE WHO ARE IN ROME. Eagerness here means READY. Paul was ready to go to visit the saints living in Rome. Paul is saying, "I can't wait until I get to Rome so that I can preach the Gospel there also." In other words, Paul is excited about his call and his commission. He is an excited Christian! Every Christian should be eager to serve the Lord. Be exited to serve the Lord. When we get to the things of the flesh: parties, football, dances, public gatherings, people seem to be exited. Why don't we get the same excitement in church, with other Christians around, and when we do whatever we do in the name of the Lord.

BEING EXCITED WHEN SERVING THE LORD.
BEING EXCITED WHEN LIVING FOR THE LORD!
BEING EXCITED WHEN PRAYING TO THE LORD!

BEING EXCITED WHEN ANNOUNCING THE GOSPEL TO THE WORLD

MY EXCITEMENT, YOUR EXCITEMENT, OUR EXCITEMENT WILL MAKE A BIG DIFFERENCE IN OUR LIVES AS WELL AS THE LIFE OF THE CHURCH.

CONCLUSION: These are characteristics every Christ should have:

1. Your FAITH should be known all over, and beyond who you are
2. You should ANNOUNCE THE GOSPEL ALL THE TIME.
3. Know that you are serving the Lord in every aspect of your life
4. Announce the Gospel for the Salvation of the world
5. You are here to share your spiritual gifts with other believers.
6. Your life must be prayerful– Pray according to the example of Paul.
7. Live a life surrendered to the Lord all your time
8. God is expecting you to BEAR FRUIT
9. Be ready be eager, be excited about Jesus all the time
   - Be sure to Always build these 8 Christian Characteristics in your life.

Machiasport October 24, 2010

(104)

Exodus 19:1—25

Text. Exodus. 19: 4-6a you, yourselves have seen what I did to Egypt, and how I carried you on eagles' wings and brought you to myself. NOW, if you obey me fully, and keep my covenant, then out of all nations you will be my treasured possessions. Although the whole earth is mine, you will be for me a kingdom of priests, and a holy nation

THEME: SINAÏ – GOD'S THREE PURPOSES TO SAVE ISRAEL: To be his treasured possessions, his Kingdom of Priests, and his Holy Nation.

INTRODUCTION: Would this church, this community, this country and the whole world be the same if the event, which took place in the book of Exodus chapter 19 could take place here today? Let us review what happened in this chapter. First, God called Moses to go and meet him in the Mount Sinai. - Just imagine, you receive a phone call from Kathy telling you that God just invited your Pastor go to and meet him in Bangor. Second, being your Pastor, I bring you this message from God. I am going to read you the message God himself sends you sitting here today: "You, yourselves have seen what I did to Egypt, and how I carried you on eagles' wings and brought you to myself. NOW, if you obey me fully, and keep my covenant, then out of all nations you will be my treasured possessions.

Although the whole earth is mine, you will be for me a kingdom of priests, and a holy nation. Then, God gave directives to Moses on how the people should prepare to meet him on the mount Sinai.

I – ISRAËL'S PREPARATION OF MEETING THE LORD. God said to Moses to tell the people to clean their clothes.(1)the people's clothes should be clean when going to meet the Lord. (2)Any married man will sleep alone two days before going to the meeting (3) When at the meeting, people should not come too close to mount Sinai because if one touches that mount when the Lord is on it, he will die or he be stoned. ISRAËL, GET READY what kind of preparations do you make because you are coming here in this place to meet and worship the Lord?

-Look at the ways the boxers train for the fight before entering the ring.-Look at the ways, from high schools to the nationals, Basketball, Soccer, Football, Olympic, all kinds of Sports Teams train. It may, sometimes take years ahead of training for some important competitions. Each year, coaches of sports teams go out and recruit new players. They look for HIGH QUALITY PLAYERS. They look for players who have the potential to bring the teams to the higher level. and even to number "ones" of their classes. God wanted Israel to be number one of all treasures he may have as the whole world is his,

-Number one kingdom of Priests

-Number one Holy nation.

II TWO REQUIREMENTS FOR ISRAËL TO BE NUMBER ONE Moses' message to the Jewish people give two requirements: (1) OBEDIENCE: If you will obey my voice; (2) KEEP THE COVENANT–I watched "SURVIVORS". Last Monday. Jimmy Johnston was one of the survivors' players. He was in the group of advanced in age. After being well known and a successful coach, he wanted to use his methods to train his team and win. By the end of the session, the other players saw in him a threat, and they voted him out. How could a team win without obedience? In order that Israel be what God is going to expect from him, he must OBEY HIM, and KEEP his covenant. Living alone or living with others, wherever you are going to be, you have to obey someone and live by the rule wherever you are. These two requirements were important to know before Israel knows God's expectations of him.

III- THE CONTENT OF THE LORD'S MESSAGE:GOD SAVED ISAREL FOR HIMSELF, AND HIMSELF ALONE: Application: What many basketball, soccer, Football, players forget is that when they are selected by these BIG TEAMS, yes, they will make BIG MONEY for themselves, but Leagues and Team Owners, make more than they. WHAT WE FORGET: When God saves you, when God saves every human being, it is to see to it that human's praise, honor, glorify, serve and worship him forever and ever. This is the job we are called to do here and the job we will continue to do in heaven after our resurrection.

If I am not number one, God would not keep me on his team. He will not keep you either. Be number one. - Treasured Possessions –

GOD WANTED ISRAEL TO BE NUMBER ONE AS HIS BEST TREASURE.

A Kingdom of Priests

-GOD WANTED ISRAËL AS NUMBER ONE AS THE TEAM OF PRIESTS. People set apart for God. People and servants of their God ; those who will bring God's teachings to all over the world; people who will bring the whole world to the full knowledge of God so that his New Kingdom will be established on earth.

-A Holy Nation –

GOD WANTED ISRAËL TO BE NUMBER ONE AS HIS HOLY NATION. Pagan nations surrounded Israel just as we are surrounded today with many who don't know Jesus or those who are fighting him wishing to make his name disappear from the face of the world. How come that we don't know history? Is it because we don't know geography and thus don't know what the VOCATION OF MUSLIM RELIGION IS ? Do we know any nation in the world where Muslim people and Christian people have lived side by side? This religion has existed since 622 after Christ. Before Islam, the whole of North Africa, in these cities the religion "Christianity" spread until the 6th century, with the exception of Rome and Ethiopia, where are all those first churches and places today?

How can we become a holy nation when Buddhism Islamic faith Hinduism, and other faiths are taking over our country? Israel was called to be number one as a holy nation. We are called as to be number one as holy people. This message is for you:

IV- WHAT GOD HAS DONE FOR YOU AS HE DID TO ISRAËL:

(1) God bore you on his eagle's wings until here.

(2) He sent his Only Begotten Son to be born for you.

(3) God's Son died on the Cross-, just for your sins

(4) you and he died and were raised -TRIUMPHAL RESURRECTION

(5) God gave you eternal life, forgiveness of all your sins.

(6) You have a place prepared for you in heaven and Jesus is coming to get you in order to bring you there. HIS PROMISE

- ARE YOU NOW HIS PARTICULAR TREASURER?

ARE WE NOW HIS KINGDOM OF PRIESTS –

ARE YOU HIS SERVANTS, TRUE WORSHIPPERS?

ARE WE HIS HOLY NATION – ARE WE IN THIS ROOM TODAY
GOD'S HOLY NATION

CONCLUSION:

1- Are you prepared to meet the Lord at the Mount Sinai?

2- Will you be obedient to God and keep his covenant?

Today, God is telling you through me, that his purposes of bearing you on eagle's wings until today are that: you be his particular treasure more precious than gold. You be member of his Kingdom of Priests – worshippers and servants.. You be member of his holy nation If you affirm today that you are God's particular treasure that you are his Priest and Servant, and that you are going to be a member of his Holy Nation forever,

PRAY THIS PRAYER WITH ME:

Prayer: O Lord God, I have answered you invitation to meet you here today through my Pastor Akoa-Mongo. I am glad that I came to this service. Now I understand why you have being carrying me on your eagle's wings until today.

From today, I promise to be obedient to your voice, to keep your covenant, to be your treasured possessions, your priest and a member of your Holy Nation forever. Lord, assist me with your Holy Spirit. Amen

Oct. 3. 2010.

(105)

Reading Exodus 32:1-

THEME: DO YOU HAVE SOME GOLDEN CALVES TOO?

INTRODUCTION: their God, Jehovah who saved them by his strong hand from the oppression, after been saved from Egypt, led the children of Israel, in the wilderness. After they have reached mount Sinai, in our sermon last week we saw how God sent Moses to the people to let them know that they should clean themselves, and get ready, because God was meeting them in two days. God also gave Moses a message to tell the children of Israel that, because he, (God) saved them from Egypt, these were the two things he was requiring from the children of Israel (1) that they obey his voice, and (2) that they keep his covenant. If they do these two things, then,

1- ISRAEL WILL BE GOD'S TREASURED POSSESSION
2- HE WILL BECOME GOD'S KINGDOMOF PRIESTS
3- HE WILL ALSO BECOME GOD'S HOLY NATION. When people heard all this, they said to Moses and to God, "YES, WE WILL". Then God called Moses to mount Sinai. With the absence of Moses for 40 days, people forgot the God who brought them from Egypt. They forgot everything God said to them including the promises he made to them if they obey him and keep his

538

covenant. They went to the second in command, Aaron, and said to him, "Moses has lasted 40 days in mount Sinai. We don't know what has happened to him, MAKE FOR US A GOD WHO BROUGHT US FROM EGYPT AND WE WILL WORSHIP HIM". Aaron ordered them to bring all the jewelry their daughters and wives brought from Egypt. He made a Golden calf with them, and the people rejoiced saying, "here is the God who brought from Egypt, from the house of slavery."

I – REASONS THE CHILDREN OF ISRAEL WANTED A GOLDEN CALF: Moses, the servant of God, the one through whom God operated miracles and saved them from Egypt, was absent for 40 days. Because he did not return from mount Sinai in 40 days, in spite of everything he did as well as God in the past, because Moses was absent, Israel felt being without God.

1-ISRAEL CONFUSED GOD WITH MOSES, THE PERSON HE USED Moses was no longer Moses became God in their eyes. If Moses were there, they would never want to have a Golden calf. But because Moses was not there, the idea of having a Golden Calf came to their mind. For them, the Golden calf replaced Moses. They did not do anything wrong, because if Moses who went to the mount was dead, they had another Moses, the Golden calf among them. What a danger to think that God, who uses people becomes those people. I have known some church leaders who have thought of themselves as being God. They were no longer humans. They could do whatever they wanted; God will always approve their actions. – You have heard about DAVID CARASH.I have known some churchgoers who have looked at their pastors, as God in their midst. Whatever they say and do was always right. They would follow them as they followed God. If they were not in their midst, it was identical as God were not there. They literally worshiped them as they worshiped God.

ARE YOU IN THAT CONDITION WITH YOUR GOD?

ARE YOU LOOKING FOR A GOLDEN CAFT IN ANY PERSON IN YOUR LIFE ?

THAT IS WRONG. DON'T LOOK ANY HUMAN BEING AS GOD

ISRAELCONFUSED THE ABSENCE OF MOSES IN 40 DAYS WITH THE ABSENCE OF GOD.

Because Moses was not with Israel in 40 days, God was not with them. Moses left with God. (1) Aaron was still there. (2) the cloud of fire was still there. If they could had moved, they would also have moved. But the could was still with them. But the person of Moses was not there. If Moses was not there, God was not there according to these people. They had to see Moses to be certain that they had God with them. They were looking for something, which proved them that God was with them. Without the presence of Moses, there was no presence of God. Is that your way of thinking of being with God of being a Christian? If you don't have your Bible, if you don't wear a cross, if you don't go to church, if you are not with other Christians, because God is not visible, he is not talking today and doing things today as in the past, because pastors don't perform miracles, your church leaders don't speak in tongues, we don't wear robes, and have a well-decorated church, there in no glamour and anything which makes God in our worship service THERE IS NO GOD. Is that your ways of thinking about God being with us?

II – WHAT DID ISRAEL DO TO FIND AN ANSWER TO THESE ABSENCE OF GOD AND MOSES? They made for themselves a Golden Calf with their own jewelry. The golden calf became Moses; the Golden Calf became God. With the Golden Calf, they had everything they needed.

1-ISRAEL CREATED THEIR LEADER AND THEIR GOD: They needed Moses. Because there was no Moses present among them, they created one. They needed God. Because there was no God present, among them, they created one

. (1)-HUMAN BEINGS ARE CREATED TO BE LED BY OTHER PEOPLE. But we should be careful about whom to choose to be our leader. Not everyone can be a good leader. Israel chose a golden calf to replace Moses. Aaron was there, the second in command. They did not choose him, they chose the golden calf. They made.

(2)-AMERICAIS GOING TO THE POLES IN FEW WEEKS. We should be careful whom we would choose to fill the vacant seats in the Congress. We know where we stand. If we choose emotionally as Israel did in this passage, we will end up with GOLDEN CALVES IN WASHINGTON. Let us be careful not to choose golden calves but real Moses.

(3)-HUMAN BEINGS ARE CREATED TO BE WORSHIPERS: But if we think that we don't have the true God, we don't believe that the one we have in the Bible is the one we should worship, that we don't believe that the one we have been preaching for century as THE WAY, THE TRUTH, and THE LIFE for the salvation of mankind, we will certainly CREATE ONE many gods AND MAKE THEM OUR GOLDEN CAFVES.

1. Some of us, HAVE MADE MONEY, OUR GOLDEN CALF
2. Some of us, HAVE MADE FREEDOM OUR GOLDEN CAFT
3. Some of us HAVE MADE DRUGS, ALCOHOL, OUR GOLDEN CALF.
4. someofusHAVEMADEINTELLIGENT,MATERTIALISM, GOLDEN CALVES.

(4)-WE THINK THAT SOUTH AMERICANS, AFRICANS, ASIANS AND OTHER PEOLE WE CALL PAGANS HAVE IDOLS, WE DON'T – WE DON'T HAVE GOLDEN CALVES IN AMERICA!

(1) Are you sure that you don't worship some golden calves in your life?

(2) DO you love God the Father, the Son, and the Holy Spirit with all your heart, with all your soul, with all your strength?

(3) Is He the one you have given yourself and everything you have?

(4) Do you trust God when sick more than you trust your doctors?

(5) Do you truly believe that God can provide for all your needs?

(6) Where are your hope, your strength, and your future? If you die today, where are you going? Are you sure to go to heaven?

5--OUR SOCIETY IS BELIEVES IN GOLDEN CALVES. WHAT ABOUT YOU ? People must worship other golden calves. If they know that Moses is with them all the time, his is not absent in spite of 40 days in the mount with God, if they know that God is till present as himself promised that I will be with you until the end of the world and he send his Holy Spirit, which is abiding in our heart, I tell you the truth, churches would be full of worshippers today. These seats would not be empty today. But because Moses is not here and God is absent, they are not here. They worship golden calves now. Conclusion: Because Moses was not there for 40 days, Israel made a Golden Calf for himself.

1- Are you looking for a leader? Don't choose a golden calf one. Moses is coming

2- Do you think that God is not present with you? What about his Holy Spirit. He abides in you. Listen to him. You are the temples of the Holy. God is here.

3- Aaron, don't be influenced by the ignorance of the people. You are second in command

4- Brother and sister, God is not absent. He left us his Church. He left us his Bible. He left us his Holy Spirit. We are his temples. He is always present with us. We should not make Golden Calves, worshipping our jobs, our banks, our freedom, our intellect, our diabolic ideas, pornography, and wherever we hope to find satisfaction in his world.

5- We were created to worship, and to worship the true God, the God of the Bible. The God who sent his beloved Son to come and die on the Cross, to make us his treasured possessions, his kingdom of Priests, and his holy nation. Let us obey and keep his covenant forever and ever. God is always with us. Amen. October 10, 2010

(106)

Reading Numbers 20:1-13, I Corinthians 10:1-12.

Numbers 20:9-11 "So Moses took the staff from the Lord's presence, just as He commanded him. He and Aaron gathered the assembly together in front of the rock and Moses said to them, 'Listen, you rebels, must WE bring you water out of this rock?' Then Moses raised his arm and struck the rock twice with his staff. Water gushed out, and the community and their livestock drank." Numbers 20:12. But the LORD said to Moses and Aaron, "Because you did not trust in me enough to honor me as holy in the sight of the Israelites, you will not bring this community into the land I give them."

THEME: WHY AARON AND MOSES NOT ENTERING THE PROMISED LAND.

INTRODUCTION: The children of Israel were living in slavery in Egypt. God appeared to Moses in the burning bush asking him to volunteer to become the Savior of his people, those he promised through their fathers Abraham, Isaac and Jacob that he will give the Promised Land. Israel has been living in Egypt for more than 700 years. The time has come to leave slavery to go to the Promised Land. God must use people to do that, and Moses, and his elder brother, who became his spoke's person, were chosen.

Moses did not want to go; but God let him know that he will be with him, and that his brother Aaron will stand by him all the time.

When Moses returned to Egypt, he and his brother did great miracles until Pharaoh let the children of Israel leave the country after the miracle of killing all the first-born children of the Egyptians. When Aaron and Moses reached the Red Sea, the Egyptian army came after them, hoping to get Israel back to slavery. But there, God, for the last time, showed his power when Moses extended his staff over the Red Sea, which made two big walls, and let the Israelites go through. When the Egyptian army followed them there, Moses extended his staff once more, and the Red Sea swallowed the whole Egyptian army.

From there, God, through Moses, met the children of Israel on Mount Sinai where he told them that, if they would obey his voice and keep his =commandments, they will become his treasured possessions, his kingdom of priests and his holy nation. The people said, "YES, WE WILL" When Aaron made the golden calf, because of Moses' prolonged absence for getting the Ten Commandments Tablets, God became mad at the people. This Moses pleaded on behalf of the people for forgiveness. God said to this Moses, I will exterminate this people and make you my new nation. Moses said to God; I would rather have my name removed from your book than to see the destruction of this people. THIS MOSES was the one who went from time to time to God, asking him to provide water, and food to this people when they rebelled and preferred the life of slavery in Egypt. THIS MOSES, the one who obeyed God all the time, risking his life, went back to Egypt where he lost his position as the future Pharaoh, just because he killed an Egyptian who was beating a young Hebrew guy. He lost everything and was sent in exile. But in this passage, God was denying Moses to enter the Promised Land, WHY?

Let us look at Aaron, Moses' elder brother. All the time when Moses and Aaron were fighting Pharaoh, Aaron was Moses' right hand. He did everything God commanded Moses. It was because of his skill, very articulate as a speaker, that both men plus God, freed the children of Israel from the land of oppression.

THIS AARON became the High Priest and stayed in the Tent of assignation all the time and was in constant communication with God. Why such a servant of the Lord should miss entering the Promised Land, WHY?HERE ARE THE MAIN REASONS MOSES DID NOT ENTER THE PROMISED LAND:

FIRST, MOSES DISOBEYED A DIRECT COMMAND FROM GOD. God had commanded Moses to speak to the rock. To hold the staff of Aaron he had in his hand, but only speak, nothing but SPEAK TO THE ROCK and the water will gush out. What did Moses do? Instead, he struck the rock with Aaron's staff twice.

. God spoke to Israel through Moses giving them two conditions: (1) If Israel would obey his voice, (2) if he would keep his commandments, Israel will become God's treasured possessions; a kingdom of priests, and a holy nation. The first requirement was the one Moses, the leader, did not observe. He became disobedient GOD HATES DISOBEDIENCE. We are called to obey God. If we don't obey him, there is nothing left to be called his » children ». The sin of disobedience was the one that blocked Moses from entering the Promised Land. IF GOD SPEAKS TO YOU TODAY THROUGH THIS MESSAGE, AND CALLS YOU TO BECOME HIS CHILD, IF YOU DISOBEY HIS VOICE,, THERE IS NO CHANCE FOR YOU TO BE HIS.SECOND, MOSES TOOK THE CREDIT FOR BRINGING FORTH THE WATER FROM THE ROCK: The way Moses and Aaron addressed people before bringing out the water was as if he and his brother were doing the people a favor. Here is what Moses said unto the children of Israel," Hear now, you rebels; must

WE(Aaron and Moses) fetch you water out of this rock? And Moses lifted up his hand, and with his rod he smote the rock twice: and the water came out abundantly, and the congregation drank, and their beasts [also]. "In verse 12 God did not leave only doubt as to why Moses and Aaron did not go into the Promised Land by stating the reason himself: TAKING THE CREDIT FOR THEMSELVES WAS A SIN. THIRD, AARON AND MOSES TOOK THE CREDIT AWAY FROM GOD. Aaron and Moses, in the eyes of these people, were those who gave them the water. If they did not want to give them the water, they would not have had any. TAKING THE CREDIT AWAY FROM GOD,WILLING TO LOOK IN THE EYES OF THE PEOPLE LIKE GOD.THINKING THAT WE CAN REPLACE GOD IN ONE WAY OR THE OTHER – IS SIN!-

This is the sin God doesn't accept. LUCIFER

ADAM AND EVE - WHEN YOU AND I SIN

God could not let such a leader take his people to the Promised Land.

FOURTH, MOSES SMOTE THE ROCK WITH THE STAFF OF AARON: The staff that stood in front of God became the staff, which smote God. What rock was it? That rock was Jesus. Moses smote Jesus TWICE with the staff of God, that staff God used to perform all miracles to save his people from Egypt.

NOT ONCE, NOT TWICE, BUT THREE TIMES 0N A SAME OCCASION: God could not keep this and of leader as the head of those who entered the Promised Land.

GOD DOESN'T FORGIVE DISOBEDIENCE, GOD DOES NOT FORGIVE THE ONE WHO TAKES HIS HONOR/GLORY/PRAISE FROM HIM, AND GOD DOES NOT FORGIVE BLASPHAMY AGAINST HIS SON JESUS ARE YOU DISOBEDIENT TO GOD? DO YOU THINK OF YOURSELF AS GOD, AND THEREFORE DON'T NEED HIM? DO YOU NEED JESUS? ARE YOU TAKING JESUS FOR GRANTED?

FIFTH, MOSES DID ALL THIS IN FRONT OF ALL ISRAELITES; He set a public example of disobedience, of taking God's Credit and of disrespecting Jesus, and of in front of all the Israelites God could not forgive all this and Moses' punishment was that he would not enter the Promised Land.

II-WHY DID ARON NOT ENTER THE PROMISED LAND? WHAT KIND OF LEADER WAS AARON:

FIRST, AARON, COULD NOT SHOW HIS TRUE LEADERSHIP QUALITY IN RELIGIOUS MATTERS. Because Moses was away for 40 days, and people came to Aaron and asked him to make a Golden Calf for them. What did Aaron do? He asked them to go back to their daughters and wives, and get jewelry, and he did caste an IDOL for them. People worshipped that idol made by Aaron. He couldn't tell them to remember the God who brought them from Egypt. He stood for nothing. He was an aloof, cold and irresponsible leader. How could a person like that be the one to lead Israel to be Promised Land?

THE PLACE THIS STORY OF WATER TOOK PLACE WAS CALLED MERIBAH, strife, conflict, disorder, discord, struggle

.SECOND, AARON WAS EASILY LED BY OTHERS- No opinion, an aloof leader. It is through strife, conflict, disorder, discord, and struggle that leaders are born. Moses and Aaron followed the instructions God gave them. God said this to them, (Numbers 20:8), "Take the staff, and you and your brother Aaron gather the assembly together. Speak to that rock before their eyes and it will pour out its water. You will bring water out of the rock for the community so they and their livestock can drink." But when they got there, Moses started speaking eloquently to the people and gave the glory and the honor of bringing water to him. Moses dared to take the rod, which was God's, and smote the rock in front of the people. Instead of blaming his younger brother, telling him that this was not what God told them to do, Aaron was standing there as a mummy. Was this a leader? NOTHING! How could he lead the people to the Promised Land?

1- God is looking for people who obey him and him alone.

2- God is looking for people who give him all his honor, glory

2- God is looking for people who know that Jesus is central for our salvation.

No blasphemy against Jesus.

4- God is looking for people who will always speak up and not say all religions are one. Why don't we just get along. Whatever God is going to do at the end, it will be up to him. He knows those who will enter the Kingdom. It is not up to us.

5- God is looking for a new generation of leaders who will continue the work he has started. Moses and Aaron have done their part and the time has come to retire them.

CONCLUSION:

YOU CAN MISS TO ENTER THE PROMISED LAND

1-YOU MAY DISOBEDING THE VOICE OF GOD.

2-YOU MAY BY TAKING CREDIT AWAY FROM GOD

3-YOU MAY BY DISRESPECTING JESUS -YOUR BLASPHEMY

NOT BELIEVING THAT CHRIST IS THE WAY,THE TRUTH AND LIFE – NO OTHER WAY TO GO TO HEAVEN.

TODAY IS DAY TO CHOOSE THE PROMISED LAND.

WILL YOU ALSO MISS IT AS AARON AND MOSES DID ? Amen.

Machiasport, October 17, 2010

107

Reading of the Scriptures Exodus 1:8-14; 2:2:1-10; 3:1-12

THEME: GOD SAVES FOR HIS OWN GLORY.

INTRODUCTION: What do you remember about the book of Exodus? I am certain that some will talk about Moses being the main character used by God to save the children of Israel from Egypt. Others will name the Red Sea, Mount Sinai, the 40 years the children of Israel spent in the wilderness. Some will say that book is one of the 5 books Moses wrote called PENTATEUCH. My intention today is to demonstrate how the book of Exodus should be well understood by every Christian, because it is not just a book found in the Old Testament, or one of the books written by Moses, but it is what the 4 Gospels and the Epistles are to the New Testament.

The way I can tell a story remains to be seen. But how Moses told the story of God saving the Jews from the hand of Pharaoh remains central to the faith of both Jews and Christians after three and a half millennia. And how you hear it will have a great deal to do with how you relate to the One that Dorothy L. Sayers called "the only God with a date in

History." God had many historical dates. And of the two most significant (the deliverance from the Egyptian oppression, and the Birth of Christ) so far, this was the first.

I – THE OUTLINE OF THE BOOK OF EXODUS:
1. The whole chapter 1 presents how the children of Israel were enslaved in Egypt - 700 years after Joseph has died, no one remembered who he was. New Pharaohs tyrannized the children of Israel.
2. Chapters 3 to 4, God Chooses Moses to be the liberator of the chosen people
3. Chapters 5 to 7:13 Moses was sent back to Egypt to convince Pharaoh to free the children of Israel.
4. Chapters 7:14-11-10 God punishes Egyptians with the 10 Plagues to show his power
5. Chapter 12:1-30 with the 10th plague, God let the Jews celebrate The Passover-before the departure.
6. Chapter 12:31 to 13:16 The Exodus: the children of Israel leave Egypt Exodus.
7. Chapters 13:17 to 15:21. It was the Crossing of the Red Sea
8. Chapters 15:22 to18 Even though, the Jews have seen how much God loved them, they started complaining in the Desert, wishing to return back to Egypt.
9. Chapters 19:1 to 24:18 The Ten Commandments and other Laws were given by God.
10. Chapters 25 to 31 The Instructions on how to build the Tabernacle given by God.
11. Chapters 32 to 34 what will happen to those who break the Law
12. Chapter 35 to 40, The Tabernacle was built -

II. WHY THE BOOK OF EXODUS IS IMPORTANT TO KNOW? THIS BOOK IS THE FOUNDATION OF THE OLD-TESTAMENT

RELIGION In order to better understand what the Book of Exodus is to the Old Testament, we are going to compare it with what we know the most of in the New Testament.

(1)- What the Cross-is to the New Testament, the Exodus event itself was to the Old Testament: God's greatest act of redemption for his people.

(2)- What the Lord's Supper is for us in the New testament, the Feast of Passover was For the Jews in the Old Testament: The Greatest memorial of our Redemption.

(3) What the Resurrection, symbolized by the Baptism is for us in the New Testament the Crossing of the Red Sea is for the Jews in the Old Testament The greatest confirmation of that redemption, and our newness of Life in Christ as we are born again.

(4) What the Church is to the New Testament, the Tabernacle is to the Old: The greatest focal point of God's presence and place of worship in the world.

(5) What the Epistles are to the New Testament, the Ten Commandments are to the Old: the greatest explanation of what life in the light of God's covenant should be like

(6) What the Four Gospels are to the New Testament, the Book of Exodus itself is to the Old: The greatest record of God's saving act. The Book of Exodus as the foundation of the Old Testament religion is to prepare the way for the coming of Christ. By understanding what happened in the book of Exodus will clear the way for all Christians to understand God's saving grace in Jesus Christ.

III-WHO UNDERSTANDS EXODUS, UNDERSTANDS THE N. TESTAMENT

(1) In order to understand the identity of God, the Nature of God, and the God who sent

(2) Jesus to come and die for our sins, we must first understand Exodus

(3) If you would like to understand John 3:16, that God sent his beloved Son to save you from the oppression you were living in, and what happened in Luke 9:31 at the MOUNT OFTRANSFIGURATION, you will understand Moses meeting Jesus in the desert in the BURNING BUSH. The Gospels continually draw parallels between Christ and the people of Israel in this book, applying to him for example the Old Testament language "Out of Egypt I called my Son."

(4) How shall we understand the Sermon on the Mount unless we have read Exodus 20-24, the Text of which is a Sermon? The Book of Exodus is absolutely the foundation of the New Testament as well, so much so that it is no exaggeration to say that without it we can never fully understand what it meant for Christ to come.

IV-EXODUS IS THE FOUNDATION OF THE CHRISTIAN LIFE.

(1) We are now in Egypt. Our Pharaoh is Satan and his agents

(2) God has a plan for our salvation. He would like to save everybody.

(3)-Moses was to save the Jews, Jesus, the Son of God, our Redeemer

(4) God can save. He saved the Hebrews, he can also save all of us.

(5) God is patient with the sinners; he is patient with us.

(6) God is holy. He wants us to be perfect and holy as he is holy.

(7) God has was his ways. We have to learn and walk in his ways not in ours to be his.

VI- GOD HAS HIS CHARACTER: THE BOOK OF EXODUS HAS THEM ALL:

(1) God is a living Being. (I am who I am)(2) God has a dwelling place: That place is in heaven 1 Kings 8:39(3) God can see and hear: " 1 Peter 3:12(4) God thinks and remembers (5) He is generous; (6) He is eager to help (7) He is approachable; (8) God is eternal; (9) God has always been and will always be; (10) God has a kingdom, and that Kingdom will be without end. (11) God is immortal: (12) God is omnipotent; (13) God is omniscient (14) He does what pleases him; (15) God is Infinite; (16) God is a loving God; (17) God is a forgiving God; (18) God knows all people - 15:11; 16:2; 21:2 (19) God is the maker of all things- 16:4(20) God controls all things- 16:33; 21:30 (21) God blesses the godly and condemns the wicked- 12:2; (22) God delights in our prayers- 15:8, 29; (23) God loves those who obey Him- 11:27; 15:9-10;(24) God cares for the poor, sick, and widows15:25; 22:22-23; (25) God purifies hearts- 17:3; (26) God hates evil- 17:5; 21:27; 28:9.

CONCLUSION: In the book of Exodus, we will see how God kept his promises; how he established a covenant with the Hebrews people; how he took care of them during difficult times for 40 years spent in the desert; how he will use his chosen leaders: Moses, Joshua, Aaron, Caleb to guide this stiff-necked people in the wilderness until they reached the promised land.

WE will also learn the BAD character of Hebrews people. The book of Exodus stands at a crossroads between the promises of the past and their culmination in the future. We are in the wilderness now; let us be obedient to God and reach the Promised Land. Amen.

(108)

Exodus 3:1-12, 4:1-20

Text. Exodus 4:17 take in your hand this staff, with which you will perform the signs.

THEME: GOD IS LOOKING FOR MOSES T0 SAVE HIS PEOPLE

INTRODUCTION: Moses was keeping the flock of his father-in-law Jethro in the wilderness. It was an ordinary day, which became extraordinary. When God steps in someone's way, that day becomes extra-ordinary. When God is present in the midst of a group of people, that group will become extraordinary.

On that day, when Moses was keeping his father-in-law's sheep, he also saw something extraordinary. The bush was burning, but not consumed. The fire was going but nothing was burning. The voice was coming inside the fire, but the person inside the fire was not burning! Moses wanted to come closer to witness what was going on. This became a confrontation between Moses and God.

Do you know that you have had many burning bushes in your life? The difference between you and Moses is that Moses had the courage, the determination, the will to get closer to it and witness, and see, and be able to know what was going on whether the bush was burning but not being consumed.

I -FIRST LESSON: IF YOU WOULD LIKE TO HAVE AN ENCOUNTER WITH GOD IN YOUR LIFE LIKE MOSES, BE COURTEOUS, COURAGEOUS, AND WILLING TO SET APART WHATERVER IS PREOCCUPYING YOU NOW.

That day, when Moses met God in the burning bush started out as a very normal day.

That day was important because it was the day God wanted to reveal it his plan the salvation of the Jewish people being oppressed in Egypt - , and to Moses, it was the true purpose of his own life. – being an agent whom God will use to save his people in Egypt.

II– DON'T REFUSE GOD'S DIVINE APPOINTMENT: The miracle of the burning bush is a picture of three important things:

1. It presents to us the Nation of Israel which is going through difficult times in Egypt.
2. It presents who God is.
3. it defines who Moses is.

III- GOD HAS A PLAN TO SAVE HIS NATION OF ISRAEL:

The person who brought the Jewish people to Egypt, Joseph was dead. It happened some 700 years ago. The Jewish people have multiplied and became a threat to the natives. The new Pharaoh was determined to eliminate that threat by killing all the baby boys of the Jewish ladies and by putting Jews into forced labor to build cities unoccupied territory. But because God was on their side, they will not be consumed, and will certainly escape.

YOU MUST FIRST MEET AND GET TO KNOW GOD For the first time, throughout the whole book of Exodus, God will allow man to get to know him very well. In order to let the whole group of the children of Israel know him, God wanted the leader, Moses to know him better. The name under which he revealed himself to Moses was, " I AM WHO I AM " I am the eternal God. The one who was, is and will be forever. I promised to save the children of Abraham, Isaac and Jacob. I have come to use you to do just that ».

You should know very well who is calling you; THE GOD » I AM WHO I AM ».

IV- THERE ARE PEOPLE WHO HAVE GONE AGAINST GOD'S PEOPLE: Pharaoh tried and failed; Nebuchadnezzar tried and failed; Hitler tried and failed. What is certain is that until the end of time, Satan and his agents have been trying, but in the end, they will fail, too. Today, as in the past, God is looking for the MOSES, people who will heed his calling and abandon everything they are doing in order to go and have an extra-ordinary encounter with him in the burning bush.

The nation of Israel, the people of God, are oppressed all over the world today. God is looking for the Moses. Would you like to be one for your family, =your city, your county your region, your country or for the whole world. Stop everything you are doing and go to the burning bush. God has a purpose for you. God has a plan to save his people and he will give it to you there. THERE IS GOD HIMSELF: Go to the burning bush and you will meet God The burning bush was where God showed his glory, his holiness, the Almighty God. Deut.33:16; the One who Himself dwelt in this bush. Exodus 3:2 . It was the "Angel of the Lord as the Old Testament calls Jesus, I believe this refers to a Christophany: an OT appearance of Jesus. This fire represented the purity and the desire of God to cleanse the people of sin, and the passion of God to save his people

V – GOD HAS ALWAYS USED MOSES TO SAVE HIS PEOPLE. Moses was a shepherd of his father-in-law's flock. Let us go back a little and see who this Moses was

   (1) It was that Moses who was Jewish by birth, but grew up in the Palace of Pharaoh

   (3) It was that Moses who, when wanting to protect the children of his race, killed the

   (4)   Egyptian and was condemned to die and to be abandoned in the desert.

APPLICATION: If all of us study our past, we will be surprised to find out that God has been with, he has protected us and, And will help us just as he did to Moses before He came and revealed himself to Moses in the burning bush. This may have happened when you were a baby, young man or woman, in your work place, in your multiple adventures in life. God has certainly protected and guided you as he did for Moses. Sure enough, you did not know that. Moses did not know that until this was revealed to him by the maid of Pharaoh's daughter, who was killed for revealing that secret that God, who protected you in the past, is revealing himself to you today and calling you to go and save his people in peril throughout the world.

V- ANSWER « YES » TO GOD'S CALLING YOU TODAY, GOD WILL USE YOU. YOU WILL LIKE IT. DO IT! DO WHAT GOD ASKS YOU TO DO AND YOU WILL LOVE IT.

Moses, who has been under God's plan for years, said to God in Exodus 5:4 , here am I'. He's not the only one who said that. Isaiah did too...but he said, 'here am I Lord, send me'...Moses said, 'here am I...who, me?' 'Can't you send someone else?' He took his shoes off, a sign of respect.
   •   I have no ability. – Who gives ability? GOD
   •   I have no message. – Who gives Messages? GOD

- I have no authority. – Who is the authority? GOD
- I have no eloquence. – Who gives the eloquence? GOD
- I have no inclination! I don't want to do this.

SOMEONE SAID:

Where God guides, He provides;

where He directs, He protects;

where He sends, He extends!

AND PAUL SAID IN PHILIPPIANS 4:13 I CAN DO ALL THINGS THROUGH CHRIST WHO STRENGTHENS ME. God will never ask you to do something you cannot do without His help! God doesn't call the equipped, He equips the called that hear and answer His voice! In Matthew 28:18-19, Jesus himself said to his disciples before he ascended to heaven," All power is given unto me in heaven and in earth. 19 Go ye therefore, and teach all nations, baptizing them in the name of the Father, and of the Son, and of the Holy Ghost".

GOD WILL GIVE YOU THE ABILITY YOU NEED

GOD WILL GIVE YOU THE KNOWLEDGE YOU NEED

GOD WILL GIVE YOU THE ELOQUENCE YOU NEED

GOD WILL GIVE YOU THE AUTHORITY YOU NEED

GOD WILL GIVE YOU THE INCLINATION AND THE LOVE TO PREACH.

That Moses, who has been under God's plan for years, said to God in Exodus 5:4, 'here am I'. He's not the only one who said that. Isaiah did too...but he said, 'here am I Lord, send me'...Moses said, 'here am I... who, me?' 'Can't you send someone else?' He took his shoes off, a sign of respect.

- I have no ability. – Who gives ability? GOD
- I have no message. – Who gives Messages? GOD
- I have no authority. – Who is the authority? GOD
- I have no eloquence. – Who gives the eloquence? GOD
- I have no inclination! I don't want to do this.

CONCLUSION: After God has appeared to Moses in the burning bush and showed him how he will use him, Moses went back to see his father-in-law, and let him know how God, the Almighty, has appeared to him and sent him back to Egypt to save the children of Israel.

You know what Moses did.

You know the way God assisted and used Moses all the way until his death at mount Nebo. God showed him the Promised Land. Even though Moses did not enter the Promised Land, he was obedient to God until death and his mission was well accomplished. Today is your day. Today is the day of the First Congregational Church of

Machiasport. God is appearing to us today to let us know that his people are still being oppressed. Let us go to « Egypt », to the world and free them. Amen.

Sept.19.2010

(109)

Scripture readings Ecclesiastes 7:1-14

Text. Eccl. 7:14 in the day of prosperity be joyful, and in the day of adversity, consider; God has made the one as well as the other, so that mortals may not find out anything that will come after them.

THEME: THINGS TO KNOW AND TO DO TO HAVE A BETTER LIFE.

LIVE IN MODERATION AS LONG AS YOU LIVE.

INTRODUCTION: In the first six chapters of the book of Ecclesiastes, Salomon has taught us what he has found in his search for the meaning of life, the life God gives us. His main conclusion was that VANITY OF VANITY, ALL IS VANITY UNDER THE SUN. Ecc. 1:12, 14; 2:11. But if one is blessed by God, and uses wisely what God has given us he or she will be happy and joyful for the rest of their life.

Through the chapter 7, Salomon would like to give us some counsels in order to live a better life. When we say " BETTER LIFE" we use the comparative adjective "better". That means, we are going to compare lives, and choose which WAYS are superior to the other ways of living. We will choose the life is better than the other. YOU ARE CALLED TO CHOOSE WHAT IS BETTER LIFE. Salomon is turning our senses, our imagination, and our mind, our WILL to many lives that we choose the best one.

I – HONOR IS BETTER THAN LUXURY, THAN WEALTH.Ecc.7:1a) What Salomon is saying is that a GOOD NAME IS BETTER THAN PARFUME.

I used to love certain perfumes. When people put perfumes on, they want others to love their smell. After the person who wears perfume has passed, or when that person leaves, the perfume also disappears little by little. This is what wealth and luxury are. They are for a moment. But good name you have, honor you carry all your life affect other lives when you are around and even when you will be no more. Salomon is advising you and all of us to choose honor, to choose good name.

APPLICATION: What are you leaving behind in this life, a perfume or the honor, and a good name? Choose good name not luxury or wealth.

II –YOUR DEATH DAY IS BETTER THAN YOUR BIRTHDAY. Ecc.7:1b the day of your birth, only your parents and your relatives rejoiced that day you were born. From that day, God has given you the time to leave marks in this world. To transform and mold others. From that day, you have fought good fights with your physical, emotional, spiritual sides, and with Satan who uses others and circumstances, and you have won by the assistance of the Holy Spirit, because you have received Jesus as your Savior.

Remember, the day of your death, radios, televisions, local and public presses, from mouth to mouth, people will talk about you. People will cry. People will see the emptiness you have left in your church family, in the community, in your family, in the world. Some will lament, some will cry without stopping, some will seem to see the sky falling. Do you really know that?

The day of your funeral or life celebration, the church will be full with people who never went to church. Some will decide to receive Jesus and be his disciples the day of your funeral. That day is more important than the day you were born.

Your obituary will be published in the local papers. Family members will gather and mourn. Have you thought about it? What will they say? What will hey miss? What effect your passing will have in other lives?

ONLY REMEMBERED

up and away like the dew of the morning,

Soaring from earth to its heavenly home,

Thus would I leave from this world and its toiling:

Only remembered for what I have done.

Only remembered, Only remembered,

Only remembered for what we have done;

Only remembered, Only remembered,

Only remembered for what we have done.

Shall we be missed when others succeed us,

reaping the fields we in springtime have sown?

Nay, for the sewer shall pass from his labor,

only remembered for what he has done.

Only the truth that in life we have spoken,

Only the seeds that on Earth we have sown,

These shall pass on ward while we are forgotten,

Only remembered for what we have done

From: <u>Randolph's Folksongs of the Ozarks.</u>

III – SORROW IS BETTER THAN LAUGHTER. Salomon is not saying that we should not laugh in this life.. But when you spend all your life laughing, is not right? Some people would like to be on vacations every day. They don't like anything serious.

When you don't want to deal with problems you face, you laugh

When putting every project for tomorrow, you laugh.

Not preparing for your retirement, the future of your children, you laugh.

Not taking care of your health, your bills, you laugh

Not saying, I AM SORRY," and change your life around, you laugh. Laughter provides temporary reprieve from the burden of life, but sorrow encourages us to make positive changes in any situation we are in.

Laugh when things are right and normal. Feel sorry when you make mistakes and take your courage to change your way. DON'T WASTE YOUR TIME.

IV- IT IS BETTER TO HEAR THE REBUKE OF THE WISE, THAN TO HEAR THE SONG OF THE FOOL.: Most of us hate when some tells us that we are wrong.

But we love when people praise us. Even I would say, few of us seek advice. I have received few calls since I became Pastor in this church than my precious church in Cameroon from people who have problem. When talking to people, old or young, you will hear them say, "I KNOW, I KNOW! I KNOW!" over and over because everyone knows, and they don't want any rebuke but praise from the fools.

Someone who would like to be wise should listen to the advice of the wise.

But someone who would like to be lost forever should always accept the praises and eulogies of the fools.

A friend or a person who does not give good advice fool

V – THE RESIGNATION IS BETTER THAN INDIGNATION: Eccl.
A. THERE ARE THINGS IN THIS WORLD WE CAN'T CHANGE:

For example, God has set his purposes for you and me, we cannot change them. We have to walk and follow them until the day we will meet him face to face. That doesn't mean that we don't have any choice, but because God is God, he knows where we are going. That is why certain names are already written in the Book of life, and others destined to eternal fire. he Serenity Prayer by Reinhold Niebuhr, the theologian the best-known form is: God, grant me the serenity to accept the things I cannot change;

Courage to change the things I can;

And wisdom to know the difference.

The extended version: God, grant us the... Serenity to accept things we cannot change, Courage to change the things we can, and the

Wisdom to know the difference

Patience for the things that take time

Appreciation for all that we have, and

Tolerance for those with different struggles

Freedom to live beyond the limitations of our past ways, the

Ability to feel your love for us and our love for each other and the

Strength to get up and try again even when we feel it is hopeless

There are certain things and situation we should not try to change in our life.

If we do, we will be covered with shame, dishonor, and live in affliction for the rest of our life. Instead of INDIGNATION, we should choose RESIGNATION.

LEARN TO LIVE WITH CERTAIN THINGS AND SITUATIONS
AND LEAVE THEM UNCHANGED BECAUSE THEY CAN BRING
YOU INDIGNATION:
KNOW THE DIFFERENCE!

1. It maybe about your sex, marriage, your children, your country, your name, your church, your wife, your husband, your job, where you life, your look,

2. CHOOSE RESIGNATION OVER INDIGNATION
CHANGE WHAT YOU CAN
KNOW WHAT YOU CAN NOT CHANGE
AND HAVE THE WISDOM TO KNOW THE DIFFERENCE.

CONCLUSION:

1. Leave a good perfume around, but that perfume should be your honor and not your wealth. Think about what people say when you are not there.

2. Preserve your honor, your respect, your faith, and your history. People will remember.

3. Always have in mind the day of your funeral. What kind of influence you will leave after you have departed from this world.

4. Accept, seek, and know that the rebuke of a wise man is better than the song of the fool, someone who doesn't care and love you will always praise you.

5. Know what you can't change, change what you can, and live with the difference. Resign yourself to something in order to save yourself from indignation.

DOING THESE THINGS, YOU WILL HAVE A BETTER LIFEHERE
ON EARTH AS WELL AS IN HEAVEN WITH YOUR LORD,
JESUS.

ILLUSTRATION: It is not too late for your and me. The Inventor and scientist Alfred B. Nobel, who invented the dynamite and ballistic power's brother Ludwig or Paul passed away. The next morning, he got his New Papers and read not his brother's obituary, but his. In it, they mentioned in the first place that he was the one who invented dynamite and the politic power known as weapons used to destroy human kind.

In order to repair the damage done to humanity, Nobel gave a large portion of his fortune to establish the Nobel Peace price in order to bring peace in the world. Today, most of the people don't know Alfred Noble as an inventor, but as the one who, each year, left the most prestigious award in the world.

You can choose and change your life and be known as a difference person for the rest of your life as Nobel. Amen.

August 22, 2010

(110)

Scripture Readings: Ecclesiastes 3:1-15 and Ephesians 5:15-20

Text. Eccl.3:10, I have seen the business that God has given to everyone to be busy with. He has made everything suitable for its time; moreover he has put a sense of past and future into their minds, yet they cannot find out what God has done from the beginning to the end. I know that there is nothing better for them than to be happy and enjoy them as long as they live. Be careful then how you live, not as unwise people but as wise making the most of the time, because the days are evil.

THEME: LIVING IS TO BE HAPPY AND ENJOY THE TIME.

INTRODUCTION: We can give the following titles to today's message: The only guaranties of life are to be happy and enjoy the time, or There is a time and a place fore everything; or In its time, or Life is full of big events, or If you waste your time, you waste your life, or Find the true meaning of time.

What the book of Ecclesiastes would like to teach us today is that no one should live as if the time is not a BIG FACTOR FOR OUR LIFE. No one should live forgetting that his/her lives in their manners of living depends on the way he or she uses, MANAGES his/her time.

Some of us when talking about time, they limit themselves to seconds, to minutes, to hours, to days, to months, to years, of life spent. The real concept of time is the SUM OF EVENTS TAKING PLACE ONE AFTER THE OTHER. If you just look at the clock, you have missed the time. An association between the time and events which take place in time is the way in which you should live your time. The only way you can better use your time is when you know how to manage what takes place within the time; then your time becomes valued, and your life will be meaningful.

I –THE FIRST LESSON EVERY SEASON HAS ITS TIME

I knew when it is winter, the snow covers roads and trees.

When it is spring trees started budding

I know now that Fall is coming, because I see leaves changing and starting to fall.

There is a place for everything in its time. Brother, sister, don't be confused by not knowing that there is a place for everything in time. The first and the biggest mistake many of us have made over the years has been that we have confused events and time. Remember, these events have been coming that way in time and they have been going leaving the time. Nothing has changed nor will change the way the events take place in time. But the time will never become events. Never !

We were born in a certain time, and we will die in a certain time.

We were young in time, and we will get old in a certain time.

We can be angry in a certain time, and we can be happy in another time.

DON'T LET ONE EVENT LAST FOREVER IN YOUR TIME, ALL THE TIME. That is, don't let seasons, events, circumstances govern your life, determine who you are

EXAMPLE: I have heard people say after they had lost a loved one: I am dead! I am dead! Do these people really die because they have lost their loved one? Be strong in any situation you are going through, because it will pass away. It has its own season.

II –UNDERSTAND THE WEATHER PATTERN IN YOUR LIFE: Learn to use the weather, the seasons, the facts of life, and keep yourself above them.

EXAMPLE: When people are sick, it looks like they have never been healthy. When they have money, they act like they have never been without. When they are made, you may believe that they have never laughed. When they laugh, you may think that they have never been sad. I love watching the Bill Cosby show. It is so real. Is that true? Is that the way Bill Cosby lives with his family?

UNDERSTAND THE WEATHER BUT DON'T BECOME THE WEATHER Keep yourself above the weather or the seasons. Don't turn yourself into the season. The season will go away and you will not go away with the season. Events will pass as anything else in your life.

III- LIFE IS FULL OF CHOICES AND CONSEQUENCES: The biggest advantage we get from so many events in time is that we can make choices for our life. God has given us the eyes to see, the mind to think, and the heart to control our emotions. The true calling of all events in our life in time is that they invite us to make choices. In order to make good choices, we MUST think; in order to think clearly, we MUST control our emotions, in order to control our emotions, we MUST put ourselves above these events. Any decision made according to the emotions will lead us into a problematic future in life.

EXAMPLE: A young man from a very poor family was talented in basketball. Just after high school, most of MBA teams wanted him. The night he was selected to play with the Boston Celtics, his friends organized a big party for him outside of his home. His father and mother embraced him before he went to the party.

That night, after drinking, smoking and doing anything you can imagine at the party, around four o'clock in the morning, his parents were called to the place of the party. He was found unconscious. They took him to the hospital where he was pronounced dead.

Be careful when facing ALL EVENTS, when going through certain seasons in your life. Be careful about any decision you would make at that time, because the season, the event will pass, but the decision you made will stick with you for the remainder of your life.

IF YOU MAKE BAD CHOICES IN TIME, YOU WILL LIVE WITH BAD CONSEQUENCES FOR THE REST OF YOUR LIFE. IF YOU MAKE GOOD CHOICES, YOU WILL LIVE WITH GOOD CONSEQUENCES ALL YOUR LIFE.

IV- DON'T MISS GOD'S TIME: EVERYTHING IS IN GOD'S TIME:

Who is in charge of history? Who determines the time in which everything is happening? Who uses those events in your life? That is God. The lesson you and I should learn is that we should not miss God's time. Each event, which is taking place in time, is something determined by God. God may not cause events, but he uses them. Romans 8:28 says that " We know that God uses everything for the good of those who love him, who are called according to his purposes".

GOD HAS A PURPOSE FOR EACH EVENT TAKING PLACE IN OUR LIVES. Ask God what does he want you to do facing this situation, facing this event, being inside this raging storm in my life? WHAT TO DO, GOD? WHAT TO DO?

There is always a lesson to be learned in each event taking place in our life.

There is always God's purpose in any event taking place in our life.

There are always some advantages in any event taking place in our life.

Ask God! Ask God! Ask him what his purpose is within the event.

Ask God! Ask God! Ask him what your profit is within the event.

Ask him what he wants you to do, where to go, how to behave during that storm.

It is here and mostly here that we miss God's timing. Don't forget God at this moment in your life. Have him face the event. Let him speak to you, and you, be ready to listen. Be obedient at that very moment, because you can easily miss his timing there.

EXAMPLE: A Christian lady was caught in a big flood. All the houses around her were under water when she woke up in the morning. Hers, too, except that she was sleeping on the second floor, and she was still in a dry room. But the longer she stayed on there, the more the whole house was going to be flooded.

From her bedroom window, one of the neighbors came to rescue her in his boat. She said to him, "no". She waited for Jesus to come and save her, and not her neighbor. When the second floor of her house was under water, she stood on the roof. A helicopter came to save her. She refused because she was waiting for Jesus to come and save her. At the end, she went down and died. She could not understand why Jesus did not come to save her.

When she saw Jesus in heaven, she asked him why he did not come to save his deaconess, who had given 10% per of her income to the church, and who believed in him. Jesus said to her, did you see the neighbor, and the pilot?

These people were Jesus. When she refused their help, she also refused Jesus' help.

God is speaking to you in every event, which takes place in your life. Listen to him.

EVERYTHING IS PART OF GOD'S PLAN.

V-FIND THE TRUE MEANING OF TIME IN EACH EVENT:

A- DON'T WASTE YOUR TIME WITHIN THE SEASON: How a person can waste his or her time within the event!

We can waste our time when we despise the event.

We can waste our time when we don't go along with the event.

We can waste our time when we don't PROFIT from the event.

B-FIND THE TRUE MEANING OF TIME IN EVERY SEASON: Everything will pass away except God and the purposes he set for human lives. God is not in time, but he is the master of the time. We live and will die within the time, but the time will not end with us.

You can't stop the time.

You can't change the time.

You can't live without the time.

But learn how to live and find a good meaning in time.

1)- Take every event as it comes knowing that it will go away.

2)- Be happy and accept every season in time as the will of God.

3)- Praise the Lord in every event every season in the time you go through

4)- Rejoice, enjoy every event in every time.

5)- Rejoice, enjoy and praise God all the time and throughout all seasons

LOOK AT EVERY EVENT AND THE TIME AS TRUE GIFTS FROM
THE LORD.

CONCLUSION:

(1)- There is a time for every season, every event, EVERYTHING.

(2)- Don't be confused in time. Distinguish seasons, and use each
appropriately.

(3)- Understand the weather pattern. If you miss it, you will be in trouble
in your life.

(4)- Life is full of choices, and these choices must be made within the
season.

Remember that good or bad choices you make during the season will
determine

Who and where you will be for the rest of your life here and the life
here after.

(5)- Don't miss God's time; everything happens in God's time and purpose.
Ask God why and what to do in his time, and in his plan for you within
each season, each event.

(6)- Find the true meaning of life, by not wasting your time,

but by taking the time and the events involved as they come,

but by being happy in each time and each event in your life,

but by praising and glorifying God all the time in all seasons.

And by rejoicing and enjoying all events in all time as true gifts from
God.

THIS WILL GIVE YOU THE TRUE MEANING OF LIFE. Amen.

August 15,2010

(111)

THEME: THE BEATITUDES, 8 MARKS OF THE KINGDOM.

Readings: Matthew 5:1-12, and 7:24-27.

Seeing the crowds, he went up on the mountain, and when he sat down his disciples came to him. And he opened his mouth and taught them, saying:

"Blessed are the poor in spirit, for theirs is the kingdom of heaven.

"Blessed are those who mourn, for they shall be comforted.

"Blessed are the meek, for they shall inherit the earth.

"Blessed are those who hunger and thirst for righteousness, for they shall be satisfied.

"Blessed are the merciful, for they shall obtain mercy.

"Blessed are the pure in heart, for they shall see God.

"Blessed are the peacemakers, for they shall be called sons of God.

"Blessed are those who are persecuted for righteousness' sake, for theirs is the kingdom of heaven.

"Blessed are you when men reviled you and persecute you and utter all kinds of evil against you falsely on my account. Rejoice and be glad, for your reward is great in heaven, for so men persecuted the prophets who were before you."

QUESTIONS WE WILL LIKE TO ANSWER TODAY:

(1) WHAT ARE THE BEATITUDES?

(2) DO THEY TEACH CONDITIONS WE MUST MEET IN ORDER TO INHERIT ETERNAL LIFE?

(3) DO THEY CELEBRATE THE POWER OF GOD IN THE LIFE OF THE DISCIPLES? Matthew 4:23 gives us THE SUMMARY OF THE EARTHLY MINISTRY OF JESUS. "And he went about all Galilee, teaching in their synagogues and preaching the gospel of the kingdom and healing every disease and every infirmity among the people."

    1) Jesus came to PREACH THE COMING OF THE KINGDOM

    2) Jesus came to TEACH THE WAY OF THE KINGDOM

    3) He came to DEMONSTRATE THE PURPOSE OF THE POWER of the Kingdom by healing the sick. - Preaching, - Teaching - and Healing.

Matthew 9:35. Repeats it" And Jesus went about all the cities and villages, teaching in their synagogues and preaching the gospel of the kingdom, and healing every disease and every infirmity.

The Sermon on the Mount Matthew 5-7 was a typical teaching of the Lord concerning the way of the kingdom, and chapters 8-9 some typical healings and miracles to demonstrate the power of the kingdom.

The Matthew's story recalls us that Jesus who is teaching in the Sermon on the Mount, is the same who called these disciples, and his desire is that as his followers, and disciples, those who receive this teaching are those who are going to depend on him all their lives.

When Jesus was teaching his disciples, there was a CROWD THERE; that is the hearers, the passive audience. We had two groups here; the disciples of Christ, and those who were there just to be there; the inner circle, and the outer circle of the "crowds." Matthew 7:28,
There is nothing wrong with listening, to be there. But Jesus' goal then as now is that those who listen to his Word be also the doers of it. They be transformed by the power of his Word. Jesus LIKES THE CROWD, BUT HE LOVES HIS DISCIPLES.

Let me mention here that this is the way our Sunday services at Machiasport are conceived. Primarily the Word is prepared to feed, strengthen and inspire THE WORSHIP AND LIFE OF GOD'S PEOPLE. Our prayer is that more and more of those who come to hear these messages, will become more curious, the skeptical, the searchers, the doubters who come to the First Congregational Church of Machiasport who seem to be the crowds gathered in behind the disciples on the mount. The Spirit will make the preaching of the Word of God more reaching in their hearts to awaken unbelievers to the truth and beauty of Christ. The Word from Christ to us will awaken the desire in others to come to Christ.

THE BEATITUDES: You can see that there are 8 beatitudes from verse 3 to verse Notice the promise of the first beatitude in verse 3: "Blessed are the poor in spirit, for theirs is the kingdom of heaven." And the promise of the 8th beatitude in verse 10: "Blessed are those who are persecuted for righteousness' sake, for theirs is the kingdom of heaven. Both of them have the identical promise, "For theirs is the kingdom of heaven."

But the other six beatitudes sandwiched between these two are all different. Verse 4: "For they shall be comforted." Verse 5: "For they shall inherit the earth." Verse 6: "For they shall be satisfied." Verse 7: :For they shall obtain mercy." Verse 8: "For they shall see God." Verse 9: "For they shall be called the sons of God."

I -ALL BEATITUDES ARE GOD'S PROMISES FOR HIS DISCIPLES:

(1) Verse 3: Theirs is the Kingdom of heaven –
    THE POOR IN SPIRIT
(2). Verse 4: "For they shall be comforted." -
    THOSE WHO MOURN
(3) Verse 5: "For they shall inherit the earth."
(4) THE MEEK
    Verse 6: "For they shall be satisfied."
    THE HUNGER FOR RIGHTEOUSNESS
(5) Verse 7: :For they shall obtain mercy."
    THE MERCIFUL
(5) Verse 8: "For they shall see God."
(6) THE PURE IN HEART
(7) Verse 9: "For they shall be called the sons of God."
(8) THE PEACEMAKERS
(9) Verse 10: They shall inherit the earth...
    THE PERSECUTED FALSELY

REMARK: The promises of the first and last beatitudes in verses 3 and 10 seem to relate to the present, and the future: the disciples are assured that "theirs is the kingdom of heaven."

II THE BEATITUDES ARE WHAT THE KINGDOM OF GOD BRINGS:

(1) The Kingdom brings comfort,

(2) The Kingdom gives earth ownership,

(3) The Kingdom brings satisfied righteousness,

(4) The Kingdom brings mercy,

(5) The Kingdom brings God's presence in our lives,

(6) The Kingdom brings our new Status as Children of God

(7) The Kingdom brings the kingdom of heaven on earth, and
the Kingdom of God on earth to be the same as the one in Heaven.

III-THE BEATITUDES SHOW THAT JESUS HAS BROUGHT THE KINGDOM OF GOD FROM HEAVEN TO EARTH.

We can enjoy the foretaste of what will be ours in heaven.

You can see exactly what this means right here in the beatitudes.

IV – THE KINGDOM OF HEAVEN IS BOTH PRESENT AND FUTURE: verses 3 and 10 assure us that "theirs is the kingdom of heaven." But verses 4-9 promise that the kingdom

blessings are still in the future. IT IS BOTH NOW AND IN THE FUTURE.

THE MOST IMPORTANT THING ABOUT THE CHRISTIAN FAITH IS THAT WE ARE MEMBERS OF THE KINGDOM OF GOD WHICH IS AND IS TO COME.

V- ALL THE PROMISES OF THE BEATITUDES BELONG TO THE DISCIPLES NOW – THIS IS THE GOOD NEWS, THE GOSPEL JESUS CAME TO PROCLAIM.

(1) If you know the gospel of the kingdom (4:23; 24:14),

(2) If you know the Good News that the kingdom has already come and is now at work, gathering in its members(13:47-50) –

(3) If you know that the power of the kingdom is already present here as it will be in the future, then you will know that "our becoming merciful" is (right now!) a work of God's kingly mercy.

GOD IS NOT WAITING LIKE A JUDGE TO FULFILL HIS PROMISES. THEY ALL ARE OURS NOW.

(1) God brought you to Christ.You didn't come by yourself

(2) Jesus chose you first, (John 15:16). You didn't come to him first.

(3) You didn't recognizeChrist first, He opened your eyes (Matt. 6:l7).

(4) It is by God's mercy that you are saved .(Romans 9:16).

VI- THE BEATITUDES ARE INVITATIONS ADDRESSED TO ALL THE DISCIPLES TO BECOME LIKE CHRIST HIMSELF.

"Ohowfortunateyouare,mydearbrothers!Ohowfortunateyouaretobechosen of God, to have your eyes opened, to be drawn to the Savior,

(1)to be poor and mourning and meek and hungry and merciful and pure in heart and peacemaker! Rejoice! Rejoice and give thanks, my beloved disciples, that you are this kind of person, for it is not your own doing! It is the reign of God in your life."

VII - THE BEATITUDES ARE WORDS OF CELEBRATION:.

1)-Let us celebrate as members of the kingdom, being poor in sprit.

2)-Let us celebrate the comfort, because we mourn in this earth.,

3)-Let us celebrate the ownership of the earth, being meek

4)-Let us celebrate being filled being hungry, thirst for righteousness.

5)-LET US CELEBRATE MERCY because we are merciful

6)-Let us celebrate as we see God, because we are pure in heart.

7)-Let us celebrate as sons of God, because we are the peace makers

8)-Let us celebrate as members of the Kingdom of God

because we are persecuted falsely here on earth.

CONCLUSION:

The beatitudes are the pure Gospel of the Kingdom Jesus came to establish here on earth. If you are his disciples, these should be THE MARKS, WHICH DIFFERENCIATE YOU FROM THOSE WHO ARE NOT JESUS' DISCIPLES. You have become who you are because the power of the Holy Spirit is operating in you.

(2) All beatitudes are God's promises for his disciples..

(3) The Beatitudes are what the kingdom of God brings to the disciples

(4) The Kingdom of God is both Present and in the Future.

(5) All beatitudes are for the disciples. If you are his, they belong to you

(6) All the Beatitudes are invitations addressed to the disciples by Christ so that they become like Christ himself.

(7) BEATITUDES, WORDS OF CELEBRATION – Celebrate who you have become: a member of the Kingdom, comforted, owner of this earth, filled, living in God's grace, being with God, God's child, and a member of the Kingdom of God now and to come

QUESTION: Do you belong to the crowds or to the group of Jesus' disciples? BE A DOER, NOT JUST A HEARER. Amen.

Machiasport, May 23, 2010 Roque Bluffs June 13,2010

(112)

Scriptural reading: Matt. 5:17-20, and 7:24-27.

Text. Matt 5:20 " For I tell you unless your righteousness exceeds that of the scribes and Pharisees, you will never enter the kingdom of heaven."

THEME: IS DOING RIGHT THINGS MAKES YOU RIGHT? THE ANSWER IS NO. THINKING THAT BY DOING RIGHT THINGS YOU BECOME RIGHT BRINGS MORE CONDEMNATION ON ANYONE.

INTRODUCTION: Many Christians think that the aim of "Christian living" is to do right things and avoid wrong things. True Christianity is about knowing Christ. After KNOWING CHRIST, THE DOING WILL FLOW FROM THAT RELATIONSHIP WITH THE PERSON WHO IS CHRIST. When we reverse the two, we end up with nothing more than dead religious works, regardless of how admirable they may look to everybody around us.

You don't need to evaluate yourself to see whether or not you are doing the things you think you need to be doing. When we spend all our life thinking about " I SHOULD BE DOING THIS or I SHOULD " and not on "BEING IN RELATIONSHIP WITH JESUS.

I-REMEMBER THE PHARISEES! They looked right and did only the right things all their lives. Their problem was THEY WERE SPIRITUALLY DEAD .Matt. 5 :20"For I say unto you, that except your righteousness shall exceed the righteousness of the scribes and Pharisees, ye shall in no case enter into the kingdom of heaven?

In order to be a good Christian, your righteousness MUST EXCEED the righteousness of the Pharisee. Don't forget that! If you continue living as the Pharisees did, Jesus' condemnation of the Pharisees falls over you too.

OUR ASSIGNMENT TODAY IS TO FIND OU "HOW CAN OUR RIGHTEOUSNESS EXCEED THE PHARISEES RIGHTEOUSNESS.

II- HOW DO WE DEFINE RIGHTEOUSNESS? Righteousness is a legalistic lie that implies you make your own way toward greater righteousness by doing the right things. DO YOU KNOW WHAT WE CALL CHRISTIAN PHARISEES? Christian Pharisees are all of us who LIVE ACCORDING TO RELIGIOUS RULES, and HAVE A LIST OF THINGS WHICH ARE CONSIDERED RIGHT OR WRONG, AND SPEND ALL THEIR ENERGY AND EFFORTS ON CHANGING OUTWARD BEHAVIOR, AND IN SIN MANAGEMENT.

III- CHRISTIAN'S LIFE IS FOCUS IN HIS UNION WITH JESUS CHRIST. His life exists in HIS UNION WITH JESUS CHRIST, from which everything else just follows.

A- I am certain that you have heard many preachers talking about the way our "ACTIONS SPEAK LOUDER THAT OUR WORDS" you have heard many of us preaching on "CHRISTIAN MORALITY" There is nothing wrong about that; but what is wrong is that IT IS OUR UNION

WITH THE PERSON OF JESUS which makes possible those outward changes in us As long as the person is not yet in union with Christ, nothing can take place. He or she will remain the same person forever.

B- ON THE OTHER HAND, some Christians truly believe that BY DOING CERTAIN THINGS and –BY NOT DOING CERTAIN THINGS AS LONG AS THEY LIVE – they know for certain that eternal life is theirs. WHAT A LIE!

IV--MANY OF US ARE CONSUMED BY OVERCOMING SINFUL ACTIONS IN OUR LIVES. Overcoming sinful actions in life consumes the thoughts and energy of many sincere Christians. Our thoughts and our actions are centered on "WHAT TO DO IN ORDER NOT THE SIN. WHILE OUR MOTIVES ARE CERTAINLY PURE, OUR GOAL AND FOCUS ARE COMPLETELY MISGUIDED. CHRISTIANS ARE CALLED NOT TO FOCUS ON SIN, NOT TO SPEND TIME (1) AND ENERGY ON MANAGING SIN, and trying to ELIMINATE SINS IN OUR LIVES. That is wrong in our part. LET US FOCUS ALL OUR ATTENTION, AND DEVOTING OUR EFFORT AND ENERGY ON THE PERSON OF CHRIST.

V- JESUS IS OUR CONQUEROR!HE HAS CONQUERED SIN-. SELF-DISCIPLINE IS LEGALISTIC. When practicing that disciple, we create some EGO-CENTRICISM IN OURSSELVES. " I did it. Why he or she can't do it?"" I, MYSELF CAN " " I AM CAPABLE OF…"Pride, self-confident, looking down on those who don't; thinking of oneself as better than…No humility in us this way. This creates in us a false hope that there is something we can do ourselves to contribute for our salvation; to defeat Satan, and to live according to the will of our heavenly FATHER.

VI _ WE SHOULDN'T STRIVE TO DO WHAT HAS BEEN ACCOMPLISHED.

Jesus has done everything for our salvation. Jesus has overcome Satan; Jesus has paid the price we can't pay for our eternal life. Anything we try to do on our own is just LEGALISTIC METHOD TO SAY THAT I DID IT MYSELF.

The only way to enjoy VICTORY OVER SIN IS TO REST ON THE VICTORY THAT IS ALREADY OURS IN CHRIST JESUS.. JESUS DEFEATED SIN ONCE FOR ALL. The transformation will come to our lifestyle when we simply believe that REALITY
AND SROP TRYING to do something that He has already done.

A-WHY DID JESUS COME?

Jesus did not come to help us KEEP RELIGIOUS RULES in the ways of the Pharisees and the Scribes. HE CAME TO DELIVER US FROM THAT SYSTEM.

B-CHRIST HAS DONE IT ON THE CROSS

B-WE HAVE DIED WITH CHRIST ON THE CROSS–Therefore, we are dead in the law. Because of our co-crucifixion with Jesus Christ, we have no relationship to the law.

(1) WE ARE DEAD TO THE LAW. (Rom.3:28 For we hold that a person is justified by faith apart from works prescribed by the law.

(2) OUR COMMITMENT IS TO CHRIST ALONE.

(3) WE SHOULDN'T STRIVE TO REDUCE OUR FREQUENCY OF SINNING. Sin will not be in our lives if we focus on Jesus.

C- THE REASON YOU ARE GODLY IS BECAUSE THE SPRIRIT ABITES IN YOU.

The Holy Spirit came into you. Jesus said, "It's necessary for me to go away, so that the Holy Spirit can come." And when the Holy

Spirit came into you, He said: "I'll never leave you, or forsake you." Since the Spirit if God has come and has made his downing in you, you are is house, his home and you have become HOLY and CHRIST HIMSELF IS HOLY. That is why you are a GODLY PERSON, THIS HAS BECOME YOUR IDENTITY BECAUSE GOD'S SPIRIT ABIDES IN YOU.

D- WE HAVE BEEN GIVEN A NEW LIFE IN CHRIST, WE ARE HOLY:

"For if by the transgression of the one (Adam), death reigned through the one, much more those who receive the abundance of grace and the gift of righteousness will reign in life through the One, Jesus Christ. Rom.5 :17

VII – RIGHTEOUSNESS, OUR RIGHTEOUSNESS IS A GIFT !
You can know that you are holy right because the Bible says so. (II Cor. 5 :21. For our sake, he made him to be sin, who knew no sin, so that in him WE MIGHT BECOME THE RIGHTEOUSNESS OF GOD. Eph. 4 :24..and to clothe yourselves with the new self, created according to the likeness of God IN TRUE RIGHTEOUSNESS AND HOLINESS. Also see Rom. 5 :19.
A-WHAT IT REALLY MEANS TO BE A GOOD CHRISTIAN?
(1)-NOT AVOIDING TO DO WHAT IS WRONG.
(2)-RECEIVERS OF THE FINISHED WORK OF JESUS-
As long as we look for our self-righteousness and not embracing Jesus Christ's righteousness, we will not be different from Adam and Eve and the Pharisees.

-DO YOU KNOW WHAT WAS THE FIRST SIN OF ADAM AND EVE? - an attempt to do something right to do something to become more like God. We all know where that path led. Consequently, today we see the same prevalent sin. Religious people who have a form of godliness and who try to do the right things, but they've missed the whole point. The point is that God never calls on you to focus on doing right and avoiding wrong. Godly behavior exists in a totally different dimension than good behavior and most of mankind has stayed in trouble since the fall because he is blinded to the difference.

OUR RIGHTEOUSNESS IS NOT ABOUT US, IT IS ABOUIT CHRIST!

It's not about figuring out what will please God and dedicating ourselves to whatever we imagine that to be. No, THE GOSPEL IS THE GOOD NEWS because the Father, the Son and the Holy Spirit have finished to work , and we rejoice by living their victory.

CONCLUSION: DOING RIGHT THINGS DOESN'T BRING LIFE. ACCEPTING THE RIGHT THING WHICH WAS DONE FOR YOU ON THE CROSS ONCE FOR ALL BRINGS LIFE AND IN ABONDANCE. Our calling is not to avoid sinning. Our calling is not to live the life of the Pharisees who were RELIOUS but not SPIRITUALS. Our calling is to be SPIRITUALS. To be spirituals in focusing on Jesus; in establishing good and strong relationship with the person of Jesus.

 If we let his Spirit live in us, if we live his life and not ours, if we become holy, as he is holy, our OUTWARD will resemble him, sand all our actions as well as our thoughts will resemble him and our RIGHTEOUSNESS WILL INDEED SURPASS THE PARISEES. FOCUS IN JESUS, AMEN Machiasport, June 6, 2010

SUMMARY. Today's message is about our righteousness surpassing the righteousness of the Pharisees and the scribes.

 If I ask you right now to tell me what WE call "good Christian", I already know what you will say. You will give me a long list of what he does and another list of what he doesn't do. What is true is that as long as

Christianity is still based on DO and NOT DO, we are not far from what the Pharisees did and the way they lived. If so, we are Christian-Pharisees. The question is if this is really what we, in this church, believe and do, are we going to enter the kingdom of heaven?

Jesus came to change that lifestyle and thought. We are not called to look for the way to avoid sin; we are not called to manage sin in our lives; we are not called to do what is right because what is right has already be done in our behalf by Jesus on the Cross. Our calling is to accept the good News of the Gospel which offers to the children of God the VICTORY OF JESUS AND HIS RIGHTEOUSNESS. It is when we FOCUS on Jesus and establish strong relationship with his person, that his Spirit, the Holy Spirit of God, comes to reside in us and we become holy as himself is holy. It is through that holiness that out outward actions and thoughts let the flow of obedience and submission come naturally. This will not be the fruit of the law, but of the new birth in Christ Jesus. It will not be about our righteousness, but of Christ righteousness for us his saved ones. This way, our righteousness will exceed the Pharisees' and we will certainly enter the kingdom of heaven.

Amen.

(113)

Readings Matt. 5:21-48 and 5:24-28

Text: Matt 5:20, 27, 48 For I tell you that unless your righteousness surpasses that of the Pharisees and the teachers of the law, you will certainly not enter the kingdom of heaven. You have heard......But I tell you... Be perfect, therefore, as your heavenly Father is perfect.

THEME: THE TRADITION,THE LAW, CHRIST'S OR THE SPIRIT OF THE LAW.

INTRODUCTION: Jesus reminds us in the passage we just finished reading that he came, not to abolish the law, but to fulfill it. He came to reveal the full meaning of the law. The Old and New Testaments have the same goal. THE TEACH MAN ABOUT THE LAW. The Old Testament's application of the law has become THE TRADITION. The way we have been doing things. If we do it as we have done before, we have accomplished the law. This is what we call tradition. When what we call "law" IS OBSERVED TO THE LETTER. When a man believes that by doing what the law says, he or she has accomplished the law, is what the Pharisees and the teachers of the law did best.

But Jesus, through the New Testament and in particular, through the Sermon on the Mount, is teaching us the fulfillment of the law by reaching deep down in our hearts and WRITING THE SPIRIT OF THE LAW THERE.

1) The SPIRIT OF THE LAW IS THE LAW OF CHRIST.

2) The spirit of the law fulfills the intention of the law.

3) The spirit of the law is the foundation of Christianity.

4) The spirit of the law once written in our hearts, leads us Christians, and disciples of our Lord Jesus Christ, to live the life of righteousness that surpasses the righteousness of the Pharisees and the teachers of the law.

I -THE TRADITION OR THE LAW ACCORDING TO THE PHARISEES:

I love traditions. I wish my children would never forget the way we lived in Africa. I remember the way my family used to celebrate Christmas. My wife will decorate the house; Christmas Music will be heard from November 15th. By the way, we just took down Christmas decoration. Christmas lights are still there. I remember the way things used to take place in church: (1) preparation of communion for all church members; (2) children's baptism; (3) Easter celebration; (4) Church discipline – I remember the positions of a Deacon, and of an Elder; the work of the session . I remember classical music -

TRADITION – TRADITION. If things are not done the way they used to be done, they loose value- ceremonies – conformities

EVEN IN OUR CHURCH - IN OUR FAMILIES -IN OUR MARRIAGES - IN OUR INDIVIDUAL LIVES, we value these ways. The ways of doing become true worship. No care about the spirit of what we do; but the ways of doing it become the most important.

II – THE LAW OF CHRIST, THE SPIRIT OF THE LAW:

A-The law of Christ recognizes that IMMORALITY BEGINS IN THE HEART. Some of us say that I never kill anyone; I never commit adultery, therefore I am innocent of all that. The question is what about in your heart? Have you hated anyone? Have you looked with a lust in your heart at anyone from the opposite sex. Immorality begins in the heart.

    (1) Where did the intention of killing Abel start in Cain? It started in his heart.

    (2) Where did the intention of sleeping with Beersheba start in David? in his heart.

    (3) Where did the intention of eating the fruit of life start in EVE ? In her heart.

B-What the law of Moses, the law according to the tradition calls sin is THE LETTER OF THE LAW. But the sin we commit in our heart is THE SPIRIT OF THE LAW, which is the LAW OF CHRIST.

    (1) I kill according to the spirit of the law when I hate someone.

    (2) I commit adultery according to the spirit of the law when I look lustfully at The person of the opposite sex. I am no longer innocent but GUILTY OF SIN.

    (3) I avenge myself according to the spirit of the law when I fight for my own interests.

    (4) I am not different from the Pharisees according to the spirit of the law when I don't love, and pray for my enemies, and people who persecute me.

    (5) I make false vows according to the spirit of the law when I don't always tell the truth and nothing but the truth in my life as someone who follows Christ.

C. THE LAW OF MOSE IS THE LETTER OF THE LAW:

The reason Christianity has not made a difference in our lives is that we still behave as Pharisees and the teachers of the law. Practicing the law according to the letter, what says the law has become the goal of all Christians. Our hearts are empty. The law of Christ is not written in our hearts. Jesus came and taught his disciples to have his law WRITTEN IN THEIR HEARTS. He came to teach us to live according to the spirit of his law. Jesus is against double minded Christians. Those who do things differently from what they think. We should always do what our hearts say and ask us to do.

D- PERSISTANCE IN IMMORALITY DAMNS OUR SOULS. - (REPENT)

Jesus gives us wonderful advice in this passage. Some of us would say, " I WAS TAUGHT AND I GRAW UP HIDING MY THOUGHTS AND ACTING CERTAIN WAYS. I have been living this way all my life; how can I change now, Pastor? Verses 29-30 say, » If you right eye causes you to sin, gauge it out, and throw it away. It is better for you to lose one part of your body than for your whole body to be thrown into hell. And if your right hand causes you to sin, cut it off and throw it away. It is better to lose one part of your body than for your whole body to go into hell ».

Jesus is telling us that THE DRASTIC ACTIONS WE TAKE NOW IN ORDER TO SAVE OUR SOULS ARE BETTER THAN CONSEQUENCES THAN ALLOWING SINS TO REMAIN IN OUR HEARTS, THEN LOSE OUR SOULS AT THE END.

God will not be cruel when we will go into hell; it will be our own choice to go where we do not belong. Jesus came to correct the way the Pharisees were misinterpreting the law. He came to fulfill the law in order that you and I who are his disciples, we live the spirit of the law and not the letter of the law of God.

(1) Take a drastic measure today to live by the spirit of the law.

(2) Let the law of Christ be written in your heart.

(3) Coordinate your action with your heart.

(3) Take a drastic measure today by letting the Spirit dictate what you do and not your emotions and your own natural desires.

III –THE PURPOSE OF THE LAW OF CHRIST WRITTEN IN THE HEARTS IS PREPARING MEMBERS OF THE KINGDOM TO BE PERFECT;

1.THE PURPOSE OF THE SPIRIT OF THE LAW IN THE HEARTS LEADS TOOBEDIENCE OF THE LAW : OBEYING AND TEACHING OTHERS THE LAW.

Once we have let Christ write his law in our heart, we will be surprise how our actions will coordinate with our thoughts.

(1) Our hearts will never desire anything contrary to the Spirit of God.

(2) Never again our actions will be different from our thoughts.

(3) Never again our natural man will dictate what we desire and do.

(4) We will never live according to the letter of the law, but the spirit

THAT WAY: Others will see our actions as reflections to the will of God in our life and actions. Others will learn from us. Our actions will go along with our words and the teachings of Christ. WHAT A DIFFERENCE WE WILL MAKE IN THIS WORLD!

2-AS DISCIPLES OF CHRIST, WE'LL PURSUE HIS RIGHTEOUSNESS:

Everything we will say and everything we will do will be the reflect who Christ is in our lives. Not only that Christ righteousness will be impute to us because of his forgiveness, but also that we will have and live his righteousness after being conformed to him from the inside out of our existence. Rom 8:29 For those God foreknew, he also predestined to be conformed to the likeness of his Son...

3- AS DISCIPLES, WE'LL BE COMPLETELY LOYAL TO HIM.

Jesus will be our King of kings and our Lord of lords, because of our complete commitment to our Lord and Savior.

4-AS DISCIPLES, WE'LL SURRENDER EVERYTHING :

5-AS DISCIPLES, WE WILL BE FOCUSED ON HIM ALONE

II Cor. 3:18 We, with unveiled faces all reflect the Lord's glory, are being transformed into his likeness, with ever-increasing glory, which comes from the Lord, who is the Spirit.

CONCLUSION:

1) Jesus came not to abolish the law of the Old Testament, but to fulfill it; to make it perfect and complete. All the laws of the Old Testament aimed at Jesus. He came to fulfill them all as they were misinterpreted and applied. 2) The law the Pharisees and the teachers applied and lived accordingly was the LETTER OF THE LAW. We can also call it the TRADITION.3) The law of Christ or THE SPIRIT OF THE LAW is the intention of the law, the law Christ came to leave with his Kingdom,

and with is disciples, us. 4) That law of Christ MUST BE WRITTEN IN OUR HEARTS.

ONCE THAT LAW IS WRITTEN IN THE HEARTS OF CHRIST'S FOLLOWERS:

1) THEY BECOME CAPABLE OF OBEYING CHRIST,& TEACHING HIS LAW.
2) THEY BECOME CAPABLE OF PURSUING GOD'S RIGHTEOUSNESS.
3) THEY BECOME COMPLETELY LOYAL TO CHRIST.
4) THEY TOTALLY SURRENDER THEIR LIVES TO THEIR SAVIOR AND REDEEMER.
5) THEIR LIVES BECOME FULLY FOCUSED ON AND REFLECT JESUS.

QUESTION: How have you decided to live from today after hearing this message?

1- Will you continue living according to the LETTER OF THE LAW as a Pharisee?
2- or will you let Jesus and his Holy Spirit write THE SPIRIT OF THE LAW in your heart and let them take over your life as his disciple? By choosing to have the Spirit of the law being written in your heart today,

(1) The Spirit of Christ will also reside in you from today.

(2) Your actions and your thoughts will be identical from today.

(3) You will live a life, which glorifies Christ from today.

And you will be perfect as your heavenly Father is perfect from today. Amen.

Machiasport, June 13, 2010

(114)

Reading of the Scripture. Matt. 6 :5-15 The Lord's Prayer, Part I
Text. Matt. 6 :9-10 Pray then in this way : Our Father in heaven, hallowed by your name. Your Kingdom come. Your will be done on earth as in heaven.

THEME: THE THREE FIRST PETITIONS OF THE LORD'S PRAYER : Your name hallowed. Your kingdom come Your will be done on earth as in heaven.

INTRODUCTION : Jesus was a great teacher as well, as a great healer. There is no other place in the Bible where he taught his disciples to recite anything except the Lord's prayer. He said, » pray then in this way ». The manner to pray; the substance of a prayer; important elements which should be found in our prayers are learned in the Lord's prayer. If we would like to pray differently from the Pharisees and the Scribes, the Lord's prayer is the way.

SOME REMARKS CONCERNING THE LORD'S PRAYER :
(1) The Lord's prayer is a part of our worship. When you say the Lord's prayer, you
Worship God the Father, God the Son and God the Holy Spirit.

(2) The Lord's prayer: you show that you are a part of the group. No selfish attitude; you include yourself in the group of the believers. That is why you say « OUR FATHER » Even if you are alone when you pray this prayer, know that you and others are praying to the same Father, the one who loves you and them at the same time in the same manner.

(3) The Lord's Prayer starts with God and God alone. The introduction and the three first petitions are about God, not about yourself, the person who prays.

I – THE INTRODUCTION OF THE LORD'S PRAYER: We say in the beginning of the Lord's prayer, « Our Father who art in heaven »

1)-The person to whom we address our prayer is « Our Father » because

a) He created us. We are people created in his own image as Genesis 1 :26 tells us.

b) He loves us : When we sinned in our father and mother Adam and Eve, he sent his beloved Son to come and save us. John 3 :18

c) He resides in us. The Holy Spirit, after Jesus ascended in heaven, came down on the day of Pentecost, and elected his residence in our heart. Today , we are illuminated, capable to hear and understand the Scripture, and receive the truth of the Bible

d) because the Spirit of God abides in us.

(e) We call him ABBAH, Father. He has adopted us, and we are members of his family, members of his kingdom; the kingdom Jesus came to establish on earth.

(2) That Father is in « heaven ». He is different from our earthly fathers

a) He is Holy, honored, respected, feared, pure, majestic, loving, and merciful. The person who prays should be sure that he knows to whom he addresses his prayer.

We are not praying to the gods. We are not praying to the idols. We are not praying to the imagination; we are praying to the LIVING AND PERSONAL GOD. he God who is eternal, omnipotent, omniscient, omnipresent. Be sure that you know to whom you pray in the beginning of your prayer by calling his name.

We come to God, then, with the confidence that He loves us as His children and will hear our prayers. But we also come to the One who is majestic and glorious. His home is in heaven because He is the transcendent God, Lord over all. When we come to Him in prayer, we must remember His greatness no less than His Fatherhood. We must remember His holiness no less than His love. Jesus teaches not to forget God's reverence.

II – FIRST PETITION : HALLOWED BE YOUR NAME :(Mat. 6:9-13)We look at God, and we look at ourselves. God is the holy One. He is up there! We are down here. There are six petitions : The first three deal with God; the last three deal with man. We use SUBJUNCTIVE: It is necessary; it is important; it is a MUST that the name of the Most High be hallowed: honored; respected; sanctified; set apart.

May your name be sanctified;

May your name be glorified

May your name be set apart;

May your name be holy

APPLICATION: There are certain names, when we pronounce them, we get the feeling of respect, of dignity, of intelligence, of honor: When you say Abraham Lincoln; Einstein; General De-Gaulle; General Eisenhower; President Kennedy; Prime Minister Churchill. And if, after calling their names, you say, such and such said," People will pay attention because their names become associated with what they said.

1- The person who prays tells the world that for himself, the name of God is already hallowed in his heart.

2- The Person who prays, invites all human beings in hallowing God's name in their lives.

3- your first petition is your WISH, YOUR DREAM, and YOUR PURPOSE HERE.

APPLICATION: Do you hallow the name of God in your life? This first petition is fundamental in our Christian faith: God must be honored, sanctified, respected, set apart; and holy all the time. IN OUR PRAYER: We seek these conditions in our lives and in the lives of all human beings. We are praying that all human beings know our Father who is in heaven as the holy One, the glorified One, the sanctified One, the pure One. THE SINFUL MAN WE ARE: Must be transformed by the Holy Father who is in heaven. We are worshipping the real and perfect God and we see ourselves in his presence.

III – THE SECOND PETITION: YOUR KINGDOM COME: The first petition is the foundation of the second. Because God is recognized as holy, sanctified, pure, set apart, now our wish, our hope, our expectation is that "HIS KINGDOM COME HERE NOW" God's glory is manifested and His name praised when his kingdom comes.

The whole created world is God's kingdom and He has ruled it from the time He made it, as many of the Psalms make clear.

BUT THE KINGDOM OF GOD WAS RUINED: When Satan temped Adam and Eve, and they wanted to be like God, with their fall, they brought the ruin of God's Kingdom, and the loss of man's position as the king under God

1) When we pray, "YOUR KINGOM COME", we are wishing that we go back to the first state of all humanity

(2) We reclaim a new covenant with our Father who is in heaven.

(3) We seek a restoration, because the world is rebelling

(4) We renounce Satan and are reclaiming Jesus as our Savior.

(5) We look for the salvation of the individual and the world.

THEREFORE, WHAT WE ARE PRAYING FOR IS:

(1) That the Kingdom of God may GLOW

(2) That the nations of the world may be converted to the Faith of Christ

(3) That we become obedient to his commandments.

IV – THE THIRD PETITION: "Your will be done" (Mat. 6:10b)

1- Christians should pray for the will of God be done in their lives.
We are not perfect; we need perfection and that perfection can be attained only when we do the will of God in our daily lives. Pray this prayer, sinful men.

2- We need God's help by making ourselves available to him – May your will be done we have been redeemed from sin. But the sin is always present in our lives.
This is a painful reality. We fight against Satan and the desires of the flesh. Prayer is the most important weapon we have to win this war. Romans 7:14-25

1) When we pray that the will of God be done on earth as in heaven:

(1) We pray as individual followers of our Savior Jesus Christ

(2) We are praying, wishing that our church's community shine.

VI – WHAT IS THE WILL OF GOD WE SEEK?

(1) We seek to fulfill the law of God as Jesus taught it: "You shall love the

(2) Lord thy God with all your heart, and with all your soul, and with all your mind. This is the first and great commandment. And the second is like unto it, you shall love your neighbor as yourself.

(3) What we are seeking in order to do the will of God is to be ABLE TO LOVE GOD, AND TO LOVE ALL OTHER HUMAN BEINGS. DOING THE WILL OF GOD WILL BUILD HIS KINGDOM

  (1) For the Christians, doing the will of God is our first obligation.

  (2) God has saved us so that we might become lovers.

  (3) Our priority is to OBEY CHRIST'S COMMANDMENTS

  (4) The Bible says, "Seek the Kingdom of God" –We are the seekers of his kingdom.

CONCLUSION: Jesus taught is disciples the Lord's Prayer. It is a prayer we say every day. That prayer has six petitions or six requests we, as believers, address to God everyday.

  1. we call God « OUR FATHER » because He is the one who created, saved, and abides in us by his Holy Spirit. He loves us and is holy, omnipotent, omniscient, and omnipresent

  2. Our first petition is about his name which MUST BE set apart, holy, respected, revere, pure. Our wish is that starting with us, God be the God of the whole world.

  3. His Kingdom comes. The kingdom our fathers destroyed by becoming selfish, wishing to be like God. It is that Kingdom we reclaim in our prayer. We renounce Satan and claim Jesus as our Savior and King. We pray that every human being receive Jesus and be saved by his blood.

  4. The Third petition is that the will of God be done on earth as in heaven. The will of God is that we love him with all our heart, with all our mind, with all our soul, and that we love others as ourselves. Love! Love! Love is what we would like to see and seek all our lives. Love is what can prove that we are members of the Kingdom of God.

5. By praying this prayer, we convene with God that he is the Master of our lives. By praying this prayer, we asking that our Holy Father transform our sinful nature forever. By praying this prayer, we promise to the Father that we will be his agents to facilitate the establishment of his Kingdom on earth where his will must be done as in heaven. This prayer teaches us the most essential elements our daily prayers should have. We thank Jesus for teaching us how to pray. Amen.

Machiasport, June 27, 2010

(115)

Readings Matt. 7:7-14

Text. Matt. 7: In everything Do to others as you would have them do to you; for this is the law and the prophets.

THEME: THE GOLDEN RULE: DO UNTO OTHERS, WHAT YOU WANT THEM TO DO TO YOU.

INTRODUCTION: A man is a social animal. You need others as they need you. No one would be happy to live alone without having some people he or she interacts with. After God created everything in six days, and had given all authority to man over all his earthly creation, the Bible tells us that, after God had put man (ADAM) in the beautiful garden of Eden, he said , "IT IS NOT GOOD THAT THE MAN SHOULD BE ALONE, I WILL MAKE HIM A HELPER AS HIS PARTNER", Gene. 2:18

A man needs a woman; a child needs parents; parents need children; Wherever we live, we need neighbors; At the work place, we need colleagues; in the society, we need friends; bosses need employees; employees need a boss; We have a saying in Africa, "one can't climb a tree with one hand". As human beings, we need each other. In order to live as human beings and not as things or animals, we need to know how to communicate, to relate to each other, with dignity, respect, and honor.

I -EXAMPLES OF SELFISH RULE, I, ME AND MYSELF RULE: Our society promotes other rules I call, Selfness; the I, Me, and Myself rule: As long as I am on top, that is good. I must profit; I must be the WINNER. If I win. I wonder about the kind of morals and society we will leave to future generations.

We have certain shows on TV. "SURVIVORS" , " AS THE WORLD TURNS ", " DESPERATE HOUSE WIVES ", " OPRAH", and the majority of the Hollywood production. Children's games! Our "POLITICS". Our ECONOMICAL SYSTEM: CAPITALISM! HOW CAN WE APPLY THE GOLDEN RULE IN OUR SOCIETY? DO UNTO OTHERS WHAT YOU WOULD WANT THEM DO TO YOU!

Jesus provides to all his followers a helpful TOOL in all circumstances. If you don't know what to do at any moment, do to others what you would want them to do to you:.

ACCORDNING TO THE GOLDEN RULE:

1- One must always tell the truth, expecting others to tell but the truth.

2- The CEO'S should pay their employees, what they are receiving.

3- Husbands, address to your wives with respect, honor, and dignity as you would like to be addressed with respect, honor, and dignity.

4- Parents, listen to their children as they should listen to you.

5- Give to others things you want them to give to you.

6- Do to God what you want him to do to you. "TRY to ALWAYS put yourself under the SKIN of everyone who receives your actions"

DO UNTO OTHERS WHAT YOU WOULD WANT THEM TO DO TO YOU.

II. THE "GOLDEN" RULE VS. THE "SILVER" RULES

There is another RULE, which is different from the golden rule, called the SILVER RULE: Many non-Christian religions and some philosophers of the world taught that rule.

1. The HINDU religion taught: This is the sum of duty: do naught to others which if done to you would cause you pain. The Mahabharata

2. The BUDDHIST religion taught: Hurt not others with that which pains yourself

Udana-Varga

3. The JEWISH traditions taught: What is hateful to you, do not to your fellow men. That is the entire Law; all the rest is commentary. - The Talmud

4. The MUSLIM religion taught: No one of you is a believer until he desires for his brother that which he desires for himself. – Hadith (no action)

5. The BAHA'I faith teaches: He should not wish for others that which he does not wish for himself, nor promise that which he does not fulfill. - The Book of Certitude

6. SOME THINKERS TOO: a. Do not that to your neighbor that you would not suffer from him . Pittacus of Lesbos (650-570 BC) b. What you do not want others to do to you, do not do to others. Confucius (551-479 c. Do not do unto others what angers you if done to you by others- Isocrates (436-338 d. "Tzu-kung asked, 'Is there a single word which can be a guide to conduct throughout one's life?' The Master said, It is perhaps the word "shu". Do not impose on others what you yourself do not desire."- Analects, 15.24. e. Treat your inferiors as you would like them to treat you. - Seneca (4 BC-AD 65)

IV. WHAT MAKES THE GOLDEN RULE TOTALLY DIFFERENT.
1. Jesus requires TO DO POSITIVE FAVORABLE THINGS TO OTHERS FIRST. These religions and philosophers ONLY PROHIBIT FROM DOING UNFAVORABLE THINGS TO OTHERS.

The Golden rule recommends every human being to do what is good; what is positive; what is right. To be engaged; to be active; to start and show an example. Do what you would want another person to do to you. You should initiate good actions and continue doing good actions until the other person would get the message, and do the same thing.

EXAMPLES:
(1) I have seen CATS AND DOGS BEING GOOD FRIENDS
(2) If not the cat, the dog started that friendship
(3) I have seen on TV. A dog and a cow being friends
(4) If not the dog, the cow started that friendship
(5) I have seen on TV. Female dog-nursing little kitten.
(6) If not the female dog, the kitten wanted to nurse.

2.THE GOLDEN RULE TEACHES TWO LESSONS:
(1) Our actions, and reactions should always be positive, good, correct, models.
(2) All the time we should only transmit POSSITIVE MESSAGES in all interactions with other human beings as long as we live.

3. OTHER RELIGIONS/PHILOSOPHERS INVITE US TO:
(1)- Think first on the NEGATIVE SIDE BEFORE ACTING
(2)- JESUS TEACHES TO BE KIND TO OTHERS. Kindness, goodness, Right, just, loving, respect, honor. These are things we should apply in our lives.

(3)- When you don't do what is bad, because you expect other to do good to you; When you don't hate others because you don't want them to hate you; That means you stop at "DON'T", you will remain inactive in your life. THIS IS "THE SILVER RULE"

Jesus' teaching was new compared to what world religions and philosophers have taught before him. They taught the "DO NOT ". Jesus taught the "DO".

   a. Christianity is a religion of action.
   b. Christianity is a practical living principle.
   c. Christianity invites the followers of Christ to be those who change the world for the better, and destroy evil, and sin.
   d. Christianity is a positive religion. (I don't like the word religion because religion means rules and regulations. Christianity is a living principle).

IV. GUIDELINE FOR RIGHTEOUS CONDUCT

Jesus, in this sermon on the mount, teaches his disciples to live righteously compared to the life of the Pharisees and the Scribes (Matt.5:20-48) therefore

   a) He teaches the STANDARD OF RIGHTEOUSNESS for the whole world..
   b) He teaches what is in HARMONY with the Laws and the Prophets

Read. Matt. 7:12 Everyone do to others as you would have them do to you; for this is the law and the prophets. – The summary of all is here!

   a. "Love your neighbor as yourself" is the summary of the Law
   b. Paul says in Romans 13:8 Owe no one anything, except to love one another; for the one who loves another has fulfilled the law. When

you do to others what you would want them to do to you become the proof that you love them as you love yourself..

V- JESUS IS INVITING US TO BE READY TO DO WHAT IS GOOD: EXAMPLES: Have you known good artists? Good carpenters? Good painters?

Ex. Michel Angelo and the 16th Chapel

(1) They always pay attention to the little details.

(2) They always sit back and look at what they have done.

(2) They will start all over their art until they are satisfied themselves.

Jesus is teaching us to always be ready to be kind, to do good, and to be models to others in everything we do in this life.

(1) It should be that way with friends as with enemies.

(2) It should be that way with acquaintance, as with strangers.

(3) That way of life should become our character, and our identity.

(4) Doing good and being kind should be our life.

DO TO OTHERS AS YOU WOULD WANT THEM TO DO TO YOU.TREAT OTHERS AS YOU WOULD WANT THEM TO TREAT YOU

VI. JUST IMAGINE That we all in this church, members of the First Congregational church of Machiasport will live and act this way all the time: Doing to others as we want them to do to us.

1. All husbands and wives
2. All teachers and all students.
3. All Palestinians and Jews.
4. All Arabs and all Jews.
5. All Rich and poor
6. All family members

7. All Christians in the world.

8. If everyone in the world could apply the golden rule, we would be in Paradise here.

CONCLUSION

LIVE BY THE GOLDEN RULE, AND NOT BY THE SILVER ONE:

1. Jesus came to teach us the golden rule. Let us live by it and we will change the world.

2. If Christians live this golden rule, Christianity would have a real impact in the world.

3. You don't have to go to Washington, or to Augusta. Start applying this GOLDEN RULE at your home, and with whomever you have contact with from today.

4. The Golden rule will transform our lives, and the lives of those who are closest to us. 5. We have committed the Golden Rule to memory; let us now commit it to life.

6. If we live by the Golden Rule, Christ will become ever present in our lives.

Amen. Machiasport, July 11,2010.

(116)

THE SERMON OF THE MOUNT: THE SUMMARY OF CHRISTIANITY.

INTRODUCTION: The Sermon on the Mount is an amplification of the Ten Commandments. It is the "Law of the Kingdom" Jesus came to establish on earth.

It is the highest teaching of the practical ETHIC of the Bible. It is the way of life of those who have been chosen, and who are members of the Kingdom of God. It is the demonstration of what happens to the person whose heart has been won by the WILL OF GOD. When Jesus, the one who taught with authority will return on earth. we will see the total application of the Sermon on the Mount. Don't lightly consider these three chapters of Matthews in your Christian life, but devout yourself to apply these teachings as a member of the Kingdom of God on earth.

HERE ARE THE MAIN TEACHINGS OF THIS SERMON:

1.THE BEATITUDES Matthew 5:1-12 The word Beatitude is not found in the Bible but means "Blessings" from the Latin word," MAKKARIOS". These verses deal with attitudes, WAYS OF THE HEARTS, and OUTLOOKS OF LIFE of the disciples of the Lord Jesus Christ. These should be our attitudes and our outlooks of life as Christians.

A-CHARACTER COMES BEFORE CONDUCT. What we are determines what we do * 'Poor in spirit' (v.3): produces " the Kingdom of heaven. The need of the person who is poor in spirit is the Kingdom of heaven 'Mourn'(v. 4): for sin, a true sorrow for sin. Produces "God's comfort" 'Meek'(v. 5): our attitude toward others produces "the inheritance of this earth" 'Hunger and thirst'(v. 6): our attitude toward God is expressed; we receive his righteousness by faith because we ask for it. 'Merciful'(v. 7): We have a forgiving spirit and love others, you receive mercy. 'Pure in heart'(v. 8): We keep our lives and motives clean. Holiness, SEE GOD. Peacemakers'(v. 9): We bring peace, between people and God, Children of God Persecuted" (v. 10): All who live godly lives will suffer persecution. "You receive the Kingdom of God"

B-THE NUMBER 8 IN THE BIBLE REPRESENTS A NEW BEGINNING.

The rest of the Sermon on the Mount shows the results of the new life in the believer:

II – THE SALT OF THE EARTH

Ye are the salt of the earth: but if the salt have lost his savior, wherewith shall it be salted? It is thenceforth good for nothing, but to be cast out, and to be trodden under foot of men - Matthew 5:13 the salt is a preservative material preserving from corruption. Salt also creates thirst and introduces flavor. Salt speaks of inward character that influences a decaying world. Salt describes our TASK TO KEEP OUR LIFE PURE in order to change the world.

III -THE LIGHT OF THE WORLDL

Ye are the light of the world. A city that is set on a hill cannot be hid...Let your light so shine before men, that they may see your good works, and glorify your Father which is in heaven.- Matthew 5:14, 16 Light speaks of the outward testimony of good works that points to God. Our calling is to shine in the dark world and bring Christ in it. The Higher Righteousness. Whosoever, therefore, shall break one of these least commandments, and shall teach men so, he shall be called the least in the kingdom of heaven... For I say unto you, that except your righteousness shall exceed the righteousness of the scribes and Pharisees, ye shall in no case enter into the kingdom of heaven.- Matthew 5:19a, 20.

4 LESSONS TO LEARN ABOUT THE COMMANDMENTS:
1) You can't break the commandments and get away with it
2) But you cannot keep the commandments in your own strength either.
3) The only way you can keep them is to come to Jesus Christ for salvation, power, and strength.
4) The commandments are not a way of salvation but a means to show you the way to salvation - through the acceptance of the work of Jesus Christ.

IV- JESUS FULFILLED THE LAW OF MOSES
Jesus became our sacrifice and shed His own sinless blood on our behalf. He offered himself once for all for the sins of all mankind Hebr. 2:27; 9:12). He taught, not the letter of the law but the SPIRIT of the law, its intention

A- THE LAW OF CHRIST:
Jesus did not set aside the Law of Moses, He fulfilled it! He takes the Law of Moses, interprets it in the extreme, and in an absolute sense. And then He absolutely fulfills it! Remember that your salvation does not accrue because of your ability to fulfill Matthew 5, 6, and 7, but because Jesus

did - and you can appropriate His achievement to your benefit. Do it now, in the privacy of your own will.

B- LIVE ACCORDING TO THE LAW OF JESUS: The Law of Moses, the law the Pharisees and the Scribes were living by, is what we call "the letter of the law".

If the law says "don't kill", as long as you never shed the blood of someone and cause his death, you would say ,"I NEVER KILL; THEREFORE I AM INNOCENT OF THAT LAW". The law of Jesus is living according to the spirit of the law. Know that if you hate someone, you have killed him. Therefore, live the kind of life loving everybody, but hating what he or she does.

- The law of Jesus is the best because it teaches us that we are sinners. We can't fulfill the law of Christ. Therefore, we need Jesus
- The Law of Moses let individuals believe that by their own will and power, they can fulfill the law, and they don't need Jesus.

The law of Christ makes us humble; the Law of Moses fills us with pride.

The law of Jesus points us to Christ, the Law of Moses points us to Satan.

The Law of Moses satisfies our will, the law of Jesus satisfies the will of the Father

V-JESUS CAME TO FULFILL THE LAW OF MOSES: The intention of the Law of Moses was to teach us that we are sinners, and we need a Savior. As the Old Testament is the shadow of the New, the law given to Moses in Exodus, being the foundation of the Old Testament, The SERMON OF THE MOUNT, which in Matthew is the deepening of the intention of the Law of Moses in the New Testament.

-Augustine, Thomas Aquinas, Martin Luther, Calvin, as well as many modern Theologians and students of the Bible believe that what the Law of

Moses was for the Old Testament, that is what the Sermon on the Mount is for the New Testament. Jesus came to fulfill the Law of Moses going from the letter to the spirit of the law.

- Transforming anger and hatred into murder -Matt.5:21-26
- Transforming lust into adultery
- Transforming adultery into marriage
- Teaching us to love our enemies, to pray for them all.
- Transforming oaths into sin 5:33-37
- Transforming eye for eye into turn the other cheek 5:38-

VI-THE LORD'S PRAYER:

The Lord's Prayer teaches us how to pray.

(1) Making God the Father of all those who believe in Jesus
(2) Teaching us to hallow, make HOLY, to honor, to praise, to speak about who God is First in our prayers.
(3) To ask God to provide for all our daily needs, not asking for our wants.

VII-THAT WE ACCUMULATE OUR THREASURE IN HEAVEN:

Jesus teaches us that believers should not accumulate wealth on earth.

He teaches us to live knowing that everything we have here will perish.

He teaches us to live knowing that here is our treasure there is our heart.

He teaches us to accumulate our wealth in heaven where will also be our hearts.

VIII- THE TESTIMONY OF THE CHURCH:

1- St. Augustine claimed that Jesus fulfilled the Law of Moses by furthering the intention of the law.
2- Aquinas in the medieval church followed Augustine

3- The Reformers claimed that Jesus' interpretation of the law was the pure and the sole true and correct one.

All agree that the sermon on the Mount emphasizes the way of life for one already saved by the grace of God

IX- BE A WISE BUILDER:

In our entire life, we do one thing: to build a house, our own house. It depends on the material and the foundation on which we build that house. THE RIGHT BUILDER IS The « ROCK » the other one built is house was Jesus. Build your on Jesus.

QUESTION: WHERE IS YOUR HOUSE BUILD NOW? Give an answer. Amen.

Machiasport, July 25th, 2010_____

(117)

Blessed be the name of God ,

Habakkuk 1 :1-4 & Luke 18 :1-8Text. Heb. 1 :1 and Luke 18 :8

How long, O Lord must I call for help, but you do not listen? Or cry out to you »Violence ! » but you do not save?...However, when the Son of Man comes, will he find faith on the earth?

THEME: PERSEVERANCE, - FAITHFULNESS, - ENDURANCE, - DEDICATION

ILLUSTRATION : Young William Wilberforce was discouraged one night in the early 1790s after another defeat in his 10 year battle against the slave trade in England. Tired and frustrated, he opened his Bible and began to leaf through it. A small piece of paper fell out and fluttered to the floor. It was a letter written by John Wesley shortly before his death. Wilberforce read it again: "Unless the divine power has raised you up... I see not how you can go through your glorious enterprise in opposing that (abominable practice of slavery), which is the scandal of religion, of England, and of human nature. Unless God has raised you up for this very thing, you will be worn out by the opposition of men and devils. But if

God be for you, who can be against you? Are all of them together stronger than God? Oh, be not weary of well doing. Go on in the name of God, and in the power of His might."

INTRODUCTION : Each one of us has gone through many stages in this life. You remember when you thought that your father, mother, or whoever raised you was the most powerful human in the world. You remember when you thought that anyone who has reached 50 years was old.

You also remember the time you thought that you were the most beautiful human being, when you could do anything, you are going to change the world; you know it all; you are invincible. You know those years and what you did then.

You can also remember the time you did many things and affirmed yourself as a strong man, strong woman. Many people, including your friends and relatives knew and appreciated your accomplishments.

You do remember the time of discouragement, the time of frustration, the time of lost hope, the time of willing to give up, the time of fear, the time you almost lost your faith in God; the time God seemed far away; the feasible things impossible; the time dreams disappeared, feelings were hidden, and you wanted to say « I CAN'T DO IT ».Today's message is about :
PERSEVERANCE, - FAITHFULNESS, - ENDURANCE, - DEDICATION

I – DEFINITIONS OF THESE TERMS :

PERSEVERANCE : The act or the habit to persist, to continue to try to do something in spite of difficulties FAITHFULNESS : Loyalty, truthfulness, consistency ENDURANCE : The ability/the power to bear up or last continued effort, hardship.

DEDICATION :Set apart for something, devote to, consecrate.

There will be no perseverance, no faithfulness, no endurance T – T – T-We need tests, trials, and temptations in order to produce perseverance, endurance, faithfulness, and dedication. Don't be discouraged, don't be afraid, don't try to give up, don't feel alone, forgotten by your God because you are going through a hard time. It may be because of finance; it may be because of your work; it may be because of your health and your age; it may be because of the situation in your marriage, don't give up, the time we live in these days in history.

If you give up, you will never know the quality we call perseverance.

If you give up, you will never be able to know what is faithfulness

If you give up, how will you acquire the ability to bear up? endurance

If you give up, how can you cultivate the quality of dedication?

II – THREE IMPORTANT QUESTIONS TO ASK YOURSELF:
Every time you face great difficulties as long as you live, here are the three important questions you should ask yourself. If the answers of these questions are positive, you are on the right path.

1) IS THE CAUSE BEFORE YOU, A RIGHT ONE? Is the difficult thing I am trying to do a cause which is worthy? If what I am trying to do is done, will that make a difference in my family, in my community, in my church, in my life?

2) AM I TRYING TO DO THIS FOR MY OWN SAKE ? Am I selfish by doing this? Is this for God of for myself? Is what I want to do for my own sake or for others?

3) AM I ON GOD'S SIDE? DO I FEEL CALLED TO DO THIS? Am I answering God's call in doing what I am doing, or am I an agent of Satan?

IF YOUR THE ANSWERS ARE « NO » This is the time to give up.

IF ALL THE ANSWERS ARE « YES » - Never, never, never give up! Go ahead!

III – THREE REASONS TO CONTINUE PERSEVERING, BEING FAITHFUL, A.ENDURING EVERYTHING AND BEING DEDICATED TO GOD ARE :

KNOWING THAT GOD IS WITH YOU A person who is on God's side should not be discouraged. He should not be afraid; he should not feel alone.

(1) God was with Moses; We know what Moses did from the time he left Egypt to the mount Nebo where God himself buried him.

(2) God was with Joshua : He conquered the promised land and gave it to the children of Israel by defeating the 7 nations who occupied the land before.

(3) God was with David when he defeated Goliath and brought peace to the nation of Israel for 400 years and established Jerusalem as the capital of the nation.

(4) God was with ALL the prophets : Remember Isaiah, Jeremiah, Daniel. When God is with you, everything is possible. Have faith, be courageous, endure, persevere, be faithful. God is on your side.

Every great servant of the Lord has known and knows that the Lord was or is with him/her. Do you want to rank among them? Be certain that he is with you.

B.NO ONE CAN WIN AGAINST THE ONE WHO IS ON GOD'S SIDE: When you are on God's side, who can defeat you ? Will it be Satan, his angels, people, circumstances, money? Who can prevail against you? Name the one who can win!

We are more than conquerors through Christ who strengthens us! Rom.8 :37

Verses 4 – Hymn 409 – Who is on the Lord's side?

Fierce may be the conflict, strong may be the foe,

But the King's own army, none can overthrow.

Round his standard ranging, victory is secure.

For his truth unchanging makes the triumph sure.

Joyfully enlisting, by thy grace divine.

We are on the Lord's side – Savior we are thine.

Philippians 4 :13I can do anything through Christ who strengthens me.

Should a Christian believe in magic?

Should a Christian trust doctors first and the prayer last?

Should Christian refuse to give to God first because of fixed income?

Should children say they don't have the time to go to church

to pray, to read the Bible, to witness because of too much work ?

God can do anything as, when he wants it. by you. God is God.

If you let God be God in your life, he will perform miracles with you.

ONLY BELIEVE!.HYMN 585 ONLY BELIEVE, ONLY BELIEVE.

ALL THINGS ARE POSSIBLE ONLY BELIEVE! (Bis)

C.LOOK AT YOUR PROBLEM AS YOUR CALLING FROM GOD :

Jesus' calling on earth was to save all human beings from sins. Each one of us has his calling which may be his GOLIATH which will stimulate his PERSEVERANCE,

HIS FAITHFULNESS, HIS ENDURANCE, and HIS DEDICATION TO THE LORD.

Whatever is trying to bring you back to where you were before receiving Jesus as your Savior, it is your calling to demonstrate that :

YOU BELIEVE IN JESUS,

YOUR HAVE FAITH IN JESUS

YOU TRUST JESUS,

YOU DEVOTE YOURSELF, YOUR TIME, AND YOUR LIFE TO HIM. JESUS IS YOUR MASTER AND YOUR LORD.

IV- YOUR PROBLEM IS YOUR CALLING FROM GOD :
AS a Christian, when you are convinced that the cause of your trial, trouble or temptation is just, fear not, God is with you. God has put you in that position for a reason. Through that situation, you are going to exercise your calling.
BE STRONG. GOD IS WITH YOU.

When Hitler was killing Jews and eliminating Christians in Germany, a young dynamic pastor named Bonhoeffer had many opportunities to leave Germany and go to the United States. Princeton University offered him a professorship as many American universities did for German intellectuals at that time. But Bonhoeffer refused to come to the States because he felt called to be in Germany and fight the Nazis. He said that if he left the country, he would be ashamed of himself. Yes, he was put in jail and killed by the Nazis by hanging. Whatever you are facing, my brother, my sister, look at that as your calling. God is expecting you to glorify him in it.. Don't give up. This is where you should show your : PERSEVERANCE, - FAITHFULNESS, - ENDURANCE, - DEDICATION WHETHER THE TIME IS FAVORABLE OR UNFAVORABLE.

CONCLUSION : Perseverance, Faithfulness, Endurance, and Dedication are all that we need as those who have been called to serve God on this earth.

A- NO OBSTACLE, NO PERSEVERANCE, NO FAITHFULNESS, NO ENDURANCE AND NO DEVOTION :There is no way we can persevere, be faithful, endure, and be dedicated if we don't face difficulties; if we don't have trials and temptations. It is through those works of Satan that we will be more than conquerors.

621

B- BURDENED, LET'S GO TO JESUS, DON'T TRY TO GO
ALONE :Jesus said, « Come to me all you who are heavy laden,
and I will give you rest. Take my yoke upon you, and learn from
me. My yoke is easy, and my burden light. Matt. 11 :28

ILLUSTRATION : About the first pilot to fly across the United States
from coast to coast. On September 17 1911 Galbraith Perry Rogers left
Long Island, New York and on November 5th he arrived in Pasadena,
California. The time Captain Perry spent in the air was only 3 days and
10 hours and 14 minutes. Along the way he crashed 39 times and made
30 other unscheduled stops. The only parts of the original plane that were
left when completed was the trip were the rudder and the drip pan. Pray
always and do not lose heart, Feed upon the word of God Be persistent
whether the time be favorable or unfavorable, Br faithful to the Lord. He
will never leave you nor forsake you. Endure everything. Be dedicated to
your God until death and our Lord will give you his yoke and his burden,
Remember the Day the Lord will come, and he will say to you, WELL
DONE, Then, you may take your seat in his Kingdom in heaven. Amen.
May 15, 2010

(118)

Reading II Timothy 4:1-8

II Timothy 4:2 Preach the Word; be prepared in season and out of season; correct, rebuke and encourage – with great patience and careful instruction.

THEME: YOU ARE CALLED TO PREACH THE WORD; TO PREACH JESUS.

INTRODUCTION: In the world today, there are many churches. I am certain that as we are inviting you to be more aggressive in witnessing the salvation we have received in Jesus Christ, people will ask you this question. WHAT IS THE SUBSTANCE OF YOUR MESSAGE? WHAT IS THE F0UNDATION OF THE MESSAGE OF THE FIRST CONGREGATIONAL CHURCH OF MACHIASPORT? This should be your answer: WE PREACH THE WORD; WE PREACH JESUS CHRIST WHO DIED AND WAS ROSE FROM THE DEAD. It is important that we let people know why our MESSAGE is different from others.

(1) We are different because of our understanding of the purpose of the church. (2) We are a lighthouse pointing men, women, boys and girls to Calvary '

(3) We point people to the saving grace of Jesus Christ.

(4) We are a congregational church governed by our local congregation, not some ecclesiastical hierarchy.

(5) We are different responding to the commission of our Lord.

(6) We are different because we believe that the Bible is the Word of God, and the only rule for our faith and practice.

I-THE MESSAGE WE PREACH IS IMPERATIVE:

Paul, in the passage we read, commanded the young Timothy to preach the Word. He commanded him to preach the GOSPEL OF JESUS CHRIST, THE GOOD NEWS.

Our mission, the mission of anyone who has received Jesus Christ as his or her Savior, is to witness. To witness is to preach the Word of God to those who don't know Him.

(1) I Cor. 1:17 says "For Christ sent me not to baptize, but to preach …."

(2) Paul wrote to Titus 1:3 saying "God commanded him to preach …."

(3) Before Jesus ascended into heaven, his final and last order he gave to the local church was "Go ye into all the world, and preach the gospel to every creature." Mk. 16:15

TO PREACH THE WORD OF GOD IS GOD'S IMPERATIVE.

(1) Corinthians 1:18-23 For the message of the Cross is foolishness to those who are perishing, but to us who are being saved it is the POWER of God. To the Greeks, with all of their philosophy, thought that it was foolish. To the Jews, with their religious traditions and rituals, the preaching of the cross was a stumbling block.

(2) MANY TODAY THINK THAT THE WORD OF GOD IS FOOLISH...a) They say it is TOO SIMPLE = just believe that Jesus died in our place and someone might have eternal life? That's

too simple. b) Others think that they have to do this and that, and it is because they do this and that, they will have eternal life. When we remove religious traditions, they say that is not right.

II. THE MESSAGE WE PREACH IS PERSONAL: 1 Co.15:3-4
THAT MESSAGE IS CENTERED AROUND ONE PERSON, JESUS.

(1) We preach about the death, burial, the resurrection, the ascension, and the second coming of Jesus Christ according to the Scriptures. (2) We preach Jesus Christ as the CENTER FIGURE in the whole Bible.

A. Every portion of the Word of God draws us to see the Lord Jesus.

B. We don't preach ourselves but Christ. 2 Co. 4:5

C. The only person we want people to know is Christ 1Co. 2:2, "For I determined not to know anything among you, save Jesus Christ, and Him crucified."

D. We are called not to cease to preach Jesus.

E. The early church did not have any other message, except Jesus.

They preached the One who died for ALL in Calvary..

III. THE MESSAGE WE PREACH IS POWERFUL!

A- The Word of God is powerful!.

(1) Heb. 4:12, "For the Word of God is quick and powerful, and sharper than any -edged sword, piercing even to the dividing asunder of soul and spirit, and the joints and marrow, and is a discerner of the thoughts and intents of the heart."

(2) (2) The message we preach brings life to that which was dead!

(3) (3) John 11:25, "Jesus said...I am the resurrection and the life: he that believeth in me, though he were dead, yet shall he live."

B. THE MESSAGE IS POWERFUL; IT IS FROM THE HOLY SPIRIT.

(1) It does not come from the person who is the preacher.

(2) It does not depend on the style of the preacher,

(3) It does not depend on the personality of the preacher

(4) It reaches men and women, the sinners through the Holy Spirit. If you who brings the Word to the one in front of you believes and acts on this foundation, the result will be a powerful faith in those who believe.

(5) The message we preach is powerful because it is through the Spirit of God.

IV. THE MESSAGE WE PREACH IS PRACTICAL.

A- The message we preach works. Ask those who have put their faith and their lives in God's hands. They will tell you that it works. Lives have been transformed because of the Message we preach. Preach the Word. That message is practical because it does what it says.

(1) If you confess your sins, you will be forgiven.

(2) If you receive Jesus as your Savior and Redeemer, you will be saved.

(3) Any child of God will never stand in judgment.

(4) Every promise made in the Bible for those who believe in Christ will be accomplished. I Cor.1:21b. It pleased God by the foolishness of preaching to save those that believe.

C. The message we preach is practical because anyone can understand it. Little children , old men, people from all nations, of all languages of the world, educated and uneducated, white, and black. Everyone can understand this message.

BELIEVE IN JESUS CHRIST AND YOU WILL BE SAVED THERE IS WHAT WE CALL A SIMPLE PLAN OF SALVATION.

We can summarize it by saying, God doesn't want anyone to perish, but that all might come to repentance. John 3:16, "For God so loved the world, that he gave his only begotten Son, that whosoever believeth in Him should not perish, but have everlasting life." Acts 16:31, "Believe on the Lord Jesus Christ and thou shall be saved." Ro. 10:13, "For whosoever shall call upon the name of the Lord shall be saved."

CONCLUSION: The message we bring to the world is imperative.

The message we bring to the world is totally personal,

The message we bring to the world is powerful,

The message we bring to the world is practical.

JESUS CRUCIFIED FOR THE SINS OF THE WORLD IS OUR MESSAGE.

DON'T LOOK FOR ANOTHER MESSAGE It will change lives;

" MESSAGE –

THE HOLY SPIRIT WILL DO HIS WORK.PREACH THE WORD!

WITNESS TO THE SINNERS. BRING CHRIST TO THEM.

LET CHRIST AND HIS SPIRIT TAKE OVER.

YOUR MISSION IS TO SHINE THE LIGHT

FOR ALL THOSE WHO ARE STILL IN DARKNESS.

GO AND BRING CHRIST TO ALL.

" Preach the word; be prepared in season, and out of season; correct, rebuke, encourage with great patience and careful instruction."

(2 Tim 4:2) Amen.

(119)

John 20:19-29

Text John 20:26-30 A week later, his disciples were in the house again and Thomas was with them. Though the doors were locked, Jesus came and stood among them and said "Peace be with you!" Then he said to Thomas, "Put your finger here; see my hands. Reach out your hand and put it into my side. Stop doubting and believe." Thomas said, " My Lord and my God." Then Jesus told him," Because you have seen me, you have believed. Blessed are those who have not seen and yet have believed."

THEME: DO NOT DOUBT, JUST BELIEVE

INTRODUCTION: We have a kind of little monkeys in Africa. They live in groups. One group may have hundreds of them. They are so dumb that they don't trust each other. If you hunt these monkeys, you could kill all of them. If one hasn't seen you, he would never go away. You have heard the expression: "Seeing is believing," or "I will believe it when I have seen it." That's the attitude of the Unknown Soldier – he believes what he sees, and what he doesn't see he doesn't worry about. Throughout history, that's been the attitude of thousands. And, in our Scripture reading, we see that is the attitude of Thomas. Thomas accepts only what he can see and touch and somehow measure and weigh. Because of this attitude, the Unknown Soldier lost his life. And because of this attitude, many lose eternal life.

I – THE KIND OF DOUBT THOMAS HAS:

A- BY NATURE, THOMAS WAS A SKEPTIC AND A PESSIMIST (John 11:16; 14:5). Thomas was not present when Jesus appeared in the flesh to the other disciples, and not as some ghost or spirit, and showed them His hands and side. The disciples told

Thomas that Christ has risen, because they have seen Him. When Thomas heard their report, he refused to believe by saying, "I will never believe." Thomas doubted the sanity of the other disciples and questioned their eye sight. He said, (John 20:25) "Unless I see the nail marks in his hands and put my finger where the nails were, and put my hand into his side, I will not believe it."

THOMAS ASKED MORE THAN WHAT WAS OFFERED TO THE OTHER DISCIPLES: Not only that he wanted to see Jesus, but he wanted to put his finger on his side. Thomas wanted to see and to feel, then he would believe in the risen Lord.

B THOMAS MUST BE REPRIMANDED, for doubting the word of his fellow disciples. He had lived and walked with them for 3 years now. He had come to know them and trust them. Yet, he refused to believe what they told him about the risen Lord.

THOMAS MUST BE CONDEMNED FOR LOOKING FOR PROOFS THAT JESUS WAS ALIVE Believing as the other disciples did just by seeing Jesus was not enough. He will believe only if he could see and touch. Remember, in Cana in Galilee, Jesus condemned the sort of attitude displayed by Thomas.(John 4:48) "Unless you people see miraculous signs and wonders," says Jesus, "you will never believe." Thomas was looking for something spectacular, wondrous, and miraculous before he will believe that Jesus really is alive.

II- THOMAS WAS WITH JESUS WHEN:

(1) He raised from the dead the widow of Nain's son (Luke 7:14).

(2) He called Lazarus out of the grave (John 11:43).

(3) Jairus' daughter was called back to life by Christ (Mark 5:41).

(4) Thomas heard from the lips of Jesus at least 3 times the predictions of his death and resurrection (Mark 8:32, 9:32, 10:33).

(5) Thomas knew that the Old Testament speaks about the Christ's resurrection (Ps 16:10).

Because you will not abandon me in the grave, nor will you let your Holy One see decay.

(6) Thomas was present when Peter made this confession: "You are the Christ, the Son of the living God" (Mt 16:16).

CONCLUSION: Thomas has seen all this, heard all this, knew all this, and yet he demanded a sign before he will believe

III – HOW CAN PEOPLE STOP DOUBTING AND BELIEVE?

The church calls those who have the mind of Thomas," the doubting Thomas." Jesus wishes that everyone who hears that he has risen from the dead, be able to believe the first witness. "Stop being an unbeliever and be a believer." That's what doubt is – being an unbeliever.

-Thomas sounded like, acted like, and thought like the unbelieving Jews.

-He was a doubter.

He knew better. Yet, he refused to believe.

He doubted the testimony of his friends and companions.

He doubted the truth of the Scriptures.

He doubted the prophecies of Christ.

He doubted the miracles he had seen with his own eyes.

My brothers and sisters, are you like Thomas?

Do you doubt the express testimony of Scriptures?

Do you demand a sign before you believe?

Do you have a "wait and see attitude," a "bring me the proof attitude"?

I hope and pray that none of us are like Thomas.

I hope and pray that none of us doubt what is written in the Scriptures.

For don't forget, to doubt is to disbelieve; to doubt is to adopt the mindset of the unbelieving. to doubt is to forfeit salvation.

IV- THE FAITH OF THOMAS:

A- One week later Thomas and the other disciples were in the same house. It is exactly the same situation as before: they were meeting secretly the door locked, the windows were blocked, and once again Jesus suddenly appeared in their midst.

After greeting and blessing those assembled, Jesus turns to Thomas and says, (John 20:27) "Put your finger here; see my hands. Reach out your hand and put it into my side." Here is the proof that Thomas demanded. He has the chance to prove to himself that Jesus really is alive. Jesus was saying to Thomas" Show yourself as a believer rather than as an unbeliever."

B- SEE WHAT HAPPENED TO THOMAS IN JESUS' PRESENCE.

At the sight, and possibly the sound, of Jesus, -all doubt was removed and unbelief was chased away. As Jesus puts it in our text, "Because you have seen me, you have believed." It was enough for Thomas to see and hear Jesus. He did not have to touch and feel Jesus. He did not have to probe into the wounds. Instead, he saw, he heard, and he said, "My Lord and my God!" Here we see that a skeptic becomes convinced, a doubter stops doubting, an unbeliever begins to believe.

V- FAITH WITHOUT SIGHT: IN JOHN 20, THERE ARE FOUR PEOPLE WHO BELIEVED WITHOUT SEEING:

(1) John who came to faith not by seeing Jesus Himself but by seeing the empty burial wrappings.

(2) Mary Magdalene saw Jesus but did not recognize and confessed Him as Lord until He called her name.

(3) The disciples saw Jesus and they believed

(4) In our text of verse 29 Jesus also tells us about another kind of faith: "blessed are those who have not seen and yet have believed." Up to this point in the Gospel, there has been only one type of faith or belief: a belief that has arisen because one has seen the glory of the resurrected Christ. But when Jesus leaves this earth and goes to the Father in heaven, there will be and there must be a new kind of faith: a belief without having a visible encounter with the resurrected Christ.

THE FAITH OF THE CHURCH, OUR FAITH

You and I don't have the benefit of seeing and hearing the resurrected Christ the way Thomas, Mary, John, and the other disciples did. You and I are called upon to believe without seeing.

WHAT IS THE FOUNDATION OF A FAITH WITHOUT SIGHT? (1Pt 1:8-9)

1- It is a belief filled with Jesus' love without seeing him.

2- It is a belief filled with inexpressible and glorious joy without seeing,

3- It is a belief on all his promises with faith, without seeing,

4- It is a belief of the salvation of your souls, without seeing.

VI – OUR FAITH CAN'T BE BASED ON SIGHT.

1- We live by faith, not by sight" (2 Cor 5:7).

1- We cannot depend on eyewitnesses – the apostles who passed away

2- Everything about Christianity comes down to faith not by sight.

NOW IS OUR TIME TO BELIEVE WITHOUT SEEING-

that there is a God

-that God made the universe out of nothing

-that Christ right now sits at God's right hand

-that there is a heaven and a hell-that there is a Spirit,

-and that He makes His home in our heart

-that there is forgiveness, but only by the blood of Christ

-that there is a resurrection of the body

-that there is life everlasting for those who believe.

THE DEFINITION OF FAITH IN (Heb 11:1) Now faith is being sure of what we hope for and certain of what we do not see.

VII – HOW CAN WE BELIEVE WITHOUT SEEING?

1- WE NEED THE HOLY SPIRIT (John 14:16, 14:26, 15:26, 16:7). Without the Spirit it is impossible to believe without seeing.

2- THE SPIRIT MUST PRODUCE FAITH IN YOU Rom 10:17; 1 Pt 1:23-25)

3- WE HAVE TO LISTEN TO THE WORD PREACHE by going to church, by hearing the Word. Through the operation of the Spirit this is how God produces faith within us. Through the operation of the Spirit this is how we can say, "Christ has risen, He has risen indeed. Alleluia!"

CONCUSION: Jesus was resurrected from the dead a longtime ago. Those we call eyewitnesses are no longer around. If we would base our faith on seeing, touching, feeling the body of Christ, and being certain that he has risen from the dead, we will never believe in Him. Are we modern Thomas by not believing the eyewitnesses, the miracles Jesus performed, the O. & New Testaments, and the witnesses of the Church over 2000 years? What would we do if Christ came today and stood among us? Would you be able to put your finger in his side, and then believe? Remember, Thomas didn't, and I am certain that you wouldn't either. Why don't you believe now as I am telling you today that CHRIST IS RISEN FROM THE DEATH, SO YOU WILL ALSO BE RAISED IF YOU BELIEVE. What is required of you, as of all those who hear this good news, is just to believe. If you can't believe, ask Jesus to send his Holy Spirit in your heart. Ask him to give you faith in him. Listen and believe to his Word that we preach from this pulpit. Jesus is risen from the dead as you will be raised yourself by the power of God. Just believe. Amen.

Machiasport, April, 18, 2010I

(120)

_ Matt. 28:1-10 and Acts 2:29-36

Text. Acts. 2: 31-32 Seeing what was ahead, he spoke about the resurrection of the Christ, that he was not abandoned to the grave, nor did his body see decay. God raise this Jesus to life, and we are all witnesses of this fact.

THEME: WE ARE ALL WITNESSES OF THE RESURRECTION.

INTRODUCTION: The whole world is celebrating the day we call EASTER, the day of Jesus' resurrection. For some, they many not go to church for the whole year, but the day of Easter, the day of the resurrection of Jesus, they will put off anything else they could do in order to go to church that day.

Last Monday, I called a colleague pastor in Cameroon. He said to me, "François, my cell phone is off this whole week because I have too much work to do. I meet and work with new members who will join the church, those who would like to baptize their children, those who will receive communion, or get married on Easter." When he said that, I went back to when was young and serving 1,800 member church in Douala. This day on Easter, 2,000 people would be sitting in front of me right now listening to this message. That is what I have known outside Machiasport.

WE ARE WITNESSES OF WHAT GOD HAS DONE BY RAISING JESUS FROM THE DEAD. AREN'T YOU? TELL ME THAT YOU ARE NOT! HOW CAN YOU TELL ME THAT YOU ARE CHRISTIAN, BUT YOU DON'T PRAISE GOD FOR RAISING JESUS FROM THE DEAD TODAY? HOW CAN YOU TELL ME THAT JESUS DIED ON THE CROSS ON FRIDAY FOR YOU AND YOU DIED WITH HIM, AND NOT REJOICE TODAY, THE DAY THE TOMB WAS FOUND EMPTY BECAUSE HE WAS RISEN?

Jesus' resurrection is a fact which has been established, verified, classified and affirmed as true. JESUS WAS RISEN, AND NOW IS ALIVE.

I –THERE ARE HISTORICAL FACTS WHICH AFFIRM THAT:

A- EVERYBODY KNEW ABOUT THE BIRTH, THE LIFE, THE MINISTRY, THE ARREST, THE CONDEMNATION, THE CRUCIFIXION OF A MAN, CALLED JESUS, IN THE BEGINNING OF THIS ERA. This is a fact well known.

B- OUR CALENDAR IS BASED ON HIS BIRTHDATE.

C- OUR CIVILIZATION IS BASED ON HIS TEACHINGS.

D- HE IS THE MOST INFLUENTIAL PERSON FOR THE DEVELOPMENT OF THE FUTURE IN HISTORY.

II –LOOK AT HIS DISCIPLES AND THEIR ENTOURAGE

(1) WE HAVE NAMES FROM THE BIBLE: Mary, the mother of James, Mary of Magdalene, Salome, Peter, John Two other disciples saw him on their way to Emmaus

(2) WE HAVE SOME LIVING WITNESSES: Those who wrote this part of the Bible we call New Testament were EYE WITNESSES: Mathew, John, Paul, Peter,

(3) THE BIBLE GIVES NUMBERS OF PEOPLE WHGO SAW JESUS: Up to 500. IS THE NEW TESTAMENT RELIABLE?

III- SOMETHINGS AMAZE ME ABOUT THIS FACT OF THE RESURRECTION OF JESUS, THE MAN OF NAZARETH.

1- THIS MESSAGE, THE FIRST TIME IT WAS PREACHED 3,000 believed.

2- THIS MESSAGE HAS BEEN PREACHED FOR 2000 years

3- THIS MESSAGE HAS BEEN PREACED ON THIS PULPIT SINCE 1831, Almost 180 years. - IS THIS MESSAGE RELIABLE?

4- THIS MESSAGE HAS CREATED WESTERN CIVILIZATION

5- THIS MESSAGE HAS SAVED LIVES ALL OVER THE WORLD.

6- THIS MESSAGE HAS TRANSFORMED PEOPLE. John Elliott criminal.

7- THIS MESSAGE HAS GIVEN PEOPLE HOPE, PEACE, and BUILT BRIDGES,

8- UNIFIED NATIONS AND ENEMIES.

9- THIS MESSAGE HAS TAUGHT PEOPLE WHAT LOVE IS

10- THIS MESSAGE IS THE ONLY HOPE OF THE WORLD.

11- THIS MESSAGE HAS BUILT BUILDINGS, - Cathedrals, Basilicas. Almost every town in America, every country in the world. Number of people who have received Jesus in the World.

12- PEOPLE OF ALL AGES , ORIGIN, SEX, LEVEL OF EDUCATION,COLOR, CONTINENTS HAVE RECEIVED JESUS AND WERE SAVED BY HIM.

IV – WHAT COULD MOTIVATE THE DISCIPLES TO CREATE A LIE WHICH, AT THE END, WOULD BRING SO MANY TO BELIEVE IT?

This was not a lie, it was the truth.

DO YOU KNOW THAT THEY WERE BEATEN, BUT
REFUSED TO DENIE THE TRUTH OF THE MESSAGE
THEY WITNESSED?
DO YOU FORGET THAT THEY WERE STONED TO
DEATH?
THAT THEY WERE TORTURED?
THAT THEY WERE CRUCIFIED, AND DIED BECAUSE OF
THEIR MESSAGE ABOUT CHRIST'S RESURRECTION?

Yet, they laid down their lives as the ultimate proof of their complete
confidence in the truth of their message. They saw the raising Christ after
his resurrection, and he was with them for 40 days until he ascended in
heaven before their proper eyes.

V- ONE QUESTION I HAVE TODAY FOR YOU IS WHERE DO
YOU STAND IN RELATION TO THIS MESSAGE OF CHRIST
BEING RAISED FOR YOUR SALVATION? ARE YOU A WITNESS,
AS I AM, OF HIS RESURRECTION?
IF YES:
(1) CHRIST IS YOUR RESURRECTED SAVIOR.
(2) YOUR SINS HAVE BEEN FORGIVEN
(3) YOUR RELATIONSHIP WITH YOUR GOD IS ETERNAL.
(4) KNOW THAT CHRIST IS ALIVE RIGHT NOW.
(5) TRUST AND LIVE FOR HIM. Amen.

Machiasport April 4,2010

(121)

Reading. Mark 11:1-11, 15-19. – Jeremiah 7:1-29

– PALM SUNDAY. Text. Mark 11:17 And as he taught them, he said," My house will be called a house of prayer for all nations. But you have made it 'a den of robbers'. In Jeremiah 7:11: Has this house, which bears my name, become a den of robbers to you? But I have been watching you! Declares the Lord. – This is the text I like the most.

THEME: THE TEMPLE IS THE HOUSE OF PRAYER.(YOUR HEART) LESSON OF THE DAY : REFORM YOUR WAYS AND ACTIONS

INTRODUCTION: If you read the whole text from Jeremiah chapter 7:1-29 you will see the WRATH OF GOD. You will understand why Jesus did what he did in the Temple of Jerusalem on Monday not on Sunday, when he came to Jerusalem for the Passover, and the time for his crucifixion.

The Passage we read in Jeremiah is titled" FALSE RELIGION WORTHLESS" Jeremiah is introducing a great Reform, which changed Judah and brought back true worship in Jerusalem.

I –THE PROPHET ADDRESSES THE WORSHIPPERS IN THE TEMPLE.

The Word of God is for everyone who lives in this world. But only those who are available to God hear his Word. You have to be in the presence of God, you have to give your time and make some sacrifice to come to the house of God so that he will address you, and let you know what he has for you. See Jer.7:2 Hear the word of the Lord, all you people of Judah who come through these gates to WORSHIP THE LORD

If I see you tomorrow and ask you, what did we learn yesterday in church, would you be able to tell me some of the important stuff we will cover here today? You have come to the house of the Lord to WORSHIP HIM, Pay attention!

II – WHAT DOES GOD SAY TO US TODAY? A lesson today for us. Vv3-

(1) REFORM YOUR WAYS AND YOUR ACTIONS. (VERSE 3 CONSEQUENCES: And I will let you live in this place

(2) DO NOT TRUST IN DECEPTIVE WORDS AND SAY, "This is the temple of the Lord, the temple of the Lord, the temple of the Lord.

(3) DON'T TRUST DECEPTIVE WORDS saying, "This is the temple of the Lord, the temple of the Lord.".

CONSEQUENCE: If you really change your ways and actions.
Then, I will let you live in this place.

III – WHAT DOES GOD ALWAYS DO TO THOSE WHO SIN AGAINST HIM?

GO TO THE PLACE IN SILOH. God's first dwelling place. Because of the weakness of Israel, God spoke to them again and again:

1) The people of Israel didn't listen. God called on them:

2) The people of Israel didn't answer.

CONSEQUENCE: WHAT HAPPENED TO SILOH, WILL IT HAPPEN TO US?

WHAT DOES THE NAME" ISRAELE" MEAN HERE? Verse 11 The house that bears my Name, the temple you trust in, the place I gave to you and your fathers.

WHAT IS GOD GOING TO DO WITH THOSE WHO DON'T LISTEN?

Verse 15. I WILL THRUST YOU FROM MY PRESENCE BECAUSE: Verse 20 " my anger and my wrath will be poured out on this place, on man, and beast, on the trees of the field, and on he fruit of the ground, and it will burn and not be quenched".

IV-WHAT IS GOD LOOKING FOR FROM SINNERS, ANY SINNER? Verse 23

(1) OBEY ME, AND I WILL BE YOUR GOD, and you will be my people

(2) WALK IN THE WAY I COMMAND YOU that it may go well with you.

(3) QUESTION: DO SINNERS LISTEN TO GOD WHEN HE SAYS THESE THINGS?

    a) Did they listen? No!

    b) They did not pay attention.

    c) They followed STUBBORN inclinations of their hearts.

    d) They went BACKWARD, and not FORWARD

V- HOW DID GOD SPEAK TO THE SINNERS IN THE PAST? Verse 26 (1) HE SENT SERVANTS- THE PROPHETS

Nobody listened to them or paid attention

People were STIFF NECKED

They did MORE EVIL than their forefather

IF YOU TELL THEM THE TRUTH OF THE PAST, WILL THEY LISTEN?

HISTORY DOES NOT CHANGE MEN.PEOPLE DON'T EVEN ANSWER.

VI-WHAT CONDITION ARE WE AFTER NOT OBEYING GOD?

Verse 28 TRUST HAS PERISHED, it has vanished.

VII-WHAT TO DO AS WE HAVE REACHED THIS LEVEL?

Verse 29

(1) WOMEN SHOULD CUT THEIR HAIR

(2) PEOPLE SHOULD LAMENT.

(3) Because the Lord has rejected them,

(4) They have been abandoned.

THIS GENERATION IS UNDER THE WRATH. "Shall be called of all nations the house of prayer" – The Temple was designed as a house of prayer. The needy could approach God in that place. The true believer, whether he was a Jew or a Gentile, could come to the Temple and pray to the Father" But ye have made it a den of thieves" – The phrase "den of thieves" can be interpreted two ways.

First, a den of thieves could refer to a cave where robbers hid themselves away from those who were searching for them.

Second, a den of thieves could refer to a place where robbers hid waiting for their unsuspecting victims to pass by . We are seeing the same things all around us today. Let's take a moment to consider a few questions that came to mind as I prepared this message.

1. Why do professing Christians refuse to pray, and read their Bibles?
2. Why do some believers seem to have such a hard time living for the Lord?
3. Why do people have the mindset that the church exists simply for their convenience?
4. Why do church members feel they can treat the church like they do? They tithe when they can afford it. They come when they feel like it. They refuse to participate in the outreach ministries of the church. They sit back and let others do the work? Why?
5. Why do believers think that they can come to worship whenever they please?
6. Why do believers think that their business is more important than God's ?
7. When God is first in your life, it will show. And, when He isn't, it will show! What does your life show about the place God holds in your heart?

CONCLUSION. The temple of Jerusalem was destroyed just as Jesus predicted it in 70 of this era. We don't need a building today to be the temple to which worship our God. Everything Jeremiah did to teach Jews people to serve and worship God, and what Jesus did in Jerusalem on the second day of his entry in Jerusalem, is what God wants us to learn today. YOU ARE THE TEMPLE WHERE THE TRUE WORSHIP OF GOD MUST TAKE PLACE RIGHT NOW HERE IN MACHIASPORT.

(1) GOD IS ANGRY AND HIS WRATH IS FINAL. Believers should take today's teaching seriously. You are the temple of God and he, and he alone should be worshipped.

(2) GOD HAS SPOKEN AND HE IS SPEAKING TODAY, What he is looking for from us is to CHANGE OUR HEARTS AND OBEY. God doesn't need anything else from a sinner, turn your

back to what you are doing wrong against God, and do what is RIGHT. Everything will be well between him and you.

(3) GOD'S PATIENCE HAS LIMITS. Look back in history, to others who have done what we are doing now, look at what happened to them. Shiloh was the best example for Israel. We have the Middle East, we have North Africa, we have Turkey, We have the DARK AGES. It can happen to us, too.

(4) LOOK HOW THINGS ARE GOING. Every true believer should see what is happening. God is abandoning us. England France, Italy, Germany, and Europe. NORTH AMERICA. Look where we stand in Christian Faith today ! Some of us say now that South America and Africa are going to be the future of CHRISTIANITY. I am from Africa and I don't believe so. THE WRATH OF GOD IS ON HAND, Let's wake up and change our ways and actions

(5) EMPTY WORSHIP brought divine judgment to the temple of Jerusalem.

(6) LOOK AT THE TEMPLE OF YOUR HEART. Where does his message find you?

(7) WHAT DOES JESUS SEE WHEN LOOKING THROUGH YOU, HIS TEMPLE? William Temple defined worship this way,

(8) To quicken the conscience by the holiness of God. Is your conscience quickened during worship by the holiness of God? Do you feel it? Are you in that level yet?

(9) To fill the mind with the truth of God, IS YOUR MIND FILLED WITH THE TRUTH OF GOD HERE?(3) to purge the imagination by the beauty of God, IS YOUR IMAGINATION PURGED BY THE BEAUTY OF GOD HERE?(4) to open the heart to the love of God, DO WE OPEN YOUR HEART

TO THE LOVE OF GOD?(5) to devote the will to the purpose of God." WHEN YOU LEAVE THIS PLACE, ARE YOU READY TO DEVOTE YOURSELF TO THE WILL AND THE PURPOSE OF GOD?

Amen. 03. 28, 2010

(122)

John 19:26-27

INTRODUCTION:

This morning, we will continue in our series on the seven sayings from the cross.

THE THIRD SAYING FROM THE CROSS IS FOUND IN (JOHN 19:26-27).

INTRODUCTION: Last week, we preached on the second word Jesus said on the Cross. Today you will be with me in Paradise. The week before was the first word he said on the cross, Father forgive them because they don't know what they are doing. Today, we will preach on the third word.

« Woman, this is your son, this is your mother. » John 19: 26-27.Last week we covered two criminals. Today it is Jesus, his mother and the beloved friend. Mary and John were with Jesus all the way to the cross. They followed everything people said, or did to Jesus from the place he left Pilate to the place of his crucifixion. They were hopeless. Nothing they could do to save Jesus.

Jesus has forgiven everyone who has taken part at this odious act. Jesus has promised eternal life to the criminal of the cross. His mother and the friend he loved have witnessed all this. What about them?

When Jesus addressed her mother, « WOMAN, » it was not because he didn't know who she was. It was not because he didn't care who she was, it was to show that she has stood for something and she is strong.

I –YOUR ATTITUDE IN SUPPERING CAN SHOW YOUR STRENGTH:

When Jesus called his mother « WOMAN » he saw in her the strong person. Someone who has endured difficult circumstances:

1- The Angel of the Lord – She has met in her life

2- Elizabeth and her pregnancy

3- The wise men

4- The Shepherds

5- Anna in the Temple

6- The death of the

7- Cana'a at the wedding

QUESTION: WHAT WILL MAKE YOU STRONG?
WHEN WILL YOU STAND YOUR GROUND
WHEN WILL PEOPLE KNOW THAT YOU CAN?

Jesus looking at his mother, he knew that she has qualified as a WOMAN.

B- JESUS AND JOHN, THE DISCIPLE HE LOVED.

Jesus remembered that John has been with him for 3 years.

1. They have been at the mount TRANSFIGURATION

2. UPPER ROOM

3. JUDAS LEAVING THEM TO BETRAY HIS MASTER

4. At the Garden where he prayed

5. The ARRESTATION

6. THE JUDGMENT

7. THE CROWD

8. THE CRUCIFICTION

I – WHEN JESUS WAS ON THE CROSS, HER MOTHER STOOD BY: THESE TWO STOOD THERE

(1) THE SUFFERING

(2) THE LOVE

Can you imagine Mary's horror as she looked up at her son who was suffering and near death? Those of you who are parents – especially those of you who have lost a child – can fully understand what Mary was going through.

III - WHERE WILL COME THE COMFORT?

MOTHER – COMFORT YOUR SON

SON, COMFORT YOUR MOTHER

III - IMPORTANT IT IS TO HONOR OUR PARENTS.

As a boy, Jesus clearly honored and obeyed His parents. I think of the words of Scripture in (Luke 2:51) where we are told that Jesus "went down to Nazareth with (His parents) and was obedient to them." Jesus respected His parents and was always obedient to them. Even on the cross Jesus showed Himself to be perfectly obedient…specifically to the fifth commandment, which teaches to honor your father and mother.

With His words from the cross, Jesus demonstrated how children of all ages are to treat their parents. In essence, Jesus asked John to provide for His mother's present and future needs. To give her shelter, food, clothing, protection, and love. Jesus arranged to have all that provided for His mother. As Christians, we have a responsibility to provide for our parents; providing them with food, shelter, clothing, protection and love.

SECOND, JESUS TEACHES US THAT WHEN GOING THROUGH DIFFICULT TIMES, BE CONCERNED ABOUT THE NEEDS OF OTHERS.

Even though Jesus was suffering on the cross, He was still concerned about others. At times, when we are struggling with difficult situations, we become self-focused. We become so absorbed with our own struggles that we neglect those around us.

But Jesus shows us that when we suffer, we should not only be concerned with our own welfare, but also with the welfare of others.

EVEN THOUGH WE SUFFER – LET SET ASIDE OUR PROBLEM ANS SHOW CONCERN FOR OTHERS.

ILLUSTRATION:

Author and lecturer Leo Buscaglia once talked about a contest he was asked to judge. The purpose of the contest was to find the most caring child. The winner was a four-year-old child, whose next-door neighbor was an elderly gentleman who had recently lost his wife. Upon seeing the man cry, the little boy went into the old gentleman's yard, climbed onto his lap and just sat there. When his mother asked him what he had said to the neighbor, the little boy said, "Nothing, I just helped him cry." Brethren, no matter what kind of trial we may be experiencing, we should still be concerned for others. We need to set aside our problems and help comfort people with their problems. We should do what that caring little child did in the story I just read…recognize a need…climb into someone's lap… and cry with them.

François Kara Akoa-Mongo

CONCLUSION:

In closing, we have learned several lessons from Jesus' third saying from the cross. We have learned how important it is to honor our parents. We have learned that even when we suffer...we should still be concerned about the needs of others. At this time, we never want to close a service without offering an invitation, so if you would like to respond, please come now as we stand and sing. Amen.

(123)

Romans 3:9-20, and 8: 33-39

Text. Rom.3:9-10 What)... shall we conclude then? Are we any better? **NOT AT ALL!** We have already made the charge that Jews and Gentiles alike are under sin. As it is written: There is no one righteous, not even one; there is no one who understands, no one who seeks God. All have turned away, they have together become worthless; there is no one who does good, not even one.

THEME: JESUS RESTORES ALL BROKEN RELATIONSHIP WITH GOD.

INTRODUCTION: We have been talking about "GOD'S WRATH". God's wrath against the non-Christians who refused to believe that God exists in spite of all the proofs they may see and have from nature, even what their conscience tells them, that they continue refusing to believe in God. The wrath of God is against the Jews, who believe that, by observing the law, they can be justified in front of God; they don't need JESUS, the one who came and died on the cross for them as well as for the Gentiles.

We also saw that the wrath of God is against us, Christians, even though we know what God doesn't like, and the punishment which will follow those who continue living in sin, we still sin and live as if God would use different measures for us. Are we dreaming?

Today, we will demonstrate that the Jews as well as the Gentiles, even we who are Christians, we are all alike as human being, because we are ALL sinners.

I- THE NAME WE SHOULD CALL OURSELVES IS SINNERS.

Paul reminds us about our nature.

(1) THERE IS NO RIGHTEOUSNESS IN US. Everything we do; every thought which comes in our mind as natural people, according to our culture, our ways of life is geared toward sin. A person, left to himself, is totally incapable of doing anything right in God's sight.

ILLUSTRATIONS:

1. Do you know that you may have been sinning this morning when you left your home to come to church? Your attitude towards those who didn't go to church may say , "**I am better than you, because I go to church and you don't.**" False!

2. Do you know that when we will give offering today, putting money on the plate, you may be sinning when you may be thinking that you have given more than someone else, and you thank yourself that you love God better than he does.. False. Know that our best Christian action is always tainted with our human side which is sin. If there is a name by which we should call ourselves, the name people should be calling us, is "**SINNERS** There is nothing righteous in our behavior from the beginning to the end.

(2) WE DON'T UNDERSTAND GOD: No one among human is capable of reading the mind of God. No one among humans can say "**I FULLY KNOW GOD**". We know him in part. We are similar to many blind men touching an elephant. The one touching the trunk would describe the whole elephant as a trunk. The one holding the ear would describe the elephant as an ear. The one touching the leg would describe the whole

elephant as a leg. WE know him in part, just as Paul says in <u>I Corinthians 13:9</u> **"For we know in part, and we prophesy in part"** Anyone who would say he knows EXACTLY what God is like or what he will do, what the future will look like, how the heaven will be, that person has not yet been born in this world. **WE DON'T UNDERSTAND EVERYTHING ABOUT GOD EVEN THOUGH WE HAVE HIS SPIRIT."**

<u>(3) NO ONE SEEKS GOD</u>: Seeking God, spending time to go after God, NO ONE. does it properly. Books have been written. Books are being written today more about God than ever before in the history of humankind. Look how the Church is divided! How many denominations and non-denominations, and independent churches do we have today? With all the theologians, theological schools. Brothers, sisters, who is really seeking God enough in his/her life today? Churches are empty today because people are not seeking God. And the Bible says so.

<u>(4) WE ALL HAVE TURNED AWAY FROM GOD AND ARE WORTHLESS</u>: 21st century Christians are subject to physical desires, corrupted environment, selfishness, ambitions, and their hearts are turned away from God. There is no morality in our society. We call ourselves Christians, but we are not different from those who are not. We know what is going on in our families, and in our churches. Last week, I heard that a priest hired someone to kill a boy he abused many years ago because that boy was going public with what he did to him. A priest is believed to be a holy man! Where is the holy woman today? Who is the best example for young people to follow today? We are worthless.

<u>(5) THERE IS NO ONE WHO DOES GOOD</u>: Pure good in our lives is an empty word. When you hear that you can buy something on credit card without interest, you may be sure that interest has been compounded in the price. When you hear **"buy one, get one free"**. The price you pay

for one is equal to the two you get. When you hear, **no strings attached**, read the fine lines, and you will see that some conditions are hidden there. When people give to church, as you know, we claim it from the income tax. There is nothing for nothing today, not even a "free' lunch.

(6) **WE DON'T FEAR GOD TODAY: DO YOU REALLY FEAR GOD?**

If our God could open the earth and swallow sinners as he did in Numbers 16:28-34 with the children of Korah and another 250 leaders who opposed Aaron and Moses.

-If the fire could come from heaven today and consume people as God did with **Elijah in II King 1:1-14,** I am sure many will fear God. (3) **If God could open the donkey's mouth** and speak to us as he did in **Number 22:28 with BALAAM,** many of us we will fear God.

(4) If Jesus could let me walk on water as he did with Peter in Matt. 14:22-33, many will be afraid of him. - We don't fear God. But the Bible says, **"The fear of the Lord, is the beginning of all wisdom."** Proverbs 9:10, and Psalm 111:10

We are lost today because the fear of the Lord is not in us.

II - WITH A NAME AS "SINNERS", WHAT CAN WE SAY NOW?
Verse 9 says we know that whatever the law says, it says it to those who are under the law, so that every mouth may be silenced and the whole world held accountable to God.
1-WE SHOULD KEEP SILENT; AND SHUT OUR MOUTH. What does being silent really mean?

(1) It means that we don't have any reason to boast.
(2) It means that we are wrong in our ways of doing things. WE ARE GUILTY.
(3) It means that we have to ask God forgiveness, REPENT.

(4) It means that we must change the course we have followed until today.

(5) That means the relationship between us and God must be restored.

- SIN SEPARATES MAN FROM GOD.

III –JESUS TO RESTORE BROKEN RELATIONS WITH GOD

How can we remove sin from our lives and be on good terms with our God? Rom 8:33 says

"WHO WILL BRING ANY CHARGE AGAINST THOSE GOD HAS CHOSEN?"

(1) IT IS IN CHRIST THAT WE ARE CHOSEN.

(2) IT IS IN CHRIST THAT WE ARE JUSTIFIED

(3) IT IS IN CHRIST THAT OUR CONDEMNATION IS NULLIFIED

(4) IN CHRIST, WE ARE UNITED WITH GOD.

CONCLUSION:

Our lives in themselves are a true disaster. There is nothing we can do in order to be right in God's sight. We don't understand or seek God We have turned away from him, and are worthless. We can't do what is good. We don't fear God in our lives. Our real name is SINNERS. Jesus came, Jesus is here, receiving Jesus is the only way our broken relationship with our Father can be restored. Let us receive HIM today, and give him our hearts so that he will remove our sins, which is the only obstacle which separates us from our Father who is in heaven. Amen. Amen. 11/28/2010

(124)

Romans 1:18-23

Text: 1:18-23 the wrath of God is being revealed from heaven against all the godlessness and wickedness of men who suppress the truth by their wickedness. Since what may be known about God is plain to them. For since the creation of the world God's invisible qualities –his eternal power and divine nature – have been clearly seen.

THEME: WHAT ARE YOUR EXCUSES NOT TO RECEIVE GOD'S FREE GIFT OF SALVATION? (The world's excuse)

INTRODUCTION: This passage starts with an expression we barely associate with God. We are accustomed to hearing about THE LOVE OF GOD, THE GRACE OF GOD, THE MERCY OF GOD, THE PRAISE OF GOD, THE GLORY OF GOD, and THE HOLINESS OF GOD - But in this verse 18, Paul speaks about THE WRATH OF GOD. Do you remember any other passage where you hear about the WRATH OF GOD IN THE NEW TESTAMENT? Yes in the Old Testament, we know that God who asked the children of Israel to slaughter all the 7 tribes of the Promised Land when they entered there. We know that God who sent fire from heaven and consumed those who did not obey him. We know that God who opened the earth and swallowed the children of Coree when they sinned against him. But in this passage, Paul speaks about the wrath of God against a certain category of people. Before we stalk about those the wrath of God is against, let's see what is the full meaning of **"WRATH"**?

The word translated **"wrath"** is the Greek word (**orge**). It's not the word used for a sudden angry outburst. Rather, the word refers to a strong settle opposition over a long period of time, to all that is evil. God is enraged. God is furious! God is out of his mind. Have you seen someone enraged? Think of that elephant, or that lion, or that whale that went after their trainers! Have you seen that in television? How these beasts became something else at those moments when they trampled, crushed, killed, mutilated those who were dear to them. Yes! That is how God is today.

I –WHAT GENERATES GOD'S WRATH?
Verse 18b **"all the godliness and wickedness of men who suppress the truth by their wickedness."**

1-WHEN A MAN KNOWS THE TRUTH, BUT DOESNT LIVE ACCORDING TO THE TRUTH HE KNOWS that generates God's
wrath. When a man can look at what God has done to let him know that he walks in darkness, and the man tells God and those who bring that truth to him that they are liars, that attitude provokes the wrath of God. When man acts as there in no light. When man lives as if God does not exist - he doesn't say that God doesn't exist, but he lives as if God doesn't exist. When someone can say, **"YES A BILIEVE IN GOD.** Yes, I am a Christian". That person is what we call **UNGOLY PERSON.** He will tell you that he believes in God. He doesn't disagree with anything you say about God. But in his daily life, he lives as if God doesn't exist

APPLICATION: Do you know anyone who lives that way? When you leave this church today, tell that person that the wrath of God is against him or her

2- WHEN A MAN TURNS THE TRUTH OF GOD INTO A LIE, BY IGNORING, OR SUPPRESSING IT. It does not indicate that men do not know the truth, but rather that they knowingly suppress the truth. The word translated "suppress" means to "to hold back or to restrain." Paul here charges the entire human race with deliberately, WILLFULLY TO TURNS AWAY FROM GOD. WHEN A MAN RESISTS GOD, REFUSES GOD - JUST STAY AWAY FROM GOD. closes his ears, shots his eyes, and decides to be who he wants to be. Even though he knows deep down in his heart that he needs God, he just says "NO, GOD." God's Wrath Is Justified because Man Is Guilty Of Willingly Ignoring The Evidence. (Vv. 19-20)

APPLICATION: Do you know anyone who lives that way? Anyone you know that he or she knows who God is, but has decided to stay away from God, who has turned his back to God, and would like to live as if God's Word is meaningless? When you leave this church today, go and tell that person that the wrath of God is against him or her.

3. WHAT GENERATES GOD'S WRATH IS MAN'S IGNORACE OF GOD'S EVIDENCE Verse 20" **for since the creation of the world his invisible attitudes are clearly seen, understood by the things God made, even his eternal power and Godhead."**

When you look at the nature, you can understand that someone, not me, not you, **BUT SOMEONE OMNIPOTENT, OMNISCIENT, REAL ENGINEER HAS MADE THIS WORLD.** You know that someone else is in control of this history. That person is GOD. Things are not happening by chance.

Science has backed the Bible in many ways. The knowledge of man is partial, limited, and superficial. God is God forever. Why doubt God when we are still discovering what he has made many millions years ago? We are still in the beginning of learning what is. Who are we do question God?

(1) God has shown us himself through the nature.

(2) He has shown himself to us through his Son Jesus Christ.

(3) He has left us his written Word to illumine our days

(4) He has given us his Holy Spirit to abide in us.

Why walk in darkness again today, O man?

APPLICATION: Do you know anyone who lives that way? Anyone you know that he or she knows who God is, but thinks that science, and his own mind can tell him what is better than God, the one who thinks that those who go to church and have given themselves to God are fools; he alone is the wise one. When you leave this church today, go and tell that person that the wrath of God is against him or her because GOD'S EVIDENCE IS VISIBLE EVERYWHERE.

II – WHAT ARE MEN EXCUSES TODAY?

I like a sermon I heard on radio many years ago. Excuses people present about not going to hear some minister.

1- they don't go because his sermons are too long,

2- because he doesn't speak too aloud,

3- because the sermon is too short

4- because he did not shack someone's hand. etc…

A-Some people don't believe in God because they have prayed and God hasn't answered their prayer.

When you pray, do you say "Not my will, but your, Lord?"

B-Some people don't serve the Lord because they are afraid to give 10%. They say they don't have enough money. Pastors expect to receive 10% from their revenues what they don't have. They prefer to stay home than to go to church. Do they know that God has the power to reduce their expenses, their problems, which take away their money? They have created some expenses in their lives the church with its teaching and the illumination of the Holy Spirit, can help them reduce with the same budget they have now and praise God with what they have.

TELL THEM TO EMPT GOD AND THEY WILL SEE

III ANY MEN'S EXCUSE TO DENY THEIR SINS, AND REFUSE TO BE SAVED GENERATES GOD'S WRATH FROM HEAVEN ANY EXCUSE, any excuse a man would present to God in order not to receive Jesus is not valuable. ---**Any excuse** a man would have in order to deny that you need salvation generates the wrath of God.

---**Any excuse** a man would use to deny that he could be saved by grace and grace alone generates the wrath of God.---**Any excuse** a man would say that HE IS NOT A SINNER, that excuse would generates God's wrath

----**Any excuse** a man would use not to believe that God loves him and he has opened all the doors for his salvation generates the wrath of God.

GO INTO THE WORLD, TELL EVERYONE IN YOUR FAMILY, TELL EVERYONE YOU KNOW THAT GOD'S WRATH FROM HEAVEN IS AGAINST ANYONE WHO DOESN'T RECEIVE HIM WORSHIP HIM, AND SERVE HIM TODAY.NOW, YOUR PERSONAL QUESTION: WHAT IS YOUR EXCUSE TODAY NOT TO STAND UP AND FALL ON YOUR KNEES AND SAY TO JESUS TODAY. I NEED YOU LORD JESUS, BE MY SAVIOR!

I THANK YOU, GOD BY SAVING ME THROUTH YOUR SON.

I THANK YOU, HOLY SPIRIT BY SPEAKING TO ME TODAY

LORD, I AM YOURS, TAKE ME AS I AM AND FOREVEN.

<u>WHAT PEOPLE HAVE BEEN SAYING</u>: (1)Many people believe that **Katrina** happened to speak to people in America in general and those of New Orleans because of their life over there.(1)People believe that **earthquake in Haiti** has a lesson for these people with their voodoo.

Same have said that 911 has a lesson for America. (3) **This economical situation** we are in has something to do with the way se see God. It may be the WRATH OF GOD FROM HEAVEN.

WE MUST REPENT, AND SAY TO GOD, WE ARE SORRY.

ILLUSTRATION: A young boy did something wrong. In order to forgive him, his father wanted him to say "**I AM SORRY**". His father sat down with him, talked to him quietly, hoping that the boy would say," **I am sorry**". He didn't He raised his voice asking him to say, "**I am sorry**". Nothing. He held him by the neck, looking at his eyes, asking him to say, "**I am sorry.**" The boy was cold as ice. His father became enraged. He gave him a blow at the chick. The boy didn't even budge. The father was out of himself ,and gave a big punch to the boy's stomach. The boy fell down and died instantly.

His father held him in his arm and said, "**MY SON, ONE THING I WANTED YOU TO SAY WAS, "I AM SORRY". WHY YOU COULD NOT SAY THOSE THREE WORDS? WHY YOU COULD SAY THOSE WORDS?**

ARE WE WAITING FOR THE LAST BLOW FROM GOD? Amen.

Machiasport November 7,2010

(125)

Reading Romans 2:1-16

<u>THEME:</u> THE WRATH OF GOD IS AGAINST CHRISTIANS.

<u>INTRODUCTION:</u> Last Sunday, we preached about the wrath of God against people who don't believe that he is God; that this natural world or the creation has enough proofs that someone more intelligent than man, that is God, is the creator of everything. He is in control of everything that is happening; that a man is a sinner and he needs salvation; that Jesus is the only road to heaven; that the Bible is where we can learn about and know God; that our own conscience tells us the difference between good and evil, but we refuse to ask knowledge from God. Therefore, those who don't receive Jesus through grace and mercy will stand into judgment.

Today, Paul is talking to us here in this church. As Christian people who have told the world and Satan that they belong to Christ, and have given themselves to him, and they live a new life according to the Spirit of Christ which abides in them. WE are numbered among those who make up the Church of Christ, those he came to save through his death at the cross, pay the price and reconcile with their Father who is in heaven.

I – <u>WE ARE NO EXCUSE FOR DOING WHAT WE CONDEMN,</u>
Chapt. 2:1 You, therefore, have no excuse, you who pass judgment on someone else for at whatever point you judge the other, you are condemning yourself, **BECAUSE …YOU DO THE SAME THINGS.**

When we see someone else doing what we do, it may be in SECRET, it may be publicly. It may even be our way of life, but when we see someone else doing that, we pass judgment.

The problem is not about passing judgment. The problem is knowing what God requires from us, and are not doing it ourselves.

Christians are people who have the privilege to know God because they have his Word, they have his Spirit; they have stood in front of this world and refuse to be under the domination of Satan. Plus, these people know that if they sin against God and ask forgiveness, God will certainly forgive them. God loves them; they are his light of the world, cities his buildings on the hill. <u>Why are they now ASHAMED TO LIVE ACCORDING TO THE GOSPEL?</u>

WHY ARE CHRISTIANS SUCH HYPOCRITES? <u>Hypocrisy is the sin the whole non-Christian world accuses us of.</u> Why to eat what we have vomited? Why to go back to the burning house, when the next one is a safe place? Why live as pagans when we have chosen a new life in Jesus Christ ?

GOD IS ASHAMED OF US. GOD DOESN'T KNOW WHAT TO DO WITH US WHEN KNOWING WHAT IS RIGHT; WE CHOOSE TO DO WHAT IS WRONG.

We violate the Ten Commandments we know so well.

God requires that we love him with all our heart, with all our soul, with all our mind, with all our strength, and with all our love, and that we love our neighbor as ourselves. We say NO!

God says that we are the temples of the Holy Spirit. We make it Satan's temple, evildoings

God wants us to serve others, but we refuse to serve, and insist on being served.

God says that we should not hate anyone. We become those who hate more than pagans.

God says that we should not worry about anything. Anti-depressants are our first remedies.

God says to trust in him and give him all our burdens. We say Yes, to Doctors not to God.

God says that we should worship him and him alone. We worship money and our jobs.

APPLICATION: Ask yourself this question. "Am I condemning what others do while at the same time I do these things myself? If your answer is "YES" know that God's wrath is against you. Change your way. Repent and God will be happy with you.

The problem is not about condemning what is wrong, BUT DOING WHAT WE KNOW THAT IS WRONG ACCORDING TO THE WILL OF GOD. We have the full knowledge that we should not do what God doesn't like. We are called to please him.

II – WHY WE SHOULD NOT DO WHAT GOD HATES?

2:2 Now we know that God's judgment against those who do such things is based on **TRUTH**.

What provokes God's wrath is that when we, Christians, do these evil things, it is as if we don't know HOW GOD WILL JUDGE THOSE WHO DO SUCH THINGS

A- QUESTIONS: *We know that God doesn't show PARTIALITY*
(Verse 11)

(1) When we go over the speed limits, what goes through our mind?

(2) Can you use an umbrella for a parachute when jumping from an airplane and be safe?

(3) Why are we playing with fire when we know what fire can do?

A Christian person knows what the Bible says about those who don't live according to the will of God. God's judgment will fall on them, and their condemnation will be eternal.

When you and I continue doing what God forbids, do we think that he will use a different standard for us on the Day of Judgment? <u>DOING WHAT IS GOOD IS WHAT GOD EXPECTS FROM US.</u>

<u>B- WE SHOULD NOT SHOW CONTEMPT FOR GOD'S GRACE.</u>
I have heard many people say that GOD IS LOVE. They don't really believe that God will be so cruel to condemn everyone who doesn't believe in Jesus.

(1) They look at the number of pagan people in the world

(2) They look at the number of Islam people

(3) They look at the number of Hindu people

(4) Those who believe in Buddhism, and other non-Christian religions.

(5) Some Christians when ask this question today : **HOW COME THAT THE LOVING GOD WILL SEND SO MANY PEOPLE TO HELL? –HE WILL NOT, they say.** This should be our question because we have the Bible! We believe in the Bible. We preach the Bible. We cannot out GUESS GOD. GOD IS GOD. HE WILL DO WHAT HE WANTS TO DO WITH THOSE PEOPLE. But for us, we believe the Bible..

Our duty is to do what the Bible says and to believe that what it says is what God says and what he will do : <u>THAT IS THE CONDEMNATION OF EVILDOERS.</u>

III – WHAT SHOULD WE DO TO MAKE GOD HAPPY?

2:5 Because of your STUBBORNESS AND YOUR UNREPENTANT HEART, you are storing up wrath against yourself for the Day of Judgment.

We know for sure that Christians will not stand into judgment. The Bible tells us that if you are a true believer in the blood of the one who died on the cross for your sins, you will never stand into judgment. But how come that this passage, talking to Christians, refers to **"STANDING TO JUDGMENT AND THE WRATH OF GOD BEING AGAINST THE CHRISTIANS?**

If you and I CHOOSE, IF WE CHOOSE to continue living, and doing what displeases God, and making that our way of life, what would be the difference between us Christians and non-Christians? The same judgment, which will fall on the non-Christians, will also be ours.

GOD IS GIVING US A WAY OUT FROM THE SAME CONDEMNATION THE NON-CHRISTIANS WILL RECEIVE THROUGH REPENTANCE.

(1) STOP YOUR STUBBORNESS: Christians who do the same things as non-Christians are stubborn. Listen to the Word of God. Listen to the messages we preach from this chair. God is speaking to you and to me now.

God will never again speak through fire as in the burning bush.

God will never again speak through dreams as with Mary and Joseph..

God will never again send prophets as Jeremiah, Isaiah and others.

Jesus will not come back again and preach here in Machiasport. The person you will hear speaking in God's name is and will always be those standing on this pulpit and preaching the Word of God. When you listen to them, be sure that you are listening to God's voice. Leave behind your stubbornness! Change your ways today!

GOD IS LOOKING FOR YOUR OBEDIENCE WHICH IS THE FRUIT OF YOUR SPIRITUAL RENEWAL (Titus 2:14)

2-<u>IT IS TIME FOR REPENTANCE</u>: What many of us do not understand is that repentance is not required only of those who come to Christ for the first time. As long as we are humans, we will sin. We will fail; we will miss the point, the goal, and the will of God. God's ways are not our ways. We are weak. We need Jesus. Every time we find ourselves against the will of God, there is only one requirement for us: TO REPENT. To say to God, "I HAVE SINNED, FORGIVE ME, LORD. I AM GOING TO CHANGE MY WAY."

3-<u>TURN YOURSELF INSIDE OUT</u>. If you were going North, go South. If you were going East, go West. Whatever you were doing which did not please God, leave it starting today and do what is right.

4-<u>GOD'S FORGIVENESS TAKES PLACE RIGHT AWAY</u>. This is the big difference between Christians and non-Christians. We can go back to our Redeemer, confess our sins, and receive his forgiveness and <u>HIS SANCTIFICATION</u>. We can be clean again.. Our relationship with Jesus can be normalized every time we go to him and confess our sin, and turn back from where we were going, and do what is right in the eyes of God.

CONFESS YOUR SINS TODAY.

RECEIVE FORGIVENESS FROM GOD TODAY.

REMOVE GOD'S WRATH AGAINST YOU TODAY.

III- WHAT IS REQUIRED FROM US IS TO DO WHAT IS GOOD:

2:7 to those who by persistence in doing Good seek glory, honor, and immortality, he will give eternal life.

Christians are saved by grace and the faith they have in Jesus. Their actions are acts of thanksgiving for their salvation. They are proofs of their salvation by grace, and mercy.

AS A GENERAL PRINCIPLE: God judges each person according to his deeds (Verse 6 –Go will give to each person according to what he has done)

YOUR GOOD ACTIONS are the result of your salvation.

YOUR GOOD ACTIONS are the fruit of your salvation.

YOUR GOOD ACTIONS are the work of the Holy Spirit in us.

YOUR GOOD ACTIONS are your thankfulness to God who has saved us.

YOUR GOOD ACTIONS are for the glory of the Lord – we seek God's glory

YOUR GOOD ACTIONS are for the honor of the Lord – we seek God's honor.

YOUR GOOD ACTIONS are for the immortality of the Lord – we seek his immortality.

PERSEVERE IN DOING WHAT IS GOOD.

Let us not become weary of doing good, for at the proper time, we will reap a harvest if we do not give up. Galatians 6:9. Matt. 24:13 but he who stands firm to the end will be saved

CONCLUSION: Christians know what God doesn't like. They know what will happen to those who do what God doesn't like. Condemning what God doesn't like and doing the same is as if we think that God will use different standards in judging all people on the Day of Judgment. By behaving this way, we provoke **GOD'S WRATH.**

God is expecting that Christians will stop their **STUBBORNNESS** and listen to him in order to change their wrong doings.

God is expecting that Christians will **REPENT**, so that they will receive forgiveness and stop God's wrath against them.

God is expecting Christians to **PERSEVERE IN DOING GOOD** in their lives until the day they will meet Christ face to face.

-DOING GOOD is our way of thanking God for what he has done.

-<u>DOING GOOD</u> is our way of glorifying, honoring, and praising the immortal God.

-<u>DOING GOOD</u> is our ways to fulfill God's expectation in our lives and the ways to show the difference between who we are and those who are not saved by the blood of Jesus Christ. This way, God's wrath against the world will not be again ourselves.. Amen. Le 14 Nov.2010

-<u>DON'T DO WHAT YOU AND GOD CONDEMN.</u>

-<u>PERSEVERE INTO DOING WHAT IS RIGHT AS CHRISTIANS.</u>

-<u>LIVING THIS WAY, WE WILL STOP GOD'S WRATH AGAINST US, CHRISTIANS.</u>

Amen . Machiasport, 14th of Nov.2010.

Book Contents

SERMONS' TITLES